CHANGES FROM OFF

Sir Ken

Rationalizing Property, Equity and Trusts

Essays in Honour of Edward Burn

Edward Burn, 1945

Head of Edward Burn
by David Wynne 1990,
The Burn Law Library,
Christ Church, Oxford

Edward Burn, 2001

Rationalizing Property, Equity and Trusts

Essays in Honour of Edward Burn

Edited by Joshua Getzler

LexisNexis™ UK

Members of the LexisNexis Group worldwide

United Kingdom	LexisNexis UK, a Division of Reed Elsevier (UK) Ltd, Halsbury House, 35 Chancery Lane, LONDON, WC2A 1EL, and 4 Hill Street, EDINBURGH EH2 3JZ
Argentina	LexisNexis Argentina, BUENOS AIRES
Australia	LexisNexis Butterworths, CHATSWOOD, New South Wales
Austria	LexisNexis Verlag ARD Orac GmbH & Co KG, VIENNA
Canada	LexisNexis Butterworths, MARKHAM, Ontario
Chile	LexisNexis Chile Ltda, SANTIAGO DE CHILE
Czech Republic	Nakladatelství Orac sro, PRAGUE
France	Editions du Juris-Classeur SA, PARIS
Germany	LexisNexis Deutschland GmbH, FRANKFURT, MUNSTER
Hong Kong	LexisNexis Butterworths, HONG KONG
Hungary	HVG-Orac, BUDAPEST
India	LexisNexis Butterworths, NEW DELHI
Ireland	Butterworths (Ireland) Ltd, DUBLIN
Italy	Giuffrè Editore, MILAN
Malaysia	Malayan Law Journal Sdn Bhd, KUALA LUMPUR
New Zealand	LexisNexis Butterworths, WELLINGTON
Poland	Wydawnictwo Prawnicze LexisNexis, WARSAW
Singapore	LexisNexis Butterworths, SINGAPORE
South Africa	LexisNexis Butterworths, DURBAN
Switzerland	Stämpfli Verlag AG, BERNE
USA	LexisNexis, DAYTON, Ohio

A CIP Catalogue record for this book is available from the British Library.

First edition 2003
ISBN 0 406 96440 8

Typeset by Kerrypress Ltd, Luton
Printed and bound in Great Britain by The Cromwell Press Limited, Trowbridge, Wiltshire

Visit LexisNexis UK at www.lexisnexis.co.uk

Preface

In common, I suppose, with most, if not indeed all, of the law students of my generation, my introduction to English property law was through the pages of the late Professor Cheshire's *Modern Law of Real Property*, then in its fifth but now, under the hand of the distinguished writer and teacher to whom this volume is dedicated, in its sixteenth edition. To the student embarking for the first time upon a study of the Law of England the appeal of the Law of Property and Trusts as a preferred field of special study is, however essential it may be to the practising lawyer's operating equipment, not immediately obvious, for it lacks the commercial familiarity of the law of contract, the human interest which forms the background to so much of the law of tort and the dramatic impact of the criminal law. On the contrary, the first-time student finds himself confronted by what appears, at first sight, to be a well-nigh impenetrable jungle of technical rules and concepts, many of which appear to him to be both archaic and arcane. Successfully to chart a course for the tyro through this daunting morass requires not only a depth of learning and understanding but also a clarity of exposition vouchsafed to few of us. For the successful teacher it requires also an appreciation of the difficulties which the student faces and the ability and understanding to help him to overcome them. It requires more, for it requires also sympathy, affection and patience. These are qualities which are, perhaps, best reflected in the affection and gratitude of those who have been privileged to benefit from them. For over half a century now, Edward Burn has taught successive generations of students, at first in Oxford, but subsequently also at the Inns of Court School of Law and the City University.

This *Festschrift* is not only a tribute to the erudition which underlies his success as a teacher and academic writer but also a testimonial of the affection and esteem in which he is held by his students, his contemporaries and his numerous friends. Of the distinguished contributors to this volume some have been his students. Some have been his colleagues. Some have been the admirers and the beneficiaries of his wisdom. All of us have been his friends – some of us for more years than we care to remember. I am grateful to the Editor and the Publishers for affording me this opportunity to pay my own inadequate tribute to an outstanding teacher and academic writer, a fellow Bencher of Lincoln's Inn and an old and valued friend.

Oliver

Aylmerton, Norfolk

Contents

Contributors

John Cartwright, Student in Law, Christ Church, Oxford

Joshua Getzler, Fellow and Tutor in Law, St Hugh's College, Oxford

Kevin Gray, Professor of Law and Fellow of Trinity College, Cambridge

Susan Gray, Solicitor, formerly Assistant Land Registrar, HM Land Registry, and Senior Lecturer in Law, University of Greenwich

Jeffrey Hackney, Fellow and Tutor in Law, Wadham College, Oxford

Charles Harpum, Barrister, Falcon Chambers, London, formerly Law Commissioner for England and Wales and Fellow of Downing College, Cambridge

Tony Honoré, Emeritus Professor of Law and Fellow of All Souls College, Oxford

Ben McFarlane, Student in Law, Christ Church, Oxford

Edwin Simpson, Student in Law, Christ Church, Oxford

Sir Christopher Slade, formerly a Lord Justice of Appeal

Ann Smart, formerly Fellow and Tutor in Law, St Hugh's College, Oxford

Lionel Smith, Professor of Law and William Dawson Scholar in Law, Faculty of Law and Institute of Comparative Law, McGill University, Canada, formerly Fellow and Tutor in Law, St Hugh's College, Oxford

Lord Templeman, formerly a Lord of Appeal in Ordinary

Graham Virgo, Reader in Law and Fellow of Downing College, Cambridge

Table of Statutes

References in the right-hand column are to page number. Page references printed in **bold** type indicate where the Act is set out in part or in full.

Foreign Statutes

Australia

New South Wales

Queensland

Canada

Table of Cases

PAGE

A

PAGE

E

F

H

PAGE

K

L

N

Introduction

The Editor

Edward Burn is the doyen of English property and trust lawyers. His texts are foundations of learning in these most difficult of legal subjects. Judges, professors and practitioners all depend on his crystalline analyses to make sense of the law. In this volume prepared in his honour, many of the leading property and equity experts of England, from bar, bench and university, have joined to celebrate his career as a searching writer and brilliant teacher.

Edward – Teddy to his many students, friends and colleagues – has exerted great influence largely from the rational strength of his legal thought, but also in good measure from a quiet charisma and empathy that strikes all who meet him. He is an extraordinary personality as well as a fine jurist, and the admiration, affection and dedication of his colleagues has been strikingly evident during the making of this volume. Whenever his name is mentioned to anyone who knows him, their immediate reaction is always to smile. Many remember the words of farewell and encouragement that Teddy offered to his students in the lecture hall at the end of their studies: 'I wish you luck in the examinations in June, but more importantly I wish you luck in your careers in whatever way you may choose to serve the law'. He has inspired his many students to serve the law with great distinction, in England and beyond.

Edward Hector Burn was born on 20 November 1922. Educated at St. Edward's School, Oxford, he went up to Wadham College, Oxford in 1941 where he read Classical Mods in one year under the Warden, Maurice Bowra. In 1942 he went to 164 OCTU at Barmouth and three months later was commissioned into the Oxfordshire and Buckinghamshire Light Infantry. He joined the 1st Buckinghamshire Battalion and landed early on D Day in Normandy. For this he was mentioned in despatches. He became GSO 3 (I) of HQ 1st Airborne Corps where he took part in the planning for an airborne landing near Bangkok. VJ Day intervened and instead he landed in Sumatra in the Dutch East Indies with 26th Indian Division where he became GSO 2 (I) with the rank of major. For this he was again mentioned in despatches.

In 1946 Teddy Burn returned to Oxford where he read Jurisprudence and a BCL. He began his teaching career at Wadham and New Colleges and in 1954 was elected to a

Studentship at Christ Church, Oxford. He remained there until his retirement in 1990, and he and his wife Helen (who died in 2000) became surrogate parents to generations of undergraduates; they were renowned for their hospitality at their Regency house and garden in North Oxford.

As an academic lawyer Teddy is the author of three books on Land Law and Trusts. With Ronald Maudsley he wrote *Land Law: Cases and Materials*;[1] and later a companion volume on *Trusts and Trustees: Cases and Materials*.[2] These works are elegant and rigorous, yet they breathe an air of worldly understanding as well as scholarship. He was asked by Geoffrey Cheshire to take over his *Modern Law of Real Property* of which he has now edited the last five editions, and it has become known as *Cheshire and Burn*.[3] This masterly book has shaped the minds of generations of common lawyers as they learn the intricacies and abstractions of English land law.

As a lecturer in the University, Teddy usually lectured at 9 a m on Roman Law and Land Law. He lectured in Christ Church on Roman Law for the BCL, with coffee in Hall between each of the one hour lectures. As an administrator he was Censor of Christ Church for six years and Tutor for Admissions for a further six. He was also Chairman of the Law Board at Oxford, leading the faculty with tact and strength during one of its most powerful phases. Outside Oxford, he became a lecturer in 1965 at the Inns of Court School of Law to a large audience of mainly Commonwealth students in the Old Hall at Lincoln's Inn. When the Inns of Court course was transferred to the City University he was transferred with it and became a Visiting Professor there.

A fine bronze head of Teddy Burn by David Wynne was presented to him on his retirement from Christ Church by his former pupils and this is now placed in the College Law Library. This library is said to be the best college law library in Oxford – or anywhere – and was created by him during his years there. In memory of this it is now called the Burn Law Library.

On his retirement from Christ Church Teddy has remained very active in his service to the law. He became a lecturer at St Hugh's College, Oxford (from which he retired in 2001 on his leaving Oxford to live in London) and continued as a Professor of property law at the City University from whom he received an Honorary degree of DCL. He was also made an Honorary DCL in Canada at the King's University in Halifax Nova Scotia. There were less formal honours too. At the end of the academic year his students at City University always give him a standing ovation; and one year the entire class wore t-shirts bearing a photograph of Teddy, emblazoned fittingly with the caption 'Equity's Darling'.

Teddy Burn is no stranger to the Bar. He was called by Lincoln's Inn in 1951 and was made an Honorary Master of the Bench in 1980. For the last fifteen years he has been the property consultant to the London firm of Linklaters.

1 Now in its seventh edition, Butterworths, London, 1998.

2 Now in its sixth edition, Butterworths, London, 2002, edited (with Edward Burn as consulting editor) by Graham Virgo, once a graduate student at Christ Church.

3 Now in its sixteenth edition, Butterworths, London, 2000.

Happily Teddy's life has taken a new turning; he has recently married Marilyn Kennedy-McGregor, herself a barrister of Lincoln's Inn. His interests are varied: extensive travelling, gardening, watching birds, collecting antiquarian books (his library is large and full of scholarly riches) and, finally, watching (but no longer playing) cricket as a member of the MCC.

The essays in this volume address topics within the three main areas of Edward's legal interests, namely trusts, land law, and Roman law. Tony Honoré in the opening chapter argues against two English dogmas: that the trust is a unique creation of the courts of equity, and that a trust necessarily involves the division of ownership in assets between a legal and beneficial owner. He shows that Civilian and hybrid systems have trust-like devices where either the administrator or the beneficiary have ownership (or neither); and that in any case *in personam* rights, powers and duties can give parties all of the necessary functions of ownership. Jeffrey Hackney in his chapter uses the comparative method in a reverse fashion, arguing that Roman *usucapio* as a doctrine of positive acquisition – at least as bequeathed to us in the possibly corrupted Justinianic texts – undermines Civilian objections to the trust as a property right defeasible by the bona fide purchaser for value without notice. Civilian and common law comparison is also found in John Cartwright's chapter. He provides an analysis of the tangled relationship of promissory and proprietary estoppels as devices to create interests in land outside the usual formalities, where some interest of justice demands informal creation. He innovates by using French doctrine as a counterpoint to the more familiar debates over estoppel in English, Australian and American contract and property law.

The next three papers turn attention towards the law of obligations. Lionel Smith's chapter on the nature of the fiduciary's duty of loyalty proposes a simple thesis: that English law measures breach of loyalty as a matter of motive, rather than as a series of prohibitions of certain results or behaviour. Here he elaborates the subjectivist approach to fiduciary obligations that has been popular with the English judiciary in recent years, though this approach may represent a departure from older equity learning and certainly remains controversial. Smith's analysis will deepen appreciation of what is at stake as law-equity fusion proceeds apace. Graham Virgo ventures onto the field of battle between restitution theory and more traditional equity jurisprudence. He casts an eirenic eye over the field and suggests that restitution lawyers' criticisms of equity can caricature their target. Equity has structure and principle; but equitable doctrine historically did not have the resources to isolate unjust enrichment as a separate cause of restitutionary remedies. That is why modern unjust enrichment theory has its place as a modification and extension of existing categories of common law and equity. Law-equity fusion is given a subtle twist in Sir Christopher Slade's paper, which gives insights into the incremental growth of solicitors' liability for errors in will-making. Sir Christopher places *White v Jones*[4] in a wide legal and policy context, and he shows that English law uses tort devices as a buttress for relationships of trust, confidence and professional expertise. Indeed the adventurous nature of the tort of negligence can be characterized as a potent form of

4 [1995] 2 AC 207.

'equity' in English law over the past twenty or thirty years, more so than those doctrines which take their source from Chancery.

Lord Templeman argues for the primacy of substance over form in much of English land law. He begins with the long-standing policy of the courts to uphold the substance of land transactions involving borrowers and tenants, and to over-ride legal forms where these create a risk of injustice and evasion of obligations. He suggests that tax cases should be decided in the same fashion, and warns of Enron-style debacles where formalistic rule-following become dominant. Edwin Simpson and Ben McFarlane pursue this theme further, in a chapter assaying the principles evolved by the courts recently to deal with tax avoidance. They also take the problems of lease characterization and avoidance of statutory tenancy regulation as a comparison. They conclude that the latest judicial approach to tax based on statutory construction will not be the solution promised, and they see a crisis of legitimacy looming if courts use purposive interpretation too aggressively to deal with avoidance. In contrast to Lord Templeman, they hint that the only correct solution lies in better-drafted legislation.

The next chapter explores the reach of legislative solutions to the legal and policy challenges of title recordation. Charles Harpum is uniquely placed to comment on the design of the new land title registration system – and also to assess the role of the judiciary in applying the legislative scheme. In his chapter he argues that the system brought in by the Land Registration Act 2002, if not quite one of statutory constitution of titles, was yet designed as a sharp break with the old-title past. He gives reasons for hoping that the House of Lords will interpret and apply the new system purposively so as to make the title register as complete and conclusive as possible.

Is land law a uniquely certain and scientific legal discipline, or is it riddled with policy questions and moral argument? This problem has hovered at the wings of many of the essays presented in this book. Kevin Gray and Susan Gray in their chapter confront the problem directly, drawing from legal and scientific philosophy, logic, social science and American legal realism in search of fresh insights into the nature of property argumentation. In a *tour de force* of scholarship, they argue that alongside the rationality of legal axiom and syllogistic deduction, there lies a rationality of rhetoric based on the shared values of the legal and wider community. They substantiate their claim in a sweeping examination of property doctrine in England and beyond.

The final chapters return to Roman law themes. Joshua Getzler's study of prescription for incorporeal rights to land looks behind the nineteenth century authorities to Roman classical law and the early common law. He shows how the radically different concepts of ownership, possession, limitation and evidence within the Roman and English systems made for bafflingly complex law when common lawyers came to adopt Roman ideas of servitude and prescription into the alien context of feudal titles. The attempted simplifications of the Prescription Act 1832 only increased the difficulties – and this provides an object lesson for reformers today. Ann Smart concludes the book with a personal description of how law was studied in Oxford a decade after the war. Roman law then enjoyed a dominant place in legal education, and was taught by scholars including Henry Lawson, HF Jolowicz, Barry Nicholas,

David Daube – and Edward Burn, who was Ann Smart's tutor in the subject. This chapter captures the excitement and challenge of learning classical law and legal reasoning with an acknowledged master.

Grateful thanks are due to the contributors who produced their chapters with care and imagination, to the Butterworths editors whose enthusiasm and professionalism brought the book to completion, and to Edward Burn himself and to Marilyn Burn for assistance with the splendid photographs and much else. A final vote of thanks is due to Lord Oliver, whose Preface expresses so well the reasons why we honour Edward Burn.

CHAPTER 1

Trusts: The Inessentials

Tony Honoré

Edward Burn and I have taught and written about trust law over many years, in his case English law and in mine South African. We also share an interest in Roman law and the civilian tradition. The South African law of property and obligations, into which its trust law has to fit, is largely civilian. To adapt trust law to a civilian system we need to ask which aspects of English trust law relating to property and obligations are essential to a trust. When a lawyer tries to expound and develop a viable system of trust law for South Africa,[1] he must decide which elements that are historically part of English trust law are not essential to trust law more widely considered. The elements that are inessential need not form part of trust law in a civilian or mixed jurisdiction. As Gretton has written in regard to Scots trust law: 'English law does not readily fit into civilian pigeon-holes. This is legitimate. But one must beware of the reverse. It does not follow that a system which has the trust must have an English pigeon-hole for it'.[2]

This brief tribute to my colleague and friend takes the form of thoughts about two inessentials of trust law. It may seem perverse to concentrate on *inessentials*.[3] But there is method in my madness. The mistaken belief that certain elements, historically connected with English trust law, are essential if trusts are to function in the sort of way in which they do in Anglo-American law, has, I believe, been harmful. It has

1 I began working on South African trust law in the early 1960s. The first edition of what is now *Honoré's South African Law of Trusts* was published in 1966, and the fifth, edited by Edwin Cameron and others, cited below as Honoré–Cameron, was published in May 2002.

2 G L Gretton, 'The Evolution of the Trust in a Semi-Civilian System', in R Helmholz and R Zimmermann (eds), *Itinera Fiduciae* (1998) 507–542.

3 For the essential elements (fiduciary position of the trustee, separate estates or patrimonies, real subrogation and trusteeship as an office) see M J de Waal, 'The Core Elements of the Trust: Aspects of the English, Scottish and South African Trusts Compared' (2000) 117 South African Law Journal 548–571; idem, 'In Search of a Model for the Introduction of the Trust into a Civilian Context' (2001) 12 Stellenbosch Law Review 63–85, to which I am much indebted. See also T Honoré, 'Obstacles to the Reception of Trust Law? The Examples of South Africa and Scotland', in A M Rabello (ed), *Aequitas and Equity. Equity in Civil Law and Mixed Jurisdictions* (1993) 793–818; 'On Fitting Trusts into Civil Law Jurisdictions' (1999) Hong Kong, at http://users.ox.ac.uk/~alls0079. G L Gretton, in 'Trusts without Equity', in (2000) 49 International and Comparative Law Quarterly 599–620, at 618, summarises my view as 'trust is patrimony plus office'.

fostered the idea that the trust is a 'uniquely Anglo-American institution'.[4] To deny this is not to denigrate the great historical achievement of Anglo-American trust lawyers. But it has hampered the reception of trust law in some civilian jurisdictions, where it could have served, or could serve, a useful purpose. This is not to argue that it should be introduced into every legal system. The main functions of a trust may already be covered by other institutions, as is arguably the case, for example, in Germany. I concentrate, therefore, on two elements that appear not to be essential to trust law. My remarks are confined to express trusts, since it is the introduction of these that some civilian systems may find beneficial. Constructive trusts are another matter. They fall largely within the law of unjust enrichment, which is already well developed in most civilian systems. It is therefore a separate question whether constructive trusts are worth transplanting and what difficulties the transplant would involve.[5] Nor will this paper be concerned with resulting trusts. Every system possesses fallback rules of the sort that give rise to resulting trusts.

But first, from what point of view is an element that has historically formed part of Anglo-American trust law to be classed as inessential at a more general level? The answer must depend on the function we attribute to trust law, not on its history. In my view, it is a branch of the law designed to allow people to set aside assets to be administered for purposes of private or public benefit in the confidence that the state, through its courts or other agencies, will, if called upon, see to it that the assets are applied for those purposes. Trust law enables private individuals and bodies to harness the power of the state, within broad limits, to ensure that the assets that they set aside are devoted to the purposes they choose. Nearly anyone can create a trust, nearly anyone can be a trustee, and nearly any lawful object can be a trust object. No other legal institution shifts the balance of power between the individual and the state so much in favour of the individual.[6] The state may, of course, itself create trusts. If, then, the functions of trust law are those described, whatever is necessary for it to fulfil those functions is an essential part of trust law, and whatever is not necessary is inessential.

The two inessentials of trust law selected for discussion are:

(i) the idea that there can be no trust except in a system that vests legal ownership in the trustee and, indeed, one that recognises dual ownership, legal and equitable; and

(ii) that the obligation of the trustee ('fiduciary obligation') and the rights of the trust beneficiary ('equitable interest') must be related to the system of law called Equity that arose in England and was historically separate from the common law.

4 E g J Langbein, 'The Contractarian Basis of the Law of Trusts' (1995) 105 Yale Law Journal 669.

5 On resulting and constructive trusts in South Africa, Scotland and Sri Lanka see Honoré–Cameron (5th edn) 128–137, see n 1 above.

6 Public and private companies also do this, but not to the same extent, since they are subject to a greater degree of state control.

If these propositions were true there could be no trust law in civilian or mixed systems.[7] But they are not.

THE FIRST INESSENTIAL: OWNERSHIP OF THE TRUST ASSETS

One ground for concern is this. Those writing about English trust law sometimes insist as a feature, supposedly essential to trust law, that there are two types of ownership, ownership at law, which is in the trustee, and ownership in equity, which is in the beneficiary.[8] According to a recent English textbook on trusts, 'this book is all about the consequences of the simultaneous occurrence of these two types of ownership'.[9] Of course, an author writing about a particular system of law may legitimately emphasise those features of the subject that are prominent, for historical or other reasons, in that system of law. But if the need for two types of ownership were a truth about trust law in general, then trusts could not exist in many systems of law, Anglo-American and civilian alike, in which they do exist.

It is not, in reality, essential to a system of trust law that either the trustee or the beneficiary should own the trust assets, still less that the assets should be subject to a dual ownership. To begin with the trustee: the main reason why it is not essential for the trustee to own the trust assets is that, even if the assets are vested in the trustee, they must, if the beneficiaries or trust objects are to be protected, be separate in law from the trustee's private assets. They must form a separate trust estate.[10] The trust estate is certainly not owned by the trustee in the same way as he or she owns his or her private assets. The estate can, it is true, be treated as nominally owned by the trustee, but it can also be treated as owned by the beneficiary or beneficiaries. It can even be treated as a separate legal entity – whether a juristic person like a nominee company or foundation, or a trust patrimony that has no owner. In practice, the location of the ownership of trust assets varies from system to system, and in at least one system (Quebec) no one owns the trust assets.[11] It is true that the title to them must be in some person or entity,[12] but title is not ownership. Like control and benefit, it is merely one

7 Apart from South Africa, Scotland and Quebec, trusts exist in such civil law (or at any rate non-Anglo-American law) jurisdictions as Liechtenstein, Mexico, Panama, Ecuador, Argentina, Peru, Venezuela and Taiwan.

8 E g P Todd and S Lourie, *Textbook on Trusts* (5th edn, 2000) 1: 'the general idea is expressed by saying that the trustee is the nominal owner of the trust property, but that the real or beneficial owner is the cestui que trust or, alternatively, that the trustee is the legal owner, the cestui que trust the equitable owner.' Many writers express similar views e g P H Pettit, *Equity and the Law of Trusts* (8th edn, 1997) 24; Underhill and Hayton, *The Law Relating to Trusts and Trustees* (15th edn, by D J Hayton, 1995) 3; Parker and Mellows, *The Modern Law of Trusts* (6th edn, by A J Oakley, 1994) 7–8; J G Riddall, *The Law of Trusts* (4th edn, 1999) 1; Keeton and Sheridan, *The Law of Trusts* (12th edn, by L A Sheridan, 1993) 3. Even if the terminology of ownership can be misleading (B Rudden, 'Things as things and things as wealth' (1994) 14 Oxford Journal of Legal Studies 81, 88), which it is, it has become ingrained in England.

9 Todd and Lourie (n 8) above.

10 Hague Convention on the Law Application to Trust and on their Recognition (1985) art 2; de Waal (2000, n 3 above) 559–563, citing K G C Reid, 'Patrimony not Equity: The Trust in Scotland' (paper given at Utrecht 18 June 1999) in *European Review of Private Law* (2000) 427–437; *Trusts in Mixed Legal Systems* (ed J M Milo and J M Smits, 2001) 19–28; Honoré, 'Obstacles' (n 3, above) 796.

11 De Waal (2001) 83, see n 3 above.

12 See nn 15–16 below.

element in the complex of rights, powers and duties that together go to make up the whole. For trust law to function the trustee must control and administer the trust assets, but need not have title to them or own them.

The law of trusts in England was built up on the basis that the trustee had the legal title to the trust assets, if the assets admitted of a legal title (ie a title enforceable at common law). Though the terminology of ownership was on the whole avoided, especially in relation to estates in land, the trustee was and is treated as in effect their owner. The beneficiary was and is treated as having an equitable estate or, in modern terminology, an equitable interest in the assets. This interest is sometimes, when the beneficiary is entitled to the capital of the trust assets, described as equitable ownership.

In this connection there is a point to be made about ownership. Ownership is important in our economic and legal culture because in the standard case the owner combines a number of rights that together amount to a monopoly over the thing owned, in particular the exclusive right to manage, enjoy, and alienate it.[13] Subject to restrictions to which he or she has agreed, and to limitations imposed by law in the general interest, the owner may do with the property as he or she pleases.

But when the incidents of ownership are divided, so that one person administers and another person or object benefits from the property, as is the case with a trust, this monopoly does not exist. Since trust assets have to be devoted to the stated personal or impersonal purpose, there is a sense in which no one owns them. The trustee as administrator has the right to manage the assets, the beneficiary or impersonal trust object to enjoy the income or capital from them and the title holder, whoever it may be, to register or transmit title to them. The administrator does not, unless given the power to do so under a discretionary trust, have the right to substitute one beneficiary or trust object for another.[14] Nor does he or she have the right to dispose of the trust assets, except in so far as the trust instrument or the general law allows it, and then only subject to the proceeds being devoted to the trust object. The beneficiary may in most cases alienate his or her interest in the assets, but cannot alienate the assets themselves, alter the trust object, or substitute one administrator for another, unless, as is the rule in some systems, all the beneficiaries agree.[15] In short, no one possesses the freedom with regard to the assets that an owner possesses in the standard case of unsplit ownership.

Nevertheless the title to trust assets must, according to conventions shared by Anglo-American and civilian systems of law, be vested in some person or entity. The property may have to be registered or alienated and, if so, must be registered or transferred in the name of some person or entity. That person or entity is often described as the owner, even if a 'bare' owner, though in fact the title, like the management and the enjoyment of an asset, can be separated from the ownership of it. Even if the trustee is entitled to alienate the assets, it does not follow that either title to, or ownership of the trust assets must vest in the trustee, because the power to alienate

13 T Honoré, 'Ownership', in *Making Law Bind* (1987) 161–192. For its economic significance see T Bethell, *The Noblest Triumph. Property and Prosperity through the Ages* (1998) 23.

14 The trustee may have the right to co-opt a co-trustee, but that is not the same thing.

15 This is possible in England under the rule in *Saunders v Vautier* (1841) Cr & Ph 240.

need not coincide with either title or ownership. Directors of a company may be entitled to sell assets that are owned not by them but by the company. Guardians of a minor may be entitled to sell assets that are owned not by them but by the minor. It is at most a convenience (and not always that) that the trustee should have title to the assets. In a unit trust the title to assets is in the trustee but the assets are managed by a separate management company. Likewise, even if the trustee has title, this need not carry with it the status of owner. In practice the ownership of trust assets is sometimes vested in the trustee, sometimes in the beneficiary, sometimes in a nominee company, sometimes in the assets themselves considered as a juristic person, such as a foundation. Sometimes the trust estate is treated as a patrimony owned by no one. When rights are split, the relations between the persons between whom they are split and between them and third parties are regulated not by rules derived from the standard attributes of ownership but by special rules that vary from one legal context and system to another.

A trust always involves a split between management/administration and benefit/enjoyment. Indeed it is a rule of trust law that the same person cannot be sole trustee and sole beneficiary.[16] In Anglo-American law it is firmly established that the title to trust assets normally vests in the trustee.[17] There are arguments in favour of this rule, though it means that ways have to be found of separating the trustee's private assets from his or her trust assets. But the rule creates a problem for many civilian lawyers. To them the title to a thing prima facie entails ownership of it and ownership carries with it the implication of a beneficial interest in the asset, even if not coupled with present enjoyment of it. This interest should be part of the owner's estate or patrimony and available to the owner's creditors and heirs. But trust assets are not available to the trustee's private creditors or heirs.[18] So it runs against the civilian grain to describe a mere administrator of assets as their owner. To do so in the case of a trust is to vest the trustee with what has been called a 'sui generis ownership'.[19] Indeed those who in civil law systems administer assets on behalf of others, in the role of guardians, curators, executors, administrators, procurators or factors, are not normally treated as owning the assets. The assets are owned by the person or persons on whose behalf they are administered. The Anglo-American rule vesting ownership in the trustee seems to turn the natural order of things upside down.

There are various ways of overcoming this obstacle, which is partly conceptual and partly psychological. Here are two illustrations, from South Africa and Quebec respectively.

16 *Re Cook* [1948] Ch 212; P H Pettit, *Equity and the Law of Trusts* (9th edn, 2001) 43; Honoré–Cameron (5th edn) 11, see n 1 above; Quebec Civil Code art 1275.

17 There are or have been exceptions, for example in the case of custodian trusteeship, the split between the tenant for life and the trustees under the Settled Land Act 1925 and, perhaps, the facility of a 'protector'. But the general principle is well established.

18 South African Trust Property Control Act 1988, s 12; Quebec Civil Code art 1261.

19 J E R Brierley, 'The Gratuitous Trust: A New Liberality in Quebec Law', *Mélanges Paul-André Crépeau* (1997) 122.

South African law

One way is to treat the beneficiary as owner. In South Africa practice has not been uniform so far as the ownership of trust assets is concerned.[20] Most trusts have been created on the English pattern, in which the ownership of the assets vests in the trustee. But some have been set up on a different pattern, adapted from Dutch law, called a 'bewind'. According to this pattern, the ownership is in the beneficiary but the assets are managed by an administrator.[21] These two patterns have been treated by South African legislatures, courts and practitioners over the years as equivalent. The legislature required that English-style trusts and Dutch-style bewinds be registered[22] and that security by the trustee or administrator be required for the due administration of the assets[23] in the same way in both cases. The courts exercised jurisdiction to appoint or remove trustees and administrators, and to modify or vary the arrangement when the object became impracticable in the same way in both cases. Practitioners drafted trust instruments according to either pattern, as their clients or convention dictated.

Nevertheless there were lawyers of a purist turn of mind who insisted that the patterns derived from English and Dutch law represented different institutions.[24] Against this view it was argued by myself and others that, since the same rules applied to both and they worked in the same way, they were two species of the same genus.[25] Functionally they were trusts, even if not trusts on the English pattern, and it was function, not origin or terminology, that was crucial. It did not matter whether the arrangement was called a trust or a bewind, or whether the person controlling the assets was called a trustee or an administrator.

In the end the legislature recognised that this was the case. It enacted a statute, the Trust Property Control Act,[26] in which a trust was defined so as to cover both patterns. It was:

> the arrangement through which the ownership of property of one person is by virtue of a trust instrument made over or bequeathed
>
> > (a) to another person, the trustee, in whole or in part, to be administered or disposed of according to the provisions of the trust instrument for the benefit of the person or class of persons designated in the trust instrument or for the achievement of the object stated in the trust instrument, or

20 For the history, see T Honoré, 'Trust', in R Zimmermann and D Visser (eds), *Southern Cross: Civil Law and Common Law in South Africa* (1996) 849–872.

21 This is also, on one view, the construction adopted in Louisiana: A N Yiannopoulos, *Trust and the Civil Law* (1965) 229; de Waal (2001) 79, see n 3 above.

22 Trust Moneys Protection Act 1934, s 2; Trust Property Control Act 1988, s 4.

23 Administration of Estates Act 1913, s 61(3); Trust Moneys Protection Act 1934, s 3; Trust Property Control Act 1988, s 6.

24 Especially C P Joubert, later a Judge of Appeal: in 'Kritiese Opvatting van Honoré se Beskouings oor die Trustreg', 31 Tydskrif vir Hedendaagse Romeins-Hollandse Reg (1968) 124–146, 262–281. There was a brief reply by the author at 32 THRHR (1969) 126–133.

25 Originally in Honoré (1st edn) 191–192, see n 1 above.

26 Act 57 of 1988, s 1.

(b) to the beneficiaries designated in the trust instrument, which property is placed under the control of another person, the trustee, to be administered or disposed of according to the provisions of the trust instrument for the benefit of the person or class of persons designated in the trust instrument or for the achievement of the object stated in the trust instrument.

The essential feature of the statutory definition is that control, not ownership, must lie with the person whom the legislature terms the trustee.[27] This point of view is also adopted in the Hague Convention, signed in 1984, which specifies that *control* should be in the hands of the trustees.[28]

The South African experience points, then, to one possible answer to the objection that a civilian lawyer may feel to treating a mere administrator of assets as their owner. Trusteeship can be an institution like guardianship or curatorship in which ownership is in the beneficiary, and the management is in the administrator.

Quebec law

It is not the only possible answer. Quebec has gone down a different route, partly marked out as early as 1932 by the French writer Lepaulle.[29] He relied on a feature that really is essential to a trust, namely that, if the beneficiaries and trust objects are to be protected, there must be a separation of the trust assets from the private assets of the trustee.[30] Since there has to be a separate trust estate – separate, for example, so far as insolvency, divorce, taxation and succession on death is concerned – one possibility is to treat the trust estate as a separate person. In that case, the trust assets are not owned either by the trustee or the beneficiaries. If the trust estate can be declared insolvent, if it can be the recipient of a testamentary bequest, if it can be taxed as a separate entity, is it not in effect a juristic person,[31] at least in these special contexts?[32]

In the end Quebec law has not quite adopted this solution. By the 1991 amendments to the Civil Code, both foundations and trusts are 'patrimonies by appropriation',[33] or, in terms more familiar to English lawyers, they consist of assets set aside so as to constitute separate estates. The property of a foundation may either be that of an

27 It would not matter if the legislature had chosen the term 'administrator' instead.

28 Hague Convention on the Law Applicable to Trust and on their Recognition (1985) art 2: 'For the purpose of this convention, the term 'trust' refers to the legal relationship created – inter vivos or on death – by a person, the settlor, when assets have been placed under the control of a trustee for the benefit of a beneficiary or for a specified purpose.'

29 P Lepaulle, *Traité théorique et pratique des trusts en droit interne, en droit fiscal et en droit international* (1932).

30 Hague Convention, (above n 10) art 2a: 'the assets constitute a separate fund and are not a part of the trustee's own estate.'

31 M J de Waal, 'Anomalieë in die Suid-Afrikaanse trustreg' (1993) 56 Tydskrif vir Hedendaagse Romeins-Hollandse Reg 1.

32 In South Africa it has been decided, however, that a trust does not in general possess juristic personality. Ownership must either be in the trustee or the beneficiary: *Commissioner for Inland Revenue v MacNeillie's Estate* 1961 (3) SA 833 (A); *Commissioner for Inland Revenue v Friedman* 1993 (1) SA 353 (A). A special statutory provision was needed to make a trust a 'person' for purposes of income tax: Act 129 of 1991 s 2(1) (b); Honoré-Cameron (5th edn) 444–445, see n 1 above.

33 Civil Code book 4 title 7.

autonomous patrimony distinct from that of the settlor or anyone else, or may be the patrimony of a juristic person.[34] The property of a trust, on the other hand, is always a patrimony by appropriation. It is autonomous and distinct from the patrimony of the settlor, trustee or beneficiary, none of whom has any real right in it.[35] This 'patrimony by appropriation' is nothing other than the trust estate, considered as a legal entity but not as a juristic person. Though it may be identified by the name of the grantor, the trustee, the beneficiary or the purpose it serves,[36] it is not owned by anyone. It does not follow that no one has title to the trust assets, since 'a trustee has the control and the exclusive administration of the trust patrimony, and the titles relating to the property of which it is composed are drawn up in his name.'[37] In South Africa it is usual to register land subject to a trust in the name of the 'trustees for the time being of the XYZ trust.'[38] But in neither South Africa nor Quebec does the customary or statutory form of registration determine who, if anyone, owns the trust assets. So long as the three elements – management, enjoyment and title – are vested in some person or entity, it does not matter who, if anyone, owns the assets.

The Quebec example shows clearly that the essential relation of a trustee to the trust assets is one not of ownership but of control. To specify how the trustee is to administer the trust assets, instead of having a special Trustee Act of the sort found in many Anglo-American jurisdictions, Quebec has a section of the Civil Code about the administration of the property of others.[39] This section applies, among other administrators, to trustees.[40] It lays down common rules for a variety of administrators: tutors, curators, testamentary executors, trustees, sequestrators, directors of corporations, co-owners and others. Trustees hold one office among others,[41] the duties attaching to which are prescribed by legislation and judicial decision and which is subject to control by the court.[42] Indeed, much the simplest way for a civilian system to introduce a law of trusts is:

34 Civil Code art 1257.

35 Civil Code art 1261. Exactly how it should be described is controversial. According to M C Cumyn, 'La fiducie, un nouveau sujet de droit?', in J Beaulne (ed) *Mélanges Ernest Caparros* (2002) it is a *sujet de droit* though not a *personne morale*.

36 Civil Code art 1266.

37 Civil Code art 1278. Under the Hague Convention (art 2b) it is a characteristic of the trust that title to the trust assets stands in the name of the trustee or in the name of another person on behalf of the trustee.

38 This form of registration, long current in practice, has recently been said by the South African Supreme Court of Appeal to be prima facie correct: *Mkangeli v Joubert* 2002 (4) SA 36 (SCA) on appeal from *Joubert v Van Rensburg* 2001 (1) SA 753 (W); Honoré–Cameron (5th edn) viii, see n 1 above.

39 Civil Code book 4 title 7 arts 1299–1370. Strictly speaking Quebec trustees do not administer the property of 'others', since the trust patrimony is not owned by anyone, but the idea is clear: the assets they administer are not their own. F Ranville, 'De l'administration du bien d'autrui', in *La Réforme du Code Civil* (1993) 1, 735–782.

40 Civil Code art 1278 'A trustee acts as the administrator of the property of others charged with full administration.'

41 On trusteeship as an office see de Waal (2000) 565–567, see n 3 above. It is because trusteeship is an office (in French 'charge': Quebec Civil Code art 1299; in German 'Amt') with a public element that a trust cannot be treated in civil law systems as a mere *fideicommissum, fiducia,* Treuhand or contract, to list some of the private law analogies that have been suggested. It is not a purely private institution.

42 Civil Code art 1277 (appointment of trustee); 1287 (supervision of the administration of a trust); 1294 (variation).

(i) to add the office of trustee to the list of offices that already exists in every system; and
(ii) to define the duties and rights attaching to it, either by a special trustee statute or by applying to the office of trustee the rules that pertain to the other existing offices.

In South Africa this was done by in the first place by judicial decision,[43] in Quebec mainly by statute.

Of course a civilian or mixed system does not have to vest ownership of the trust assets in the beneficiary or a juristic person, or to constitute them an autonomous patrimony that belongs to no one. It may, like Scotland, follow the English model and vest ownership in the trustee, if that is thought to be more convenient.[44] In Scots law, one person, the trustee, owns two estates, his private estate and the trust estate.[45] But that does not imply that a dual ownership, legal and equitable is recognised.[46] No civilian system recognises dual ownership.

In the upshot it is no obstacle to the reception of trust law that no civilian system will admit dual ownership and that some cannot stomach treating an administrator as owner of the assets administered.

THE SECOND INESSENTIAL: EQUITY

There are conceptual and historical links between what I argue are two inessentials of trust law. The English trust grew up under the aegis of a split court system, a split that led to the supposed distinction between legal and equitable ownership. There were courts of common law and courts of equity. Trusts were enforceable in courts of equity but, in general, not in courts of common law. This predictably gave rise to a terminology of common law and equitable obligations, common law and equitable interests in property, and indeed ownership at common law and in equity. For example, a leading writer in England defines a trust as an equitable obligation binding a person to deal with property over which he has control for the benefit of persons, of whom he may himself be one, any one of whom may enforce the obligation.[47] The leading American treatise speaks of a 'fiduciary relationship with respect to property, subjecting the person by whom the title to property is held to equitable duties to deal with the property for the benefit of another person.'[48]

43 *The Master v Edgecombe's Executors* 1910 TS 263, 269: 'courts administering Roman-Dutch law and the authorities adopted by those courts apply to administrators [ie in the context testamentary trustees] the same obligations and legal principles as had been transferred from the law on the subject of guardianship to the office of executors.'
44 K McK Norrie and E M Scobie, *Trusts* (1991) 1; cf G Gretton, 'The Evolution of the Trust', see n 2 above.
45 K G C Reid, 'National Report for Scotland', in D J Hayton, S C J J Kortmann, and H L E Verhagen, (eds) *Principles of European Trust Law* (1999) 67.
46 G L Gretton, 'Trust and Patrimony', in H L MacQueen (ed), *Scots Law into the 21st Century: Essays in Honour of W A Wilson* (1996) 182–192.
47 Underhill and Hayton, see n 8 above, 3; *Halsbury's Laws of England* (4th edn) vol 48 s 501: 'a trust is a purely equitable obligation, enforceable only in a court where equity is administered.'
48 A W Scott and W F Fratcher, *The Law of Trust* (4th edn, 1987) 41.

This terminology, though understandable in the context, and unobjectionable if confined to English law and cognate systems, does not represent any distinction essential to a system of trust law.[49] There is certainly a distinction between common law and equitable interests in property,[50] but there is no need for a trust beneficiary to be given a proprietary interest in the trust assets. Whether it is desirable to do so is a matter that each system of trust law can decide for itself. Finally, the contrast between ownership at common law and in equity is a metaphorical way of describing a situation where the leading incidents of ownership are split between two or more persons, one of whom has the title to the property while the other is entitled to the income and, ultimately, the capital derived from it. None of these contrasts, therefore, has any real bearing on the essentials of trust law broadly considered. There is no need to regard the notion of equity, in the sense in which it describes a separate court system or the distinctions derived from it, as essential to the law of trusts.

As to the separate court system, in England this was abolished by the Judicature Acts 1873–1875. In many other Anglo-American jurisdictions there are no separate courts of equity.[51] There are other countries[52] where, though there have never been separate courts of equity, trust law is a recognised institution, often regulated by statute.

Equitable duties?

Common law and equitable obligations were at one time recognised and enforced in different courts. Is the type of obligation to which trustees are subject specially 'equitable'? Is the fiduciary obligation of the trustee somehow different from the type of obligation that is enforceable at common law? Is it alien to a civilian system?

Certain distinctions are commonly drawn between common law and equitable obligations. Equitable duties affect all except the bona fide possessor without notice; they rest on conscience; and their existence and impact falls more in the discretion of the court than is the case with obligations at common law. But none of these suggested distinctions plays, or need play, any role in the law of express trusts. The obligations created by an express trust are not discretionary. There is nothing peculiar about the duty of honesty and loyalty that a trustee owes to the beneficiaries and the purposes set out in the trust instrument.[53] These are duties like the duties of guardians or directors of a company or parties to a contract such as partnership or agency. They are by no means uniquely 'conscientious' in requiring the trustee to subordinate his or her own

49 G L Gretton 'Trusts without Equity', see n 3 above.

50 R Goode, *Commercial Law* (2nd edn, 1995) 61, 706.

51 E g India, Pakistan, Bangladesh, Malaysia, Singapore, Hong Kong, and many ex-British African countries: G W Keeton and L A Sheridan, *The Comparative Law of Trust in the Commonwealth and the Irish Republic* (1976) 194. The Indian Trusts Act 1882 was an important landmark.

52 E g Liechtenstein, Puerto Rico, Sri Lanka, Ethiopia, Israel, Taiwan, Quebec, Mexico and a number of South American countries.

53 Quebec Civil Code art 1309: 'An administrator shall act with prudence and diligence. He shall also act honestly and faithfully in the best interest of the beneficiary or of the object pursued'. South African Trust Property Control Act 1988, s 9(i): 'A trustee shall in the performance of his duties and the exercise of his powers act with the care, diligence and skill which can reasonably be expected of a person who manages the affairs of another'.

private interests to those of the beneficiaries. Many legal institutions require a person to act in the interests of another rather than for him or herself. Each of the duties in question has, indeed, its own special features; but they share others. The duties ascribed to trustees in Anglo-American and civilian systems are in fact remarkably similar.[54] They are vindicated by proceedings for breach of the duty in question. In civilian systems the remedy for breach of trust will be in delict, and is sometimes treated as a form of Aquilian liability,[55] or for breach of a statutory duty. In Anglo-American systems it will be for breach of an equitable or statutory duty. The label does not matter and there is no need to postulate a special remedy confined to breaches of 'equitable duties.' Though actions for breach of trust happen, in England, not to be treated as actions in tort, this is no more than a historical hangover.

Finally, the persons, other than the trustee, whom the fiduciary obligation binds depend on doctrines, such as the doctrine of notice (discussed further below), which are not specifically equitable and the application of which varies from system to system.

Equitable rights?

The trust beneficiary's basic right is to insist that a trust be carried out according to its terms and that the court, if necessary, devise a scheme to ensure that this is done. Whatever person or agency supervises purpose trusts, including charitable trusts, has a similar right. It is in effect a right of a quasi-public character to specific performance of the trust.

But a trust beneficiary also needs private rights against the trustee and the trust estate. These rights could either be rights *in personam* or proprietary rights *in rem*. Is there anything specially equitable about these rights? Let us begin with the trust beneficiary's rights *in personam*.

(a) *Rights in personam*. Some lawyers misconceive the nature of a right *in personam*. Such a right is always indirectly a right that carries with it an interest of the creditor of the right in the debtor's property. This is because the security for the enforcement of a right *in personam* consists of the estate or patrimony of the debtor, against which any judgment in favour of the creditor will have to be executed. A creditor's right *in personam* is always in that sense a right against the debtor's estate. It is not, however, a right that gives a preference or exclusive claim as against concurrent creditors over the whole of the debtor's estate or any particular item in it. So it is not a right *in rem*.

In the case of a trust there are two debtor estates (and so in a sense two persons) to be considered. So far as actions for breach of trust are concerned the security for the enforcement of the beneficiary's right *in personam* against the trustee is the trustee's private estate. But so long as there is no breach of trust, the security for the payment of income or capital to the beneficiary is primarily the trust estate or patrimony. This

54 De Waal (2000) 558–559, see n 3 above.
55 Honoré–Cameron (5th edn) 362–369, see n 1 above.

remains true even though some systems of trust law provide that the trustee's private estate is liable for the payments subject to the trustee's indemnifying him or herself from the trust estate.

By the principle of real subrogation,[56] admittedly a term not familiar to English lawyers, the trust estate consists of the trust assets as they are constituted from time to time. Real subrogation, which means 'replacement of a thing by another thing', is the familiar principle that when assets in a fund are lawfully replaced by other assets, any right held by a person in relation to the former assets now attaches to the new assets. It is an idea related to 'overreaching'. It relates to the continuity of a fund despite changes in the assets of which it is constituted. In the case of trust funds, this serves to ensure the continuity of the trust estate. If an asset is lawfully sold, the proceeds of sale or reinvestment, by the principle of real subrogation, replace the former asset. It follows that a trust beneficiary has an interest in both the trustee's private estate and the trust estate as these estates are constituted from time to time. It is a mistake to explain this, as do some English authors, as resting on a right *in rem* of the trust beneficiary arising by virtue of his or her equitable interest in, or ownership of the trust assets.[57] The principle is not specially concerned with rights *in rem*. The beneficiary's right is *in personam* against the trustee in his private capacity or as owner/administrator of the trust estate. Both estates include the assets which comprise them from time to time. If one is prepared to personify the trust estate, one could think of the beneficiary's interest as being *in personas* rather than *in personam*. The beneficiary's right in relation to both estates need be neither preferential nor exclusive. It need not therefore be *in rem*. Consistently with giving the beneficiary adequate protection, it can be a right *in personam/personas* concurrent with the rights of other personal or trust creditors.

The only way in which a beneficiary's *in personam* interest in trust assets differs from a common law interest *inpersonam* is that the right of the beneficiary and other trust creditors in relation to the trust estate is protected against the claims of the trustee's private creditors. In other words, the beneficiary's rights *in personam* are clothed with an immunity that would not exist if the trust assets were really part of the trustee's private estate – if the trustee really owned the trust assets in the sense of enjoying the full monopoly described above. One can call this sort of right a protected right *in personam*.[58] The beneficiary is, in relation to the trust assets, in competition with other trust creditors but not with the trustee's private creditors. That restriction is inevitable, given the nature of a separate estate or patrimony. Incidentally, the existence of a separate trust estate not available to private creditors of the trustee cannot be put down, as one author would have it, to the 'equitable property rights of the beneficiaries in the trust property'.[59] For the immunity applies equally to creditors of the trust who are not beneficiaries, such as lawyers or accountants employed by the trustee in the proper course of trust administration. Indeed once the claims of these creditors are satisfied

56 E g Ethiopia, Civil Code art 530; Israel, Trust Law 1979, s 5.
57 E g J G Riddall, *The Law of Trusts* (12th edn, 1993) 352.
58 Honoré–Cameron (5th edn) 558–565, see n 1 above.
59 E g D J Hayton, *Vertrouwd met de Trust: Trusts and Trust-like Arrangements* (eds D J Hayton, S C J J Kortmann, A J M Nytinck, A V M Stuycken and N E D Faber) 4.

out of the trust assets, there is inevitably less available for the beneficiaries. But there is no ground on which these outside creditors could be thought to have equitable proprietary rights in the trust assets. The beneficiaries have a claim to the enjoyment of the trust assets, but it is not an exclusive right or claim and so need not be regarded as proprietary.

In the upshot nothing about the beneficiary's rights *in personam* in relation to either patrimony is inconsistent with the civilian tradition. That tradition is familiar with the idea of a debtor's separate estate or patrimony (Sondervermögen, patrimoine d'affectation) and with real subrogation, both of which are genuinely essentials of a trust.[60] Nothing 'equitable' about these ideas prevents their transplantation into civil law systems.

The principle of real subrogation, as set out above, applies to trust assets lawfully acquired. What about assets that come into the hands of the trustee as a result of an unlawful disposition, whether he or she reinvests them or mixes them with his or her private assets? Does the rule of real subrogation apply also in this case, so that the new asset, unlawfully acquired, or the mixed asset, becomes a trust asset? Can the lawful asset be traced into the unlawful proceeds into which it has been converted? In English law, though the detailed rules are rather complicated, especially when there is an improper mixing of assets, it does.[61] Provided that the proceeds of the original asset can still be identified, tracing is allowed not merely into properly acquired assets but also into unlawfully acquired ones. This rule does not on the whole exist in civilian systems, though there is much to be said in its favour. But it does not, in any event, turn the beneficiary's personal right into a real right. It concerns, once again, the composition of the trust estate in relation to which his or her right *in personam* can be exercised. If tracing is allowed, the unlawful proceeds form part of the trust estate. Once again, it is for each system of trust law to decide for itself whether to extend the protection of the beneficiary by adopting this principle of tracing. It is useful, but not essential, to a system of trust law.[62]

(b) Rights in rem. Does a system of trust law require recognition of an unusual type of interest in property, which a civilian system may find it difficult to accommodate? Must the trust beneficiary have an equitable interest in trust assets that is not merely *in personam* but *in rem*? Does he or she have a preferential or exclusive right over some trust assets? On one view 'the interests of both the trustee and the beneficiary in the subject matter are interests *in rem*'.[63] It would be a cause for concern if trust beneficiaries really had to possess unregistered and often unascertainable rights *in*

60 De Waal (2000) 557–567, see n 3 above.

61 *Clayton's Case* (1816) 1 Mer 529, 572; *Re Hallett's Estate* (1880) 13 Ch D 696; *Re Diplock's Estate* [1948] Ch 465; *Ministry of Health v Simpson* [1951] AC 251; R Goff and G Jones, *The Law of Restitution* (6th edn, 2002) Section III.

62 It is not part of South African law: Honoré–Cameron (5th edn) 30 (see n 1 above) but is of Scots law: G L Gretton, 'Constructive Trusts: I' (1997) 1 *Edinburgh LR* 282–283; Reid, 9, see n 10 above; De Waal (2000) 565 (see n 3 above) advocates its extension to South African law. But constructive trusts seem to exist only marginally and controversially in Scots law: *Mortgage Corpn v Mitchells Roberton* [1997] SLT 1305, 1310; *Bank of Scotland v Macleod Paxton Woolard & Co* [1998] SLT 158, per Lord Coulsfield at 274.

63 W Fratcher, *International Encyclopaedia of Comparative Law* VI, ch 11.

rem in relation to trust assets. And since in English law an equitable interest gives rise to a preference in insolvency over unsecured creditors, there is no doubt that in that and cognate systems a trust beneficiary has a right *in rem*.[64] It is, as adumbrated, a somewhat disturbing right *in rem*, since it need not be registered and there may be great difficulty in discovering its existence. But there is no need for a civilian system to incorporate in its trust law the equitable proprietary interests recognised in English law. Each civilian or mixed system can decide for itself whether to grant a trust beneficiary rights that go beyond those against the trustee's personal estate and the trust estate set out above – rights which certainly are essential to a workable system of trust law. These rights may of course include the right of a beneficiary to acquire from the trustee or the trust estate a right *in rem* such as ownership. Such rights of the beneficiary are not themselves rights *in rem*. They are rights *in personam* to acquire rights *in rem*.[65] They give the beneficiary no preferential or exclusive right to the trust assets.

What happens to this right if the trustee wrongfully disposes of a trust asset in relation to which the beneficiary has a right *in personam* to acquire a right *in rem*? Consider the position of the person who acquires the asset wrongfully disposed of. In this case the doctrine of notice, familiar to civilian lawyers, comes into play.[66] By virtue of this doctrine a right *in personam* to a right *in rem* binds those who acquire the assets with notice of its existence or who acquire the assets by lucrative title, without payment. The personal right avails against the acquirer as well as against the original debtor. This right corresponds rather closely[67] to the beneficiary's 'equitable' right in English trust law to follow trust assets into the hands of all save a bona fide purchaser for value without notice, a right which is explained as deriving from a constructive trust.[68] But it need not be treated as a right *in rem* and there is nothing distinctively equitable about it. Its basis is that the acquirer would be unjustly enriched if, in the circumstances, he or she were not obliged to hand back the asset. In a system with a developed law of unjust enrichment there is no need to have recourse to a proprietary remedy in these cases.[69]

The trust beneficiary does not therefore possess, and need not be given, a real right in the trust assets in any sense that should cause concern to a civilian lawyer. The law of trusts at a cross-cultural level can happily dispense with references to equitable ownership, equitable duties and equitable proprietary rights.

64 R Goode, *Commercial Law* (2nd edn, 1995) 58–61, 706–707.
65 In the technical language of the civil law, a *ius in personam ad rem acquirendam:* Honoré–Cameron (5th edn) 23, 29–30, 276, 388, 558–568, 576–580, see n 1 above.
66 For Scotland see *Redfearn v Sumervail* (1813) 1 Dow's App 50; *Taylor v Forbes* (1830) 4 Wilson & Shaw 450; 7 Bligh NS 417; W A Wilson and A G M Duncan, *Trusts, Trustees and Executors* (2nd edn, 1975) 147–148; for South Africa *Willoughby's Consolidated v Copthall's Stores* 1918 AD 1, 16; *De Jager v Sisana* 1930 AD 71, 80, 84; Honoré–Cameron (5th edn) 490–554, see n 1 above.
67 There may be argument about the distinction between knowledge and notice, but this does not affect the substantial correspondence.
68 The 'equitable' tracing right may be narrower than the doctrine of notice if it is the case that it arises only when there was initially a fiduciary relationship, as in the case of trustees. Whether this is so has not been finally settled.
69 Honoré–Cameron (5th edn) 133–136, see n 1 above.

CHAPTER 2

Usucapio and the Law of Trusts

Jeffrey Hackney

BACKGROUND

In the first quarter of the last millennium but one, a group or series of legal scholars in Rome created ways of thinking about, and terminological descriptions of the law which long survived the fall of their society and which are widely adopted today even by lawyers who profess vehement ignorance of their existence or legacy. It might be said that this particular way of thinking has become the new 'prose' of Western legal civilisation; Common Lawyers who deny all debt to Rome use the categories of tort, contract, property etc as if they were as elemental and self-evident as fire and water[1] and the Roman way of thinking can subliminally enter modern court rooms and class rooms in ways which are often helpful in organising thought, but sometimes not. This period in the history of Roman law is usually described as that of the classical law. The period some 500 years before it is described as pre-classical, and the period immediately following it, up to the time of Justinian's momentous compilation, is known as post-classical. It seems to be fairly widely assumed that classical is a term of praise but it is helpful to see that first and foremost, 'classical' is not an evaluation of quality, but a term descriptive of a particular style. In its stylistic usage, Classicism identifies a style of thought and exposition, which is dominated by rule, concept and precept. Three examples from the arts seem a good way into this, though the list could be extended.[2] The architecture of Palladio is said to be classical because his buildings are designed with close adherence to a rule book, for example on orders of pillars, capitals and pediments and their proportion. Unpopular[3] music of the mid-eighteenth century to the early mid-nineteenth is described as classical[4] because of its domination by structural compositional rules and rules governing the nature of keys and their sequences. The drama of the French playwrights Racine and Corneille is classical because it is written within the three 'unities' of place, time and plot: one

1 It was du Parcq LJ in *Re Schebsman* [1944] Ch 83, 104, who introduced most lawyers to Molière's M Jourdain from *Le Bourgeois Gentilhomme,* who was astonished to discover in his middle age that he had been unknowingly talking prose all his life.
2 Classical dance, classical painting, classical poetry, classical language would be a start.
3 To use a neutral term.
4 Preceded by baroque and followed by romantic.

place, one day, one story. The cultures of ancient Greece and ancient Rome adopted the constraints of classicism of this sort to such an extent that they are often referred to simply as the classical civilisations, without further explanation.

Exponents of classicism are open to evaluation from two groups, which overlap. First, like all human endeavour, they are vulnerable to attack using evaluations which are non-classical, that is from outside the technical criteria. In the world of the fine arts, criteria of beauty etc, however formulated would be an example. So those ignorant of classical rules can still admire a classical structure. Palladio would appear to be on the receiving end of much praise of this sort as would, say, the final movement of Mozart's 41st symphony. Those in the know get a double pleasure. Conversely both groups might consider that a perfectly conforming construct failed non-classical tests; the notion of 'classical rubbish' bluntly expresses that verdict. Much painting, architecture and music attracts such blunt attack. But classicists are also vulnerable to attack from adherents on the analytically distinct ground that they have deviated from the rule book. So an architect who put a Corinthian capital on the top of a pillar which had a Doric base, however pleasing that might seem to the non-adherent, would be criticised by classicists for having broken the rules. For some extremists, conformity with the rules will transcend all other criteria as a necessary condition for praise – beauty itself will have become a rule dependent idea.

All this may be applied to law. A classical system will lay out a rule book containing its fundamental concepts from which the structure of the law will be extruded. Institutions and concepts will have their set places, and detail will have to be referable to a governing principle. Conscious innovation, if it is allowed, will have to take place inside the framework and if this precept is ignored, serious disorder may ensue. Classicism in Roman classical law is visible on the first page of the book. Gaius' Institutes, written in the second century of the Common Era is our only surviving complete text from the heyday of Roman legal classicism.[5] Its elegance is derived from a simple sentence in the seventh paragraph of Book I, which must be the envy of all legal classicists since – 'all the law we use relates to persons, things or actions'. Every idea in Roman private law is derived from and can be compressed back into that simple sentence. Persons is the law of status; things is property and obligations – the latter being in Gaius' scheme divided into contract and delict/tort; actions is civil procedure. This is the high point of legal classicism and as an act of human ingenuity it ranks amongst the very highest. Once elaborated, we get a plan or diagram of the law which allows us, as does a genealogist's tree, to see the compartments of the law and the relationships between them. It is also an extremely ambitious scheme: it purports to place the whole of the private law inside this small phrase. It is indeed over-ambitious and Gaius soon discovers that his confidence is misplaced. Unjust enrichment looms within pages and cannot be accommodated. Attempts are made to squeeze it in and it is later to be affiliated in a bizarre way to the law of contract. Other supervening discoveries are affiliated to tort, and we finish in Justinian's day with two of the worst consequences of the closed book of Roman classicism – quasi-contract

5 Francis de Zulueta, *The Institutes of Gaius Parts I and II* (1953). This was the work which provided the backbone for the Institutes of Justinian in the sixth century.

and quasi-delict. A heavy price is being paid today for those who adopt Justinian's scheme but seek to free themselves from its folly, as concepts which are already defined in terms of each other have to admit a new dimension into their conceptual world. This cannot be done by reducing the font size: unjust enrichment spreads across the other categories and modern lawyers who have freed themselves from the foolish quasi-contract escape-hatch are discovering as much. The lesson may be that in general terms it is harder to reform classical structures than non-classical. The fairly non-classical early-modern common law would find it much easier to adopt the trust long after its main institutions were well settled.[6]

As with other forms of human expression, a particular classical legal system is reviewable by the two sets of criteria. Internally the system is evaluated by whether it conforms with its own basic structural concepts. So, coherence and consistency of the concepts will rate highly. The external assessment replaces beauty, sonority etc with justice, social fairness, adaptability etc. From this standpoint, if the original ideas are well conceived, as a response to social values of the society intended to be served, and the system adapts well to new social inputs, it will score highly in this adjudication. And if predictability of result is a classical characteristic, modern western systems in the liberal democracies will want some[7] classical qualities. At its worst however, legal classicism blinds its adherents to the important difference with the arts. If a classical composer moves between keys in a way which breaks the rules, no money is lost and deserted mothers keep their homes. But in legal systems where classical characteristics predominate, or are allowed to overwhelm selected areas, such consequences may follow. A severe classicist will attach great importance to internal elegance and consistency and the very internalised will regard the maintenance of the system as a value of its own. This can lead to such enormities as the maxim 'hard cases make bad law', and the 'law-as-game' syndrome will appear.[8] Classical Roman law is suspect on this external evaluation.

6 It is true that some believe that civilian systems knew trust like devices notwithstanding classical dogmatism: see R H Helmholz and Reinhard Zimmermann (eds), *Itinera Fiduciae: Trust and Treuhand in Historical Perspective* (1998).

7 It is easy for property lawyers to overplay this, being occupied as they so often are, with law which is essentially facultative and for which certainty of outcome is a major desired outcome. But if the rule of law is thought always to require predicted outcomes using existing norms, it is clear that it will on occasion have to be relegated to a subordinate role, in the absence of penal consequences. The most unfair and partial legal systems may conform to the abstract ideals of the rule of law. What is needed is a private legal system which can accommodate the kind of rapid and substantial moral change which the Western democracies have experienced in the last 50 years.

8 Contemporary opposition to the brilliantly creative judgment of Goff J in *Re Denley's Trust Deed* [1969] 1 Ch 373 may be a manifestation of English classicism. This judgment side-stepped the repressive and timorous invention of the so-called 'beneficiary principle' in the period 1950–60. Goff J's judgment, working within the doctrine of precedent, managed to rescue, as an option for settlors, the creation of a limited range of benevolent quasi-charitable purpose trusts. It is not free from difficulty, but the social benefits seem well worth the minimal legal effort. No serious argument seems to be raised that the *Denley* outcome is not a social consequence devoutly to be wished, but classicists are fiercely opposed to it on grounds of violation of the said principle, or perhaps worse, that it messes up some very elegant resulting trust theories. Unless we can find another solution to the problems posed by e g *Re Abbott* [1900] 2 Ch 326, we have lost sight of why legal systems exist in liberal democracies.

The contrasting system has no easy label. The post-1300 Common Law in England[9] is an example. In the early years after the Conquest, the courts of the Norman invaders began to intervene in legal matters. But a classical system was never envisaged. By the classical period, Roman law had a unitary court system and a mighty state to run it, and Gaius' 'all the law we use' ambition could be realised. The courts of the French invaders however did not initially set out to cover the whole law and their intervention was sporadic and patchwork, sharing jurisdiction with a number of autonomous or near-autonomous courts. There was no monolithic state sending out sovereign commands across the whole field of the law.[10] The first great book of the Common Law for example famously disavows any royal court interest in 'private agreements'.[11] Even though the Plantagenet lawyers borrowed heavily from Roman sources in their attempts to construct the new law – the second great book for example, *Bracton*, is divided into the three parts of persons, things and actions[12] – it must have been clear to them that their mission was distinct from that of their Roman predecessors. From around 1300 onwards however, as royal courts begin seriously to extend the range of their law, the English[13] abandon all pretence of Romanism[14] and to the despair of some of our contemporaries,[15] set out to solve such legal problems as were presented to them and which they cared to answer on a relatively unstructured basis, solving problems in disconnected categories which they abandon, or to which they add, with business-like common sense. There being no sustained attempts to lay out the whole law between Bracton's work and that of Blackstone in the late seventeenth century it does not seem unfair to label this system from the appearance of one of its dominant source materials, the Abridgements and to call it the 'alphabetical' model, as some now do.[16] The law is not in these sources organised into major

9 Patrick Glenn, *Legal Traditions of the World*, (2000), picks up the theme of common laws elsewhere.

10 The structure is clearly set out in J H Baker, *An Introduction to English Legal History* (4th edn, 2002), and is the subject of much of the theoretical work of S F C Milsom, *Historical Foundations of the Common Law* (2nd edn, 1981). For some rather scary implications see the same author's *The Legal Framework of English Feudalism* (1976).

11 G D G Hall (ed), *Glanvill* (1965) 124, 132. This is a late twelfth-century work.

12 S E Thorne (ed), *Bracton* (1977). This work was put together between the 1220s to the late 1250s. Wherever Bracton picked this up, whether from the Justinianic texts or from the medieval Romanists, it is clear he is not persuaded. Actions form the overwhelming bulk of the book compared to just over 10 per cent of Justinian's Institutes.

13 These are not the Anglo-Saxons, so beloved of our continental colleagues, with whom the break was made when the Normans put their own men into all positions of authority. Nor after 1300 does it make much sense to describe them as Anglo-Norman, a century after the break with Normandy and with an English-named King.

14 Even though traces of the language remain.

15 The closing words of T F T Plucknett, *Early English Legal Literature* (1958), sum it all up. Talking of the Year Books, which were the heralds of the new Common Law, he wrote (114): 'It was the Year Books, in this most obscure epoch, which maintained the continuity of English law. There was indeed the sun of Bracton and the moon of Littleton to illuminate the scene each in his season, but for most of the time English lawyers walked by the light of faint anonymous stars. Of science there was very little (and I have been at pains to lament it rather loudly). Nevertheless, English law plodded on, with its eyes stubbornly turned away from the glittering pages of the Digest to pursue its own course – insular, lay, and French (what French!). Altogether an odd story, which may well arouse our interest; indeed, it fascinated Maitland'. Lay indeed!

16 The exception of Littleton's tenures is not forgotten. But it is a tiny book and sets out to cover only a part of the law. It is noteworthy not only for its well-known virtue of seeking out the 'arguments and reasons' of the law, but also for its very Bentham-like definitional method of describing situations rather than concepts: eg there is not a definition of a term or years, but of a tenant for term

doctrinal groups and the difference might best be expressed to a modern lawyer by saying these works had an Index, but no Table of Contents, or at least no Table as any half decent modern scholar would want to produce. This system has the merit of great flexibility and a capacity to adjust to new social demands without the need to look over one's shoulder to see which category a new solution should belong to. One weakness of this institutionally conservative system was a reckless tendency to category swap in order to camouflage changes in the law. Nor was it at all well-serviced and the accretions had, by the eighteenth century, become an obstacle to understanding, possibly even to prosperity.[17] Blackstone in his Commentaries, which demonstrate some desire to return to classical modes of thinking,[18] also lays the foundations for much modern classical thinking with his memorable metaphor of the map of the law:[19] The student 'should consider his course as a general map of the law, marking out the shape of the country, it's connexions and boundaries, it's greater divisions and principal cities: it is not his business to describe minutely the subordinate limits, or to fix the longitude and latitude of every inconsiderable hamlet'. This is a potentially dangerous metaphor. Its disadvantage for classicists is that the location of the greater divisions and cities set out on a map only rarely has any conceptual underpinning. The cities were not located nor named according to any classical scheme and the image conjured up for the student will be misleading. More dangerously for the non-classicist, the locations are fixed and cannot be easily moved if it were thought convenient to do so. The image reinforces the conservative view of judicial made law at least, that it is there waiting to be found. Blackstone's contribution in his Commentaries was to envisage a plan, not a map, and the plan now has to be seen to be one of a virtual reality only, changeable even to its core if experience and changing moral and social codes so require. One of the characteristics of the English law which has so distinguished it from those founded on the Institutes, has been the way it has been able to adapt and to accept new ideas and it is likely that it has been this characteristic which has allowed it so readily to accept and develop the trust. This concept was allowed to grow without too much concern about whether it was located in property or obligations. Modern attempts to force it into these categories seem, to some extent, misconceived. In English law terms it is indexed under 'T', cutting across the classicists' plan.

of years: 'Tenant for term of years is where a man lets lands or tenements to another for a term of certain years, the number of which has been agreed by the lessor and lessee.' *Littleton, His Treatise of Tenures* (T E Tomlins (ed), 1841 and 1978). And H L A Hart, 'Definition and Theory in Jurisprudence' (1954) 70 LQR 37. The Romans too foreshadowed this definitional technique, see n 45 below.

17 This requires us to answer the 'what-if' question of how much more wealthy England might have become if it had had an efficient and speedy judicature. J Getzler, 'Theories of Property and Economic Development', (1996) 26 Journal of Interdisciplinary History 639, 645–650 picks up Max Weber's related speculations.

18 The structure of the Institutes is clearly laid out in the edition of William Blackstone's *Commentaries on the Laws of England* by Wayne Morrison (2001), and discussed in the Introduction. Blackstone did not approve of attempts to force English law into the Justinianic scheme but he used his four book model.

19 William Blackstone, *Commentaries on the Laws of England* (1979) I, 35.

THE TREATMENT OF GRANTS VOID FOR INFORMALITY IN ROMAN LAW AND EQUITY

For present purposes a formality is a legal requirement not forming part of the definition of the substantive transaction to which it is attached: parties need to be sure which transaction they are involved in before knowing which formality is applicable. So a grant which is void for informality will have been made by parties who have capacity; who have property capable of being conveyed; and which they intend to transfer and be transferred for an interest which the law recognises. But this transaction will lack some other, essentially irrelevant characteristic such as writing or a deed or appearance before an official. In Roman law, some property, the so-called *res mancipi*[20] could not be conveyed without the presence of the parties, witnesses, a set verbal (originally oral) formula and someone holding a pair of scales. In a world where written record was not freely available, this made a good pass at solving a serious problem in the law of grants of things of special value.

One of the questions which arises when discussing the trust with lawyers from the Civilian tradition, is whether it can replicate the notion of proprietary interests. Its free-range past is now causing some havoc, especially when those from different traditions are let loose upon it.[21] There is a classical Roman tradition, in England at least, of treating this question in highly abstract, not to say metaphorical or mystical terms. W W Buckland, having decided that a definition of ownership as the right to use, enjoy and destroy would need modification, proceeds to say that it would not do at all for that species of ownership which the Romans called *dominium*: '*Dominium* is the ultimate right, that which has no right behind it. It may [have] no practical content, but it is still *dominium*. . . '[22] Other forms of ownership, not being *dominium,* are then listed by Buckland, including most importantly for these purposes, the so-called 'bonitary ownership'. This phrase described the rights of one who had taken a conveyance which was void for informality and it explains Buckland's decision to sever *dominium* from enjoyment but to retain it as a species of ownership. Under the old civil[23] law of Rome, *dominium* of *res mancipi* could not pass without the public grant. This was a formalities problem in the sense that the substantive elements of the transaction, namely conveyance, were present, but some additional requirement for legal validity (in this case the pantomime with the kitchen scales) was missing. If the formalities were not complied with, the recipient in the old Roman law acquired only possession. The old civil law's solution to this problem had been to give possession only to the transferee, but after a period of one or two years[24] by what might be a

20 Items of property in early Roman law to which they evidently attached special economic or other importance.

21 'The *Webb v Webb* farrago'. [1994] QB 696 (European Court of Justice). See J E Penner, *The Law of Trusts* (3rd edn, 2002) 44, where it is said quite rightly, though perhaps from a different point of view, that this half-learned stuff 'still occasionally raises its bewildered head to confuse and annoy . . .'

22 W W Buckland, *A Textbook of Roman Law from Augustus to Justinian* (3rd edn, 1963) 188.

23 The ancient law of Rome was known as the civil law. The magistrates, most particularly the Praetors, in a stroke not worlds away from the intervention of the Chancellor in England, modified it by using their control of access to the courts. Unlike the Chancellor they managed to do it, not by foolishly establishing a parallel court structure, but by manipulating the writs – the *formulae.*

24 Depending on the nature of the property transferred.

species of acquisitive prescription,[25] gave *dominium* to the transferee. This prescriptive device was *usucapio.* The magistrates however, in their *ius honorarium,* (perhaps looking on that as done which ought to have been done), intervened to give the possessor interim protection greater than that normally offered to bare possessors. The possessor acquired additional rights against not only the *dominus*/owner who had granted, but also against third parties, both to retain possession and to recover it if lost. Once *usucapio* had operated, the protection of the magistrates was not needed nor offered: the possessor was now *dominus,* and his *dominium* was not only ownership but a very fine capitalist version of it. It was the Byzantines who first called the interim protection offered by the magistrates 'bonitary ownership'. So 'bonitary ownership' could not endure for more than two years. The lawyers of the classical period were more cautious and described the possessor only as having the thing as his goods.[26] It is arguable that the earlier description is more apt. The non-possessing grantor-*dominus* had title but he had no ownership.

Equally the interest of the possessing grantee non-*dominus* cannot be ownership. The classical lawyers were clear that a man could not be made owner for a time and even if an agreement were made to do such a thing, there would be only an obligation to retransfer, not an automatic reversion.[27] This may explain why Gaius does not describe this short, fixed term enjoyment as *dominium* nor seek to find any other way of describing it as ownership. At the end of the period, the possessor either becomes owner if he has satisfied the requirements of *usucapio*, or never becomes owner. Both the brevity of the enjoyment and the certainty of termination conjoin to make the term bonitary ownership misleading and inapt. In the language of the Common Law, it may have been a proprietary interest, just as a one-year lease,[28] but there seems to be no definition of ownership in use either in Rome or here which simply fits.[29] Perhaps it was the Byzantine re-designation of this useful device which helped prevent them from easily accommodating the common law's trustee, who has title and possession but no ownership.[30]

25 It is unusual to see a device which cures titles defective only in form as a thoroughbred acquisitive prescription device.

26 Gaius 1.54. It is said to be Theophilus, one of Justinian's compilers, who first coins the phrase. Buckland, 191, n 2 (see n 22).

27 Buckland, 189, n 1 (see n 22).

28 And just as it seems right to describe a lessee for 999 years as owner.

29 This is not ignoring the fact that some modern town planning legislation treats as owner people who have only time-limited interests.

30 This assumes that there is no serious definition of ownership which is rights-free. Trustees may have rights to recover trust property at common law in the narrow sense, but they have no choice and they derive no benefit from their actions. The settlement of 1616 set out in Ch 1 Rep 49–50, whatever the political spin, settled that where a common law right conflicted with an equitable duty, it was for all serious purposes the equitable duty which prevailed. This decision is widely known, but hardly ever cited and less frequently quoted; it reads as follows: 'Forasmuch as Mercy and Justice be the true Supporters of our Royal Throne, and that it properly belongeth unto us in our Princely Office to take Care and provide, that our Subjects have equal and indifferent Justice ministred unto them: And that where their Case deserveth to be relieved in Course of Equity by Suit in our Court of Chancery, they should not be abandoned and exposed to perish under the Rigor and Extremity of our Laws, We in our Princely Judgment having well weighed and with mature Deliberation considered of the several Reports of our learned Counsel, and all the Parts of them, do approve, ratify and confirm, as well the Practice of our Court of Chancery expressed in their first Certificate, as the Opinions for the Law upon the Statute mentioned in their later Certificate, the same having Relation unto the Case sent

The English Common Law treated this particular legal problem differently. Clearly a legal system cannot ignore formalities failures but equally between consenting adults such failures are not a serious threat to the integrity of the system.[31] Some kind of wrist-slap is called for. The Roman slap was to make the transferee wait his year, though he waited for increasingly little as the magistrates increased their protection.[32] The Common Law slap was to recharacterise the failed grant as a contract to make the same grant. The context in which this is most recognisable to modern lawyers is the reaction of the courts to the Real Property Act 1845. Section 3 of that Act made a deed a mandatory requirement for the creation of certain leases – without it they were to be 'void at law'. The court of Common Pleas' first reaction to this section either was, or was taken to be, to take it at face value and invalidate the transaction.[33] Counsel had argued that it could take effect as a contract for a lease even though void as a lease. This ingenious argument was based on the precedents revealing the early history of the lease as a contract. Sheppard and Bacon for instance had emphasised the contractual nature of lease creation and it had been held that for a lease, words of grant and words of contract had the same effect.[34] But section 3 was regarded by the profession, it seems, as a major 'statutory blunder'[35] and there was much unhappiness by the judges in this case at the way it seemed doomed to go. There was a saving grace in precedent terms, that the parties were held not actually to have intended a contract, but it was a slender line. The result was plainly regarded as unacceptable by the profession, and relying on the historic link between contract and lease, first the Chancery, then the Exchequer of Pleas and finally the Common Pleas itself produced

unto them by our Chancellor: And do will and command that our Chancellor, or Keeper of the Great Seal for the Time being, shall not hereafter desist to give unto our Subjects, upon their several Complaints now or hereafter to be made, such Relief in Equity (notwithstanding any Proceedings at the Common Law against them) as shall stand with the Merit and Justice of their Cause, and with the former, ancient and continued Practice and Presidency of our Chancery have done: And for that it appertaineth to our Princely Office only to judge over all Judges, and to discern and determine such Differences, as at any time may and shall arise between our several Courts touching their Jurisdictions, and the same to settle and determine, as we in our Princely Wisdom shall find to stand most with our Honour, and the Example of our Royal Progenitors in the best Times, and the general Weals and Good of our People, for which we are to answer unto God who hath placed us over them: Our Will and Pleasure is, that our whole Proceedings therein, by the Decrees formerly set down, be inrolled in Chancery, there to remain of Record, for the better Extinguishing of the like Differences and Questions that may arise in future Times. Per ipsum Regem 18 July 14, 1616.'

31 There may be fiscal consequences if taxation is linked to certain formal transactions either because they are mandatory or because they are in any event used by the profession to achieve other results. Public formalities in conveyancing law may also assist certain types of land taxation.

32 He could not originally free a slave transferred without formality, but even here the magistrates intervened to give substantial effect to a purported manumission. Buckland at 77 (see n 22).

33 *Stratton v Pettit* (1855) 16 C B 420, 139 ER 822.

34 Bacon's *Abridgment*, title *Leases and Terms for Years*, states: 'Where one by articles covenants, grants, and agrees with JS that he shall have such lands, or have, hold, and enjoy such lands for so many years, these are words sufficient to show a present contract for the lessee's enjoying of those lands, and therefore amount to a present lease of them as effectually as if there had been the words dimisit, locavit, or such like'; cited at 16 CB 429. In Sheppard's *Touchstone*, vol 2, 82 (Preston's edition), the rule is laid down thus: 'A deed that is intended and made to one purpose may enure to another; for, if it will not take effect in that way it was intended, it may take effect another way; [provided it may have that effect consistently with the intention of the parties]': cited *Stratton* (see n 33) at 433.

35 Maule J, *Stratton* at 433: 'The 7 & 8 Vict c. 765 was a notorious statutory blunder. It was incongruous and impossible of operation, and its absurdities were so great that the framers themselves had no very distinct notion of its meaning.'

the new rule that a lease void for informality would be treated as a contract for that same lease. The formalities for contracts, as indeed their substantive requirements such as consideration,[36] were still required,[37] but common law or equitable remedies were available for breach. Performance of this contract would be to grant a legal lease and it would be on the strength of that performance that the lessee would acquire the full possessory remedies at common law: the failed lease is treated as a contract for a lease, not as an agreement to occupy. The new rules do not appear to have been formulated as recharacterisations of grants as contracts, but as attempts to discover the true intention of the parties. The modern position seems to be to treat the new rules as recharacterisation; that is that all failed grants of leases should be treated as contracts for leases.[38] It is a moot point whether all failed grants of real property governed by the successor to section 3, s 52 of the Law of Property Act 1925, are also rescued as contracts to make such grants. Plainly they could not have been rescued under the original 'leases are descended from contracts' theory, though if that has been developed into a general recharacterisation theory, there would be no logic in not applying it here.[39]

This is not the place to divert into the whole, vexed issue of recharacterisation by English property judges. Grants of interests which fail because the interest is not in the list, such as a lease for the duration of the war, cannot be recharacterised as contracts to make such a grant, since the whole process would become a loop, though Lord Templeman in *Prudential*[40] is bold enough to assert, on the basis of cases of voidness for informality, that one who enters under the grant of a 'lease' for the duration of the war, and pays rent, picks up a periodic tenancy. Grants of future property, that is property not yet in the hands of the grantor, whether the property exists or not, look void for something or other, presumably substance, and we are told that Common Law judges so treated them.[41] But Chancery judges have happily[42] applied a variety of the leases rule to them and treated them, if they satisfy the demanding Equitable contracts rules,[43] as contracts to grant that property when the would-be grantor gets it. Failed

36 Assuming consideration to be part of the substantive definition of a bargain, if that is what a contract is at common law.

37 The failed grant is treated as if it were a contract, that is, it remains subject to the contractual tests: it is not deemed to be a *valid* contract.

38 R E Megarry and H W R Wade, *The Law of Real Property* (by Charles Harpum, 6th edn, 2000) 772–773; G C Cheshire and E H Burn, *Modern Law of Real Property* (16th edn, 2000), 402. The latter seems not to pick up the point that the common law also treated such transactions as contracts. Perhaps it will be picked up in the *Post-Modern Law of Real Property.*

39 *Megarry and Wade* does not mention s 52 in the section on the freehold estates. *Cheshire and Burn* picks the point up in the section on Conveyance but p 839 n 2 simply refers the reader back to the discussion of leases as if the matter is concluded there.

40 *Prudential Assurance v London Residuary Body* [1992] 2 AC 386 at 392.

41 Snell's *Equity* (30th edn, 2000) 5–28.

42 '[A]lways' apparently. Snell, *ibid.* The history is littered with cases explicable on the grounds that an element of promise was present. *Warmstrey v Tanfield* (1628) 1 Rep Ch 29 is often cited as the first case, but it has complicating features. *Theobalds v Duffoy* (1730) 9 Mod 102 looks a clear statement, but the reliable modern authorities, the dubious *Tailby v Official Receiver* (1888) 13 App Cas. 523, and *Re Lind* [1915] 2 Ch 345 all post date the corrupting influence of the leases cases. *Tailby,* which seems to cut off the doctrine from its contractual roots and reliance on specific performance, may be part of the drift away from the reasoning of the early leases cases and to fall more in line with the simple recharacterisation law which seems to have replaced them.

43 Notably value-consideration.

transfers to trustees on trust will not however be recharacterised as declarations of trust, unless the court wants to defeat the IRC.[44]

THE TREATMENT OF GRANTS BY A NON-OWNER IN ROMAN LAW AND EQUITY

Grants by a non-owner raise economic and moral issues wholly different from those raised by grants void for informality: the conflict between security of vested rights and security of transactions. The Common Law's basic rule is like the Roman basic rule: property is indefeasible. So whereas Digest 41.1 is headed 'Concerning the Acquisition of Ownership', 41.2 is headed 'Concerning the Acquisition and Loss of Possession'. The point could not be more neatly put: you keep your ownership until you decide otherwise but this is not true of possession.[45] So in general legal interests were indefeasible, except, as one would expect in an alphabetical system, where it suited otherwise. So the Common Law had its exceptions – treason, felony, flight from felony, market overt, deodand, treasure trove, waif, stray, wreck, factoring, quite apart from statutory intervention like contraband, drug profits etc.[46] Property has never been indefeasible at Common Law, but the exceptions are pragmatic and do not form a coherent whole. Equity was different. Equity allowed for the creation of its interests if conscience required it, just as the Common Law allowed for the creation of leases or life estates by people who, having the fee simple, did not have leases or life estates to dispose of. The notion of a power to create what one does not have has been silently assumed in both systems. Beneficial legal owners did not have equitable interests before the Chancellor established his jurisdiction and, under the constitutional convention governing the parallel existence of the two sets of courts, in the absence of a jurisdiction giving fact, no equitable interest could exist. This has been silently taken for granted in all the cases on the Statute of Frauds and s 53 of the Law of Property Act 1925, in that a beneficial legal owner who has disposed of property has never been required also to conform with the formalities rules, if any,[47] governing the disposition of legal interests. Some resulting trusts have caused anxiety in that the proprietary arithmetic theories[48] have been thought by some to be incompatible with this simple truth. When a settlor fails to exhaust the beneficial interest[49] by conveying a bare legal

44 There may be a good, though not overwhelming policy reason for the first part of this sentence. The latter part is based on *Re Rose* [1949] Ch 78.

45 There is a forward reference here to more recently articulated theories of definition. The titles are not 'Concerning Ownership' etc. The reference to 'more recent' is to H L A Hart's Inaugural Lecture, 'Definition and Theory in Jurisprudence' (1954) 70 LQR 37 picking up the work of Jeremy Bentham. The avoidance of 'Concerning Possession' also pre-echoes the idea in A Kocourek, *Jural Relations* (1927) ch 20 that there is no separate definition of possession: we have rules for acquiring and rules for losing, and if you have acquired and not yet lost, you may count yourself as having it, but there are no discrete rules governing the middle state.

46 Some of this looks 'public' law to a modern lawyer brought up in the Roman tradition, but in a feudal legal system bold assertions to that effect can look seriously anachronistic, not to say misconceived.

47 None for chattels for example.

48 Jeffrey Hackney, *Understanding Equity and Trusts (1987)* 153.

49 See Lord Upjohn in *Vandervell v IRC* [1967] 2 AC 291 at 313, echoed by Lord Browne-Wilkinson in *Westdeutsche Landesbank Girozentrale v Islington London Borough Council* [1996] AC 669.

estate to a bare trustee so that a trust 'resulting in pattern'[50] is created, or where he conveys a bare legal estate to trustees on trust for *A* for life, so that a 'true' resulting trust results, it will be true that he now has something he never before had.[51] But his act is not a disposition but an act of creation, similar to and the reverse of, a declaration of trust. It seems clear from the *Grey*[52] line of cases that to be a disposition for the purposes of the legislation, the disponor must have started with the interest alleged to have been disposed of and someone else must have finished with substantially the same interest. So the failing to exhaust settlor in a single act splits the legal and equitable interest just as does a settlor who declares himself trustee, and he does not dispose of the whole equitable interest. Conversely in *Vandervell*,[53] when a beneficiary of a bare trust directs his trustee to transfer the legal estate to a third party so as to make him full beneficial owner, this is not a disposition of an equitable interest, since the transferee does not get it: it is an act of destruction.[54]

The Common Law's response to the problems of the innocent purchaser of another's property was market overt as a limited mercantile exception and for the rest the possessor had to rely on the law of limitation of actions, which gave no title but barred the action of the person hitherto entitled.[55] But the Chancery went one step further and allowed its property rights to be defeasible on the same general theory as it allowed their creation.[56] The bona fide purchaser of a legal estate for value without notice takes free of prior equitable interests. This notorious feature is wholly jurisdictionally based.[57] Attempts to justify it on policy grounds, on the basis that the settlor chose this trustee and therefore his beneficiaries should lose their (proprietary) interest, are barely worth repetition in a post Old Testament world, quite apart from the fact that the

50 Peter Birks, *An Introduction to the Law of Restitution* (1985) 60–61.

51 If the act is not a disposition, where the subject matter is chattels, Law of Property Act 1925, s 53(2) does not need to be invoked. There has been no disposition of an equitable interest subsisting at the date of the disposition. The plaintiff in *Hodgson v Marks* [1971] Ch 892 was presumably in trouble under s 53(1)(a) in that she had set out to create an equitable interest in land.

52 *Grey v IRC* [1960] AC 1.

53 *Vandervell v IRC* (see n 49) above.

54 The fact that a beneficial legal owner can get an injunction to protect it in Equity does not support the view that he must therefore have an equitable interest in the property. Snell's *Equity* (1st edn, 1868), divides the Chancery jurisdiction into three: the Exclusive jurisdiction; the Concurrent and the Auxiliary. This debate takes place in the Exclusive jurisdiction where trusts are the prime feature. Remedies are in a long list of Chancery assistance offered to those who also have rights at law and are properly located in the Concurrent jurisdiction. Injunctions are in any event based on the bad behaviour of the defendant, if a need is still felt to find an equitable ground of intervention. The conduct of the plaintiff will only be relevant to bar him from relief if he has not washed his hands.

55 This is not to ignore the bona fide purchaser rules in commercial law, notably those about securities, negotiable instruments and agency.

56 *Pilcher v Rawlins* (1872) 7 Ch App 259.

57 The passages are in the judgment of James LJ at 268–269: 'such a purchaser's plea of purchase for valuable consideration without notice is an absolute, unqualified, unanswerable defence, and an unanswerable plea to the jurisdiction of this court'. It may safely be assumed that an appeal court judge in England, hearing a case involving English residents and property inside the realm would understand the difference between 'we are persuaded by the arguments of the defendant' and 'we have no jurisdiction'. The arguments from policy about the nature of the role of the settlor might fit better with parts of US trust law. See for example Uniform Trust Code 2000, Section 411(a): 'A noncharitable irrevocable trust may be modified or terminated upon consent of the settlor and all beneficiaries, even if the modification or termination is inconsistent with a material purpose of the trust . . .' English courts seem much more ambivalent about the post-trust role of the settlor. The very

beneficiaries may be infants or incapable. And arguments based on fairness apply equally to the common law situation and were, as is essential in a capitalist system, repudiated: I sell your stolen bicycle to a bona fide purchaser and he has to find me if he wants his value back after you have recovered your bike. Security of vested rights was and is the default position of judges in both jurisdictions and what is crucial in this instance is not the behaviour of the trustee or the settlor but the fact that the trustee has vested a legal title in a transferee who can prove the negative, namely that he has done no wrong, by proving the inconsistent positives – good faith, value, no notice[58] – and thereby take himself out of the jurisdiction. He is not 'Equity's darling' in that Equity shows him no favours – if James LJ is right, a Chancery court before the judicature reforms of the 1870s should not even have entered judgment in the dispute, but simply declined to hear it. Jurisdiction belonged in the Queen's Bench where judgment was automatically in favour of the party with the legal estate, as it had always[59] been.

It is this doctrine which is often cited by civilians as being evidence that trust interests cannot be proprietary.[60] The inarticulated major premiss is that property interests are indefeasible. They might as well argue of course that therefore there were no proprietary rights at Common Law (in the narrow sense) either, but it cannot be said that the Common Law of property[61] holds much fascination for modern civilians. But what they fail to recognise is the effect of *usucapio*, which led a double life. It not only cured grants void for informality but grants void for substantive failure – taking from a non-owner. *Usucapio* in the civil law of Rome, operating in true 'acquisitive prescription' mode cured such grants in favour of the grantee and so established defeasible property at the core of the Roman system. The new acquirer got ownership and he got it without the consent of the previous owner nor by transfer from him. Nor was there some presumption of a lost grant.[62] The ownership of the previous owner is defeated just as is the ownership of the beneficiary under the trust. The successful usucaptor seems to get an ownership identical to that of his predecessor, if it is the case that servitudes survive *usucapio*,[63] just as the *Pilcher* purchaser gets the title of the settlor of the trust, along with any limitations it might have, such as legal easements.

origin of powers in settlements as ways of tempering the rigours of the duties imposed by the Chancellors is a core expression of this importance. It figures again prominently in recent discussions of trustee exemption clauses: *Trustee Exemption Clauses*, Law Commission Consultation Paper 171 (2003).

58 The development of constructive notice does appear to have seriously diminished.

59 Nearly always, anyway. Common law judges may well have tried to solve some of these problems by using the writ of Account, until they gave up when the Chancery solution seemed to have done it far simpler.

60 *Webb v Webb* (see n 21) above. The view is not confined to civilians. It may have some historical truth for the period prior to the late nineteenth century, but the heavy emphasis on property which then came into the law superseded any justification for it.

61 Especially if it is real property.

62 Buckland, 242 (see n 22) above.

63 Alan Watson, *Roman Private Law* (1971) 63 suggests that in the pre-classical period only rustic servitudes could be usucapted. Barry Nicholas, *An Introduction to Roman Law* (1962) 116 n 3 says the acquirer takes subject to all servitudes, just as does the acquirer by taking of abandoned things. These two examples seem to confound classical notions that all modes of acquisition are derivative or original.

What is bizarre however is that modern commentators are unanimous in their assertion that *usucapio* was used by the Romans to solve not only the minor problem of grants void for informality but also used the same set of rules for resolving the conflict between security of vested rights and security of transactions. The *usucapio* rules operating in this context are not dissimilar to the *Pilcher v Rawlins* approach, namely by making the purchaser set up the Caesar's wife defence of total purity and regularity.[64] But if the Romans really did use the same rule in both cases, requiring similarly punishing standards from the grantee with only a formally defective title, it is a black mark on their jurisprudence and their common sense. The question is whether they actually did. The Roman law textbooks seem all to assume it.[65] The clearest account is in Thomas, as follows. *Usucapio* is ancient and the only early requirement was possession of the thing held for two years for land and one year for all else. This requirement meant that in practice the grantee from a non-owner would rarely usucapt, since the owner would be bound to catch up with him inside the period, and so *usucapio* would in practice have been limited to those who took only under a grant void for informality. But there were dangers in these short periods in the expanding Empire and so, in order to protect the owner, further restrictive requirements were imposed on *usucapio*. The developed law required that stolen things could never be acquired by *usucapio*; that the possession had to be uninterrupted; that the grantee was in good faith; and the transferee had to have acquired possession as the result of some transaction which was normally a good reason for transferring ownership, the so called *justa causa*,[66] which might not be imaginary – it had to be valid as well as thought by the parties to be valid.

This regime sets up a stiff test for the grantee from a non-owner and is heavily biassed in favour of security of vested rights. The transferee must not only be pure (good faith) but transacting ordinary business (*justa causa*) and faultless (no imaginary *causa*). What is more, the trump card is hidden in the pack and the grantee cannot see it – the thing must never have been stolen. So security of transactions may prevail, but the burden is not light. For the transferee from the owner by a grant void for informality however, the requirements are nothing short of ludicrous and the attempts by the text writers to give these simple phrases a meaning which covers both situations is silent witness to subliminal embarrassment. Good faith in its core usage means that the grantee believes the grantor has power to make the grant. Quite why the bonitary owner, who is ex hypothesi taking from the owner, has also to believe that fact, is

64 *Cæsar's wife must be above suspicion.* The name of Pompeia having been mixed up with an accusation against P Clodius, Cæsar divorced her; not because he believed her guilty, but because the wife of Cæsar must not even be suspected of crime. (Suetonius, *Julius Cæsar,* 74.) The good old days.

65 W W Buckland, 241–249 (see n 22) above; J A C Thomas, *Textbook of Roman Law* (1976) 157–163; H A Jolowicz, and Barry Nicholas, *Historical Introduction to the Study of Roman Law* (3rd edn, 1972) 151–155; Barry Nicholas, *An Introduction to Roman Law* (1962) 122. Francis de Zulueta, *The Institutes of Gaius, Part II Commentary* (1953) 70 comes closest to seeing the problem, but even he thinks all that is needed is a different formulation of the requirements.

66 Poorly phrased by Thomas at 162 as 'some transaction in consequence of which ownership would usually pass'. This makes *justa causa* and conveyance synonymous on one reading. Thomas does not mean this: a *justa causa* is the reason for the conveyance – sale, gift etc. Buckland at 246 is guilty of the same lack of precision: 'some fact which is ordinarily a basis of acquisition'. This again is fine if you know what he means, but it can mislead the unwary.

unexplained: belief seems a useful tool when knowledge fails, but just how one can be required also to believe something which one knows to be true belongs to another discipline. The *justa causa* rule makes sense in an overly regulated system where *justa causa* was required for all conveyances, even from owners of property for which there were no formalities requirements,[67] though in this case the *causa* was allowed to be imaginary. It makes sense in the context of the transferee from a non-owner to have the stiffer rule that the *causa* must be actually valid, but it is hard to see why, in the case of a transfer from an owner which is void for informality, they did not follow the same rule as for conveyances by owners of property for which no formality was required, namely that the *causa* could be putative. But this pales into logical insignificance compared with the rule that the thing may not have been ever stolen. In the case of the bonitary owner this is a logical impossibility. Finally, the length of time rule; this makes the sense which Thomas gives it in the context of the transfer from the non-owner since it gives the owner time to catch up and reclaim his rights over his things before time cuts him off. Extensions of the period in the later law reflect the growing size of the Empire. Extending the period for the bonitary owner makes no sense at all and the original purpose of the delay cannot have been to allow him time to catch up with the owner: it was the owner who transferred the thing to him and the owner could catch up in seconds. No one however thinks that that is what was wanted. The delay can only have had a penal function.

The conclusion from common sense and from our preconceptions of the high quality of classical Roman law says there must be some mistake. It is indeed possible that this is an instance where we have been stitched up by Justinian's compilers. Our access to classical law, with one famous exception, is via the compilers. They systematically went through the traditional texts bringing them into line with Justinian's law. The originals were consigned to a metaphysical if not actual bonfire. So although modern scholarship is able to make a good stab at whether particular texts have been modified, we know that we are not infallible and that error may slip through. What is of interest here is that Justinian abolished the category of things which required formal conveyance, leaving only the category of conveyance by a non-owner as the subject matter of acquisitive prescription. It would have made sense for the compilers therefore ruthlessly to have eliminated all references to those who took by a conveyance void for informality. The error might then be for us to have missed that, and knowing as we do that in the classical period there were two functions, we have assumed that the rules which survive for transfers from non-owners also applied in the classical law to both circumstances.

The exceptional refugee from the bonfires mentioned above was the said Gaius. His work escaped the censors because it was overwritten in a palimpsest which predated the compilation. Gaius 2.41 talks of *usucapio* by the man who has taken under a conveyance void for informality. 2.42 says that under the old law *usucapio* was two years for land and one year for other things. 2.43 says 'we may also acquire by *usucapio* things which have been delivered to us by one who is not their owner'. There follow the remaining rules from the *usucapio* list. It is tempting to hope that in this

67 So-called *res nec mancipi,* like English chattels, were subject to no formal requirements on transfer.

case our classical ancestors had seen the major policy differences between the two situations and that Gaius' structure is our last glimpse of this. The classical scheme might then have been that for conveyance from a non-owner, the wrist-slap is the one-year wait. This is the equivalent of the common law's recharacterisation of grant as contract. For conveyance from a non-owner, the pre-classical lawyers began with a similar scheme but with the overriding rule that there was to be no *usucapio* of a stolen thing.[68] As society grew and owners became more likely to be distanced from their property, the Romans developed a formidable list of obstacles for the transferee from a non-owner, but if he satisfied them, he got a title. But if the substantial tests in the books applied to *usucapio* by a 'bonitary owner' the system loses all claim to respect. This is a resort of desperation, since the only other conclusion is to attribute major lack of sophistication to a system in which this is not a generalised characteristic. The interpolationists' heyday is gone: we are now reconciled to the fact that Ulpian might not have got an alpha in Professor Mommsen's translation class. But the suggestion here is not one of minor interpolation or of detailed dissatisfaction with individual texts, but of wholesale excision of a branch of obsolete law. Justinian's compilers did not mislead his readers, but if this hypothesis is right, they mislead us.

68 This rule is in the XII Tables and is confirmed or amended in some way by the *Lex Atinia* of about 150 BCE.

CHAPTER 3

Formality and Informality in Property and Contract

John Cartwright

Edward Burn's first edition of Cheshire's *Modern Law of Real Property* was the 11th edition in 1972. By the time he taught me we were using the 12th edition, and I recall a little game he used to play: he would patiently hear his students give an account of topics in Land Law which kept faithfully to a point of view set out in *Cheshire* – and then proceed to demolish the point of view. From that experience we learnt, of course, always to question what we read. But it also said much about Edward Burn's view of the editorship of a book such as *Cheshire*. He took over a book which was a well-established and leading text, and the contents of which (as we discovered to our cost) he did not necessarily agree with in every detail. But it was *Cheshire*, not *Burn*. This is not to say that Edward Burn's *Cheshire* did not, right from the start, show the signs of new ideas which were meant to keep Cheshire's Law of Real Property really *Modern*; it did – for example, his very first edition brought registered land into every chapter, to reflect the reality of conveyancing. But he rightly respected the structure, principles and even, largely, the detail of the text he had inherited. But, little by little, the structure and the text changed: always keeping faithfully to the spirit of *Cheshire*, but in the 13th edition (1982) becoming in name as well as in substance *Cheshire and Burn*. By now – in the 16th edition, on the 75th anniversary of the enactment of the 1925 property legislation – relatively little of Cheshire's text remains. But it is still a thoroughly modern and revised edition of the book which Cheshire first wrote. The lineage remains apparent.

One subject at which Edward Burn has worked quietly, right from his first edition of *Cheshire*, is what would commonly be called proprietary estoppel. His 1972 edition was the first to give licences their own section within Cheshire's chapter on easements and profits; and the first edition under the name of *Cheshire and Burn* in 1982 gave licences their own chapter. A section appears headed 'licences by estoppel'; and the tentative suggestion (first written in the 1972 edition[1]) that: 'the law on this point is still in the process of development, but it seems that a new right *in alieno solo* is

1 *Cheshire and Burn* (11th edn, 1972) 573.

emerging in the twentieth century' becomes (from the 1982 edition[2] onwards): 'the law on this point is still in the process of development, but it seems that a new right *in alieno solo* has emerged in this century.' There are matters with which one might take issue: whether the creation of a novel interest in land since 1925 is compatible with the scheme of the 1925 property legislation,[3] and whether it is right now to speak of 'licences by estoppel' – perhaps it might be time to take the next step, and take 'proprietary estoppel' out of the shadow of the chapter on licences and give it its own identity.[4] But the rather cautious, historically-grounded and context-sensitive approach to proprietary estoppel which is taken by even the latest edition of *Cheshire and Burn* should not be put aside incautiously. And, in particular, it is right to continue to set the doctrine of proprietary estoppel in the context of the informal creation of interests within the law of *property*. There is a tendency in the modern law to think that estoppels have not only a life of their own, but also a unity: that there is a single, underlying principle to all estoppels and so well-established rules and limits on the application of one form of estoppel can be discarded simply by noticing that there is no such limitation in another form.

A question which continues to be asked in England – and which will sooner or later be asked of the House of Lords – is whether the well-established limits on the doctrine of promissory estoppel should be revised in the light of either (in particular) the operation of proprietary estoppel or (more generally) the recognition of a unity of principle underlying the different forms of estoppel which breaks down the limits traditionally placed on the individual forms of estoppel. Most commonly the question is whether the rule, generally held to have been established by the decision of the Court of Appeal in *Combe v Combe*,[5] that promissory estoppel cannot be 'used as a sword' can withstand the development that proprietary estoppel can be so used. The Court of Appeal[6] has recently declined to take this step, and has said that any such development must be made by the House of Lords. Promissory estoppel could indeed be developed to allow enforcement of promises which are unsupported by consideration; and there is much to be said in favour of such a development. But such issues will not be the focus of this brief article, which contains instead a short and simple message: that the 'unity of estoppels' argument should not be the basis of that development. It is far too simplistic to argue that, just because proprietary estoppel can be 'used as a sword', promissory estoppel should also. Proprietary estoppel must be understood in its context within the law of property; there is a more subtle web of links between proprietary estoppel and other areas of the law of property, both real and personal, which cannot be ignored.

2 *Cheshire and Burn* (13th edn, 1982) 569.

3 Lawson and Rudden, *The Law of Property* (2nd edn, 1982) 220; Megarry and Wade, *The Law of Real Property* (6th edn, C Harpum, 2000) 733–734.

4 *Megarry and Wade* ch 13, and esp 750–751.

5 [1951] 2 KB 215, [1951] 1 All ER 767, CA. The statement that proprietary estoppel can be 'used as a sword' is itself too simple because – as discussed later in this paper – it is used defensively to prevent the original property owner from relying on his own failure of formality to create the (new) property right alleged – and so to prevent the original owner from asserting his prior property right.

6 *Baird Textile Holdings Ltd v Marks & Spencer plc* [2001] EWCA Civ 274, [2002] 1 All ER (Comm) 737 (estoppel by convention, but also discussing promissory estoppel and proprietary estoppel).

THE ROLE OF 'PROPRIETARY ESTOPPEL'

This is not the place to give a detailed account[7] but, in brief, 'proprietary estoppel' – or estoppel by 'encouragement' or 'acquiescence' – covers the case where the owner of land causes the claimant to believe that he has, or will have, an interest in his land; and in reliance on this the claimant acts in such a way that it becomes unconscionable for the landowner to insist on his strict legal rights in such a way as to deny the claimant the interest he believed he would have.[8] The belief may be created not only by an express assurance by the landowner that he has, or will have, the interest in land,[9] but also by the landowner allowing ('acquiescing in') the claimant to continue in his own mistaken belief about his rights.[10] It is often said that the claimant must have relied to his detriment on the landowner's assurance, or on his own mistaken belief, that he has or will have the interest; but what in substance this means is that the claimant's conduct in response to the assurance (or his belief) is such that, if the owner were now allowed simply to deny the expectation he has caused or allowed to continue, it would be prejudicial (or 'unconscionable') to the claimant.[11] It is, however, clear that the remedy which follows upon the claimant's establishing a proprietary estoppel is not necessarily the full protection of the claimant's expectation. The remedy is at the court's discretion: and it has generally been said that the court will do what is appropriate to satisfy the equity which has arisen by virtue of the claimant's reliance. This may be to order that the landowner grant the claimant the interest which he expected to receive,[12] but it may be less than that.[13] The Court of Appeal has recently emphasised the (principled) discretionary nature of the remedy, and that there must be proportionality between the expectation and the detriment: where the claimant's expectations are uncertain, or extravagant, or out of proportion to the detriment he has suffered, the court will satisfy the equity in another (and generally more limited) way, whilst not necessarily awarding simply the equivalent of the claimant's detriment.[14]

7 Cheshire and Burn, *Modern Law of Real Property* (16th edn, 2000) 649–659; *Megarry and Wade*, ch 13.

8 *Taylors Fashions Ltd v Liverpool Victoria Trustees Co Ltd* [1982] QB 133n at 151, [1982] 1 All ER 897 at 915; *Lim Teng Huan v Ang Swee Chuan* [1992] 1 WLR 113 at 117, PC.

9 *Pascoe v Turner* [1979] 2 All ER 945, CA, [1979] 1 WLR 431 ('the house is yours and everything in it').

10 *Ramsden v Dyson* (1866) LR 1 HL 129 at 168 (Lord Wensleydale); *Taylors Fashions Ltd v Liverpool Victoria Trustees Co Ltd* [1982] QB 133n at 145–147, [1982] 1 All ER 897 at 910–912 (Oliver J discussing *Willmott v Barber* (1880) 15 Ch D 96). In a case of passive acquiescence it is probable that the landowner must know, or at least suspect, the true position: *Taylors Fashions* at 147, 912.

11 *Lim Teng Huan v Ang Swee Chuan* [1992] 1 WLR 113 at 117, PC; *Fontana NV v Mautner* [1980] EGD 184 at 874; *Gillett v Holt* [2001] Ch 210 at 232, [2000] 2 All ER 289 at 308, CA.

12 *Pascoe v Turner* [1979] 2 All ER 945, CA, [1979] 1 WLR 431 (order for conveyance of fee simple).

13 *Dodsworth v Dodsworth* (1973) 228 EG 1115, CA (defendants led to believe they could live in property: claimant could get possession on payment to defendants of sums they had spent on the property). It might appear from *Crabb v Arun District Council* [1976] Ch 179, [1975] 3 All ER 865, CA, that the remedy might even give the claimant *more* than his expectation: there, the claimant was led to believe he would be given right of access to, and right of way over, the defendant's land in return for payment; but the order was for the grant of rights without payment. However, this can be explained as compensation for the loss of use of the right of way until the time of the court order: Gardner (1999) 115 LQR 438 at 445.

14 *Jennings v Rice* [2002] EWCA Civ 159, esp at [21], [36], [43], [50].

For present purposes, however, it more important to notice that proprietary estoppel is a doctrine by which a claimant may acquire an interest in land in circumstances where the formalities normally necessary for the creation of such an interest have not been complied with.[15] In a typical case of proprietary estoppel the claimant asserts that he has a right in land by reason of the landowner either promising that he has it (or will acquire it), or allowing him to act on the belief that he has it (or will acquire it). By statute, no interest in land can be created except by writing signed by the person creating it,[16] yet the claimant has no writing to which he can point. So he seeks the assistance of the court to grant him a remedy to side-step the formal defect in the means by which he claims to have acquired his interest in land. And the court sees the 'equity', raised by the claimant's reliance on the landowner's assurance that (or acquiescence in the claimant's belief that) he has or will acquire an interest in land, as deserving of protection in spite of the failure of formality.

THE CONFLICT BETWEEN FORMALITY AND INFORMALITY

This conflict between formality and informality is familiar to most legal systems. Formalities are set for particular types of transaction – property transactions and contracts, for example – for good reasons of policy. But hard cases arise where a party who seeks to enforce a property right or a right arising under a contract can strictly be met with a defence that the necessary formality requirement was not respected; yet the policy underlying the formality requirement appears to be counterbalanced by some other policy which points towards giving force to the transaction in spite of the failure of formality.

This can be seen in Roman law where the Praetor intervened to protect a possessor of property who did not strictly have title to it. For reasons of policy the law required a formal transfer ('*mancipatio*') of property rights in certain assets which had particular importance within Roman society ('*res mancipi*') and the transferee received only possession, not ownership, if the formality was not complied with.[17] Yet cases arose in which the possessor needed legal protection to which, according to the strict rules of law, he was not entitled because he had not acquired the full legal title. To take perhaps the strongest case, it would be outrageous if the transferor, who had himself failed to use the formality requirements required by law, could rely on the absence of formality to reclaim the property which he had willingly transferred. So the Praetor devised remedies to protect the possessor in certain circumstances as if he were the owner – at least, against the transferor and third parties although not against a person, other than

15 Slade, *The Informal Creation of Interests in Land* (The Child and Co Oxford Lecture, 1984). On this view, proprietary estoppel is not itself a new interest in land but only the means by which a recognised interest in land can be created. The remedy is not necessarily proprietary: e g *Dodsworth v Dodsworth*, n 13 above. But where the award is of a proprietary interest, it is made in circumstances where the interest has not been created through the normal formality.

16 Or by his agent, or by will, or by operation of law: Law of Property Act 1925, s 53(1)(a). However, the statute builds in an exception in s 53(2) for interests arising through the creation or operation of resulting, implied or constructive trusts. If, therefore, proprietary estoppel takes effect as a constructive trust, the failure to create the interest through the normal formality is in a sense a *permitted* informality.

17 Jolowicz and Nicholas, *Historical Introduction to the Study of Roman Law* (3rd edn, 1972) 137–139, 143–149; Buckland, *A Textbook of Roman Law* (3rd edn, revised Stein, 1963) 235–241.

the transferor, who had the full right of property in the asset.[18] This undercut the formality requirements, and indeed allowed their wholesale evasion. But it could be done because the policy in favour of the transferee outweighed the policy in favour of enforcing strictly the formality. As long as the rights of a real owner who was not himself involved in the informal transaction was protected, the transferee's position (his possession) should be given priority.

In French law, too, we can see the courts' recognition of the need to balance the requirements of formality with the merits of the hard case in which the formality has not been used. For example, an *inter vivos* transaction[19] embodying a gift ('*donation*') must be notarised; failure to comply with this renders the transaction a nullity.[20] But in applying this rule, and in exploring the circumstances in which exceptions can be made to it, the French writers and the courts have examined the underlying purpose of the formality.[21] In one respect the requirement of notarisation is intended to protect the donor – to ensure that he has reflected on the transaction. But it is also intended to provide a more general protection for those members of the family who might expect to inherit on the donor's death: France has rules limiting the extent to which certain family members can be deprived of their inheritance, and gifts made *inter vivos* are brought back into account on the donor's death:[22] so gifts must be properly traceable. Moreover, there is a public interest in the identification of valid gifts, which are subject to taxation, both *inter vivos* and on death.[23] But it can happen that a person who wishes to make a gift fails to comply with the formality requirements. The French courts have sometimes allowed such a transaction to have effect as being a *donation déguisée* (a 'disguised donation'): for example, where the transaction is not really a sale, but is a gift dressed up as a sale – either because it has all the appearance of a sale contract, but the transaction is a sham in that the price is not intended to be paid; or even where a nominal purchase price is inserted in a contract of sale.[24] As long as it

18 *Jolowicz and Nicholas*, 263–267; *Buckland*, 191–195. The possessor could defend a claim by the transferor ('*exceptio rei venditae et traditae*': D. 21.3.3) and, if he lost possession, could bring a claim ('*actio Publiciana*': G. 4.36; D. 6.2) in which the judge was to assume (fictionally) that the period of uninterrupted possession had been sufficiently long to give him the right of ownership by *usucapio*. The real owner, if not the transferor, could however assert his rights by a positive claim ('*vindicatio*') if out of possession, or by a defence ('*exceptio iusti dominii*') if he regained possession, unless he had in fact lost his right of ownership, eg by a real (rather than fictional) passage of time sufficient for *usucapio*.

19 Including a contract of gift, which is recognised in French law: C civ art 1105.

20 C civ art 931: 'Tous actes portant donation entre vifs seront passés devant notaires, dans la forme ordinaire des contrats; et il en restera minute, sous peine de nullité' – ie the original of the document must be kept by the notary.

21 The laconic form of a French judgment (particularly a judgment of the Cour de cassation) generally inhibits the reader from seeing the detail of the reasoning lying behind it, but commentators discuss the issues fully: see, eg Ghestin, *Traité de droit civil, La formation du contrat* (3rd edn, 1993) 396–401; Malaurie and Aynès, *Droit civil, Obligations*, vol 2, *Contrats et quasi-contrats* (11th edn, 2001), 107–114; Terré and Lequette, *Droit civil, Les successions, Les libéralités* (3rd edn, 1997) 368–370; Grimaldi, *Droit civil, Libéralités, Partages d'ascendants* (2000) 199–201.

22 C civ art 913, 920.

23 Malaurie and Aynès, *Droit civil, Les Successions; Les Libéralités* (4th edn, 1998) 571–586.

24 Because of the policies relating to gifts, the French courts are suspicious of a gift which is dressed up as a sale, and they seek to re-characterise the transaction to reflect the parties' real intentions. Similarly, Roman law was suspicious of nominal consideration in a sale contract and required a contract of sale to have at least a 'real' price (though not necessarily the 'right' or 'market' price), so as to ensure that a transaction which was in substance a gift (*donatio*) was so treated in law:

fulfils the formal requirements of the 'pretended' transaction it will be given effect and the (in substance) donee can enforce it.[25] But although the courts will allow the formality rule to be evaded to that extent, it does not mean that the *donation déguisée* evades the other consequences of a gift: it cannot take effect so as to evade the inheritance or tax rules.[26] So some policies can be avoided, whilst others continue to be enforced.

Similarly, if proprietary estoppel is to be analysed in English law as a means by which a court can give effect to a transaction which has failed to comply with a particular formality requirement, one would expect the court to examine whether or to what extent the policy underlying the formality requirement would be undermined by allowing the (informal) transaction to be given effect. This is, indeed, what can sometimes be seen in the cases. In *Yaxley v Gotts*,[27] for example, where the question was whether an oral agreement to grant an interest in property was enforceable where there was no contract in writing in accordance with section 2 of the Law of Property (Miscellaneous Provisions) Act 1989, the Court of Appeal considered the underlying policy of the 1989 Act. Beldam LJ said:[28]

> The general principle that a party cannot rely on an estoppel in the face of a statute depends upon the nature of the enactment, the purpose of the provision and the social policy behind it. This was not a provision aimed at prohibiting or

Buckland, 253–256, 485–486. English law, however, has different policies, and in the case of a sale at a nominal consideration is content to allow the transaction to be given its effect as a sale, since the donor's decision to squeeze into the model of a sale contract, a transaction which is in substance a gift, is a considered decision which should therefore be given effect (and so the absence of ('real') consideration should not be a bar to the enforceability of the transaction).

25 Civ 1re 29 mai 1980, D 1981 273: 'les libéralités faites sous le couvert d'actes à titre onéreux sont valables lorsqu'elles réunissent les conditions de forme requises pour la constitution des actes dont elles empruntent l'apparence, les règles auxquelles elles sont assujetties quant au fond étant celles propres aux actes à titre gratuit'.

26 In the case of the spouses, the code itself prevents a donation (including a *donation déguisée*) taking effect so as to frustrate the inheritance rules: C civ art 1099: 'Les époux ne pourront se donner indirectement au delà de ce qui leur est permis par les dispositions ci-dessus. Tout donation, ou déguisée, ou faite à personnes interposées, sera nulle'. But in other cases the courts will identify the essentially gratuitous character of the transaction and so re-characterise it in law to apply the inheritance or tax rules: Malaurie and Aynès, *Droit civil, Les Successions; Les Libéralités* (8th edn, 1998) 236–239; and see, eg Com 8 juill 1970, JCP 1971 II 16597 (transfer of shares re-characterised as *donation*: tax payable and fine for dissimulation of the real character of the transaction); Com 14 janv 1992, JCP 1992 IV 782 (burden of proof on the tax authorities to show that the transaction is really gratuitous).

27 [2000] Ch 162, [2000] 1 All ER 711, CA.

28 At 191. See also Robert Walker LJ at 175 and Clarke LJ at 181–182. It should be noticed that, although such a case involves a *promise* to create or transfer an interest in land, it is still properly seen as a case of proprietary estoppel rather than promissory estoppel (below). Such a promise is different from a promise unrelated to land, because a promise to create or transfer an interest in land: (a) if enforceable, itself creates an equitable interest: *Cheshire and Burn*, 130–131; and (b) has its own special statutory formality rules for validity: Law of Property (Miscellaneous Provisions) Act 1989, s 2; *Cheshire and Burn*, 126–130. The development of promissory estoppel by the High Court of Australia in *Waltons Stores (Interstate) Ltd v Maher*, below, was made in the context of a contract for the sale of land but where it was the buyer, rather than the seller, who was estopped from denying his (informal) promise: it was not therefore a case of proprietary estoppel. A promise to *sell* property is in this context different from a promise to *buy*, since the promisee buyer can acquire property rights in the subject-matter of the sale arising from his right to enforce the seller's promise. In general, the seller's rights against the buyer are necessarily only personal.

outlawing agreements of a specific kind, though it had the effect of making agreements which did not comply with the required formalities void. This by itself is insufficient to raise such a significant public interest that an estoppel would be excluded.

Where (as is generally the case) the formality is a statutory requirement, the court must construe the statute. In *Yaxley* the court was able to hold that the statute by its own language, as well as by its context as evidenced by the background to its enactment, indicated that to give effect to an informal agreement through the doctrine of proprietary estoppel would not necessarily undermine the policy requiring written contracts for the sale of land.[29]

PROTECTION OF TRANSACTIONS WHICH FAIL TO COMPLY WITH FORMALITY REQUIREMENTS

It was suggested above that proprietary estoppel is an example of the courts allowing property rights to be created by informal means. This is not the only area in which the English courts have developed such a principle: admitting that a claimant has an enforceable right in property even though he is met by a defence that he cannot have acquired a right because the formality required by an applicable statute prohibits it. There are a variety of situations in which the courts have admitted that a defendant, who has received property on the basis that he will allow the claimant to have rights in that property, holds his own property rights subject to the claimant's rights. The technique often employed by the courts in such cases is to say that the defendant holds the property on constructive trust for the claimant,[30] a constructive trust which takes effect independently of the operation at law of the strict formality requirement.

29 The Court relied on s 2(5), which provides that the section does not affect 'the creation or operation of . . . constructive trusts'; and the Law Commission's report which proposed the provision, Law Com No 164, *Formalities for Contracts for Sale etc of Land* (1987), which at 18–20 discussed estoppel as a means of giving effect to an agreement which would not comply with the formality. For the link between proprietary estoppel and constructive trusts – and, indeed, on the issue of whether proprietary estoppel takes effect as a constructive trust – see *Grant v Edwards* [1986] Ch 638 at 656, [1986] 2 All ER 426 at 439, CA; *Lloyds Bank plc v Rosset* [1991] 1 AC 107 at 132–133, [1990] 1 All ER 1111 at 1118–1119, HL; *Stokes v Anderson* [1991] 1 FLR 391 at 398–399, CA; *Lloyds Bank plc v Carrick* [1996] 4 All ER 630 at 640, CA; Slade, *The Informal Creation of Interests in Land* (1984); Hayton [1990] Conv 370 (taking however the view that it is a discretionary remedial constructive trust, and not the perfection of an imperfect gift). But for the view that an oral contract for the transfer of an interest in land cannot be given effect through the doctrine of estoppel *by convention*, see *Godden v Merthyr Tydfil Housing Association* (1997) 74 P & CR D1, CA (Balcombe LJ: the argument was 'that as both parties contracted in ignorance of the provisions of the Act, the [defendant] was estopped from relying on those provisions. This argument, if accepted, would drive a coach and horses through a recent Act of Parliament enacted for very specific reasons of public policy'). And where the question is whether the underlying policy of a statute permits a construction which in effect side-steps the formality requirement, judges can inevitably take different views in different contexts: on s 2 Law of Property (Miscellaneous Provisions) Act 1989 cf *United Bank of Kuwait plc v Sahib* [1997] Ch 107, CA. For constructive trusts as an exception to the requirement of writing for the creation of an interest in land, see Law of Property Act 1925, s 53(2); see n 16 above.

30 Oakley, *Constructive Trusts* (3rd edn, 1997) 53–63.

This appears to be the basis on which *Binions v Evans*[31] can be accepted as good law. When the Binionses bought, from the former employers of Mrs Evans' deceased husband, the cottage in which Mrs Evans was living they agreed with the vendors to allow Mrs Evans to continue to live there, and in consequence paid a reduced price. For various reasons[32] the Court of Appeal held that the Binionses were not entitled to evict Mrs Evans; but it is now generally accepted that the better analysis of the case is that although the licence originally granted to Mrs Evans to live in the house after her husband died did not itself create an interest in land, the purchase by the Binionses in circumstances where they undertook in favour of the vendors to give effect to Mrs Evans' rights of occupation, coupled with their having obtained a reduction in the purchase price, gave rise to a constructive trust in her favour: in those circumstances the Binionses' conscience was affected.[33] The details of such a constructive trust need not concern us here, beyond noticing that, if it created an interest in land, it would not fall foul of the general rule in section 53(1) of the Law of Property Act 1925 requiring writing, because section 53(2) provides that that general rule does not affect the creation or operation of resulting, implied or constructive trusts.

It can also be argued that secret trusts and mutual wills involve the operation of similar underlying principles.[34] In the cases of a secret trust the testator, instead of naming in his will the beneficiaries he intends to benefit, names another person who is to hold the property for their benefit. The person named as beneficiary in the will, who has agreed to this arrangement before the testator's death, cannot be allowed to take the full beneficial interest under the will, and is made to hold the property on trust for the beneficiaries intended by the testator. Whether or not such an arrangement is clear on the face of the will,[35] to allow the (unnamed) beneficiaries to have enforceable rights is to side-step the formalities required by the Wills Act 1837 by giving effect to the testator's intention which is not in the form required by the Act for a valid will. The courts have long found that a remedy is necessary in such a case, and have held that, although the Wills Act has its proper effect to allow only the beneficiary named in the

31 [1972] Ch 359, [1972] 2 All ER 70.

32 Megaw and Stephenson LJJ, following *Bannister v Bannister* [1948] 2 All ER 133, CA, held that the original agreement gave Mrs Evans a life interest so she held as tenant for life under the Settled Land Act 1925; and Megaw LJ added that, if this were wrong, it might be argued that the Binionses would be prevented by injunction from evicting Mrs Evans because that would be (the tort of) knowingly to interfere with Mrs Evans' contractual rights against the vendors (her original licensors). Lord Denning MR held that the Binionses were bound by Mrs Evans' licence, *either* because the original grant of the licence created an equitable interest which bound the Binionses as purchasers with notice of it, *or* a constructive trust arose on sale to the Binionses of the property 'subject to' her rights. It is a version of this last explanation that is accepted in *Ashburn Anstalt v Arnold,* see n 33 below.

33 *Ashburn Anstalt v Arnold* [1989] Ch 1 at 22–26, [1988] 2 All ER 147 at 164–167, CA (Fox LJ emphasising that it is not sufficient that the sale was 'subject to' the licensee's rights; beyond that the circumstances must be shown which affect the purchaser's *conscience* if he were to fail to respect the licensee's rights); *Lloyd v Dugdale* [2001] EWCA Civ 1754, [2002] P & CR 13 at [52]; *Megarry and Wade*, §17–019 at 1056–1057; *Cheshire and Burn*, 648–649; Martin, *Hanbury and Martin: Modern Equity* (15th edn, 1997) 321.

34 *Oakley*, ch 5; *Hanbury and Martin*, ch 5.

35 If there is no indication, it is a 'fully secret trust'; if it is clear that the named beneficiary is to take for the benefit of (in the will unidentified) beneficiaries, it is a 'half-secret trust'. But in either case, the strict requirements of Wills Act 1837, s 9 are not fulfilled because the beneficiaries are not named in the will.

will to take the legal title to the estate, he is made to hold the estate on trust for the intended beneficiaries – a trust which operates outside the will.[36] Just like in *Binions v Evans*, the person who, in strict law, has full title to the property is not to be allowed to deal with his property as a full, unencumbered owner: as a condition of its acquisition he undertook that he would give effect to the claimant's rights, and he is required to do so. As Viscount Sumner said in *Blackwell v Blackwell*:[37]

> A Court of conscience finds a man in the position of an absolute legal owner of a sum of money, which has been bequeathed to him under a valid will, and it declares that, on proof of certain facts relating to the motives and actions of the testator, it will not allow the legal owner to exercise his legal right to do what he will with his own . . . For the prevention of fraud equity fastens on the conscience of the legatee a trust . . .

Similarly, where two persons have made mutual wills which provide for each to leave property to the other, and on the death of the second of them the property is to be distributed in a particular way, but after the death of the first the second person changes his or her will so that it will no longer pass in accordance with the original agreement, the courts have held that the personal representatives are subject to a trust to give effect to the original agreement.[38] The survivor received property from the first to die on the basis that it would be dealt with in a particular way; and therefore he or she no longer had an unfettered freedom to treat the property as his or her own:

> a court of equity will not permit a person to whom property is transferred . . . on the faith of an agreement or clear understanding that it is to be dealt with in a particular way for the benefit of a third person, to deal with that property inconsistently with that agreement or understanding.[39]

This is not the place to discuss these areas in detail; nor is it suggested that the examples discussed in this section are all part of a single unitary doctrine. But it appears that there are common themes – a common principle – which underlie them. They are all cases where a person has acquired property subject to an undertaking to give effect to a third party's rights; but for reasons of policy, reflected in rules of formality, the undertaking in favour of the third party is not in law effective. But the benefit which the defendant has received, in circumstances where it is unconscionable not to give effect to the third party's expectations, gives rise to a constructive trust of the property in favour of the third party.

36 *Re Young* [1951] Ch 344 at 350, [1950] 2 All ER 1245 at 1250.
37 [1929] AC 318 at 334–335, HL.
38 *Re Green* [1951] Ch 148, [1950] 2 All ER 913.
39 *Re Cleaver* [1981] 2 All ER 1018 at 1024, [1981] 1 WLR 939 at 947 (Nourse J, referring to both mutual wills and secret trusts, and approving the argument of counsel, E G Nugee, in *Ottaway v Norman* [1972] Ch 698 at 701: 'secret trusts . . . [is but an example] of a wider category of cases in which a court of equity will not permit a person to whom property is transferred, whether by deed or by will, on the faith of an agreement or understanding that it is to be dealt with in a particular way for the benefit of a third person, to commit a fraud on that third person by treating the property as his own'). On the difficulties of analysis of mutual wills, however, see *Oakley*, 263–272; *Hanbury and Martin*, 305–312; McGhee, *Snell's Equity* (30th edn, 2000) paras 9-32–9-37.

How, though, does this relate to proprietary estoppel? An analogy was drawn by Edward Nugee QC sitting as the trial judge in *Re Basham*:[40]

> The rights to which proprietary estoppel gives rise, and the machinery by which effect is given to them, are similar in many respects to those involved in cases of secret trusts, mutual wills and other comparable cases in which property is vested in B, on the faith of an understanding that it will be dealt with in a particular manner, of which Nourse J said in *Re Cleaver*:[41]
>
>> The principle of all these cases is that a court of equity will not permit a person to whom property is transferred by way of gift, but on the faith of an agreement or clear understanding that it is to be dealt with in a particular way for the benefit of a third person, to deal with that property inconsistently with that agreement or understanding. If he attempts to do so after having received the benefit of the gift equity will intervene by imposing a constructive trust on the property which is the subject matter of the agreement or understanding.
>
> The factor which gives rise to the equitable obligation in the cases to which Nourse J referred is B's receipt of the property on the faith of an understanding. In cases of proprietary estoppel the factor which gives rise to the equitable obligation is A's alteration of his position on the faith of a similar understanding. A third situation in which the court imposes a constructive trust is where A and B set up house together in a property which is in the name of B alone, and A establishes a common intention between A and B, acted on by A to his (or more usually her) detriment, that A should have a beneficial interest in the property: see the statements of principle by Nourse LJ and Browne-Wilkinson V-C in *Grant v Edwards*.[42] Here too, if the two elements of common understanding or intention and detrimental acts on the part of A are established, they give rise to an equitable obligation enforceable against B which is in the nature of a constructive trust. A common theme can be discerned in each of these classes of case; and although different situations may give rise to differences of detail in the manner in which the court will give effect to the equity which arises in favour of A, one would expect the general principles applicable in the different situations to be the same unless there is a sound reason to the contrary.

In cases where the defendant undertook to grant a right to a third party, therefore, the 'unconscionability' arises by virtue of the defendant's receipt of property – the defendant's *benefit* – on the basis that he would give effect to the third party's right. There is also a corresponding detriment suffered by the transferor who was encouraged to transfer the property to the defendant on the basis that he would give effect to the third party's rights, and once the transfer has been made to the defendant it is too late to recall it and give effect to the third party's rights by other means. But the

40 [1987] 1 All ER 405 at 410, [1986] 1 WLR 1498 at 1503–1504. See also his argument in *Ottaway v Norman*, see n 39 above.

41 See n 39 above.

42 [1986] Ch 638, [1986] 2 All ER 426, CA.

cases have tended to focus on the defendant's benefit as the basis of the equity which binds him. Proprietary estoppel, however, is different. It is not the defendant's receipt of the property which underpins the claimant's equity: in the usual case, the defendant already had the property before he made the representation on which the estoppel is based. So here the focus shifts from the defendant's benefit to the claimant's *detriment*: it is because the defendant has induced the claimant to incur a detriment that the defendant is required to give effect – in some measure, at least[43] – to the representation. This shift of emphasis from the defendant's benefit to the claimant's detriment is inevitable because of the circumstances in which proprietary estoppel generally arises. But it is possible still to see a link of principle between these different doctrines: and so to accept that in proprietary estoppel, just as other cases of constructive trusts which arise to enable a party to obtain rights in property, is a principle under which the courts give effect to transactions which fail to comply with the formalities normally required for the creation or transfer of property rights. Viewed in this way, it is understandable that the courts have (perhaps instinctively) limited the operation of the doctrine of proprietary estoppel to cases where the representation is about the rights a claimant has or will acquire in *property*.[44] The estoppel operates to prevent the defendant, as the owner of property, from exercising his prima facie right to do what he will with his own. Before such a restriction can be held to have been placed on him it must be shown that he granted, or undertook to grant, rights to the claimant in respect of the property in circumstances where it would now be unconscionable for him to deny it. And given that the creation or transfer of rights in property is in many contexts – and, in particular, in the context of land – subject to requirements of formality which are designed both to facilitate such transactions but also to protect the property owner from being deprived of his property too easily,[45] it is not surprising that the courts have developed such doctrines carefully, but in such a way as, in effect, to permit the avoidance of the formality requirements where justice (or, literally, 'Equity') on the facts so demands. But the question then arises as to whether a further step can be taken: can the principles, or the reasoning underlying the principles, of proprietary estoppel be applied also to the context usually covered by the doctrine of *promissory* estoppel?

'PROMISSORY ESTOPPEL' IN ENGLISH LAW

At first sight, promissory estoppel operates very differently, and in a very different context, from proprietary estoppel. In English law,[46] the doctrine is limited to preventing a party from reneging on a promise not to enforce his existing rights under

43 Depending on how the equity is to be satisfied on the facts, according to the decision of the court: above, text to nn 11–14.

44 In *Western Fish Products Ltd v Penwith District Council* [1981] 2 All ER 204 at 218, CA, Megaw LJ explicitly rejected the extension of proprietary estoppel outside the context of property, although he did accept that it might extend beyond land.

45 On the policies underlying formalities for contracts for the sale of land, see *Formalities for Contracts for Sale etc of Land* (Law Com no 164, 1987) part II. For a discussion of the functions performed by legal formalities generally, but also with particular reference to the doctrine of consideration, see Fuller, 'Consideration and Form' (1941) Colum L Rev 799 and esp at 799–806.

46 For the approach in other jurisdictions, see below.

(usually) a contract. So it only applies where there is already a legal relationship[47] – usually a contract[48] – between the claimant and the defendant, and the claimant has, by an unequivocal representation,[49] led the defendant to believe that he will not enforce against him the rights he has under that relationship. If the defendant has altered his position on the faith of that representation,[50] he can defend the claimant's claim to enforce the original contract, in so far as the claim is inconsistent with his representation, unless and until the claimant has given the defendant a reasonable opportunity of placing himself again in the position of performing his obligations. So the doctrine of promissory estoppel only normally has the effect of suspending the enforceability of existing contractual rights.[51] It does not give the representee a claim in his own name to new rights: in that sense it can be said to operate as a 'shield', not as a 'sword'. *Combe v Combe*[52] is still authority at the level of the Court of Appeal that where the defendant promised to make payment to the claimant, and the claimant relied on that promise but without giving consideration for it, the claimant cannot enforce the promise under the doctrine of promissory estoppel.[53] As Denning LJ said:[54]

> That principle does not create new causes of action where none existed before. It only prevents a party from insisting on his strict legal rights, when it would be unjust to allow him to enforce them, having regard to the dealings which have taken place between the parties.

So there appear to be very significant differences between promissory estoppel and proprietary estoppel: promissory estoppel is limited to the variation of an existing relationship between the parties, not the creation of a new one; and normally it only

47 *Ajayi v R T Briscoe (Nigeria) Ltd* [1964] 3 All ER 556 at 559, PC, [1964] 1 WLR 1326 at 1330.

48 But not necessarily: another obligation owed by the defendant to the claimant can, in principle, be suspended under the doctrine of promissory estoppel: *Durham Fancy Goods Ltd v Michael Jackson (Fancy Goods) Ltd* [1968] 2 QB 839 at 847, [1968] 2 All ER 987 at 991 (personal obligation on director under Companies Act 1948, s 108, now Companies Act 1985, s 349, where he signs a bill of exchange without properly mentioning the company's name).

49 *Woodhouse AC Israel Cocoa Ltd SA v Nigerian Produce Marketing Co Ltd* [1972] AC 741, [1972] 2 All ER 271, HL; *The Post Chaser* [1982] 1 All ER 19, [1981] 2 Lloyd's Rep 695.

50 *Ajayi v R T Briscoe (Nigeria) Ltd* see n 47 above. For the most limited view of this requirement, see the judgment of Lord Denning MR in *W J Alan & Co Ltd v El Nasr Export and Import Co* [1972] 2 QB 189 at 213–214, [1972] 2 All ER 127 at 140, CA.

51 The representation can become final and irrevocable (and therefore the contract is permanently varied in the terms of the claimant's representation) if the defendant cannot, even if he is given a period of time to do so, place himself in the position of performing the original contractual obligations: Lord Hodson in *Ajayi v R T Briscoe (Nigeria) Ltd*, see n 47 above, at 1330, at 559.

52 [1951] 2 KB 215, [1951] 1 All ER 767, CA.

53 There are a few hints in the English cases that promissory estoppel might operate, or might be developed to operate, to create new rights: *Pacol Ltd v Trade Lines Ltd* [1982] 1 Lloyd's Rep 456 at 466–467; *Crabb v Arun District Council* [1976] Ch 179 at 193, CA (Scarman LJ, preferring not to separate promissory and proprietary estoppel into separate categories); *Re Wyvern Developments Ltd* [1974] 2 All ER 535 at 542–543, [1974] 1 WLR 1097 at 1104–1105; *Williams v Roffey Bros & Nicholls (Contractors) Ltd* [1991] 1 QB 1 at 13, 17–18, [1990] 1 All ER 512 at 520, 523, CA. However, the Court of Appeal itself has recently said that the line of cases which hold that promissory estoppel does not create new rights is binding and can now be changed only by a decision of the House of Lords: *Baird Textile Holdings Ltd v Marks & Spencer plc* [2001] EWCA Civ 274, [2002] 1 All ER (Comm) 737.

54 [1951] 2 KB 215 at 219, [1951] 1 All ER 767 at 769, CA.

suspends the representor's rights against the other party. This is clearly a much more limited doctrine than proprietary estoppel, which can be used by a representee to claim that he should be granted a remedy in respect of the (property) rights he was led to believe he had or would be granted.

PROMISSORY ESTOPPEL 'AS A SWORD' IN OTHER JURISDICTIONS

However, there is no logical reason why this limitation on the operation of the doctrine of promissory estoppel should be maintained. It would be possible to free the doctrine from its limitation to being a defensive doctrine – a 'shield' – and instead to allow the representee as claimant to enforce the representation on the basis that it would be unconscionable to allow the defendant to deny the claimant a remedy given the representee's reliance on the representation. Other common law jurisdictions have accepted such a role for promissory estoppel. Most notably, in the United States promissory estoppel has long been admitted as an alternative to consideration as a mark of enforceability of a promise.[55] And the High Court of Australia[56] has held that there is no reason why the limitations of *Combe v Combe* should be maintained in Australian law, and so it is now accepted that a promise which is not supported by consideration can be enforced by the representee under the doctrine of promissory estoppel where it would be unconscionable for the representor to deny it. If promissory estoppel is accepted as an alternative to consideration, various questions follow, such as: In what circumstances will it be 'unconscionable' for the defendant not to give effect to his promise – what kind of reliance by the claimant will suffice? What remedy will be awarded? If damages, what measure will be appropriate? Or might it be appropriate, other than by an award of damages, to give effect to the parties' legal relationship *as if* the defendant had fulfilled his promise? How much discretion can or should be given to the court in awarding the remedy? What is the consequence for the doctrine of consideration – for example, will the courts take a more restrictive approach to consideration given that estoppel is available alongside?[57] This is not, though, the place to answer such questions.[58]

The approach taken by the High Court in Australia in *Waltons Stores (Interstate) Ltd v Maher*[59] was to develop promissory estoppel by reference to the underlying principles it identified in a number of cases, and in particular by the unification in principle of

55 Restatement of Contracts Second, §90(1): 'A promise which the promisor should reasonably expect to induce action or forbearance on the part of the promisee or a third person and which does induce such action or forbearance is binding if injustice can be avoided only by enforcement of the promise. The remedy granted for breach may be limited as justice requires.' The principle first appeared in the first Restatement in 1933. See generally Farnsworth, *Contracts* (2nd edn, 1998) §2.19. But for an enlightening account of the development of the theory of reliance-based enforcement of promises from the first to the second Restatement, see Gilmore, *The Death of Contract* (ed Collins, 1995) 76–81.

56 *Waltons Stores (Interstate) Ltd v Maher* (1988) 164 CLR 387. It must, however, be noted that the judgments in this case do not speak with one voice as to how the (extended) doctrine of promissory estoppel should work. See also *Commonwealth of Australia v Verwayen* (1990) 170 CLR 394.

57 The courts might, for example, be less disposed to 'invent' consideration in order to make a promise enforceable: Treitel, *The Law of Contract* (10th edn, 1999) 67–68.

58 These questions have been asked in US law: see e g the discussion in *Farnsworth* §2.19.

59 See n 56 above.

promissory and proprietary estoppel. For example, in their judgement Mason CJ and Wilson J reviewed a number of English and Commonwealth cases on both promissory and proprietary estoppel, and concluded:[60]

> One may therefore discern in the cases a common thread which links them together, namely, the principle that equity will come to the relief of a plaintiff who has acted to his detriment on the basis of a basic assumption in relation to which the other party to the transaction has 'played such a part in the adoption of the assumption that it would be unfair or unjust if he were left free to ignore it'[61] . . . Equity comes to the relief of such a plaintiff on the footing that it would be unconscionable conduct on the part of the other party to ignore the assumption.

But this approach looks for, and then gives effect to, a unity between promissory and proprietary estoppel, without taking full account of the differences between them: and in particular the fact that proprietary estoppel is a doctrine under which a *property owner* has fettered his property rights. There is a danger in seeing only the '*unity of estoppels'* without seeing also that there are other links, such as the link between proprietary estoppel and the other circumstances in which the courts impose constructive trusts of property, set out by Edward Nugee QC in *re Basham* and discussed earlier in this paper. Seeing proprietary estoppel as part of the law of *property,* and for that reason fundamentally different from promissory estoppel, is not just an exercise in pedantic line-drawing or legal categorisation. The defendant owns property, and his rights cannot be interfered with except by a person who has had another, overriding right validly created in his favour. In a case of proprietary estoppel, similarly to the other cases of constructive trust discussed in this paper, the defendant is estopped from denying the claimant's rights to his property because, although he did not create those rights through the legal formalities normally designed for their creation, he has induced the claimant to believe that he has them, and to act accordingly. Although proprietary estoppel can be used by a representee to assert new rights, and therefore can be used 'as a sword', there is a sense in which it is still a limited sword, and the estoppel is still being used defensively: the claimant asserts a right to or in the defendant's property; the defendant responds that he has a superior property right and that the claimant has no right carved out of that superior property which has been created by a formality recognised by the law; but the defendant is estopped from asserting this because of his contrary representation and the claimant's reliance. The defendant in a proprietary estoppel claim is, in effect, estopped from setting up his own legal property rights which are inconsistent with those claimed by the claimant.[62] But in the case of promissory estoppel, if it is to be allowed to be used

60 At 404. See also Brennan J at 420, 426. Gaudron J at 459–460 left open the question whether proprietary and promissory estoppel are discrete categories, but thought that there was much to be said for the view of Scarman LJ in *Crabb v Arun District Council*, see n 53 above, that they are not.

61 Quoting Dixon J in *Grundt v Great Boulder Pty Gold Mines Ltd* (1937) 59 CLR 641 at 675, a case of common law estoppel, not equitable (promissory) estoppel.

62 This is clearest in cases where the courts simply give negative protection by way of refusing the (paper) owner's claim to possession from the representee: *Inwards v Baker* [1965] 2 QB 29, [1965] 1 All ER 446, CA.

generally to create new rights, the most that can be said is that the defendant is estopped from not giving effect to the promise: he is estopped from changing his mind. The promissory estoppel simply creates a new obligation: a very sharp 'sword'.[63]

THE WAY FORWARD IN ENGLISH LAW

How, then, might an English court approach the question whether the limitations on promissory estoppel, established in *Combe v Combe,* should be removed so as to allow – to some extent, at least[64] – a promisee who has given no consideration for the promise, but has relied on it, to bring a claim to enforce it? The simple message of this paper is that it is not adequate to say that, because proprietary estoppel can be used 'as a sword', then promissory estoppel should be able to do so too. That is far too simplistic.

One approach would be to go back to the themes set out earlier in this paper, and ask what policies underlie the legal rule which would be circumvented by allowing promissory estoppel to create an obligation. In this case, it is not simply a formality rule; and it is not a statutory rule. It is the rule that, for a promise to be binding in English law, either the promisee must have provided consideration or the promisor must have set out his promise in the form of a deed. We see an analogy here,[65] with the application of proprietary estoppel: there is a formality provided by the law to make enforceable a promise which not supported by consideration, but the promisor has not used it: so, just as we ask whether the representee's reliance on the representor's statement that he has, or will acquire, an interest in land should override the policy of the statute that normally requires a formality for such a right to be created, so we could ask whether the need to use a deed to make enforceable a promise which has not been bargained for can be overridden by the promisee's reliance on the promise.

Moreover, another analogy can be found which supports the argument that reliance by a beneficiary of a gratuitous promise might be a sufficient reason for allowing it to be

63 For a detailed account of the 'unity of estoppels' argument in both Australian and English law, and the rejection of its extension to the enforcement of promises, see Finn, 'Equitable Estoppel' in Finn (ed) *Essays in Equity* (1995) 59–94.

64 If such a step is taken, it will involve the courts' taking decisions not only on the principle that a promisee's reliance (without consideration) entitles him to enforce the promise, but also on the scope of and limitations on such a new principle, as mentioned earlier in this paper. No doubt in doing this the experience of other jurisdictions would be of assistance (such as the US experience in relation to Restatement Second §90: *Farnsworth* §2.19), but these questions are too large to consider in a paper of this kind. One might also wonder, however, whether an English court would prefer to see legislative reform in this area, rather than judicial reform, just as the reform of privity was better achieved through the Contracts (Rights of Third Parties) Act 1999 so as to cover all the consequential changes necessary upon such a radical change in basic legal doctrine.

65 The analogy is not, of course, exact: there is no statutory rule that a deed must be used for a contract – only a rule of the common law, coupled with (now) a statutory definition of what constitutes a valid deed: Law of Property (Miscellaneous Provisions) Act 1989, s 1. And the solution which can be employed in the property context is the constructive trust, which is itself recognised by some, at least, of the statutes imposing formality as an exception to it: see n 16 above. However, this is not a significant difference: given that it is a common law rule that governs the enforceability of a promise, there need not be any statutory basis or recognition of an exception to that rule.

enforced. The reform of the law of privity in the Contracts (Rights of Third Parties) Act 1999 has created the principle that a third party beneficiary to a contract, who has himself given no consideration for the benefit which the contracting parties expressly, or through implication, intend him to be able to enforce, acquires the right of enforcement which cannot be taken away without his consent when:[66]

(a) the third party has communicated his assent to the term to the promisor,
(b) the promisor is aware that the third party has relied on the term, or
(c) the promisor can reasonably be expected to have foreseen that the third party would rely on the term and the third party has in fact relied on it.

Although there must be consideration between the contracting parties themselves, the third party's right to enforce a term becomes irrevocable when he has either accepted it, or – for present purposes more significant – relied on the term and the promisor either knows about or ought reasonably to have foreseen that reliance. This does not cover the case we are considering, in which the promisee has relied on the promise without there being any consideration provided, either by himself or by another person. But there is certainly an analogy which might form one of the building blocks of a development of the doctrine of promissory estoppel to permit it to create new obligations. Earlier in this paper a number of cases were discussed which involve third parties: *Binions v Evans*, secret trusts and mutual wills. In each of these cases, property was acquired by a person who had undertaken to give effect to a third party's intended rights: and the recipient of property was required to give effect to that undertaking. In those cases the emphasis was on the benefit received by the defendant through receipt of the property, as a significant factor in the creation of the trust of property in his hands in favour of the third party whose rights he had agreed to respect. The Contracts (Rights of Third Parties) Act 1999 might sometimes now allow a *contractual* solution in such cases, although it would focus not on the benefit received by the contracting party but on the acceptance, or reliance, by the third party. So Mrs Evans would be able to say that she was a third party beneficiary of the contract between the Binionses and her deceased husband's employers; the contractual term under which the Binionses undertook to allow her to remain in the cottage created in her a right which, once she had communicated to them her acceptance, or had relied[67] on the term to their knowledge or in circumstances where they should have foreseen it, became irrevocable without her consent and so she could enforce it and obtain the usual contractual remedies in the event of breach.[68] Just as there is a link of principle between the doctrine of proprietary estoppel and property cases in which constructive trusts are imposed such as *Binions v Evans*, secret trusts and mutual wills, so one could see that the development of third party contractual rights which are now enforceable sometimes by virtue of the (gratuitous) third party's reliance on the term

66 Contracts (Rights of Third Parties) Act 1999, s 2(1).

67 It is not, though, clear what would constitute sufficient reliance on the facts of *Binions v Evans*.

68 Contracts (Rights of Third Parties) Act 1999, s 1(5). If, however, the claim based on constructive trust gave her a better remedy through the law of property than simply relying on contractual remedies, a claimant in Mrs Evans' position would still have an interest in pursing the property claim.

which was inserted for his benefit might form a link to a development of the doctrine of promissory estoppel so as to allow reliance to become a source of new rights.

There is no doubt that the House of Lords could take such a step; and could allow promissory estoppel to sit alongside the doctrine of consideration as a principle under which a promise becomes binding on the promisor by virtue of the promisee's reliance on it, even though the promisee has provided no consideration, and the promise is not contained in a deed. But if such a step is to be taken, it should be done with care, with full consideration of the policy issues governing the enforceability of promises under English law as it stands today, and with a full analysis of the policy issues involved in extending the role of reliance as a mark of enforceability of promises. What must certainly not happen is to hide an extension of the doctrine of promissory estoppel behind the argument that it is simply part of a general doctrine of estoppel, and that, just because proprietary estoppel can create new property rights, promissory estoppel must necessarily be able to create new obligations.

CHAPTER 4

The Motive, Not the Deed

Lionel Smith

. . . The Light of Lights
Looks always on the motive, not the deed,
The Shadow of Shadows on the deed alone.[1]

I learned a lot from Edward Burn in the years during which it was my privilege to be his colleague. One of my enduring memories will be of interviewing would-be undergraduates with him. Interviewing is a difficult process; Teddy taught me by example. He had many ways of exploring a candidate's analytical skills. One was to ask them about lying. What is a lie?, he would ask, and, usually with some gentle prompting, the candidate would be led to the conclusion that the essence of a lie is not in the falsehood, but in the intention to deceive. And then he would press just a little more: What then is a white lie?[2] Again, often with a little assistance, the student would come to the understanding that in this case, everything turned on motive. Even the teller of a white lie intends to deceive; but he does so with some well-meaning motive. As often as not, this would lead to a discussion of the analytical difference, crucial in the criminal law, between intention and motive. Motive, of course, is generally irrelevant to criminal liability, while intention is always justiciable and often essential.

In this paper I will try to isolate the essence of the fiduciary obligation, and I will argue that it lies in the justiciability of motive. In this, I will depart from those who take the

1 W B Yeats, *The Countess Cathleen* (7th edn, 1912), scene 5. This play, first performed in 1899, is based on an old Irish folk tale set in a time of starvation. The people begin to sell their souls to the Devil's agents; the Countess redeems their souls by selling her own. Even so, she escapes damnation, for the reason given by an angel in the passage quoted. In his notes to this edition, Yeats observes that one of several things to which some audiences took objection was the Countess's escape from Hell despite her transaction.

2 Of course one could ask some difficult and interesting questions about the cultural significance of the term 'white lie'. It is also true that not every candidate had a shared understanding of what the term meant. One example proffered was that in the case of a roadside breakdown, one might call an assistance service using the membership information of a friend or relation. 'Sounds like good old-fashioned fraud to me', was Teddy's response.

view that it is impossible, or at least not useful, to try to identify the heart of the fiduciary obligation.[3] I am not going to address the difficult question of when fiduciary obligations arise; I will largely confine myself to trustees and company directors, where the obligation uncontroversially exists. Suffice it to say that I follow what I take to be the dominant view, that such relationships arise through a voluntary undertaking on the part of the fiduciary.[4] This is either an undertaking to put another person's interests ahead of one's own, or an undertaking to accept some position to which the law has attached the fiduciary duty.[5] Given the presence of a fiduciary relationship, I will try to isolate what it is that is special or characteristic about fiduciary obligations. That may sound overly ambitious, or alternatively trite, and so I will begin by showing that there is arguably a certain equivocation on this question, before I try to provide my own answer.

On the terminological plane, for the sake of variety as well as to disengage occasionally from the historical roots, I will sometimes refer to the duty of loyalty. Within the common law tradition, I mean this to be the same as the fiduciary duty. It is the duty to put another's interests ahead of one's own interests.[6] Such duties can also be found within the civil law, even though that tradition lacks the historical foundations that underpin the fiduciary obligations known to the common law. The phrase 'duty of loyalty' therefore serves as a neutral term which can work in either tradition. Although the duty of loyalty grew and developed within equity

3 In this, with some trepidation, I will depart from the arguments of P D Finn, *Fiduciary Obligations* (1977), who says on the first page of his groundbreaking book that the use of the term 'fiduciary' provides 'a veil behind which individual rules and principles have been developed. . . . These rules are everything. The description "fiduciary", nothing'. There are many of Finn's points with which I agree; but I will argue that the rules and principles he identifies all rest on a coherent and articulable basis. Similarly I will disagree with J Glover, *Commercial Equity: Fiduciary Relationships* (1995). His argument (especially at 42ff) is that the best that we can hope for is to find 'family resemblances' among different kinds of fiduciary relationships. My own thought, to the contrary, is that a common label is unjustified unless it corresponds to a common referent; and indeed the appeal to 'family resemblances' might be thought to support this and so to work directly against Glover's argument. The members of any group of people among whom we would expect to find family resemblances *do* share a single characteristic, namely descent from a common ancestor (and hence shared genetic material). If we consider resemblances in characteristics which are learned rather than inherited (Glover's quotation from Wittgenstein mentions gait), the common characteristic is habitational proximity.

4 A Scott, 'The Fiduciary Principle' (1949) 37 Cal LR 539, 540; *Hospital Products Ltd v United States Surgical Corpn* (1984) 156 CLR 41, 96–97.

5 Normally when obligations are voluntary, we expect that the content of the obligation will correspond to what was voluntarily undertaken. This expectation, which I will call the 'correspondence principle', will re-appear in the analysis below.

6 In this regard I do not follow the terminology of those who identify three different kinds of fiduciary duty: those of loyalty, of influence, and of confidence. See J Glover, *Commercial Equity: Fiduciary Relationships* (1995) 6–10; P Millett, 'Equity's Place in the Law of Commerce' (1998) 114 LQR 214, 219–221; G Virgo, *The Principles of the Law of Restitution* (1999) 524–534; cf PD Finn, *Fiduciary Obligations* (1977) ch 15. The enterprise of distinguishing the three is clearly necessary, as they arise in different situations and according to different juristic principles. The idea that they should all be called 'fiduciary' is less obvious. I agree with P Birks, 'The Content of Fiduciary Obligation' (2000) 34 Israel LR 3, 8, that it is unhelpful to use 'fiduciary' to mean only that there is something in common with the rules governing trusts; that would make the term so wide as to be unhelpful. My terminological choice, which I think is shared by many (see for example *Lac Minerals Ltd v International Corona Resources Ltd* [1989] 2 SCR 574, 61 DLR (4th) 14; *A-G v Blake* [2001] 1 AC 268; *Coulthard v Disco Mix Club Ltd* [2000] 1 WLR 707), is to confine the label 'fiduciary' to the duty of loyalty.

jurisprudence, my proposed understanding of the nature of the duty is applicable whether the duty arises in equity, or from statute (as in Canadian corporate law), or in a civil code.

A CIRCULAR CONCEPT?

Very often, the core of the duty of loyalty is thought to be the duty to avoid certain situations. These duties are sometimes called 'proscriptive' duties because they forbid the fiduciary from being in certain situations; they do not require him to do anything.[7] And according to some commentators, this is what is special about fiduciary duties. For example, Patrick Parkinson writes:

> Essentially, however, fiduciary obligations prescribe what it is impermissible to do, not what ought to be done.[8]

There are notoriously two main things that a fiduciary may not do. The 'no-conflict' rule says that a fiduciary must avoid any conflict of interest and duty, and indeed any conflict of duty and duty. The 'no-profit' rule requires the fiduciary to avoid making any profit out of the fiduciary relationship, except where expressly authorized by the constitutive act (such as the deed of trust), or by the court. Either rule can be displaced by the fully informed consent of the beneficiaries, before or after the fact.[9] And of course there is some debate about whether the two rules are distinct, or whether one reduces to the other.[10] But so central are these two rules that most textbook accounts of fiduciary duties simply begin with them, without any suggestion that they rest on something more fundamental.[11]

If we agree that a fiduciary has committed a breach of duty simply by being in (for example) a conflict of interest and duty, then clearly something unusual is going on here.[12] Normally if a person owes a duty, he is (obviously) not allowed to breach the

7 They are called 'negative principles' by C Harpum, 'Fiduciary Obligations and Fiduciary Powers: Where Are We Going?' in P Birks (ed), *Privacy and Loyalty* (1997) 145, 147.

8 P Parkinson, 'Fiduciary Obligations' in P Parkinson (ed), *The Principles of Equity* (1996) 325, 331–332. See also A J McLean, 'The Theoretical Basis of the Trustee's Duty of Loyalty' (1969) 7 Alta L Rev 218.

9 The effectiveness of consent after the fact, without any additional consideration to make a promise not to sue binding, may be explicable on the basis of estoppel: J Payne, 'Consent' in P Birks and A Pretto (eds), *Breach of Trust* (2002) 297, 299–300.

10 See especially A J McLean, 'The Theoretical Basis of the Trustee's Duty of Loyalty' (1969) 7 Alta L Rev 218; and C Harpum, 'Fiduciary Obligations and Fiduciary Powers: Where Are We Going?' in P Birks (ed), *Privacy and Loyalty* (1997), 145, 147–149.

11 In *Bristol and West Building Society v Mothew* [1998] Ch 1, CA, Millett LJ, as he then was, said that the obligation of loyalty has several facets, including the no-conflict and no-profit rules. Later, he identified other rules and principles: the 'double employment rule', the 'duty of good faith', the 'no inhibition principle', and the 'actual conflict rule'. My argument is that all of the other principles he describes grow out of the basic one, which I am trying to isolate in this paper, and which I believe corresponds to his 'duty of good faith'. However, in my view, 'good faith' is not a suitable term here. See n 58 below, and text.

12 This calls for a word on the 'self-dealing' and 'fair dealing' rules, which respectively (and in brief) prevent a trustee from buying (in his personal capacity) trust property from himself (in his capacity as trustee), and from buying (in his personal capacity) a beneficiary's interest under the trust of which he is trustee. In company law, these rules find their analogues in rules regarding directors'

duty. In the fiduciary situation, he is not only not allowed to breach the duty, he is further not allowed to be in a position where he might be tempted to breach the duty. We have a logical structure which could be compared to that of gun control. The thing we want to prevent with gun control is people getting shot. We control possession of handguns, even though we also have all sorts of laws against the use of unlawful force, simply because handguns are things which are designed to allow the rapid infliction of serious harm. In addition to forbidding the harm, we attempt to set up a zone of exclusion around the harm, and forbid people even from entering that zone.[13]

So this unusual case of a 'prophylactic' rule in private law is often identified as the hallmark of the fiduciary duty. And if it is a breach of fiduciary duty to be in a conflict, then it might seem naturally to follow that the prophylactic duty to avoid conflicts (and profits) *is* the fiduciary duty.

I am not sure this is right. We can notice that in a classic conflict of interest and duty, there are two appearances of the word 'duty': the duty to avoid the conflict (call that *duty 1*), and the duty which is not to be allowed to come into conflict with the fiduciary's self-interest (call that *duty 2*).[14] In other words, there is a *duty 1* to avoid a conflict of interest and *duty 2*. Are these duties referring to the same idea, or different ideas? *Duty 1* is the prophylactic rule. It is the duty not to allow one's self-interest to conflict with *duty 2*. They must be different duties. It would be a logical circle to say that you have a duty to avoid a conflict of self-interest and duty, if the duty that must not be allowed to conflict with your self-interest was the duty to avoid conflicts of self-interest and duty. The prophylactic *duty 1* must be different from the *duty 2* that is not to be allowed to conflict with self-interest (or indeed with other duties of loyalty).

Everyone knows that the prophylaxis (*duty 1*) is understood to have a very wide scope. It is imposed to protect against something, but the prophylaxis is so wide that it overshadows independent analysis of the harm against which it protects.[15] This is what has happened, I would argue, when the duty to avoid conflicts (along with the duty to avoid profits, if that is thought to add something) is said to be the core or the heart of the fiduciary duty. I would say, instead, that it is the most obvious protection of the fiduciary duty, but it is not the fiduciary duty itself. The fiduciary duty is *duty 2*. I will try to show this by providing an independent analysis of the *duty 2*. If my

contracts with the corporation of which they are directors. Richard Nolan has argued that these rules are not responses to a breach of duty, but rather are responses to unjust enrichments: 'Conflicts of Interest, Unjust Enrichment and Wrongdoing' in W R Cornish, et al (eds), *Restitution: Past, Present and Future: Essays in Honour of Gareth Jones* (1998) 87. In my own view, they are simply particularly clear examples of conflicts of interest and can be understood according to the same principles. It is true that in self-dealing the transaction is voidable by the beneficiary, while in fair dealing it is not automatically so. This, however, can be understood on the basis that the fully informed consent of the beneficiary is always a defence to a breach of the prophylactic duty. The non-voidability of a contract within the fair dealing sphere requires the fully informed consent of the beneficiary who contracted, and so displaces the prophylactic rule.

13 See also P Birks, *An Introduction to the Law of Restitution* (rev edn, 1989), 340–343.

14 Of course there may be even more. In a conflict of duty and duty there are at least three: the two which conflict, and the duty to avoid the conflict.

15 An exception is P Birks, *An Introduction to the Law of Restitution* (rev edn, 1989) 340–343, who takes the view that the prophylactic duty protects against harm caused to the beneficiary. See now the further development of this argument in P Birks, 'The Content of Fiduciary Obligation' (2000) 34 Israel LR 3, which is discussed below.

argument be correct, then it would be logically possible to have a *duty 2* which was not protected by a prophylactic rule. I will therefore have to offer an independent justification for the prophylactic rule.

The wide scope of the prophylactic rule is sometimes seen as problematic.[16] There is a related problem of indeterminacy: not only is the prophylactic rule wide, but it is difficult to find its outer limits. This is especially thought to be a problem in company law. We know that the duty of loyalty owed by a director is not a duty of absolute selflessness: rather, it is accepted that being a director is not a full-time job, and the director may lawfully devote the bulk of his energy and ingenuity to other affairs, including the affairs of other companies. And for trustees we know this is also true. Being a trustee is not necessarily a full-time job; and a trustee may be trustee of more than one trust.

ACCENTUATE THE POSITIVE

There is one way in which to break the circle and to conclude that the fiduciary duty is the prophylactic duty to avoid conflicts (*duty 1*). Part of the explanation for the breadth of the prophylactic rule (*duty 1*) might be that the underlying duty (*duty 2*) involves, at least much of the time, a duty to act. If it was merely a duty not to cause harm, like the majority of duties in criminal law and in the law of civil wrongs, we might not need a prophylactic rule. But fiduciaries often have duties to act, like the duty of a trustee to insure the trust property, or the duty of a company's managing director to seek out business opportunities for the benefit of the company. We might think that the breach of such a positive duty is likely to be less visible than the breach of a duty not to cause harm, and so requires an extra layer of protection.

An analysis along these lines can be found in the dissenting speech of Lord Upjohn in *Boardman v Phipps*:[17]

> 2. Once it is established that there is such a [fiduciary] relationship, that relationship must be examined to see what duties are thereby imposed upon the agent, to see what is the scope and ambit of the duties charged upon him.
>
> 3. Having defined the scope of those duties one must see whether he has committed some breach thereof and by placing himself within the scope and ambit of those duties in a position where his duty and interest may possibly conflict. It is only at this stage that any question of accountability arises.

Although this was a dissenting speech, it was taken as representing the law by Roskill J in *Industrial Development Consultants Ltd v Cooley*,[18] on the basis that the other Law Lords only disagreed as to the application of the law to the facts. In *IDC Ltd v Cooley*, the defendant managing director of IDC Ltd was approached by Smettom with a business opportunity. Smettom wanted to deal with Cooley personally, and not

16 See for example the dissenting speeches in *Boardman v Phipps* [1967] 2 AC 46.
17 [1967] 2 AC 46, 127.
18 [1972] 2 All ER 162, [1972] 1 WLR 443.

with IDC Ltd. After some negotiations, Cooley resigned his position and took up the opportunity personally. He was held to have breached his fiduciary obligations to IDC Ltd, and was required to disgorge his gains.

This approach, which I will call the 'positive duty approach,' is a common one.[19] It is frequently called in aid by those who take the view that the 'no-conflict' rule is distinct from the 'no-profit' rule. Consider another famous case, *Regal (Hastings) Ltd v Gulliver*.[20] The plaintiff company decided (through its board of directors) to establish a subsidiary, which was to acquire some leases. The landlords, however, required the personal guarantees of the directors, unless the subsidiary should have £5,000 in paid-up capital. The plaintiff company could only afford to subscribe £2,000 for shares of the subsidiary. The directors did not wish to give personal guarantees, so they subscribed their own money, £500 each from four of them. Another £500 was subscribed by the company's solicitor, acting at the board's request, and the final £500 from outside parties. Later these shares in the subsidiary were sold at a large profit. At the same time, control of the plaintiff corporation changed hands, and it successfully sued the former directors for disgorgement of their profits. This kind of case is often put forward as illustrating a violation of the 'no-profit' rule without any violation of the 'no-conflict' rule. There is no conflict because the fiduciary has done his duty to the full. Directors of a corporation have no duty to guarantee the debts of its subsidiaries, or to risk their own capital by investing in a subsidiary.[21] What is implicit in the positive duty approach is that the 'duty' in the phrase 'conflict of interest and duty' is some positive duty that the fiduciary owes to the beneficiary.

The positive duty approach clearly separates *duty 1* and *duty 2*. It requires us to find a positive duty, a duty to do something, which is *duty 2*. Then, if that duty conflicts with the fiduciary's self-interest, we have a breach of *duty 1*. This approach has the very important double virtue of breaking the logical circle described above, and of helping us to define the limits of the amorphous no-conflict rule (*duty 1*). The defendant in *IDC Ltd v Cooley* had a positive contractual duty, as managing director, to bring to the corporation the business opportunity of which he became aware, even though he became aware of it in his private capacity. In other words, it was his job to seek out such opportunities for the corporation. So his self-interest in taking the opportunity conflicted with this duty.[22] The approach also brings the hope of clearer limits on the prophylactic rule. The managing director in *IDC Ltd v Cooley* was liable because he had a positive contractual duty, as *managing* director, to find business opportunities. A director who did not also have a contract of employment with the corporation – a

19 This appears to be the approach in P D Finn, *Fiduciary Obligations* (1977) 203.

20 [1967] 2 AC 134n, [1942] 1 All ER 378.

21 So too in the foundational case of *Keech v Sandford* (1726) Cas temp King 61, 25 ER 223: the trustee had done his duty, by trying to secure a renewal of the lease for the benefit of his beneficiary. This case is similarly put forward by some as a case of profit without conflict.

22 See the argument in B Welling, *Corporate Law in Canada: The Governing Principles* (2nd edn, 1991) 408–414. Welling attempts to make sense of the cases by distinguishing between situations of actual conflict, potential conflict, and no conflict. The distinction is based largely on the contractual duties of the fiduciary.

non-executive director – would not have the same positive duty.[23] We know that being a non-executive director is not a full-time job. If you are a non-executive director, it is not your job to seek out business opportunities. It is your job to provide, along with the other directors, strategic leadership. This approach therefore helps us toward what seems to be the correct position, that the scope for accountability for misappropriating a corporate opportunity will be wider in the case of a managing director, or an executive director, than in the case of a non-executive director. Shortly after *IDC Ltd v Cooley,* the Supreme Court of Canada decided a similar case in *Canadian Aero Services Ltd v O'Malley*.[24] The defendants in *Canadian Aero* were senior officers, and they were also held accountable for appropriating an opportunity.[25] As officers, they owed a duty of loyalty to the corporation, regardless of whether or not they were directors.[26] Professor Prentice evaluated these two decisions in a note.[27] He asked, 'Are there now positive obligations on directors to advance the interests of the company?'[28] To one who adopts the positive duty approach, this question has things backwards. It was the positive duties already incumbent on the defendants in *IDC Ltd v Cooley* and *Canadian Aero* that led to breaches of the no-conflict rule. Those duties were the positive contractual duties incumbent on them as officers. A trustee's position is somewhere in between that of an executive and a non-executive director, in this sense. He does not (generally) have any duties that we would call contractual; but he usually has certain positive duties that come with his office, an office that he consensually assumed.[29] An example would be the duty to insure the trust property. No one would call a failure to insure a breach of the duty of loyalty. On the other hand, if he purchased insurance from a firm in which he had a financial interest, there would be a conflict.[30]

By breaking the logical circle, the positive duty approach therefore allows us to say that the prophylactic no-conflict duty (*duty 1*) is the fiduciary duty (or is part of it, when combined with the no-profit rule). It is the duty to avoid a conflict between self-interest and some positive duty. It is not clear, however, that this approach explains enough. At a basic level, it does not seem quite right to say that the duty of

23 I take it as fundamental that the relationship between a company and its director, as such, is not a relationship of employer–employee or master–servant (despite some of the language in the Companies Act 1985, ss 319–320). Far from the company having the power to give directions to the director, it is the directors who decide what the company will do. In this regard (as in many others) directors are like trustees, and this translates into the rule that they are not entitled to remuneration unless authorized by the corporate constitution or the court (*Guinness plc v Saunders* [1990] 2 AC 663, [1990] 1 All ER 652). By contrast, the most exalted President or Chief Executive Officer, as such, is an employee. This yields a different approach to compensation (*Craven-Ellis v Canons Ltd* [1936] 2 KB 403).

24 [1974] SCR 592, 40 DLR (3d) 371.

25 In North American terminology, a senior employee holding a defined office in the corporation (such as President or Chief Financial Officer) is called an officer. Hence a managing director (a term which is not commonly used in North America) would be described as both an officer and a director.

26 The extension of the fiduciary duty to officers has now been codified in all Canadian jurisdictions.

27 'The Corporate Opportunity Doctrine' (1974) 37 MLR 464.

28 'The Corporate Opportunity Doctrine' (1974) 37 MLR 464, 468.

29 Of course this is not true of trustees who become such by operation of law, but such trustees do not usually owe fiduciary obligations. See A W Scott and W F Fratcher, *Scott on Trusts,* vol V (4th edn, 1989) 304; R Chambers, *Resulting Trusts* (1997) 194–200; L Smith, 'Constructive Fiduciaries?' in P Birks (ed), *Privacy and Loyalty* (1997) 249, 264–267.

30 Cf *Williams v Barton* [1927] 2 Ch 9.

loyalty, the fiduciary duty, *is* a duty to avoid certain situations. Those situations are ones where loyalty might be tested, and it might be in doubt, but avoiding those situations is not the heart of what we mean by being loyal. There is more to loyalty than avoiding things. Furthermore, this approach does not readily provide an explanation of why we need the prophylactic rule, given the presence of a positive non-fiduciary duty on the defendant. It is true that breaches of fiduciary duty allow gain-based remedies.[31] But it would be backwards to justify a right because of its remedy; and anyway, the response of disgorgement is no longer seen as exceptional. It is clearer and clearer that there are plenty of civil wrongs that allow disgorgement of a defendant's gain as an alternative to compensation for the plaintiff's loss.[32] Even a breach of contract, that most quotidian civil wrong, may permit it.[33] Disgorgement can be understood as a response that is appropriate for some wrongs as a matter of corrective justice.[34] What remains unique in fiduciary obligations is the prophylaxis.

The positive duty approach to fiduciary obligations therefore needs to be supplemented by an explanation of the prophylactic rules. Of course, accounts have been offered over the years. Perhaps the most frequently heard explanation for the prophylactic rules is that they are designed to prevent fiduciaries from being tempted.[35] There are a couple of difficulties with this explanation, which amounts to saying that prophylaxis operates as a deterrent. First, a rule that only takes away the defendant's gain is not much of a deterrent. Any economist will tell you that the rational self-serving defendant knows that he will not be caught and sued to judgement every time he puts himself in a conflict of interest and duty. If the chance of that is 70 per cent, and if even when he is caught he will have to give up only his gains from the times he is caught, his incentive is to go ahead, because he will keep 30 per cent of his gains. Unless the odds of being held accountable are 100 per cent, a functional deterrent would require a penalty (for that is what it would be) in excess of

31 In fact, the position seems to be that any juridical act performed by the fiduciary in breach of the prophylactic duty and affecting the beneficiary is voidable at the instance of the beneficiary; and, any gain acquired by the fiduciary must be disgorged to the beneficiary; and, any loss caused to the beneficiary must be compensated. Disgorgement or compensation can be combined with avoidance if the beneficiary wishes. The avoidance of any juridical act may raise other issues: for example, it may be subject to the rights of another party to the transaction. Applying general principles, we should expect that if A Ltd contracts with B, but the contract is voidable by A Ltd because its directors acted in breach of their fiduciary duties, nonetheless B could resist the avoidance unless it knew or ought to have known of the breach: see *Barclays Bank plc v Boulter* [1993] 4 All ER 513, [1999] 1 WLR 1919, HL; D Friedmann, 'The Objective Principle and Mistake and Involuntariness in Contract and Restitution' (2003) 119 LQR 68, 81–84. For a slightly different approach, see *Criterion Properties plc v Stratford UK Properties LLC* [2002] EWCA Civ 1783, [2003] All ER(D) 280 (DRC). Avoidance may further require restitution in the sense of giving back, as where the price paid under a contract must be returned if the contract is avoided.

32 See P Birks, 'Civil Wrongs: A New World' in *Butterworths Lectures 1990–1991* (1992) 55.

33 *A-G v Blake* [2001] 1 AC 268.

34 E J Weinrib, 'Restitutionary Damages as Corrective Justice' (2000) 1 Theoretical Inquiries in Law 1. Disgorgement is sometimes explained as having a deterrent function; functionalism, however, is inconsistent with understanding private law as based on corrective justice (E J Weinrib, *The Idea of Private Law* (1995) 3–8 and *passim*). Even on a functionalist approach to private law, deterrence does not provide a good account of disgorgement, as I seek to demonstrate in the next paragraph in relation to prophylaxis.

35 A famous statement in these terms is that of Lord Herschell in *Bray v Ford* [1896] AC 44, 51–52. The judgment of King LK in *Keech v Sandford* (1726) Cas temp King 61, 25 ER 223 also seems to be premised on the avoidance of temptation.

the gain. Secondly, an explanation based on deterrence is inconsistent with the internal rationality of private law.[36] The reason is that deterrence looks outside of the relationship between plaintiff and defendant, and their conduct that gave rise to the litigation. To the extent that it seeks to influence the conduct of others in the future, it is effectively a public law principle.[37]

More broadly, this approach must drive us to ask, Why are we so concerned about fiduciaries' being tempted? Why not have a prophylactic rule for breaches of contract or for the tort of negligence? We do not particularly relish or invite breaches of any of those obligations. We might say that one of the characteristics of the fiduciary relationship is the vulnerability of the beneficiary.[38] This vulnerability requires a special protective rule. I am not sure this works. First of all, not every beneficiary is particularly vulnerable to his fiduciary. A multinational corporation with a board of 15 directors is not particularly vulnerable to a single non-executive director, but that director clearly owes fiduciary obligations to the corporation. Conversely, if prophylaxis was premised on vulnerability, we should have a lot of prophylaxis outside fiduciary relationships. A pedestrian on a crossing is extremely vulnerable to motorists, but is protected only by the ordinary law of negligence.

The fiduciary relationship is best understood as premised on a voluntary undertaking to assume an office to which the law attaches fiduciary obligations, or, outside of that, on a voluntary undertaking to put another's interests ahead of one's own.[39] Its content should correspond to what is undertaken.[40] In order to explain prophylaxis within the positive duty approach, we need to say that the fiduciary's undertaking directly creates the no-conflict and the no-profit rules. It creates these proscriptive obligations as a way of throwing up an extra ring of protection around the fiduciary's positive duties. In other words, some other (non-fiduciary) duties are effectively super-protected. This approach is perhaps best captured by the famous words of Cardozo J in *Meinhard v*

36 E J Weinrib, *The Idea of Private Law* (1995).

37 I realise that many would disagree with this view. The view implies that punitive damages, when used to fulfil a deterrent or retributive function, represent an incursion of public law into the private law sphere. See also the discussion of the jurisdiction to use the civil law in aid of the criminal law in *A-G v Blake* [2001] 1 AC 268. So I accept that such incursions are possible. But even so, I do not accept that this could give a satisfactory account of the prophylactic principle in fiduciary law; no one suggests that it operates in a retributive way, or otherwise in aid of the criminal law, and as the text explains, a deterrent function is implausible. See now *Harris v Digital Pulse Pty Ltd* [2003] NSWCA 10, where however, the discussion is largely in terms of a semi-theological debate about the fusion of law and equity.

38 See for example *Frame v Smith* [1987] 2 SCR 99, 136, 42 DLR (4th) 81, *per* Wilson J. This was a dissenting judgment, but it was adopted by the majority in *LAC Minerals Ltd v International Corona Resources Ltd* [1989] 2 SCR 574, 599-600, 61 DLR (4th) 14, 63, who said: 'The one feature, however, which is considered to be indispensable to the existence of the relationship, and which is most relevant in this case, is that of dependency or vulnerability.' The majority drew support from the judgement of Dawson J in *Hospital Products Ltd v United States Surgical Corp* (1984) 156 CLR 41, 142. Note however that in *Hodgkinson v Simms* [1994] 3 SCR 377, 117 DLR (4th) 161, a majority of the court rejected the idea that vulnerability is always required for a fiduciary obligation. See L D Smith, 'Fiduciary Relationships – Arising in Commercial Contexts' (1995) 74 Can Bar Rev 714.

39 See text above at n 5.

40 See n 6 above.

Salmon, which seem premised on the idea, not that fiduciary law imposes qualitatively different obligations, but rather that it imposes extraordinarily high standards in respect of ordinary obligations:

> Many forms of conduct permissible in a workaday world for those acting at arm's length, are forbidden to those bound by fiduciary ties. A trustee is held to something stricter than the morals of the market place. Not honesty alone, but the punctilio of an honor the most sensitive, is then the standard of behavior. As to this there has developed a tradition that is unbending and inveterate. Uncompromising rigidity has been the attitude of courts of equity when petitioned to undermine the rule of undivided loyalty by the 'disintegrating erosion' of particular exceptions. Only thus has the level of conduct for fiduciaries been kept at a level higher than that trodden by the crowd.[41]

The positive duty approach has most recently been advocated by Professor Birks.[42] He argues that the prophylactic rules represent nothing more than the highest level of a tripartite division of obligations, which classifies them according to how altruistic the person who owes the obligation must be. At the lowest level, as in the ordinary law of negligence, he must simply avoid wrongfully inflicting harm. At the middle level, he has a positive duty to improve the condition of another, usually according to a promise he has made. At the highest level, where the prophylactic rules operate, he has a duty to improve the condition of another, but in a disinterested way. It is central to Birks' argument that the 'obligation of disinterestedness' cannot be understood independently of some other obligation. It is only a standard of care for another obligation, a rung on a ladder of standards.[43]

So the positive duty approach must explain prophylaxis as a tool to provide extra protection for beneficiaries of fiduciary obligations. This extra protection corresponds well to the fiduciary's undertaking. Even so, I will try to show that this account is incomplete. My argument will be that the duty of loyalty is quite distinct from other duties, in particular duties of care and diligence, but also from the positive duties on a trustee arising out of the terms of the trust.[44] It is distinct in character, and is not just a particularly high standard that goes with some other duties. This is true in ordinary language. There can be loyal carelessness, as where a trustee acting from the purest motives makes an unreasonably risky investment decision. Negligence is not

41 249 NY 458, 464, 164 NE 545, 546 (1928).

42 P Birks, 'The Content of Fiduciary Obligation' (2000) 34 Israel LR 3, 28: 'The trustee shall not pursue any interest of his own which might possibly conflict with his duty to the beneficiary, scilicet his duty to promote and preserve the interest of the beneficiary'. On this account, the prophylactic rules protect the duties of care and diligence.

43 (2000) 34 Israel LR 3, 28–29: '. . . while the obligation of care can exist on its own, the obligation of disinterestedness cannot . . . The obligation of disinterestedness is meaningless without the obligation to preserve and promote'. Elsewhere (e g at 38) he calls the duty of disinterestedness 'parasitic'.

44 I mention these separately from the general duties of care and diligence because in many cases they can be violated regardless of the degree of care taken. An example would be the duty to pay a beneficiary upon reaching a certain age, if the terms of the trust so require. The terms of the trust may mitigate the default rule of strict liability, and the court may have a statutory discretion to relieve the trustee.

disloyalty.[45] So too, if a properly motivated trustee misunderstands the terms of the trust, there can be a loyal breach of trust.[46] Conversely, there can also be careful disloyalty, as where a fiduciary chooses what is, objectively, a perfectly good investment opportunity for his beneficiary, not revealing that he has a personal interest.[47] I will argue that it is also analytically true that the duty of loyalty is distinct from fiduciaries' other duties, because the inquiry into what makes a breach is totally different in each case; and I will try to show that the law reflects this analytical distinctiveness, most revealingly when the judicial control of fiduciary powers is considered.

First, a slightly different account must be considered. The positive duty approach says that the proscriptive rules *are* the fiduciary obligation. If the no-conflict rule says that there is a *duty 1* to avoid a conflict of interest and *duty 2,* it says that *duty 1* is the fiduciary obligation, and *duty 2* is some non-fiduciary duty. In line with a recent formulation of Professor Burrows, we might say that the fiduciary obligation *is* the voluntarily assumed obligation to act in the interests of another.[48] I am not sure that those who espouse the positive duty approach would see this account as inconsistent with their own, or indeed as very different at all. There is, however, an important difference. Burrows' description tells us that the fiduciary duty is *duty 2.* It sets it apart from the prophylactic duty (*duty 1*). On Burrows' account, the fiduciary duty is the positive duty to advance the interests of the beneficiary. This is protected by a prophylactic rule that forbids the fiduciary from being found in a position in which he might breach that fiduciary duty for the sake of his own interests. Thus, the prophylactic rule is not the fiduciary duty itself, but is an added layer of protection for the beneficiary against the breach of a fiduciary duty.

I agree with Burrows that the prophylaxis is not itself the fiduciary duty, but rather is something that exists to try to prevent a breach of the fiduciary duty. Burrows' approach is more convincing in finding the heart of the duty of loyalty, not in the prophylactic rules, but in a duty to advance another's interests. I would argue,

45 *Girardet v Crease & Co* (1987) 11 BCLR 2d 361; *Bristol and West Building Society v Mothew* [1998] Ch 1, CA. It would be possible, albeit strained, to understand obligations of care, skill and diligence as arising out of the idea of loyalty: we might say that a loyal person takes reasonable care, and exercises his skills diligently; and it may well be accurate that historically, these ideas were not clearly separated: see J Getzler, 'Duty of Care' in P Birks and A Pretto (eds), *Breach of Trust* (2002) 41. My argument, however, will try to show that the law follows the ordinary use of language in testing loyalty by subjective motive. This is fundamentally different from a liability based on a prohibited result, possibly filtered through some objective standard of care. It follows that an attempt to understand result-based liabilities as growing out of disloyalty would inevitably require us to lose sight of the essential differences between the two. The same effect would result from the reverse strategy of trying to understand loyalty as nothing more than a particular standard to be associated with a duty of care.

46 Loyalty can even have the effect that an omission which would otherwise constitute murder is instead a lawful act: *Airedale National Health Service Trust v Bland* [1993] AC 789; [1993] 1 All ER 821.

47 *Hodgkinson v Simms* [1994] 3 SCR 377, 117 DLR (4th) 161. It is a distinct issue whether the principles governing the causation of any loss suffered should differ depending on which duty has been breached (see *Canson Enterprises Ltd v Boughton & Co* [1991] 3 SCR 534, 85 DLR (4th) 129).

48 A Burrows, 'We Do This at Common Law But That in Equity' (2002) 22 OJLS 1, 8–9.

however, that his account still needs more detail.[49] One development that it would require is something to control the scope of the fiduciary duty. If we say that the trustee has a positive duty to advance the interests of his beneficiary, where does it stop? Some commentators, implicitly or explicitly adopting a version of Burrows' approach, have begun to ask whether fiduciary duties impose particular positive duties to act.[50] Taken at its widest, it would exclude the trustee from doing anything in his own interests or those of anyone other than the beneficiary. The account also needs some more detail in order to explain the prophylaxis. It is not uncommon for one person to have a positive duty to advance the interests of another. If I make a contractual promise to you that I will put a new roof on your house, I have a positive duty to advance your interests. We do not impose prophylaxis in this case. It seems to me, therefore, that Burrows would also have to take a line similar to the one described above: that is, the fiduciary duty to advance another's interests is a duty of loyalty, unlike the duty to put a new roof on your house. This is the feature which demands that it be super-protected by the prophylactic rules.

There is something shared by Burrows' account and the positive duty approach. Both try to express the fiduciary duty in terms of results. There is a duty to do, or not to do, something. On the positive duty approach, the fiduciary duty is captured by the 'proscriptive' rules that require that the fiduciary not do certain things. On Burrows' account, the fiduciary duty is a positive duty to do something – advance the interests of the beneficiary – which in turn is super-protected by the proscriptive rules, which are duties not to do certain things. This represents a very strong impulse. We want duties to be expressed in terms of results, in terms of what you may or may not do. That is how most duties work.[51]

My own argument is that there is more to a fiduciary relationship than the prophylactic rules. In this I agree with Burrows. What I hope to add to his account, and what will differentiate my account both from his and from the positive duty approach, is this: I will try to show that the heart of the fiduciary obligation lies in the justiciability of motive. Inaction, or action, may be a breach of fiduciary obligation, but not because there was a duty to act, or not to act; rather, because the inaction or action was improperly motivated.

49 The account that he gives is clearly not put forward as a complete theory of fiduciary law, and so when I say that it needs more detail, this should not be seen as a critique of the article I am citing, but merely as a way of developing my own argument.

50 See the discussion in R P Austin, 'Moulding the Content of Fiduciary Duties' in A J Oakley (ed), *Trends in Contemporary Trust Law* (1996) 153, 159–161.

51 P D Finn, *Fiduciary Obligations* (1977) is effectively the perfection of this impulse. Finn's position is that the rules which grow out of the fiduciary duty are 'everything' (see n 3 above), and his book is a detailed analysis of those rules, understood as defining what the fiduciary may or may not do. The argument in P Birks, 'The Content of Fiduciary Obligation' (2000) 34 Israel LR 3 is also built on the assumption that duties must be expressed in terms of results; at 17 he says, 'What the law requires when it requires altruism is at most action in the interest of others, outcomes, not motives'. This view, with which I would venture to disagree, leads to his formulation of the 'duty of disinterestedness' as nothing more than a standard applicable to the positive duties of care and diligence. The project of asking whether fiduciary obligations impose positive duties to act (see the previous note) is based on the same impulse.

A COMPARATIVE INQUIRY

The civil law tradition, like the common law tradition, has a variety of ways to classify obligations. One classification, which is second nature to civil lawyers, arranges obligations by their 'intensity'.[52] The classification is not one that is familiar to common lawyers, but it translates reasonably well and may be very revealing to common lawyers, who find they have never thought of it quite this way.[53] There are three intensities:

- An obligation of *means*. This means that the obligation is only to use the appropriate means (usually, reasonable skill) to try to bring about a result. The classic example is the obligation of a professional, like a doctor or a lawyer, to meet the client's needs.
- An obligation of *result*. Here the result must be secured. The fact that you used reasonable skill is no excuse for a failure. But *force majeure* will be an excuse. Most contractual obligations (say, the seller's obligations in a sale of goods) fall into this category.
- An obligation of *guarantee*. Here the result must be secured, and even *force majeure* will not excuse the debtor. The typical example is that of a contract of insurance, but some quality guarantees in sales contracts are in this category.

This typology starts from the existence of duties which are defined according to some result in the world, and then it classifies such duties by the extent to which the debtor is held to what she is supposed to do. Some have tried to understand the obligation of loyalty through this kind of lens, as a particularly intense obligation.[54] This is based on a strong impulse that every duty is properly understood in terms of a result to be brought about in the world. This impulse explains why fiduciary obligations are frequently expressed in terms of a duty not to do: not be in a conflict, not make a profit. But I would argue that the attempt to understand the duty of loyalty in terms of results will always fail, because the duty is not directed to any result, not even a negative one. Rather, it is a required *manner* of doing what one does, or not doing what one does not do. I will try to demonstrate that the duty of loyalty is one that is met or not met based on the motives with which the fiduciary acts. It is a duty to act (or not) with the right motive.

52 See for example P A Crépeau, *L'intensité de l'obligation juridique* (1989); D Lluelles and B Moore, *Droit québécois des obligations,* vol 1 (1998) 45–50. Of course there are other ways to classify obligations in the civil law just as in the common law; for example, by their source. The classification in the text would cut across such a classification.

53 Common lawyers would typically reach the same results through an analysis of the allocation of risk, done by the law if not by the parties.

54 Professor A Burrows argues that the duty of loyalty (understood as a duty to advance another's interests) may be strict, or a duty to use reasonable care: 'We Do This at Common Law But That in Equity' (2002) 22 OJLS 1, 8. This reflects an attempt to distribute the fiduciary obligation into a classification by intensity. Presumably Professor Burrows is referring respectively to the strict liability which follows on a trustee's failure to follow the terms of the trust, and the liability based on failure to take care which follows on an act of negligence causing loss. I would argue that neither of those liabilities necessarily arises from disloyalty, and so neither is properly called a breach of fiduciary obligation: see the text at nn 44–46. Similarly, Professor Birks argues that the best understanding of the duty of loyalty is as imposing a special standard of 'disinterestedness' onto some other duty: 'The Content of Fiduciary Obligation' (2000) 34 Israel LR 3.

The civilian typology of intensity omits any reference to motive. In respect of any obligation, it does not ask the question: With what motive must you act? The common law is notoriously indifferent to this.[55] We might be tempted to say that it is not a question which a legal system asks; whatever inquiries may be mandated by morality, the law only judges results. The law addresses the deed, not the motive. But this seems untenable. The civil law routinely inquires into motives, under the rubric of good faith.[56] The common law tradition also knows good faith in a wide range of situations, particularly but not exclusively in the equitable jurisdiction.[57] The idea of good faith, I suggest, involves an inquiry into motive, which may be one reason why common lawyers, who prefer to understand duties in terms of results, have difficulty in assimilating it. But the demands of good faith do not generally reach to the heights of the fiduciary obligation. An obligation to act in good faith does not import a duty of loyalty.[58] But both obligations show the incompleteness of a classification based on intensity; in other words, of a classification which presupposes that all obligations involve results in the world. If someone is under an obligation to act in good faith, does anyone inquire whether he must take reasonable care to act in good faith, or rather whether he is strictly liable to act in good faith? The question hardly makes sense, because the obligation is fulfilled, or not, according to motives, not results. And the same is true of the obligation of loyalty.

55 *Bradford Corpn v Pickles* [1895] AC 587.

56 See for example the Civil Code of Quebec, arts 6, 7, 1375. Article 7, on the abuse of rights, seems to change the prior law. In *Houle v Canadian National Bank* [1990] 3 SCR 122, 74 DLR (4th) 577 the Supreme Court of Canada confirmed the existence of a doctrine of abuse of contractual rights under the old Civil Code of Lower Canada. It furthermore specified that an abuse of rights could be established without showing bad faith (see especially para 144). Article 7 of the current Code seems to require bad faith for an abuse of rights.

57 The most general incarnation is in the equitable defence available to a good faith purchaser who acquires a legal interest for value without notice of a prior equitable interest. Good faith appears in a similar role in the common law, but not in a general way; for example, in the case of a sale of goods by a non-owning seller who is in possession with the consent of the buyer (Sale of Goods Act 1979, s 24). Most Canadian statutes reforming lending secured by personal property have a general obligation of good faith for transactions within the statute (see for example *Personal Property Security Act,* RSA 2000, c P-7, s 66(1)). The US Uniform Commercial Code § 1–203 imposes a duty of good faith on all transactions within the code. For a comparative study within Europe, see R Zimmermann and S Whittaker, *Good Faith in European Contract Law* (2000), reviewing the English position at 39–48.

58 The Civil Code of Quebec implicitly recognises this; while there is a general obligation of good faith (arts 6, 7, 1375), there are only particular duties of loyalty. The precise language varies, but differently worded duties of loyalty can be found in arts 322 (company directors), 1309 (administrators of the property of another, which includes trustees in Quebec), 2088 (employees), 2100 (entrepreneurs), 2138 (mandataries, which includes partners and company officers), 2270 (directors of an association). In the absence of the language of loyalty, the Code also requires a person to act in the interests of another in arts 12 (consent to treatment given for another person) and 33 (decisions concerning children). The common law tradition also recognises, in a similarly implicit way, that the standard of good faith is less exacting than the standard of loyalty: there are many instances in which good faith is required in the common law (as discussed in previous note), but no one would classify those as duties of loyalty.

THE MOTIVE, NOT THE DEED

I would argue that the heart of the fiduciary obligation is the surveillance and the justiciability of motive. Whatever powers a fiduciary has, he must exercise them (or not exercise them) with a particular motive. He must act (or not act) in what *he perceives to be* the best interests of the beneficiary. This is demonstrated by the existence of an entire body of fiduciary law that has nothing to do with prophylaxis: with the 'no-conflict' rule or the 'no-profit' rule. It is applied routinely to company directors and to trustees, and I would say to all other fiduciaries as well. These are cases in which the motives of fiduciaries are under investigation, even without any allegation of a conflict of interest or a profit. In the law of trusts, the cases are collected under the rubric of 'fraud on a power.' In company law, they are collected under the rubric of the 'proper purposes' doctrine. Both bodies of law would better be called the 'proper motives' doctrine.

Most treatments of fiduciary obligations leave aside the control of fiduciary powers, and focus on the prophylactic aspects of fiduciary law. An attempt to understand fiduciary obligations on the basis of just that material will naturally lead to an understanding which focuses entirely on explaining the prophylactic rules.[59] Under the influence of the impulse to understand obligations in terms of prohibited results, those rules will become the heart of the fiduciary obligation; that is the positive duty approach. But that understanding will be incomplete, because there is more to the fiduciary obligation than the prophylactic rules. By contrast, Professor Finn devoted a large section of his book to the judicial review of fiduciary powers.[60] And his epigrammatic statement of the essence of the fiduciary obligation is one with which I agree: 'A fiduciary must act honestly in what he alone considers to be the interests of his beneficiaries'.[61] But again, the lawyer's natural desire to define obligations in terms of results arises. In the context of powers, Finn proceeds to translate his principle into further obligations defined in terms of results: the duty not to delegate, the duty not to act under another's dictation, and so on, finding eight duties in all. My argument is that these are all outgrowths from the core duty, which can only be evaluated in terms of motive and not results. The outgrowths are important, but it would be a mistake to lose sight of the core duty, for it is the foundation not only of any existing particularized rules, but also of future development.[62]

59 For example, P Birks, 'The Content of Fiduciary Obligation' (2000) 34 Israel LR 3, leaves aside the question of powers (at 9) and focuses on obligations, primarily the prophylactic rules and the duties of care and diligence.

60 P D Finn, *Fiduciary Obligations* (1977) Part I. See also C Harpum, 'Fiduciary Obligations and Fiduciary Powers: Where Are We Going?' in P Birks (ed), *Privacy and Loyalty* (1997) 145, 160ff.

61 P D Finn, *Fiduciary Obligations* (1977) 15.

62 As Finn himself notes: P D Finn, *Fiduciary Obligations* (1977) 15. One consequence of the atomization of the general principle into particularized duties may be that one loses sight of commonality and difference regarding which general principle underlies which particular duty. The arrangement of the two Parts of Finn's book, for example, suggests that the review of fiduciary powers is based on one principle, while the prophylactic rules are based on another, since these latter are discussed in a separate Part dealing with 'duties of good faith'. I would disagree. Conversely, Finn places the law relating to undue influence and breach of confidence under the duties of good faith, but these fields are not based on duties of loyalty and are not judged by an examination of motive.

It is almost universally the case that a person who owes fiduciary obligations holds a number of powers by which he can affect his beneficiary's interests; trustees, in particular, have various powers to dispose of trust property. But of course the exercise of these powers is reviewable. It is reviewable not only as to action (the exercise of the power) but as to inaction (the failure to exercise). But paradoxically, the starting point is that the trustee's decisions in this regard are not reviewable as to their wisdom. They are not reviewable substantively. The reason is that the power belongs to the trustee, not to the court. There is a strong parallel to the judicial review of administrative action, where courts are asked to review decisions which belong, not to the court, but to some person or agency.[63] Even if trustees ask the court, on an application for advice and directions, how they should exercise a power, they will be sent away and told to do their fiduciary duty.[64] As in administrative law, the grounds for review are limited. An argument that the decision was substantively a bad one is, on its own, simply not a justiciable argument. Not every unfortunate investment makes a trustee liable. The exercise of a power is reviewable, for reasons relating to the fiduciary obligation, and for other reasons. Consider some of the other reasons first. Clearly, a power may not be exercised beyond its scope; a power to pay money to a person for his or her education does not allow a payment to help the person to buy a house. That kind of review does not owe anything to the duty of loyalty.[65] A purported exercise outside the scope of the power would be void. It might also be that the exercise of a power, or more likely its non-exercise, is reviewable as arising out a breach of another non-fiduciary obligation of the trustee. Even here, the structure of the allegation will not be, simply, that the decision is now revealed to have been a bad one. The argument must be that, according to what was known at the time the decision was made, the defendant failed to meet some objective standard. Motive is irrelevant. For example, a trustee might neglect to insure trust property out of sheer inattention. That non-exercise of his power to expend trust money constitutes a breach of his duty of care, and the beneficiary could justly implead the trustee and recover any resultant loss.

Other challenges to the exercise of powers are based on the duty of loyalty.[66] It is essential to understand that these challenges owe nothing to any allegation of the breach of any objective standard of care. Taking the easy case first, it is clear that if a power was exercised in a situation that violates one of the prophylactic rules, the exercise is reviewable. This is best illustrated by the 'self-dealing' principle. A trustee may have the power to sell trust property, but if he sells it to himself in his personal capacity, he is in a conflict of interest and duty, and the transaction is voidable. But crucially, even in the absence of any violation of the prophylactic rules, the exercise

63 As noted by P D Finn, *Fiduciary Obligations* (1977) 3, and ch 9. An excellent example of this parallel is *Re Hastings-Bass* [1975] Ch 25, 41, CA: the exercise of a power can be reviewed if the fiduciary failed to consider matters which he ought properly to have considered, or considered matters which he ought not. See now *Barr's Settlement Trusts, Re, Abacus Trust Co (Isle of Man) Ltd v Barr* [2003] EWHC 114 (Ch), [2003] 1 All ER 763. No such inquiry is made in cases involving allegations of the breach of a duty of care.

64 *Re Burger Estate* [1949] 1 WWR 280 (Alta SC). For a full collection of cases which illustrate the principle, see J Mowbray et al, *Lewin on Trusts* (17th edn, 2000) 760–761; A W Scott and W F Fratcher, *Scott on Trusts,* vol IIIA (4th edn, 1988) 409–410.

65 G Thomas, *Powers* (1998) ch 8.

66 G Thomas, *Powers* (1998) ch 9.

(or non-exercise) of a power is reviewable if the trustee acted with an improper motive. If so, the exercise will again be voidable.[67] It is this which shows that the fiduciary obligation is not confined to the prophylactic rules, and which demonstrates that the real heart of the fiduciary obligation is in the justiciability of motive. Loyalty is not measured by results.

It is normal to distinguish the 'dispositive' powers of trustees from their 'administrative' powers. Examples of administrative powers are powers to insure and powers to invest. These administrative powers are held for the benefit of the trust beneficiaries. They are therefore constrained by the duty of loyalty owed to those beneficiaries: the trustee must exercise the power (or not) in what he perceives to be the best interests of the beneficiaries. Sometimes the exercise (or non-exercise) of these administrative powers is challenged on the ground of disloyalty.[68] Such challenges are more common in the case of dispositive powers. An example is where property is held in trust for A, but the trustee holds a power of appointment in favour of B. These powers have objects whose interests can potentially be *opposed* to the interests of the trust beneficiaries.[69] The fiduciary obligation of loyalty requires the fiduciary to act with a particular motive: in general, she must act (or not act) in what she perceives to be the best interests of the person to whom the duty is owed. This applies directly in the case of administrative powers, which are held for the benefit of some beneficiary, and which are constrained by the same fiduciary duty that is owed to that beneficiary. But where the fiduciary holds a dispositive power, the position is different.[70] The trustee has express authority to favour the interests of one or of some over the interests of others, and so it would not make sense to control the power through the duty of loyalty, not even with the help of the 'even hand' rule that assists when the duty of loyalty is owed to more than one person.[71] The dispositive power authorizes uneven treatment. Moreover, the objects of the power may not even be trust beneficiaries; in this case, the power authorizes the trustee to advance the interests of a non-beneficiary over those of a beneficiary. In exercising a dispositive power, therefore, the fiduciary's motive need not be what he perceives to be the best interests of one or more beneficiaries, or objects of the power; instead, he should be motivated

67 *Barr's Settlement Trusts, Re Abacus Trust Co (Isle of Man) Ltd v Barr* [2003] EWHC 114 (Ch) [2003] 1 All ER 763, possibly subject to the rights of a third party: see *Criterion Properties plc v Stratford UK Properties LLC* [2002] EWCA Civ 1783 [2002] All ER (D) 280 (Dec) and n 31 above.

68 See *Williams v Barton* [1927] 2 Ch 9.

69 It is often the case that the objects of the power are the same as the beneficiaries of the trust, in which case the opposition is less clear. Even here, though, their interests as objects of the power are quite distinct from (and opposed to) their interests as trust beneficiaries. In *Re Brooks' Settlement Trusts* [1939] Ch 993, a beneficiary's settlement of his beneficial interest did not include (even though it was intended to) what he later received as object of a power of appointment.

70 D W M Waters, *The Law of Trusts in Canada* (2nd edn, 1984) 788.

71 The 'even hand' rule exists to regulate the case of multiple beneficiaries; the fiduciary must act in what he perceives to be the best interests of all the beneficiaries. One function of corporate personality is to obviate the need for such a principle for company directors. In fact the even hand rule applies in situations that on their face constitute a conflict of duty and duty and so appear to make any action by the fiduciary voidable. Probably the best analysis is that if a conflict of duty and duty is created by the terms of the trust, the prophylactic rule against such a conflict does not apply; it is implicitly excluded. See *Kelly v Cooper* [1993] AC 205, PC; E Simpson, 'Conflicts' in P Birks and A Pretto (eds), *Breach of Trust* (2002) 75.

by fulfilling the purposes for which the power was granted.[72] But in either case, the fiduciary's motives for action (or inaction) are reviewable.[73] And it is important to see that they are reviewable even in the absence of any conflict. For example, if a trustee refuses to exercise a power out of spite, there is no conflict, but the non-exercise is reviewable.[74]

The same principles apply, with some modifications, in company law. It is a basic principle that the court will not second-guess the business judgment of directors. Courts sometimes note that they are not equipped to manage business organisations, but what is more germane is that the decision does not belong to the court but rather to the directors. This was well expressed in *Burland v Earle*:

> It is an elementary principle of the law relating to joint stock companies that the Court will not interfere with the internal management of companies acting within their powers, and in fact has no jurisdiction to do so.[75]

In the US, the term that has evolved to capture this idea is the 'business judgment rule'.[76] Although this terminology has not been used much in the Commonwealth jurisprudence,[77] the principles are the same. A decision is not reviewable as to substance alone. Although the utmost care is not always taken with the language used, this means that a decision is *not* reviewable on the basis that, with hindsight, it can be seen that it was not in the best interests of the company. Not every bad business decision is an unlawful act. As with trustees, only some arguments are justiciable. Clearly it is a justiciable argument to allege that the directors lacked the power to do what they purported to do. Also justiciable is the argument that a decision involved a violation of the duties of care, skill and diligence. Finally, there is the argument that the decision involved a breach of the fiduciary obligation of loyalty, or of the prophylactic duties which protect the obligation of loyalty.[78]

Any argument based on a breach of the duties of care, skill and diligence requires proof that a particular objective standard was not met. Motive is irrelevant. Looking at the fiduciary obligation, we find the reverse. The exercise of a power can be set aside

72 *Vatcher v Paull* [1915] AC 372, 378, PC; *Klug v Klug* [1918] 2 Ch 67; *McPhail v Doulton* [1971] AC 424, 449, 457; *Re Hay's Settlement Trusts* [1982] 1 WLR 202, 209; *Turner v Turner* [1984] Ch 100; *Re Beatty* [1990] 1 WLR 1503, 1506; *Hayim v Citibank NA* [1987] AC 730, 746, PC.

73 See especially *Re Hastings-Bass* [1975] Ch 25, 41, CA; *Barr's Settlement Trusts, Re, Abacus Trust Co (Isle of Man) Ltd v Barr* [2003] EWHC 114 (Ch), [2003] 1 All ER 763.

74 *Klug v Klug* [1918] 2 Ch 67; A W Scott and W F Fratcher, *Scott on Trusts,* vol III (4th edn, 1988) §§ 187.4–187.5.

75 [1902] AC 83, 93, PC. This statement is simply no longer accurate as a matter of company law, due to the appearance of procedural tools by which stakeholders can invite discretionary judicial oversight of internal corporate affairs. In England this is governed by the Companies Act 1985, s 459; in the reformed Canadian statutes, the corresponding provisions are even wider. For an excellent overview, see J J Chapman, 'Corporate Oppression: Structuring Judicial Discretion' (1996) 18 Advocates' Quarterly 170. However the statement in *Burland v Earle* remains a useful expression of the attitude of the courts towards the review of fiduciaries' powers; indeed it was this attitude which led legislatures to enact the provisions for discretionary judicial oversight.

76 *Smith v Van Gorkom* (1985) 488 A2d 858 (Del).

77 As often happens, this terminology has started to creep into Canadian cases: e g *UPM-Kymmene Corp v UPM-Kymmene Miramichi Inc* (2002) 214 DLR (4th) 496 (Ont SC).

78 *Aronson v Lewis* (1984) 473 A2d 805, 812 (Del).

for a breach of the duty of loyalty if the power was exercised (and presumably if a decision was made not to exercise a power) with the wrong motive. Like administrative powers of trustees, the powers of directors are given to them, and held by them, for the benefit of the company. In a challenge based on a breach of the duty of loyalty, the crucial question is whether the directors exercised the power in *what they perceived to be* the best interests of the company. If they did not, the exercise is voidable at the instance of the company.[79] And again, it is essential to notice that this occurs even if there is no allegation of a conflict of interest or any other aspect of the prophylactic rules. It is the control of fiduciary powers which shows that there is more to fiduciary law than the prophylactic rules.

In order to substantiate this argument, it is necessary to take issue with some aspects of certain English decisions. In *Hogg v Cramphorn*,[80] the directors of a company issued shares to foil a takeover bid. The share issue was set aside, on the basis that the directors could not use their power to issue shares in order to affect the control of the company, regardless of whether or not the directors were motivated by what they thought were the best interests of the company. The basis of the reasoning is that such an action would be incompatible with the idea that the majority of the shareholder collective controls the corporate destiny. I would suggest that this reasoning is inconsistent with the principle of corporate personality, and inappropriately identifies the majority of the shareholders with the corporate person. *Hogg v Cramphorn* was not followed in *Teck Corpn v Millar*,[81] which also dealt with a share issue to fend off a takeover attempt. Berger J held that so long as the directors acted in what they perceived to be the best interests of the company, their action was proper.

Hogg v Cramphorn gives rise to what is called the 'proper purposes' doctrine. The idea is that a power can only be used for proper purposes. The upshot of this reading of *Hogg* is that 'affecting the control of the company' is never a proper purpose for the power to issue new shares; 'raising capital' is a proper purpose for that power. The effect of *Teck* is that this inquiry is misguided, and the real doctrine is 'proper motives'. So long as the directors acted in what they perceived to be the best interests of the company, their acts are valid. In my own view, *Teck* is preferable to *Hogg* on this point. The approach in *Hogg* has since been followed by higher courts in England.[82] My argument would be that the control of the exercise of directors' powers *on the basis of their fiduciary obligations* cannot be based on the 'proper purposes' reasoning. The English decisions could be criticised for failing to make a careful distinction between the company and its shareholders.[83] The power to issue shares

79 Who speaks for the company on this point becomes crucial; the legislation mentioned in n 75 above illustrates one solution, while the Delaware cases cited in n 84 below reveal another. Note also that voidability may be subject to the rights of a third party: see *Criterion Properties plc v Stratford UK Properties LLC* [2002] EWCA Civ 1783, [2002] All ER (D) 280 (Dec) and n 31 above.

80 [1967] Ch 254.

81 (1972) 33 DLR (3d) 288 (BCSC).

82 *Howard Smith Ltd v Ampol Petroleum Ltd* [1974] AC 821, [1974] 1 ALL ER 1126 PC; *Lee Panavision Ltd v Lee Lighting Ltd* [1992] BCLC 22, CA.

83 In other words, it is not enough to observe that the majority of shareholders elect the directors, and so it should follow that the directors may not frustrate the wishes of the majority of shareholders. That seems especially to have been the reasoning in *Lee Panavision Ltd v Lee Lighting Ltd* [1992] BCLC 22, 29–30, CA. That line of reasoning would change totally the way companies are run.

belongs to the directors, and their fiduciary obligations which condition that power are owed to the company, not to the majority of shareholders. Alternatively, the holdings in those cases could be understood to be correct, but not be based on the directors' duty of loyalty to the company. If the power held by the directors is actually a limited one which can only be used for certain purposes, then of course it cannot be used for other purposes; but its failure when an attempt is made to use it for an improper purpose is not based on the fiduciary obligation. It is simply based on the fact that the power has a limited scope. It would be as if a trustee held a power of appointment to appoint property to the children of the donor, and attempted to appoint property to one of the donor's nephews. The attempt fails – it is wholly void – but not due to any breach of the duty of loyalty.[84]

If that be correct, then while there are various ways to challenge the exercise of a power held by directors, not all of them are based on the directors' fiduciary obligations. As to fiduciary obligations, we can say this. If the power was exercised in a situation within one of the prophylactic rules, its exercise is reviewable. But the fiduciary obligation is wider, because even if there was no violation of the prophylactic rules, the exercise can be challenged on the basis of the directors' motives. The exercise of the power fails unless they were motivated by what they perceived to be the best interests of the company. Although I have argued that the case itself was either wrongly decided or should have been decided on a different basis, my conclusion is supported by *Hogg v Cramphorn* itself. Buckley J said:

> The power to issue shares was a fiduciary power, and if, as I think, it was exercised for an improper motive, the issue of these shares is liable to be set aside.[85]

84 In the terminology of G Thomas, *Powers* (1998), this would be a case of 'the excessive execution of a power' (ch 8), while a case of exercising a fiduciary power with a motive other than the best interests of the beneficiary would be 'fraud on a power' (ch 9). The same distinction is discussed in different terms in P D Finn, *Fiduciary Obligations* (1977) ch 9. The Delaware cases on defensive tactics by corporate directors separate these issues equally carefully, first analysing whether the directors had the relevant power, and then, if they did, whether they exercised it lawfully: see e g *Unocal Corp v Mesa Petroleum* (1985) 493 A2d 946 (Del); *Moran v Household International Inc* (1985) 500 A2d 1346 (Del); see also *Zapata Corp v Maldonado* (1981) 430 A2d 779 (Del), in the context of the board's decisions about corporate litigation. Such decisions also involve the exercise of a power constrained by a fiduciary obligation.

85 [1967] Ch 254, 269. This passage is difficult to square with Buckley J's opinion that it was irrelevant that the directors were acting in what they thought were the best interests of the company. One way to understand this, perhaps providing another way to reconcile the English cases with *Teck,* would be to say that the decisions differ as to whether directors' powers should be analogised to administrative powers or dispositive powers of trustees. The *Teck* approach treats them like administrative powers: they must be exercised in what the directors perceive to be the best interests of the company, which is the beneficiary of the obligation of loyalty. The English cases might be said to treat them like dispositive powers: the directors' motivation is scrutinised, but only to see whether they acted in line with what they perceived to be the purpose for which the power was granted. Between those two choices, however, it seems that the former must be correct. The different control of dispositive powers is based on the incontrovertible fact that the creation of the power is an explicit authority to subordinate the beneficiaries' interests to the interests of the objects of the power (see n 70 above and text). The granting to directors of a power to issue shares cannot be understood as authorizing the directors to subordinate the interests of the company to the interests of some other.

My argument is that this is the heart of the fiduciary obligation: the scrutiny of motive. If this be correct, then the prophylactic rules (no-conflict and no-profit) can be viewed in a different light. The prophylactic rules are not themselves the fiduciary obligation. The fiduciary obligation is a duty to act (or not to act) with a particular motive: you must act (or not) in what you perceive to be the best interests of the beneficiary.[86] The prophylactic rules protect against a violation of this fundamental obligation. They protect against the compromising of the fiduciary's motive. Earlier, I said that the no-conflict rule creates a *duty 1* to avoid a conflict of self-interest and *duty 2*. My argument is that *duty 2* is the fiduciary duty to act in what you perceive to be the best interests of the beneficiary. *Duty 2* is the fiduciary duty, and the duty to avoid a conflict (*duty 1*) merely protects against a breach of that fundamental obligation.[87] The prophylactic duty is not the fiduciary duty. One effect of this is that the question whether or not there is a difference between the no-profit rule and the no-conflict rule becomes uninteresting. Both situations call into doubt one's motive. Both rules therefore exist to protect against the same breach, which is acting with an improper motive. This approach also squares very well with the idea that carelessness as such is never a breach of the duty of loyalty.[88] A careless action (or inaction) is not one to which we generally ascribe any particular motive.

SYNTHESIS: PROPHYLAXIS AND ITS LIMITS

My thesis is that the fiduciary obligation is a kind of adjectival obligation. It does not require the fiduciary to do or not to do anything. There are other duties that impose such obligations. Those duties are judged by result. A trustee breaches a trust, or does not, based on the things that he does, or does not do. A company director breaches his obligations of care, skill and diligence, or does not, based on the things that he does, or does not do. But breaching those duties is never a breach of fiduciary obligation. It does not amount to disloyalty. Disloyalty is a matter of motive. It is never judged by result.

The first challenge is to give an account of prophylaxis under this approach, because the prophylactic duties *are* judged by result. The second challenge is to give an account of the limits of prophylaxis. Consider the simplest case of a self-dealing contract. The company director is buying company property, or the trustee is buying (in his personal capacity) property from himself (in his capacity as trustee). The duty of loyalty requires the fiduciary to act in what he perceives to be the best interests of the beneficiary. But because of the conflict, the transaction is voidable as of right by the beneficiary, unless there has been fully informed consent.[89] The 'business

86 Or, in the case of dispositive powers, you must be motivated by the fulfilment of what you perceive to be the purpose for which the power was given.

87 In the case of conflicts of duty and duty, there is a *duty 1* to avoid a conflict between *duty 2* and *duty 3*, where both *duty 2* and *duty 3* are duties of loyalty, to act in what you perceive to be the best interests of the respective beneficiaries.

88 See n 45 above and text.

89 In the case of companies, self-dealing contracts are subject to specific regulation in most jurisdictions (e g Companies Act 1985, s 317, 320–322). There remains a difficult issue about who speaks for the company as far as giving informed consent. See M A Jacobson, 'Interested Director

judgment rule', and its trust law equivalent, fall away completely in the presence of a violation of the prophylactic rules. There is no longer any deference to the fiduciary's exercise of his powers. And yet there has not necessarily been a breach of the fiduciary obligation as I have defined it. It is possible that the fiduciary *was* acting in what he perceived to be the best interests of the beneficiary. The transaction is still voidable. I have already argued that the usual position, which ascribes the existence of the prophylactic rules to a desire to remove temptation from the fiduciary, is unsatisfactory.[90] I need to provide my own account for those rules.

Prophylaxis cannot be explained on the basis that the exercise of the fiduciary's powers was, or was presumed to be, a bad one as far as the interests of the beneficiary are concerned. The reason is that the decision to exercise the powers is not substantively reviewable. That is, even if it was proved or conceded that the decision was substantively not a good one, it would not follow that the fiduciary had done anything wrong. Not every unfortunate investment decision by trustees is a breach of trust; not every failed business venture entails liability for the company's directors. Prophylaxis, therefore, does not protect against any particular result, such as harm. It protects against disloyalty, which is not evaluated by harm as such, but by motive.

I have argued that the fiduciary obligation is an obligation relating to motive. At the best of times, motives can be inscrutable. The prophylactic rules are triggered by situations in which it may be especially difficult to know with what motive the fiduciary acted, because the fiduciary is subject to conflicting motivational pressures.[91] We might say that when he is within one of the prophylactic situations, there is an irrebuttable presumption that he acted with an improper motive.[92] Irrebuttable presumptions, however, are always obscure and generally a bad idea.

Transactions and the (Equivocal) Effects of Shareholder Ratification' (1996) 21 Delaware J Corp L 981; J Payne, 'A Re-Examination of Ratification' (1999) 58 CLJ 604; S Worthington, 'Corporate Governance: Remedying and Ratifying Directors' Breaches' (2000) 116 LQR 638. In Canada the issue is largely moot, because reformed statutes make it clear that a shareholder vote is not determinative: B Welling, *Corporate Law in Canada: The Governing Principles* (2nd edn, 1991) 428–438. Provisions which allow shareholder ratification of self-dealing contracts, where disclosure was not properly made, also preserve this position: even if the shareholders have approved by a special resolution, the contract is voidable and the fiduciary must account, unless the contract was 'reasonable and fair to the corporation': e g Canada Business Corporations Act, RSC 1985 c C-44, s 120(7.1). See however Civil Code of Quebec, art 323, which allocates approval of at least certain breaches to the shareholders, possibly only for the case of approval in advance.

90 See n 36 above and text.

91 The argument that the no-profit rule is distinct from the no-conflict rule becomes, on my approach, somewhat uninteresting but also difficult to make (although it is easier to make on other approaches: see n 20 above and text). All of the prophylactic situations are cases in which the fiduciary's motives are called into doubt by some external motivational pressure. It does not really matter whether this is another duty of loyalty, or the fiduciary's own self-interest. And since the underlying fiduciary duty is a duty to act with the right motive, the performance of this duty is called into doubt by a personal profit just as much as it is called into doubt by any other self-interest.

92 Lord Eldon LC said, in *Ex p James* (1803) 8 Ves 337, 345, 32 ER 385, 388: 'This doctrine, as to purchases by trustees, assignees, and persons having a confidential character, stands much more upon general principle than upon the circumstances of any individual case. It rests upon this; that the purchase is not permitted in any case, however honest the circumstances; the general interests of justice requiring it to be destroyed in every instance; as no Court is equal to the examination and ascertainment of the truth in much the greater number of cases.' This was followed in *Chan v Zacharia* (1984) 154 CLR 178, 204, per Deane J.

There is no point saying that everything turns on motive, but in these cases there is an irrebuttable presumption as to motive, because that would mean that far from everything turning on motive, motive would be totally irrelevant. Another possibility would be that there is a rebuttable presumption as to a bad motive; or, perhaps the same thing put differently, a reversal of the burden of proof in respect of this issue. This does not really work either, because it would mean that if the self-dealing fiduciary could prove that his motive was pure, he would be allowed to retain the benefit of the transaction, and this is clearly not the law.[93]

It may be enlightening to elaborate the special effects of the prophylactic rules, and work backwards to their relationship to the underlying duty of loyalty, understood as an obligation to act with the right motive. If we take a simple case of a non-fiduciary obligation, like a contractual obligation to deliver goods of a particular quality, we can envisage a dispute about whether the obligation has been performed. It generally falls to someone who makes an allegation to prove it. So if the buyer admits that the goods were delivered, but argues that their quality was deficient, he will have to prove that. He has an entitlement to goods of the right quality, but he may have to undertake litigation risks and expenses in order to prove that the obligation was not fulfilled. Now consider a duty of loyalty. The duty requires the fiduciary to act in what he perceives to be the best interests of the beneficiary. If the beneficiary wants to argue that this duty has been breached – that the fiduciary acted with an improper motive – then outside of the prophylactic situations, he will have to prove this. But the effect of the prophylactic rules is that within their domain, the beneficiary does not have to prove improper motive; he only has to prove that the fiduciary was in a conflict or made a profit from his position. So we could say that the effect of the prophylactic rules is to relieve the beneficiary from certain litigation risks and expenses. The beneficiary is owed a duty of loyalty; this means that he has an entitlement *that the fiduciary shall act with the right motive.* The prophylactic rules give the beneficiary more than just some evidentiary assistance with that entitlement; they effectively give him a second entitlement. Motive, the crucial issue in the first entitlement, is immaterial in this second entitlement created by the prophylactic rules. We could describe the second entitlement in this way: the prophylactic rules entitle the beneficiary *not to have to wonder about the fiduciary's motive*.[94]

Understood in this way, it seems to me that prophylaxis can be seen to grow properly out of the voluntarily undertaken duty of loyalty.[95] Upon an undertaking that generates a duty of loyalty, the fiduciary must act with the proper motive. But

93 *Keech v Sandford* (1726) Cas temp King 61, 25 ER 223; *Regal (Hastings) Ltd v Gulliver* [1967] 2 AC 134n, [1942] 1 All ER 378; *Boardman v Phipps* [1967] 2 AC 46.

94 This idea may be best captured by the well-known words of James LJ in *Parker v McKenna* (1874) 10 Ch App 96, 124, who said that the no-profit rule 'is an inflexible rule, and must be applied inexorably by this Court, which is not entitled, in my judgment, to receive evidence, or suggestion, or argument as to whether the principal did or did not suffer any injury in fact by reason of the dealing of the agent; for the safety of mankind requires that no agent shall be able to put his principal to the danger of such an inquiry as that'. The sanction for breach of either entitlement is the same: the beneficiary may (but need not) avoid any legal act transacted in breach (possibly subject to the rights of third parties: see n 31), *and* may demand disgorgement of any gain acquired by the fiduciary via the breach, or compensation of any loss suffered by the beneficiary.

95 That is, it complies with the correspondence principle: see n 5 above.

furthermore, his undertaking to be loyal is inconsistent with his taking an adversarial litigation stance *vis-à-vis* the beneficiary, at least where other motivational pressures are in play. He is not allowed to say, 'I am obliged to act with the right motive, but you must prove that I did not'. His undertaking issues directly in the fiduciary duty to act in what he perceives to be the best interests of the beneficiary. But, albeit less directly, it also issues in the prophylactic rules. It would be a kind of disloyalty to leave your beneficiary wondering whether you had been disloyal, or to force him to prove disloyalty in such cases. In other words, the undertaking of a duty of loyalty is special in two ways; but both seem to grow naturally out of the idea of loyalty. First, it creates an obligation that is reviewable on the basis of motive. Secondly, it requires not only that this duty as to motive be done, but that it be seen to be done. This creates another prophylactic duty (or set of duties) that is not judged by motive but by events in the world, because it forbids the fiduciary from being found in any situation that is liable to make his beneficiary wonder whether the fiduciary's motives were pure or impure.

This brings us to the second challenge: the limits of prophylaxis. My account here will be informed by a version of the positive duty approach, which I earlier rejected to the extent that it suggests that prophylaxis is the heart of the fiduciary obligation. It is notoriously difficult to find limits to the prophylactic principle. The classic cases on profiting from opportunities and information illustrate this.[96] And the courts are arguably more and more sensitive to conflicts of interest and duty.[97] This is especially a problem when the fiduciary duty is defined as a duty to advance another's interests, because an open-ended obligation to advance another's interests does not tell you when you are allowed to stop.[98] Every self-interested act is in conflict with an undefined obligation to advance another's interests.

My suggestion for finding the limits of the prophylactic principle, while keeping it in contact with the nature of the underlying fiduciary obligation, is this: The fiduciary duty, as a duty to act with the correct motive, is a kind of adjectival duty that controls

96 *Regal (Hastings) Ltd v Gulliver* [1967] 2 AC 134n, [1942] 1 All ER 378; *Boardman v Phipps* [1967] 2 AC 46; *Industrial Development Consultants Ltd v Cooley* [1972] 1 WLR 443, [1972] 2 All ER 162; *Canadian Aero Services Ltd v O'Malley* [1974] SCR 592, 40 DLR (3d) 371.

97 In *Hogg v Cramphorn* [1967] Ch 254 and *Teck Corpn v Millar* (1972) 33 DLR (3d) 288 (BCSC), directors were resisting takeover attempts and yet it was conceded that the directors were not trying to entrench themselves. More recently, the courts have taken the view that defensive measures in the face of a takeover bid are inherently rife with the conflict between the fiduciary duty to the corporation, and the self-interest of a board which knows it will be deposed if the bid succeeds: see for example *Unocal Corpn v Mesa Petroleum* (1985) 493 A2d 946, 954 (Del); *Olympia & York Enterprises Ltd v Hiram Walker Resources Ltd* (1986) 59 OR (2d) 254; affd (1986) 59 OR (2d) 281 (Div Ct). If the court takes the view that a decision was made by the board while the members were in a conflict of interest and duty, then the decision is voidable. This has led to the practice of having such bids (and other transactions involving potential conflicts) evaluated by a committee of the board, which is made up entirely of non-executive directors. Seen in the light of the analytical framework in this paper, this is an attempt to shift the decision back into the domain of the 'business judgment rule.' If the decision-makers were not in a conflict, then their decision can be reviewed only by proof that they were actually improperly motivated, or that they breached their duties of care, skill and diligence. Courts have taken different approaches to this strategy. See *Zapata Corpn v Maldonado* (1981) 430 A2d 779 (Del); *General Accident Assurance Co of Canada v Lornex Mining Corpn* (1988) 66 OR (2d) 783; *Brant Investments Ltd v Keeprite Inc* (1991) 80 DLR (4th) 161 (Ont CA).

98 See text after n 49.

the fiduciary's actions (or inactions). The fiduciary obligation proper never obliges the fiduciary to act or not to act. It controls his decision-making processes. It is an obligation to make decisions in a particularly motivated way. So the question becomes, to which decisions does it apply? I dissent from the often-expressed view that there are different 'intensities' of fiduciary obligations.[99] The obligation of loyalty is irreducible and cannot be put on a scale. It applies, or it does not, to a particular decision. On the other hand, I agree entirely with the view, which is significantly different, that just because a person owes a duty of loyalty in respect of some things which he does, it does not follow that he owes a duty of loyalty in respect of everything which he does.[100]

The duty of loyalty seems best understood as something that constrains the fiduciary's decision-making power in respect of some of his decisions relating to the things he may choose to do, or not do. Everyone has rights, powers, privileges (or liberties) and immunities.[101] It is trite that the powers of fiduciaries to affect the legal positions of their beneficiaries are constrained by the duty of loyalty. But so too may be rights, liberties and immunities.[102] So the key to understanding the limits of prophylaxis lies in understanding to what extent a fiduciary's freedom of action is hampered by the duty of loyalty. In *Industrial Development Consultants Ltd v Cooley*,[103] the defendant was a managing director. This meant that he had not only the duties and powers of every director, but duties and powers arising out of an employment relationship with the corporation, and a very significant employment relationship at that. The employment relationship gave him a whole range of rights, powers, liberties and immunities; but because he was a fiduciary employee, all of those were constrained by a duty of loyalty. That was surely the nature and extent of his voluntary undertaking of loyalty.[104] Assume for a moment that he was not a fiduciary. When he met with Smettom, who wanted to contract with him, it is probably true that he was obliged by his employment contract to offer that opportunity to IDC Ltd, and his failure to do so was a breach of contract. He had the power to so breach the contract, but if he were not

99 One of the most frequently cited passages in this regard is from the judgement of Fletcher Moulton J in *Re Coomber* [1911] 1 Ch 723, 728–729. But the judge was expressing the view that not every fiduciary obligation imports a presumption of undue influence. That presumption, while it may often overlap with the incidence of the duty of loyalty, has a different juristic basis and implements a different norm. See n 6 above.

100 *Hodgkinson v Simms* [1994] 3 SCR 377, 464, 117 DLR (4th) 151, 216, per Sopinka and McLachlin JJ, dissenting: '. . . not every act in a so-called fiduciary relationship is encumbered with a fiduciary obligation . . .'. See also *Plus Group Ltd v Pyke* [2002] EWCA Civ 370, at para 80: 'The fiduciary duty of a director to his company is uniform and universal. What vary infinitely are the elements of fact and degree which determine whether the duty has been breached.'

101 This terminology comes from W W Hohfeld, *Fundamental Legal Conceptions* (reprint 1964), and was adopted in § 1–5 of the *Restatement of the Law of Property* (1936). Glanville Williams, 'The Concept of Legal Liberty' (1956) 56 Col LR 1129, suggested 'liberty' for Hohfeld's 'privilege'. The reference is to something which one may do but which does not (like a right) correspond to another's obligation; for example, one has the privilege or liberty to walk down the street. A power is an ability to change legal relationships (for example, by making a contract, or terminating one, even unlawfully). An immunity is from someone else's power.

102 My account here is similar to that of J C Shepherd, 'Towards a Unified Concept of Fiduciary Relationships' (1981) 97 LQR 51. See also E J Weinrib, 'The Fiduciary Obligation' (1975) 25 UTLJ 1; J Penner, 'Exemptions' in P Birks and A Pretto (eds), *Breach of Trust* (2002) 241, 245 n 14.

103 [1972] 2 All ER 162, [1972] 1 WLR 443.

104 And so complies with the correspondence principle: see n 5 above.

a fiduciary, that breach would not have been disloyal.[105] But since Cooley *was* a fiduciary employee, the decision to breach the contract was conditioned by the fiduciary obligation to act in what he perceived to be the best interests of the company, and so it was disloyal; and since there was a clear self-interest, the prophylactic rules were activated, and the company did not even need to prove his faulty motivation. This also applies to his resignation, which occurred later. Every employee has the power to resign, and when a non-fiduciary employee resigns, he is not being disloyal. But Cooley's decision to resign was encumbered by his fiduciary obligation; again, it was disloyal, and again, because of his self-interest, the prophylactic rules were activated.[106] So Cooley's breach of fiduciary obligation actually occurred before he profited from it by contracting with Smettom.

Similarly in *Canadian Aero Services Ltd v O'Malley*,[107] the fact that the defendants had resigned did not save them. Their resignations were improperly motivated and were themselves breaches of fiduciary duty. Some recent cases have started to draw the limits around this, and established that a resignation that was not improperly motivated is not a breach of the duty of loyalty; nor is it necessarily a breach of the prophylactic rules, if the conflicting motivational pressure generated by self-interest is not present at the time of the resignation.[108] The resignation issue, in fact, is usually something of a red herring where the opportunity in question arose before resignation. The reason is that if a fiduciary is at liberty to take personal advantage of an opportunity, then he need not resign to do so; whereas if he is not, resigning in order to do so will not change anything, because the resignation itself will be disloyal, and in any event will breach the rule against conflicts of self-interest and duty.[109] Resignation is relevant only in respect of opportunities arising after the resignation, which do not involve information acquired during the tenure of the fiduciary office. In such a case, the resignation, if it was properly motivated, will allow the former fiduciary to take the opportunity for himself.[110]

If we contrast this with the case of a non-executive director, who has no employment relationship with the company of which he is director, we see that the rights, powers,

105 To the extent that a breach of contract can give the plaintiff a gain-based remedy (*A-G v Blake* [2001] 1 AC 268), the fiduciary character of the employment becomes less crucial; but a breach of contract which is not a breach of fiduciary obligation does not attract the prophylactic rules.

106 It might be going too far to suggest that the power of a fiduciary to resign her position is like an administrative power, being one which can only be exercised in what the fiduciary thinks is the best interests of the beneficiary. It might be more appropriate to treat it like a dispositive power: the fiduciary must be motivated by fulfilling what she perceives to be the reason for which the power was given (see n 70 above and text). Either way, the motive for the resignation is justiciable; and even on the narrower view, Cooley's resignation could be considered disloyal. The general law of fiduciary powers is clearly to the effect that if the holder of a dispositive power exercises it with the motivation of acquiring some indirect personal benefit, the exercise is voidable as a violation of the fiduciary obligation: D W M Waters, *The Law of Trusts in Canada* (2nd edn, 1984) 1083; G Thomas, *Powers* (1998) 463–466.

107 [1974] SCR 592, 40 DLR (3d) 371.

108 *Island Export Finance Ltd v Umunna* [1986] BCLC 460; *Balston Ltd v Headline Filters Ltd* [1990] FSR 385. The former case is especially valuable for the discussion (at 481–482) of the fiduciary's freedom to take up opportunities after resigning.

109 See B Welling, *Corporate Law in Canada: The Governing Principles* (2nd edn, 1991) 414–419.

110 As in *Island Export Finance Ltd v Umunna* [1986] BCLC 460 and *Balston Ltd v Headline Filters Ltd* [1990] FSR 385.

liberties and immunities which he holds are constrained to a much lesser extent by the duty of loyalty. His duty of loyalty conditions his directorial functions, but not his private life.[111] The duty of loyalty also conditions what the director can do with information he acquires in the course of exercising his directorial functions. I would argue that this is a proper extrapolation from the fiduciary's voluntary undertaking, that his duty of loyalty should extend to hamper his liberty in respect of information that he acquires through his fiduciary office.[112] But if he learns of it privately, his liberty is not so constrained. He does not have an open-ended positive duty to advance the interests of his beneficiary; rather, his fiduciary duty of loyalty conditions some, but not all, of his latitude for action. This position is analogous to that of most trustees: they are allowed to have a private life in which they are free to be self-interested. Their fiduciary obligations condition what they do as trustees, and this reaches to what they do with information obtained in their office.[113] In either case, non-executive director or trustee, the analysis of resignation is the same as for executive directors: if the fiduciary is at liberty to take the opportunity, then there is no need to resign in order to do so; if not, resignation in order to take it will be disloyal and in any event will be a breach of the prophylactic rules. But for non-executive directors and trustees, it is far more likely than for executive directors that the fiduciary will be at liberty to take the opportunity without resigning, because they are not constrained in what they do with privately acquired information. This is why being a trustee or a non-executive director is not a full-time occupation, and why the holders of such offices can pursue their own lines of business. The taking of the opportunity is self-interested; but in this case, because of the more limited scope of the duty of loyalty, the self-interest does not conflict with the duty of loyalty, and so the prophylactic rules are not transgressed.

But the position is different in the case of a director (such as a managing director or an officer) who also has positive contractual obligations to the company. This person cannot rely on the distinction between information obtained privately, and information obtained in the board room; even in the former case, the fiduciary obligation conditions his decisions, since his relationship with the company includes positive contractual duties to benefit the company, and his freedom to decide whether or not to fulfil those duties is constrained by his fiduciary duty.[114] And once the duty of loyalty is in play in respect of such information, the prophylactic rules swoop down. Of course, it is common that the same person is both an executive director of one company, and a non-executive director of one or more other companies. Where the

111 Even this narrow version of the principle was enough to catch the non-executive directors in *Regal (Hastings) Ltd v Gulliver* [1967] 2 AC 134n, [1942] 1 All ER 378, since the opportunity arose in the boardroom.

112 This account is therefore built on the correspondence principle (see n 5 above) and does not depend on characterising information as property, a pointlessly tendentious exercise.

113 As with the defendant fiduciaries in *Boardman v Phipps* [1967] 2 AC 46, although they were not actually trustees.

114 *Canadian Aero Services Ltd v O'Malley* [1974] SCR 592, 40 DLR (3d) 371, like *Industrial Development Consultants Ltd v Cooley* [1972] 2 All ER 162, [1972] 1 WLR 443 before it, established a wider test of liability than the one applied in *Regal (Hastings) Ltd v Gulliver* [1967] 2 AC 134n, [1942] 1 All ER 378, as noted for example by D Prentice, 'The Corporate Opportunity Doctrine' (1974) 37 MLR 464. But it was entirely appropriate to use a wider test in those cases, dealing with executives or managing directors, than the test which had been used in *Regal (Hastings) Ltd v Gulliver* in respect of non-executive directors.

businesses of the companies compete in any way, this state of affairs is probably untenable.[115] The non-executive directorships do not preclude the person from taking the full-time job of executive director with another company; they only require her loyalty in respect of her directorial functions, and information so obtained. But this person is far more likely to breach the wider prophylactic duties arising out of her executive directorship, even if the breach comes about through a conflict of duty and duty rather than a conflict of duty and interest.

This framework can be tested against the decision in *Peso Silver Mines v Cropper*.[116] A mining opportunity was presented to Cropper, the managing director of the plaintiff company. He properly offered it to the company, but the company (through its board) declined to take it up. A couple of months later, the opportunity was offered to Cropper personally. There was a finding that at this time it had passed completely out of his mind, which may not seem credible, although such opportunities were considered by the plaintiff at the rate of two or three a week. Cropper now took it up, and profited. The plaintiff asked him to disgorge his gain; he refused, and resigned from the plaintiff, and was sued by it for an accounting. He was held not liable. The company's decision not to take up the opportunity, of course, did not quite amount to an informed consent that Cropper himself should take it up, and so that defence was unavailable. It seems clear that the initial decision by the board of the plaintiff (including Cropper) to reject the opportunity was not improperly motivated; Cropper made full disclosure. The finding that he then forgot entirely about the opportunity seems to be the basis for a holding that when the opportunity arose a second time, it came to Cropper independently of his role in the plaintiff company. So he did not use information that he had acquired through his fiduciary office. That might have been enough if he was a non-executive director; but at the time, he was still managing director of the plaintiff. That is, even if the first offer had never happened, the facts surrounding the second one are effectively those of *Industrial Development Consultant Ltd v Cooley*.[117] I would therefore join those who disagree with the decision.[118] Cropper should have done the second time exactly what he did the first time: offer the opportunity to his beneficiary.

CONCLUSION

Most accounts of fiduciary obligations do not try to identify what is characteristic about the obligations as such, but instead try to describe the results which must or must not be brought about. In order to take account of the control of fiduciary powers, as well as the more familiar territory of the prophylactic rules, this requires a large number of rules addressed to particular situations. The solving of real problems through the generation of multiple, fact-specific rules certainly has the virtue of being pragmatic. But the rules must come from somewhere, and it is always wise to try to

115 *Scottish Co-operative Wholesale Society v Meyer* [1959] AC 324, 366–368; *Plus Group Ltd v Pyke* [2002] EWCA Civ 370, [2003] 2 BCLC 201; P L Davies, *Gower's Principles of Modern Company Law* (6th edn, 1997) 622–623.

116 [1966] SCR 673, 58 DLR (2d) 1.

117 [1972] 2 All ER 162, [1972] 1 WLR 443.

118 See K P McGuinness, *The Law and Practice of Canadian Business Corporations* (1999) 751–752.

keep track of the underlying principles. There is even a pragmatic reason for this seemingly anti-pragmatic effort to identify the heart of the fiduciary obligation: disputes will always arise which are outside the existing fact-specific rules. Only a solid sense of the underlying bedrock of principle gives the judge the ability see whether and how the rules may be developed.

Anyone who has tried to teach the prophylactic rules along with the control of fiduciary powers will have been forced to confront the question, What do they have in common? How can the rules about conflicts of interest be said to rest on the same basis as the rules controlling the exercise of fiduciary powers? The answer is that the essence of loyalty is motive. I hope that Teddy Burn would agree that a white lie is an act of loyal deceit.[119]

119 I acknowledge with gratitude the financial support of the Social Sciences and Humanities Research Council of Canada.

CHAPTER 5

Restitution Through the Looking Glass: Restitution Within Equity and Equity Within Restitution

Graham Virgo

Over a decade ago Beatson described the integration of equitable doctrine and remedies into the law of restitution as 'unfinished business.[1] The extent to which equity is, and should be, integrated within the law of restitution remains an important question, but perhaps more important is the question viewed from a different perspective, namely to what extent is restitution integrated into equity? It is clear that restitutionary principles operate within equity and have done so for hundreds of years. Indeed, the key equitable remedies of account of profits and declaring that property is held on a constructive trust are restitutionary, because they are assessed with reference to the value of a benefit obtained by the defendant following the commission of an equitable wrong; this being the essence of a restitutionary remedy, namely that it focuses on the defendant's gain rather than the claimant's loss.

Although restitution clearly operates within equity, the way in which it does so has proved to be increasingly controversial. There is a sense, amongst certain members of the judiciary and certain academics, that the young upstart of the law of restitution, created by the common law, is seeking to take over the long established principles of equity and subvert them.[2] This has been expressed recently by Gummow J in *Roxborough v Rothmans of Pall Mall Australia Ltd*,[3] a decision of the High Court of Australia. He said of the recognition of the unjust enrichment principle that it:

> may distort well settled principles in other fields, including those respecting equitable doctrines and remedies, so that they answer the newly mandated order of things. Then various theories will compete, each to deny the others.[4]

1 *Use and Abuse of Unjust Enrichment* (1991) 257.
2 In *Westdeutsche Landesbank Girozentrale v Islington London Borough Council* [1996] AC 669, 685 Lord Goff of Chieveley referred to the 'tension between the aims and perceptions of "restitution lawyers" and "equity lawyers".'
3 (2002) 185 ALR 335.
4 (2002) 185 ALR 335, 355.

Much of this concern is misplaced.[5] Restitutionary principles already exist within equity anyway and the identification of these principles, both at common law and in equity, often provides a coherent explanation of the law. As Sir Anthony Mason has recently said, restitution 'serves an important purpose in informing equitable principle.'[6]

But, despite this, there are three real concerns about the operation of restitution within equity. First, there is a sense amongst certain commentators, but sometimes the judiciary as well, that we must constantly strive to ensure that the law is rational and consistent.[7] If it is not then it is wrong and needs to be changed and the law of restitution can provide the peg on which a new coherent law can be hung. But there is a real danger in losing both baby and bath-water. For example, there is a tendency to assume that equity and the common law must be consistent and, to the extent that they are not, then equity must change to comply with the common law. But analysis of the historical origins of equity and, more importantly, its function today, may mean that differences of approach are justified.[8]

Secondly, a particular problem with the operation of restitution within equity derives from the application of the unjust enrichment principle, a principle which does not always fit happily with the equitable way of doing things. In fact, the unjust enrichment principle can be characterised as a common law invention and it is a matter of particular importance to determine whether it is applicable within equity.[9] Equally, it is important to determine whether equity has a role in the interpretation of that principle.[10]

Thirdly, there is a tension between approaches grounded on rules and approaches grounded on discretion. There has been a tendency to assume that the law of equity is discretionary whereas the common law is much more dependent on rules. According to this view, the importation of the common law rules of restitution into equity may result in a more rule-based approach, whereas the importation of equity into the common law rules of restitution may result in a watering down of those rules by reference to the exercise of vague discretion. But this apparent difference between law and equity does not exist now, and probably never existed, for equity consists of rules in the same way as the common law. The crucial debate therefore, which applies both to the common law and equity and especially as regards the law of restitution, is to determine to what extent it is appropriate to rely on a discretionary approach to temper the application of strict rules.

5 *Westdeutsche Landesbank Girozentrale v Islington London Borough Council* [1996] AC 669, 685 (Lord Goff of Chieveley).
6 Foreword to Parkinson (ed) *The Principles of Equity* (1996) vi.
7 See especially the writings of Birks, including *An Introduction to the Law of Restitution* (1985), and Burrows, especially (2002) OJLS 1.
8 See text at n 147 below.
9 See Lord Nicholls of Birkenhead, 'Knowing Receipt: the Need for a New Landmark' in *Restitution: Past, Present and Future* (eds Cornish, Nolan, O'Sullivan and Virgo) 245. See also text at n 30 et seq below.
10 See text at n 45 et seq below.

This essay will examine how restitution operates within equity and equity within restitution; whether there is a real tension between the two and, if there is, how that tension can be removed.

CLARIFYING TERMINOLOGY

One of the main difficulties in having a meaningful debate about the interaction of restitution and equity arises from confusion as to terminology. It is vital at the outset to be clear about the appropriate meaning of key concepts.

The meaning of restitution

Essentially the law of restitution is that body of law which is concerned with the award of remedies which are assessed with reference to gains obtained by the defendant rather than losses suffered by the claimant. So, for example, where the defendant has received property in which the claimant has an equitable proprietary interest, the law of restitution operates to restore to the claimant either the property itself, this being a proprietary remedy, or the value of the property, a personal remedy. Here the effect of the restitutionary remedy is to restore to the claimant what he or she has lost, assessed by reference to the defendant's gain, albeit that what the claimant recovers from the defendant may be different in value from that which was lost. There are other circumstances, however, where the restitutionary remedy does not *restore* what has been lost, but rather requires the defendant to *disgorge* to the claimant what the defendant has gained. This is exemplified by cases involving breach of fiduciary duty where, for example, a fiduciary has obtained a bribe from a third party which induces the defendant to act against his or her principal's best interests, and the defendant is required to give up the bribe to the principal.[11] The principal lost nothing, so nothing could be restored. Instead the defendant is required to disgorge the benefit because he or she is not allowed to profit from the wrongdoing. Although it has been argued by some that it follows that the disgorgement remedy should not be treated as restitutionary, because literally nothing is restored,[12] it is still appropriate to characterise this as restitutionary in a wider sense, since the remedy is assessed with reference to what the defendant gained rather than what the claimant lost. Further, there will be cases where the defendant has committed a wrong which involves taking property from the claimant and where the award of a restitutionary remedy will operate to restore either the value of the property or the property itself to the claimant.

The notion of restitution has also been used in a different sense in equity, especially in the context of breach of trust. For example, in *Target Holdings Ltd v Redferns*,[13] the House of Lords described the remedy of ordering the reconstitution of a trust

11 See *A-G for Hong Kong v Reid* [1994] 1 AC 324. See text to n 96, below.
12 See especially Smith (1992) 71 CBR 672, 696.
13 [1996] AC 421.

following a breach of trust as 'restitutionary'.[14] But the remedy of reconstituting a trust can usually be characterised as compensatory, so it was not appropriate to describe this as restitutionary other than in a very descriptive, and potentially misleading, way.[15] What the House of Lords probably meant was that the remedy of compensation in equity operated to restore to the trust what it had lost, namely what the trust fund would have been but for the breach of trust. This may have been the same as what the defendant had gained from the breach of trust, but need not have been. Since the focus was on the loss suffered by the trust it was not appropriate to describe this remedy as restitutionary: the substantive law of restitution (meaning that body of law which is concerned with the award of remedies assessed with reference to the defendant's gain[16]) is not operating in this type of case.

The meaning of equity

The notion of 'equity' has many different meanings. As Sherwin has identified:

> It can refer to individuation of justice and overriding of rules; it can refer more generally to what is morally fair; or it can refer to the rules and practice of English . . . courts of equity.[17]

The first notion of equity, in the sense of overriding or correcting the effect of rules, explains the origins of part of that body of law which is now called Equity, where the Chancery Courts provided relief for procedural and substantive unfairness at law.[18] As the law developed, equitable principles became more rigid. The legitimacy today of equity being used to modify the application of common law rules is doubtful.[19] The second notion of equity is often used interchangeably with the notions of good conscience and natural justice.[20] The third notion is the more acceptable one, being 'the technical system of Equity as administered by the Court of Chancery.'[21] Even though this system of equity is no longer confined to the Chancery courts, it is this technical sense which represents the essence of equity as it is taught in the law schools and is generally applied in the courts. But, as will be seen, the other two senses of equity are still at play, especially in respect of restitutionary claims.

14 Lord Browne-Wilkinson at 434. See also *Swindle v Harrison* [1997] 4 All ER 705, 726 where Hobhouse LJ described equitable compensation for breach of fiduciary duty as 'restitutionary'; *Day v Mead* [1987] 2 NZLR 443, 451 (Cooke P).

15 Chambers, 'Liability' in Birks and Pretto (eds), *Breach of Trust* (2002) 15. See also Elliott [1998] RLR 135.

16 See Virgo, *The Principles of the Law of Restitution* (1999) 1–2.

17 (2001) 79 Texas LR 2083, 2088–2089. See also Hackney, 'More Than a Trace of the Old Philosophy' in Birks (ed), *The Classification of Obligations* (1997) ch 6; Tudsberg (1913) 29 LQR 154; *Great Peace Shipping Ltd v Tsaritis Salvage Ltd* [2002] EWCA Civ 1407, [2002] 3 WLR 1617, 1660.

18 Baker, *An Introduction to English Legal History* (4th edn, 2002) 97–115. See *Story's Equity Jurisprudence* (14th edn, 1918) 3–7.

19 Sherwin (2001) 79 Texas LR 2083, 2100–2101.

20 *Story's Equity Jurisprudence* (14th edn, 1918) 1.

21 Winfield, *The Province of the Law of Tort* (1931) 129. See also Maitland, *Equity* (1936, revised edn, J Brunyate) 1.

The essential principles underlying the law of restitution

Although the matter remains controversial it seems that, following the decision of the House of Lords in *Foskett v McKeown*,[22] the orthodox view of the law of restitution should be rejected. This orthodox view, sometimes known as the quadration theory, was that the law of restitution equated with the unjust enrichment principle, in the sense that all cases involving the award of restitutionary relief were triggered by the fact that the defendant was unjustly enriched at the expense of the claimant.[23] Instead, restitutionary remedies should now be treated as triggered by three separate principles.

Unjust enrichment

Where the defendant has been unjustly enriched at the expense of the claimant he or she will be required to make restitution and no other types of remedy are available. For most claims, especially those arising in equity, the notion of enrichment will usually be easy to establish because such claims often involve the receipt of money, which is always an enrichment, or other property which can easily be valued. Equally, the requirement of the enrichment being at the claimant's expense is usually easily established because it will have been derived directly from the claimant.[24] It is the element of injustice which requires careful definition. The use of the word 'unjust' is not an invitation to the courts simply to determine whether it is fair and just to require the defendant to make restitution. Rather, it must be defined in a much more principled fashion by reference to recognised grounds of restitution, such as mistake, undue influence or total failure of consideration.[25] Crucially these grounds of restitution are properly analysed, in most cases at least, as focusing on whether the claimant's consent to the transfer of a benefit to the defendant can be considered to be absent, either because it has been vitiated or because it was qualified by a condition which has not been satisfied.[26]

Wrongdoing

Restitution for wrongs is distinct from restitutionary claims grounded on the reversal of unjust enrichment. This is because, where the defendant has committed a wrong and seeks a restitutionary remedy, it is the commission of the wrong itself which constitutes the cause of action. It is not necessary to establish that the defendant has been enriched at the claimant's expense and that a recognised ground of restitution

22 [2001] 1 AC 102.

23 As was assumed by the House of Lords in *Lipkin Gorman v Karpnale Ltd* [1991] 2 AC 548, 578 (Lord Goff of Chieveley). Burrows wishes to retain this quadration of restitution and unjust enrichment: [2000] RLR 257 and, most recently, *The Law of Restitution* (2nd edn, 2002) 5. See also Goff and Jones, *The Law of Restitution* (6th edn, 2002) 3.

24 See Virgo, *The Principles of the Law of Restitution* (1999) 105.

25 Similarly in equity where the unconscionability principle is relied on, it is vital that the principle is structured clearly. See Getzler (1990) 16 Monash ULR 283. See text at n 68 below.

26 See Virgo, *The Principles of the Law of Restitution* (1999) 119–125; Birks, *An Introduction to the Law of Restitution* (1985) 140–264.

applies. Rather, the claimant only needs to establish the commission of a wrong for which restitutionary relief is available. The equitable wrongs for which restitutionary relief may, but need not, be available include breach of trust, breach of fiduciary duty and breach of confidence.[27]

The recognition that restitution for wrongs has nothing to do with the unjust enrichment principle is important for a number of reasons. For example, it establishes what needs to be pleaded and proved in court. It also affects the defences which are available, since the appropriate defence will be one which relates to the wrong, on which the claim is founded, rather than unjust enrichment.

Vindication of property rights

This has proved to be the most controversial aspect of the modern law of restitution, namely whether there is a separate principle grounded on protecting property rights or whether this is only relevant to the extent that the defendant has been unjustly enriched. The House of Lords in *Foskett v McKeown*[28] has now accepted that the vindication of property rights is a distinct principle. Even so, this remains controversial and the validity of this approach will be considered later[29] since this debate is crucial to the consideration of how restitution operates within equity.

THE UNJUST ENRICHMENT PRINCIPLE AND EQUITY

The action for money had and received[30]

Much of that body of law which is now described as being founded upon the reversal of the defendant's unjust enrichment has involved the action for money had and received, one of the old common counts.[31] Many of the cases which recognised and developed this cause of action appear to involve equitable principles. For example, in the leading case of *Moses v Macferlan*,[32]Lord Mansfield described the gist of the action for money had and received as being 'that the defendant, upon the circumstances of the case, is obliged by the ties of natural justice and equity to refund the money.'[33] In *Clarke v Shee*[34] he described this action as 'a liberal action in the nature of a bill in equity; and if, under the circumstances of the case, it appears that the

27 There are other types of equitable wrongdoing, such as dishonest assistance in a breach of trust and certain estoppels, such as proprietary estoppel, but the remedies which are awarded are invariably not restitutionary since they are not assessed with reference to the gain made by the defendant.

28 [2001] 1 AC 102.

29 See text at n 108 below.

30 See generally Kremer (2001) 17 J Contract Law 93.

31 The language of the common counts is still used today, even though these forms of action were abolished in 1852 by section 3 of the Common Law Procedure Act.

32 (1760) 2 Burr 1005, 1012.

33 See also the Roman jurist Pomponius: 'this by nature is equitable, that no one be made richer by another's loss.' See Dawson, *Unjust Enrichment: A Comparative Analysis* (1951) 3. In *Towers v Barrett* (1786) 1 Term Rep 133, 134, Lord Mansfield described this as the principle of 'eternal justice'. Sir William Evans said that the obligation arising under the action for money had and received was 'enforced according to the general principles of natural equity': 'An Essay on the Action for Money Had and Received' (1802), reprinted [1998] RLR 1, 4.

defendant cannot in conscience retain what is the subject-matter of it, the plaintiff may well support this action.'[35] In *Straton v Rastall*[36] Buller J went well beyond the mere drawing of an analogy with equity and stated that, in order for the action to succeed, the plaintiff had to show that 'he has equity and conscience on his side, and that he could recover it in a Court of Equity.' During the later eighteenth century and into the nineteenth century there was a general tendency to fuse or confuse equity with the law.[37] This 'myth' that the action for money had and received was equitable, was eventually exploded by Pollock CB in *Miller v Atlee*,[38] who said that it was a 'perfectly legal action, and no good can result from calling it an equitable one.'

Characterisation of the action of money had and received specifically, or the unjust enrichment principle more generally, as founded on notions of equity, conscience or natural justice continued throughout the twentieth century. So, for example, in *Royal Bank of Canada v R*,[39] Lord Haldane referred to the common law principle of 'justice and equity'.[40] Similarly, Lord Clyde has described the unjust enrichment principle as 'equitable in the sense that it seeks to secure a fair and just determination of the rights of the parties concerned in the case.'[41]

For much of the history of the law of restitution there has been a tension between whether this body of law should be treated as principled, being grounded on rules, or whether it is simply a matter of vague discretion. The assumption in a number of cases that the award of restitutionary remedies depended simply on whether or not the defendant had been enriched in circumstances of injustice was one of the main obstacles to the recognition of the law of restitution as an independent body of law. So, in *Holt v Markham*,[42] Scrutton LJ described the history of restitution as a 'history of well-meaning sloppiness of thought'. In *Baylis v Bishop of London*,[43]Hamilton LJ said:

34 (1774) 1 Cowp 197, 199-200. See also *Sadler v Evans* (1766) 4 Burr 1984, 1986; *Dale v Sollett* (1767) 4 Burr 2133, 2134; *Atkins v Hill* (1775) 1 Cowp 284, 288–289; *Longchamp v Kenny* (1779) 1 Doug KB 137, 138.

35 See also *Greville v Da Costa* (1797) Peake Add Cas 113, 114 (Lord Kenyon); *Kelly v Solari* (1841) 9 M & W 54, 58 (Parke B), 59 (Rolfe B); *Shaw v Jakeman* (1803) 4 East 201, 205 (Lord Ellenborough); *Smith v Jones* (1842) 1 Dowl NS 526; *Tregoning v Attenborough* (1830) 7 Bing 733; *Rogers v Ingham* (1876) 3 Ch D 351; *Phillips v London School Board* [1898] 2 QB 447, 453.

36 (1788) 2 Term Rep 366, 370.

37 See Winfield, *The Province of the Law of Tort* (1931) 129 et seq; Holdsworth (1929) Harvard LR 1, 8–13, 21–24.

38 (1849) 13 Jur 431. See *Sinclair v Brougham* [1914] AC 398, 456 (Lord Sumner). See also *Cooth v Jackson* (1801) 6 Ves 12, 39 (Lord Eldon); *Johnson v Johnson* (1802) 3 Bos & P 162, 169 (Lord Alvaney CJ).

39 [1913] AC 283.

40 See also *Jacobs v Morris* [1901] 1 Ch 261, 268–269 (Farwell J); *Re Bodega Co Ltd* [1904] 1 Ch 276, 286 (Farwell J); *Lodge v National Union Investment Co Ltd* [1907] 1 Ch 300, 311–312 (Parker J); *Fibrosa Spolka Akcyjna v Fairbairn Lawson Combe Barbour Ltd* [1943] AC 32, 65 (Lord Wright); *National Commercial Banking Corpn of Australia Ltd v Batty* (1986) 160 CLR 251, 268 (Gibbs CJ).

41 *Banque Financière de la Cité v Parc (Battersea) Ltd* [1999] 1 AC 221, 237. Similarly in America, for example: *Myers v Hurley Motor Co* 273 US 18, 24 (1927) (Sutherland J); *United States v Jefferson Electric Manufacturing Co* 291 US 386, 402–403 (1934) (Supreme Court); *Atlantic Coast Line Railroad Co v Florida* 295 US 301, 303 (1935) (Cardozo J).

42 [1923] 1 KB 504, 513.

43 [1913] 1 Ch 127, 140.

> To ask what course would be *ex aequo et bono* to both sides never was a very precise guide, and as a working rule it has long since been buried . . . Whatever may have been the case 146 years ago, we are not now free in the twentieth century to administer that vague jurisprudence which is sometimes attractively styled 'justice as between man and man'.

Now that we have a well-recognised principle of unjust enrichment firmly embodied in English law, it would appear that reliance on notions of equity and conscience, implying a discretionary approach to the determination of unjust enrichment, need no longer be of any significance in determining the award of restitutionary remedies. This was well put by Winfield, albeit writing over 70 years ago and speaking of quasi-contract rather than unjust enrichment:

> the main heads of quasi-contract have become so well settled that there is much less room for exercising in it the purely creative side of judicial discretion as compared with the merely interpretative side of it in applying technical rules embodied in scores of decisions . . .[44]

However, in *Roxborough v Rothmans of Pall Mall Australia Ltd,*[45] Gummow J has emphasised the equitable nature of restitution, particularly the action for money had and received. After analysing a number of English, Australian and American cases he asserted that regard should be had to the general considerations recognised in *Moses v Macferlan* and that 'if those general considerations resonate with equitable notions, then in a system in which equity prevails that cannot be a source of surprise'.[46] Later he explained that 'notions derived from equity have been worked into and in that sense have become part of the fabric of the common law'.[47] He emphasised, correctly, that there is a distinction between an action of an equitable nature and an action in equity, and that the action of money had and received is only of an equitable nature.[48] But he was able to deduce from this that the action was properly founded on the notion of unconscientious receipt, rather than unjust enrichment,[49] and concluded that restitutionary relief would be available if the defendant's retention of money, which had been paid in circumstances where the parties had expected it to be paid over to the revenue authorities, could be characterised as unconscionable.[50]

44 *The Province of the Law of Tort* (1931) 134. See also *Sinclair v Brougham* [1914] AC 398, 456 (Lord Sumner).
45 (2002) 185 ALR 335. See Beatson and Virgo (2002) 118 LQR 352; Grantham [2002] Singapore JLS 388.
46 (2002) 185 ALR 335, 362. See also Sir Anthony Mason, in Parkinson (ed) *The Principles of Equity* (1996) vi: Lord Mansfield's 'approach to good faith and to restitution has always seemed to me to reflect the spirit of equity rather than what its admirers refer to as the genius of the common law'. See also Kremer (2001) 17 J Contract Law 93.
47 (2002) 185 ALR 335, 363.
48 Relying on *Sinclair v Brougham* [1914] AC 398, 452, 455–456 (Lord Sumner); *Chapman v Fornes* 26 NE 3, 5 (1890) (New York Court of Appeals).
49 See also *South Australian Cold Stores Ltd v Electricity Trust of South Australia* (1957) 98 CLR 65, 75 (Dixon CJ, McTiernan, Williams, Webb and Taylor JJ); Dietrich, *Restitution: A New Perspective* (1998); Jackman, *The Varieties of Restitution* (1998). Cp *Baltic Shipping Co v Dillon* (1993) 176 CLR 344, 359 where Mason CJ equated unjust enrichment with unconscionability.
50 (2002) 185 ALR 335, 365.

There is some evidence that this reliance on conscience as a principle is being adopted in England as well. In *Vedatech Corpn v Crystal Decisions (UK) Ltd*,[51] the claimant sought restitution in respect of work it had done for the defendant in the expectation that a contract would be made when no contract was concluded. The claim was described as 'a quantum meruit or unjust enrichment claim'.[52] Although the case was primarily concerned with the valuation of the services provided, Jacob J did consider the elements of the claim which needed to be established. He concluded that the elements were 'benefit, at the plaintiff's expense, and unjust' and concluded that all three were present in the case. But he did not define what the ground of restitution was. Rather, he said that the defendant got the benefit of the work and 'it would be unjust for it to have it for nothing'. This looks very much like the ground of total failure of consideration. However, he went on to state:

> The principle of unjust enrichment is in large part founded on conscience. Can the receiver of a benefit in all conscience hang on to it without paying? If he cannot, then he is unjustly enriched.[53]

But this emphasis on conscience is a real cause for concern, because it is being used as a principle in its own right. According to Jacob J the defendant will be unjustly enriched if conscience, and maybe not even the defendant's conscience, requires restitution to be made. But this is not a principle. It is a vague notion, a mere cipher which enables the judge to assess the facts, but without any indication as to what weight should be given to them.

The reality is that, although the action of money had and received clearly involved the incorporation of equitable principles into the common law, it does not follow that this enables the courts today to temper the law by the application of vague discretion. Equity is more rigid than that. True, unjust enrichment claims can be tempered by the defendant relying on defences, because justice demands the recognition of such defences,[54] but these too have to be interpreted in a principled fashion and it is not possible, or appropriate, for the defendant simply to refer to any matter or circumstance which show that his or her receipt or retention of money was not unjust.[55] For how can those matters or circumstances be assessed in the abstract, without reference to established principles which help to determine their weight and legitimacy? It is for this reason that the reliance in Australia,[56] and other jurisdictions, on the notion of unconscientious receipt, sometimes in preference to unjust

51 [2002] EWHC 818 (Ch), [2002] All ER (D) 318 (May).

52 Quantum meruit was another of the common counts. Whereas money had and received related to the recovery of money, quantum meruit was a claim for the value of services provided.

53 [2002] EWHC 818, para 74. He said later that 'the concept of unjust enrichment . . . depends on all the circumstances'.

54 See *Moses v Macferlan* (1760) 2 Burr 1005, 1010 (Lord Mansfield).

55 Cf *David Securities Pty Ltd v Commonwealth Bank of Australia* (1992) 175 CLR 353, 379 (Mason CJ, Deane, Toohey, Gaudron, McHugh JJ).

56 See *Commercial Bank of Australia v Amadio* (1983) 151 CLR 447; *Legione v Hateley* (1983) 152 CLR 406; *Muschinski v Dodds* (1985) 160 CLR 583, 619–620 (Deane J); *Stern v McArthur* (1988) 165 CLR 489; *Baltic Shipping Co v Dillon* (1993) 176 CLR 344, 359 (Mason CJ), 376 (Deane and Dawson JJ); *Bridgewater v Leahy* (1998) 194 CLR 457: *Roxborough v Rothmans of Pall Mall Australia Ltd* (2002) ALR 335.

enrichment, can be criticised. 'Unconcionability', although being an equitable concept, is too uncertain to constitute a cause of action in its own right[57] and is inconsistent with the notion at the heart of equity that its 'principles are fixed and certain',[58] although those principles are, of course, subject to judicial development.[59] Kremer's assessment of the function of conscience is particularly pertinent:

> 'conscience' is used as a concept to underlie and structure the operation of an area of the law; it provides a generative, basal principle which is in turn used to construct rules . . . It is those rules which are applied judicially in determining a dispute. Conscience is thus not a determinant; it is a reference concept, a purpose, which is used to generate determinants.[60]

But this is not how the notion of conscience was used by Gummow J in *Roxborough*[61] and Jacob J in *Vedatech*. For these judges it was sufficient that the defendant's conduct could be characterised as unconscionable without any clear indication as to why this was so. There is nothing inherently unacceptable about basing recovery on the concept of 'against conscience', but, if it is to serve any useful purpose in rationalizing the law, some way of defining the principles which underpin the concept must be identified. That is the advantage of the unjust enrichment principle, at least when it is used as a substantive rather than merely a descriptive principle. As Birks has said:

> There is no future for the gut reaction, not for any form of mystical 'experience' which inarticulately claims the right to trump good intellectual order.[62]

It does not follow, however, that conscience has no useful role as a way of rationalizing the law. Indeed, conscience has had a long-standing role in equity. Probably the most important statement of the significance of conscience is a dictum of Lord Browne-Wilkinson in *Westdeutsche Landesbank Girozentrale v Islington London Borough Council*:[63]

> Equity operates on the conscience of the owner of the legal interest. In the case of a trust, the conscience of the legal owner requires him to carry out the

57 But note the recent reliance on the notion of unconscionability by the English Court of Appeal for the purposes of determining fault for the action of unconscientious receipt in *Bank of Credit and Commerce International (Overseas) Ltd v Akindele* [2001] Ch 437. Cp *Dubai Aluminium Co Ltd v Salaam* (2002) UKHL 48, [2002] 3 WLR 1913, 1933 (Lord Millett). See also *Pennington v Waine* [2002] EWCA Civ 227, [2002} 4 All ER 215, [2002] 1 WLR 2075.

58 See *Story's Equity Jurisprudence* (14th edn, 1918) 20 et seq.

59 *Re Hallett's Estate* (1879) 13 Ch D 696, 710 (Jessel MR).

60 (2001) 17 J Contract Law 93, 107.

61 Conscience has been used in this way in other Australian cases. See, for example, the doctrine of equitable estoppel in *Waltons Stores (Interstate) Ltd v Maher* (1988) 164 CLR 387, where conscience was identified by Mason CJ and Wilson and Brennan JJ as a general notion which gave content to the key principle of detrimental reliance. See Kremer (2001) 17 J Contract Law 93, 107.

62 (1999) 23 Melbourne University LR 1, 21. He goes on to say, at 22, that 'conscience of the intuitive kind is . . . antithetical to the rule of law.'

63 [1996] AC 669, 705. See also *T Choithram International SA v Pagarani* [2001] 1 WLR 1, 12 (Lord Browne-Wilkinson); *Gillett v Holt* [2001] Ch 210, 225 (Robert Walker LJ).

> purposes for which the property was vested in him (express or implied trust) or which the law imposes on him by reason of his unconscionable conduct (constructive trust).

But the reliance on conscience by itself is never sufficient to recognise a trust, of whatever kind. Rather, it is a foundation upon which legal principles can be built.[64] This is particularly well illustrated by the law on constructive trusts. Although the defendant's unconscionable conduct is the foundation for the recognition of such trusts, it is not enough for a claimant simply to assert that the defendant has acted unconscionably. This is too vague to operate as a unifying principle for constructive trusts. Instead, the courts must determine whether the defendant's conduct falls within recognised categories. For example, the constructive trust has been used to enforce mutual wills,[65] to ensure that an executor de son tort does not benefit from abuse of position[66] and where a defendant has acted unconscionably by denying property or a share in property to a claimant where there was a common understanding of shared ownership.[67] Recently a new category has been identified, which is consistent with the established categories, but which threatens to swamp them. This has simply been called 'unconscionable conduct'. Although unconscientiousness is at the heart of this category it remains distinct because there is no vague reliance on notions of unconscionability. Rather, the courts have sought to identify the nature of unconscionability with a degree of precision by focusing on the identifiable fault of the defendant. It is this form of constructive trust which was explicitly recognised by Lord Browne-Wilkinson in *Westdeutsche Landesbank Girozentrale v Islington London Borough Council*,[68] when examining the earlier decision of *Chase Manhattan Bank v Israel-British Bank (London) Ltd*.[69]In that case the plaintiff had mistakenly paid the defendant the same amount of money twice. Goulding J held that the plaintiff had an equitable proprietary interest in the money because 'a person who pays money to another under a factual mistake retains an equitable property in it and the conscience of the other is subjected to a fiduciary duty to respect his proprietary rights'.[70] The result, but not the reasoning, was endorsed by Lord Browne-Wilkinson in *Westdeutsche*. He suggested that the plaintiff may have had an equitable proprietary interest in the money because the defendant knew that the plaintiff had paid the money to it by mistake within two days of the defendant having received the money. As Lord Browne-Wilkinson said:

64 Like notions of 'reasonableness' in tort and 'proportionality' for cases concerning the application of the European Convention on Human Rights.
65 *Re Cleaver* [1981] 2 All ER 1018, [1981] 1 WLR 939.
66 *James v Williams* [2000] Ch 1.
67 *Lloyds Bank plc v Rosset* [1991] 1 AC 107, [1990] 1 All ER 1111; *Yaxley v Gotts* [2000] Ch 162, [2000] 1 All ER 711; *Banner Homes Group plc v Luff Developments Ltd* [2000] Ch 372, [2000] 2 All ER 117.
68 [1996] AC 669, 714.
69 [1981] Ch 105.
70 See n 69, at 119.

> Although the mere receipt of the moneys, in ignorance of the mistake, gives rise to no trust, the retention of the moneys after the recipient bank learned of the mistake may well have given rise to a constructive trust.[71]

Although the emphasis on the knowledge of the defendant means that this category of constructive trust purports to be principled and predictable, there remains an inherent uncertainty within it. For example, what degree of fault is sufficient for the defendant's conscience to be affected so that he or she holds the property on trust? Presumably, since emphasis is placed on the defendant's conscience, fault is to be determined subjectively, so it would encompass knowledge, belief and even suspicion of the circumstances with reference to which the claimant will have a restitutionary claim.[72] But this remains unclear. Also, at what point must the defendant's conscience be affected?[73] What if the defendant became aware of the mistake months, or even years, later and the property or its product is still identifiable in the defendant's hands? Must a constructive trust still be recognised in such a case? Although this category of constructive trust requires clarification, it does at least purport to be principled, and so is consistent with the general trend of restitutionary relief within equity. All the categories of constructive trust are linked by the defendant's unconscionability. New categories of constructive trust can be recognised, but only by reference to the established categories and the general notion of unconscionability.

So if unconscionability has proved to be a useful, albeit uncertain, concept for the purpose of rationalizing the law on constructive trusts, should it have a similar role in rationalizing the law relating to the action for money had and received, in preference to the unjust enrichment principle? The answer should be a categorical 'no', at least as regards those grounds of restitution which are not characterised as equitable in origin.[74] The test of unconscionability requires a fundamentally different focus from that of unjust enrichment, a focus which is inappropriate to personal restitutionary claims at common law. In particular, the focus on the injustice of the defendant's enrichment rather than the state of the defendant's conscience, emphasises that questions of fault are, for the most part,[75] irrelevant to establishing unjust enrichment. The essence of the unjust enrichment principle, as embodied in the action for money had and received is that liability is strict and focuses on whether the claimant's consent to the transfer of the enrichment can be considered to have been vitiated or qualified in some way, rather than whether the defendant was at fault in retaining the enrichment received.[76]

It follows that conscience and unconscionability should have nothing to do with the future development of the unjust enrichment principle at common law. That principle is now clearly recognised as existing in English law and it is vital that it be affirmed as

71 [1996] AC 669, 715.

72 See Virgo, *The Principles of the Law of Restitution* (1999) 633.

73 See Virgo, *The Principles of the Law of Restitution* (1999) 633–634.

74 See text at n 84 below.

75 Fault is relevant to the defence of change of position. See *Lipkin Gorman (a firm) v Karpnale Ltd* [1991] 2 AC 548, 580 (Lord Goff). See text at n 134 below. Fault will also be relevant to establishing those grounds of restitution which are equitable in origin. See text at n 84 below.

76 See Grantham [2002] Singapore JLS 388, 398. See also text at n 26 above. Cp text at n 84 below.

a common law principle, rather than one which is by its very nature equitable.[77] And, as the Court of Appeal has recently recognised in a different context, 'the premise of equity's intrusion into the effect of the common law is that the common law rule in question is seen in the particular case to work injustice, and for some reason the common law cannot cure itself'.[78] But the unjust enrichment principle does not cause injustice and so does not need to be cured by equity. This is not to deny the influence equity has had on the action for money had and received and, more recently, unjust enrichment, but the meaning of equity in this context needs to be carefully defined. The reference to 'equity' should be interpreted as not referring to that body of law and procedural rules which have been administered in the Court of Chancery, properly characterised as 'Equity', but, rather, as a reference to the *jus naturale* of Roman law[79] or simply to the notion of doing what is reasonable.[80] This can still be considered to underpin the modern law of unjust enrichment, but it is far too vague to provide a basis for developing that principle. Ultimately, however, regardless of how the equitable influence is analysed, the real issue, which is of vital importance to the future development of the law of restitution, is that the unjust enrichment principle is rule-based and is not a passport to do whatever is considered to be fair and just.[81]

This exclusion of equitable influences from the modern interpretation of the common law notion of unjust enrichment does not mean that that principle should have no application in contexts typically associated with equity. So, for example, where a trustee pays money by mistake, that money can be recovered without needing to prove fault on the part of the recipient;[82] restitution can be justified by reference to the strict liability unjust enrichment principle.[83] But in such cases, unjust enrichment is not operating within equity as such, but only in contexts associated with equity.

Equitable grounds of restitution

Although the unjust enrichment principle is essentially a common law invention, it does not follow that equity has had no distinctive influence on the recognition and development of particular grounds of restitution. A number of such grounds emerged in parallel at law and in equity, such as what we would now call the ground of mistake, including especially misrepresentation, and total failure of consideration.[84] But today the overt equitable influence on the interpretation of these grounds has disappeared. There are only a very few grounds of restitution which can still be described as

77 *Roxborough v Rothmans of Pall Mall Australia Ltd* (2002) 185 ALR 335, 392 (Callinan J).
78 *Great Peace Shipping Ltd v Tsavliris Salvage Ltd* [2002] ECWA Civ 1407, [2002] 3 WLR 1617, 1660.
79 *Baylis v Bishop of London* [1913] 1 Ch 127, 133, 136–137 (Farwell LJ); Birks (1984) 37 Current Legal Problems 1; Sir William Evans, 'An Essay on the Action for Money Had and Received' (1802), reprinted [1998] RLR 1, 4.
80 Winfield, *The Province of the Law of Tort* (1931) 140.
81 *Lipkin Gorman v Karpnale Ltd* [1991] 2 AC 548, 578 (Lord Goff).
82 *Re Diplock* [1948] Ch 559; *G L Baker Ltd v Medway Building and Supplies Ltd* [1958] 1 WLR 1216. See text to n 162 below.
83 See also Nolan, 'Conflicts of Interest, Unjust Enrichment and Wrongdoing' in Cornish, Nolan, O'Sullivan and Virgo (eds) *Restitution: Past, Present and Future* (1998) 87 et seq.
84 Ibbetson, A *Historical Introduction to the Law of Obligations* (1999) 273–276.

explicitly equitable and they tend to be those grounds which can be characterised as grounded on the defendant's exploitation of the claimant. For example, where the defendant has been enriched by unduly influencing the claimant, this undue influence will ground a restitutionary claim.[85] The equitable origin of undue influence was identified by Millett LJ in *Dunbar Bank plc v Nadeem*:[86]

> The court of equity is a court of conscience. It sets aside transactions obtained by the exercise of undue influence because such conduct is unconscionable.

But, although the ground of restitution is recognised because of the defendant's unconscionable conduct, it is not inherently uncertain because the courts have sought to expound the requirements of actual and presumed undue influence in some detail.[87]

Similarly, although the point remains controversial, there appears to be an equitable ground of restitution which depends on the identification of unconscionable conduct.[88] This will apply where the defendant has unconscientiously exploited his or her superior bargaining position to the detriment of the claimant who is in a much weaker position. Again, this is not a vague ground of restitution which simply turns on the assertion of unconscionability. Rather, the claimant must be suffering from a special disability or be placed in a situation of disadvantage as against the defendant, such as being poor or ignorant[89] or an expectant heir,[90] and the defendant must be considered to have been at fault, either because he or she knew or should have known of the claimant's disability or disadvantage.[91]

The recognised grounds of restitution which are clearly equitable in origin are limited. It might be wondered why it matters that grounds of restitution are still treated as operating either within the common law or in equity. It does matter because those grounds which arise in equity are clearly more dependent on considerations of fault, whereas those which are characterised as existing at law involve strict liability. So, for example, if the claimant has paid money to the defendant by mistake, the defendant must make restitution to the claimant, subject to the operation of defences such as change of position, even though the defendant was unaware of the claimant's mistake. Where, however, the claimant wishes to establish a claim grounded on undue influence or unconscionable conduct, it is an important part of that claim that the defendant was at fault in some way, although this can be presumed in cases involving undue influence. But even though actual and presumed fault are relevant to the

85 Virgo, *The Principles of the Law of Restitution* (1999) 251–265.

86 [1998] 3 All ER 876, 884.

87 See, for example, *Bank of Credit and Commerce International SA v Aboody* [1990] 1 QB 923; *CIBC Mortgages v Pitt* [1994] 1 AC 200; *Barclays Bank plc v O'Brien* [1994] 1 AC 180; *Royal Bank of Scotland plc v Etridge (No 2)* [2001] UKHL 44, [2002] 2 AC 773.

88 *Earl of Chesterfield v Janssen* (1751) 2 Ves Sen 125; *Lloyd's Bank v Bundy* [1975] QB 326; *Hart v O'Connor* [1985] AC 1000, 1024 (Lord Brightman); *Crédit Lyonnais Bank Nederland NV v Burch* [1997] 1 All ER 144, 151 (Nourse LJ). Cp *National Westminster Bank plc v Morgan* [1985] AC 686, 708 (Lord Scarman). See generally Capper (1998) 114 LQR 479.

89 *Cresswell v Potter* [1978] 1 WLR 255n; *Crédit Lyonnais Bank Nederland NV v Burch* [1997] 1 All ER 144.

90 *Earl of Aylesford v Morris* (1873) 8 Ch App 484.

91 Virgo, *The Principles of the Law of Restitution* (1999) 286–297.

definition of these equitable grounds of restitution, it does not follow that they operate differently from other grounds of restitution. In particular, it is still possible to justify the recognition of these grounds of restitution on the basis that the claimant's intention to transfer a benefit to the defendant has been vitiated, in the same way that the grounds of mistake and duress are justified.[92] It is simply that liability cannot be characterised as involving strict liability, since the equitable influence requires proof of unconscionability before these grounds of restitution can be established.[93]

Conclusions

Although equity has had a significant influence on the unjust enrichment principle, this influence must not be over-played. Today there is only very limited application of overtly equitable concepts within the law of unjust enrichment[94] and equity should not have any influence on the interpretation of that principle. This does not mean that the relevance of equity within the law of restitution is insignificant, because the equitable influence is much more important in respect of the other two categories of restitutionary claim.

RESTITUTIONARY RELIEF FOR EQUITABLE WRONGDOING

Where the defendant has committed certain types of equitable wrongdoing, notably breach of trust, breach of fiduciary duty and breach of confidence, the usual remedy which will be awarded is restitutionary,[95] either as a personal remedy to account for the profits made by the commission of the wrong, or a proprietary remedy by virtue of which the profits are held on constructive trust for the claimant. The award of such remedies is long-standing and not controversial. Here, restitution is fully integrated within equity.

What is controversial concerns the determination of whether a personal or proprietary remedy is appropriate. The most important case which focuses attention on this issue is the decision of the Privy Council in *A-G for Hong Kong v Reid*.[96] In that case the defendant fiduciary held a number of public offices in Hong Kong, including that of Director of Public Prosecutions. He accepted a number of bribes to induce him to frustrate the prosecution of certain criminals and he purchased land with this money. The plaintiff claimed that it had an equitable proprietary interest in the land, since it was purchased using money obtained by the defendant's breach of the fiduciary duty which he owed to the plaintiff. The Privy Council agreed and concluded that the land was held on constructive trust. This decision was reached in the following way. First, a fiduciary who receives a bribe in breach of duty is liable to account to the principal for

92 See Birks and Chin, 'On the Nature of Undue Influence' in Beatson and Friedmann (eds), *Good Faith and Fault in Contract Law* (1995), 57. Cf Bigwood (1996) 16 OJLS 503.
93 Virgo, *The Principles of the Law of Restitution* (1999) 252–253.
94 See Dietrich, *Restitution – A New Perspective* (1998) 140.
95 Compensatory remedies, in the form of equitable damages, are also recognised. See *Target Holdings Ltd v Redferns* [1996] AC 421.
96 [1994] 1 AC 324, [1994] 1 All ER 1.

the value of the bribe immediately it is received. This is a personal liability to account. Secondly, by virtue of the equitable maxim that equity treats as done that which ought to be done, equity presumes that the fiduciary has accounted for the value of the bribe immediately it is received. Thirdly, it follows that equity considers the principal to have an equitable proprietary interest in the bribe once it is received, with the result that the defendant holds the bribe on constructive trust for the principal.

Even though the application of the equitable maxim in this way is open to criticism,[97] the effect of this decision is far-reaching. Assuming that the decision is not confined in its application to the receipt of bribes,[98] it follows that in any case where a defendant is liable to account for profits in equity, that personal liability can be converted into proprietary relief simply by virtue of the application of the equitable maxim.[99] But the legitimacy of this approach needs to be considered carefully. Is it really appropriate for the victim of a breach of fiduciary duty, or some other equitable wrong, to obtain proprietary restitutionary relief, with the consequent advantage of gaining priority over other creditors of the defendant? Two distinct approaches to this question can be identified.

First, the operation of equity and its equitable remedies should be regarded as a technical matter involving the application of clearly recognized principles.[100] If the principles of equity operate in such a way as to give the victim of a breach of fiduciary duty proprietary relief, then so be it. This does not mean that the law should not be criticised and that underlying policy objectives should be ignored. What it means is that the recognition of principle is vital for the clarity of the law, especially when property rights are involved. If the recognition of proprietary interests cannot be justified in all cases, then qualifying principles need to be developed to ensure that appropriate results are achieved. One way of doing this, for example, is to reject the reliance on the equitable maxim that equity considers done what ought to be done, and instead conclude that proprietary relief is appropriate only when the defendant has interfered with the claimant's proprietary rights. Then the profits obtained by the defendant can be considered to represent the fruits of the claimant's property.[101] Alternatively, a proprietary remedy can be justified whenever the property obtained by the defendant would have been obtained by the principal had the defendant not breached his or her fiduciary duty, the so-called 'deemed agency gain'.[102] Here the justification for proprietary relief is that the demands of the fiduciary relationship are such that it should be assumed that the defendant obtained the property for his or her

97 Crilley [1994] 2 RLR 57, 65–66.

98 Peter Gibson LJ in *Halifax Building Society v Thomas* [1996] Ch 217, 229 assumed that the decision was of general significance.

99 The result is consistent with *Boardman v Phipps* [1967] 2 AC 46, where Wilberforce J held that shares which the defendant fiduciary had purchased in breach of duty should be held on constructive trust. Nothing was said by the Court of Appeal or the House of Lords to suggest that this was wrong. Cf *Regal (Hastings) Ltd v Gulliver* [1967] 2 AC 134n and *Industrial Developments Consultants Ltd v Cooley* [1972] 2 All ER 162, [1972] 1 WLR 443, where the fiduciaries were only liable to account for profits made in breach of fiduciary duty.

100 Birks (1999) 28 UWALR 13, 58.

101 Virgo, *The Principles of the Law of Restitution* (1999) 539.

102 Goode, 'Property and Unjust Enrichment' in Burrows (ed), *Essays on the Law of Restitution* (1991) 230.

principal rather than for him or herself.[103] The effect of recognising either, or both, of these principles would be that proprietary relief would not have been awarded in *Reid*, because the defendant had not interfered with the plaintiff's property and had not obtained property which would otherwise have been obtained by the plaintiff. From the perspective of policy this must be right. There is no obvious reason why the principal should obtain priority over the fiduciary's unsecured creditors if the principal has no obvious interest in the property obtained by the fiduciary. But, regardless of the result, this mode of analysis is at least principled. A principle is identified, which is consistent with desired policy, and which can then be applied consistently.

The alternative approach is that awarding equitable remedies should be a matter for the discretion of the court. This is the view of Finn in particular,[104] who considers that the function of the courts is to determine the remedy which is most appropriate to the facts of the case, having regard to a range of factors, such as proportionality and unjust enrichment. But is this sufficiently certain to determine when remedies should be awarded, especially as regards the decision to award personal or proprietary restitutionary relief? Surely this is a descent to confusion and unrestrained discretion.[105] Whilst it is legitimate to have a range of remedies available where the defendant has committed an equitable wrong, it is important to award such remedies in a principled way. Predictability is important, both because it encourages resolution of disputes out of court and because it is a legitimate function of the law to ensure that like cases are decided in a similar way. So, as regards restitution for wrongs, the nature of the wrong needs to be considered to determine whether restitutionary relief is appropriate and only then should the nature of that relief be considered, especially as to whether personal or proprietary relief should be awarded, but also, for example, as to whether the defendant should be awarded an equitable allowance[106] or whether the defendant should be required to disgorge all benefits obtained from breaching his or her fiduciary duty, including those obtained indirectly, for example by investing the profits obtained directly.[107] This cannot be determined on a case by case basis, but by reference to a variety of principles. This is actually how equity operates as regards the award of all its remedies, whether they be restitutionary or specific performance or injunctions.

The restitutionary principles within equity probably need clarification, especially following the decision of the Privy Council in *Reid*, but what is clear for present purposes is that principles are discernible and that restitution is securely integrated within the law of equitable wrongdoing.

103 See *Keech v Sandford* (1726) Cas temp King 61; *Cook v Deeks* [1916] 1 AC 554.

104 'Equitable Doctrine and Discretion in Remedies' in Cornish, Nolan, O'Sullivan and Virgo (eds), *Restitution: Past, Present and Future* (1998) p 251 et seq. See also Wright [2001] Singapore JLS 301; Davies, 'Restitution and Equitable Wrongs: An Australian Analogue', in Rose (ed), *Consensus Ad Idem* (1996).

105 See Birks (2000) 29 UWALR 1.

106 See *Boardman v Phipps* [1967] 2 AC 46. See also *Warman International Ltd v Dwyer* (1995) 128 ALR 201.

107 See Virgo, *The Principles of the Law of Restitution* (1999) 544. See *Maguire v Makaronis* (1997) 144 ALR 729, 761 (Kirby J).

VINDICATION OF EQUITABLE PROPRIETARY RIGHTS[108]

In *Foskett v McKeown*[109] the House of Lords drew a crucial distinction between the law of unjust enrichment and the law of property. The case concerned a claim brought by the beneficiaries of a trust to recover part of the proceeds of an insurance policy. A trustee of the trust had misappropriated trust money to pay at least two annual premiums of a life assurance policy. After five annual instalments had been paid the trustee committed suicide and his children received a payment of just over £1 million. The beneficiaries of the trust claimed a proportionate share of this sum, amounting to £400,000. The House of Lords held by a bare majority that this claim should succeed since the beneficiaries' money was used to assist in obtaining the £1 million.

The analysis of the judges is of profound importance to our understanding of the operation of restitution within equity. Lord Browne-Wilkinson in particular distinguished between unjust enrichment and proprietary claims and held that the restitutionary claim in the case had nothing to do with unjust enrichment and everything to do with the vindication of property rights. It was, he said, a matter simply of hard-nosed property rights.[110] Lords Hoffmann and Millett adopted a similar approach.[111]

This decision has been subject to vigorous criticism. Birks in particular has been critical of the decision.[112] Essentially his criticism focuses on the fact that the beneficiaries were claiming restitution of a substitute for their property. To claim that substitute it is necessary to show that the claimant has a right to it and, Birks asserts, the beneficiaries could only establish that by means of the unjust enrichment principle and not simply by the assertion of property rights. At the heart of Birks's argument is the fundamental distinction, drawn in a number of his recent writings,[113] between events and responses. According to Birks, in the law of civil obligations it is necessary to identify an event before considering the appropriate response. The law, he asserts, recognises four events, namely consent, wrongs, unjust enrichment and other events. Where the event of unjust enrichment can be established, the response is restitution. Vindication of property rights is not an event and so, he concludes, restitution cannot respond to it.[114] As he says:

108 The analysis in this section is elaborated in Virgo, 'Vindicating Vindication: *Foskett v McKeown* Reviewed' in Hudson and Dignam (eds), *The Idea of Property and Obligations in Law* (2003).

109 [2001] 1 AC 102.

110 *Foskett v McKeown* [2001] 1 AC 102, 109.

111 *Foskett v McKeown* [2001] 1 AC 102, 115 (Lord Hoffmann), 129 (Lord Millett).

112 [2002] CLP 231. See also Burrows (2001) 117 LQR 412.

113 See especially (1996) 26 UWALR 1, 8–10, [2002] CLP 231.

114 Birks has acknowledged, however, that, although his classification is derived from Roman law, the Roman classification was confined to personal rights and did not encompass proprietary rights: (1996) 26 UWALR 1, 9.

> The key point is that the law of property is not formed in answer to a question about causative events: 'How do rights arise?'. It is formed in response to the quite different question: 'Against whom are rights exigible?'[115]

He goes on to say that:

> . . . it is an error of logic to force a choice between the law of property and the law of unjust enrichment.

Much of the recent debate about the legitimacy of vindication of property rights has got stuck on the question of language. 'Vindication of property rights' is obviously not an 'event'. It is a principle which is simply not framed in those terms. But the title could be changed to convert it into an event. For example, the event could be that the defendant has interfered with the claimant's property rights in some way. There are a number of responses to that event, including compensation, but the most important involves the award of restitutionary remedies, either personal or proprietary. This semantic debate about the nature of events is not unimportant, but of more interest and practical significance is the question whether there are any substantive consequences of rejecting the notion of vindicating property rights and emphasising instead that the triggering 'event' is unjust enrichment. This requires consideration of a number of separate issues.

Can property rights in substitute property derive from unjust enrichment?

There is no case which explicitly recognises that property rights can derive from the fact that the defendant has been unjustly enriched. Birks[116] considers that *Foskett* was such a case, even though the language of the judges contradicts this, and that there are others, including *Sinclair v Brougham*,[117] but this has been overruled,[118] and *Chase Manhattan Bank v Israel-British Bank*,[119] but this case has been re-interpreted by the House of Lords.[120] Further, neither of these cases explicitly recognises that property rights can derive from unjust enrichment. As Gummow J said in *Roxborough v Rothmans*:[121]

> To the lawyer whose mind has been moulded by civilian influences, the theory may come first, and the source of the theory may be the writing of jurists not the decisions of judges. However, that is not the way in which a system based on case law develops; over time, a general principle is derived from judicial decisions upon particular instances, not the other way round.

115 [2002] CLP 231, 241.
116 [2002] CLP 248. See also Grantham and Rickett (2000) 63 MLR 905, 908 who acknowledge that property rights can arise from unjust enrichment.
117 [1914] AC 398.
118 *Westdeutsche Landesbank Girozentrale v Islington London Borough Council* [1996] AC 669, [1996] 2 All ER 961.
119 [1981] Ch 105.
120 *Westdeutsche Landesbank Girozentrale v Islington London Borough Council* [1996] AC 669, [1996] 2 All ER 961.
121 (2002) 185 ALR 335, 355.

There is simply no empirical evidence to support the suggestion that property rights can derive from the defendant's unjust enrichment and so the recognition of such a principle would be despite, rather than because of, the case law.

Should rights in substitute property derive from unjust enrichment?

Although there is no empirical evidence to support the recognition of the theory that restitution of substitute property should depend on the defendant's unjust enrichment, it is still necessary to determine whether this would be appropriate as a matter of principle and policy. There are, in fact, four objections to such an approach.

Carving up proprietary restitutionary claims

Birks and others wish to draw a distinction between so-called 'real property rights' and rights in substitute property. The effect of this distinction is that, if the claimant wishes to recover the property in which he or she has a subsisting proprietary interest, then restitution is a matter for the law of property, whereas if the claimant wishes to recover substitute property this will depend on the claimant establishing that the defendant has been unjustly enriched. But why should the law of proprietary restitutionary claims be carved up in this way? If the claimant has a property right, the restitutionary claim should be based on that right regardless of the property which is being claimed.

Difficulties in establishing unjust enrichment

Unjust enrichment analysis does not fit easily with the nature of the restitutionary claim to substitute property. Typically such a claim would arise where a trustee has misappropriated property from a trust and used this to purchase an asset which is given to the defendant. To establish an unjust enrichment claim, the claimant will need to show that the defendant has been enriched. Since the claim relates to property this will often be easily established.[122] Secondly, this enrichment must be at the claimant's expense. The claimant would rely on the tracing rules to establish this. Thirdly, the claimant would need to establish a ground of restitution. Presumably the existing grounds of restitution will be applicable. So, if the claimant transferred property to the defendant by mistake, then the ground of restitution will be satisfied. But does it follow that proprietary relief is available in all cases of mistake? If it does, then proprietary relief will tend to give the claimant excessive protection, because the consequences of such relief include giving the claimant priority over the defendant's other creditors and enabling the claimant to claim increases in value. Why should a

122 But not always so. There may be circumstances where the defendant may have given full value for the property which he or she has received, and so will not have been enriched by the receipt of the property, but the defendant may still be required to make restitution to the claimant if he or she had notice of the claimant's beneficial interest. In other words, the defendant's notice of the interest will mean that he or she is not able to rely on the defence of bona fide purchase. See *Foskett v McKeown* [2001] 1 AC 102, 129 (Lord Millett).

claimant who made a mistake be allowed such proprietary protection? A reason would need to be identified to distinguish between different types of mistake, to determine the particular circumstances in which mistakes will trigger proprietary relief, and it is surely far better to do this explicitly within the established principles of the law of property. After all, this is how equity traditionally operates.[123]

But there is an additional difficulty to the unjust enrichment analysis of claims to substitute property, which is that in many of the traditional cases in equity where a beneficiary wishes to recover property misappropriated from a trust, the established grounds of restitution will not be applicable. The property will not have been transferred as the result of a mistake, duress or exploitation because the beneficiary will be unaware of the misappropriation. So what ground of restitution would be applicable? Birks has suggested that absence of consent should be the ground of restitution[124] and Burrows is content to rely on a specific ground of ignorance.[125] But no case has recognised such grounds of restitution.

This absence of recognition of grounds of restitution relevant to restitutionary proprietary claims is not surprising, because it is not necessary to rely on the unjust enrichment principle at all.[126] It is sufficient that the defendant has received property in which the claimant has an equitable proprietary interest at the time of its receipt, if the claimant seeks a personal restitutionary remedy, or continues to have a proprietary interest in it, if the claimant seeks a proprietary restitutionary remedy. The tracing rules are relevant to establish this, since they enable the courts to identify proprietary rights in mixtures and substitutions.[127] Once the proprietary right in the substitute can be identified, the claimant can then 'vindicate' it either by personal or proprietary restitutionary remedies.

For Birks, the fact that one asset is substituted for another is a new event. It follows that it is necessary to find a reason to assert proprietary rights over the new asset, and unjust enrichment provides that reason. Lord Browne-Wilkinson in *Foskett v McKeown*[128] disagreed. He asserted that the original property right can be transferred to the new asset without needing to identify any new event.[129] This is the preferable view. The unjust enrichment principle is unsuited to establishing claims to substitute property.

Encouraging the exercise of discretion

A further unfortunate consequence of reliance on the unjust enrichment principle might be the conclusion that the recognition of proprietary rights lies in the discretion of the court whenever the defendant's receipt can be considered to be unjust. There is a tendency in some of the literature to assume that the recognition of proprietary rights

123 See text at n 132 below.
124 [2002] CLP 231, 246.
125 *The Law of Restitution* (2nd edn, 2002) ch 4.
126 *Foskett v McKeown* [2001] 1 AC 102, 127 (Lord Millett).
127 See *Boscawen v Bajwa* [1996] 1 WLR 328, 334 (Lord Millett).
128 [2001] 1 AC 102.
129 *Foskett v McKeown* [2001] 1 AC 109.

should be a matter of discretion, sometimes characterised as the exercise of policy, involving a normative discourse,[130] and the reliance on the unjust enrichment principle may encourage such a view.[131] This is similar to the notion that the action for money had and received turns on the defendant's conscience. This discretionary approach is even more unacceptable as regards the recognition of proprietary rights, since the consequence of recognising such rights is so important, especially since it gives the claimant priority over the defendant's creditors. The recognition of principles is just as important here as it is in respect of unjust enrichment claims and restitution for wrongs, so any resort to vague discretion to create proprietary rights should be rejected. This view was strongly expressed by Lord Browne-Wilkinson in *Foskett v McKeown*:[132]

> The rules establishing equitable proprietary interests and their enforceability against certain parties have been developed over the centuries and are an integral part of the property law of England. It is a fundamental error to think that, because certain property rights are equitable rather than legal, such rights are in some way discretionary.

Consistent with this assertion of principle and rejection of the discretionary approach is the fact that the remedial constructive trust, namely a trust which arises through the exercise of discretion rather than principle, does not and should never form part of English law.[133] It is alien to the equitable way of doing things.

Application of the defence of change of position

In the real world the importance of the debate as regards the proper characterisation of proprietary restitutionary claims and remedies is especially relevant to the application of the defence of change of position.[134] Although that defence has been recognised for over a decade, we still know very little about it. In *Lipkin Gorman v Karpnale Ltd*[135] the House of Lords recognised change of position as a defence to claims founded on unjust enrichment. This was at a time when the prevalent view about the law of restitution was that restitution and unjust enrichment quadrated and so were

130 See Burrows (2001) 117 LQR 412, 423–428 and Burrows, *The Law of Restitution* (2nd edn, 2002) 70–72. Such views are expressed in various papers in Rose (ed), *Restitution and Insolvency* (2000), such as Finch and Worthington, 1–20; Rotherham, 113–133; Wright, 206–219; and McCormack, 261–275. See also Rotherham, *Proprietary Remedies in Context* (2002), especially 343–347; Wright, *The Remedial Constructive Trust* (2000). This is not to deny the importance of normative analysis as a critical device, but such analysis should not be converted into the principle for determining whether property rights will be recognised.

131 Birks does not support such an approach: (2000) 29 UWALR 1.

132 [2001] 1 AC 102, 109. See also Lord Millett, *Foskett v McKeown* [2001] 1 AC 102 at 127.

133 It was rejected in *Re Polly Peck International plc (No 2)* [1998] 3 All ER 812. See also *Fortex Group Ltd v MacIntosh* [1998] 3 NZLR 171. Cf *Westdeutsche Landesbank Girozentrale v Islington LBC* [1996] AC 669, 716 (Lord Browne-Wilkinson).

134 The characterisation may also be significant in respect of private international law, in determining which court has jurisdiction and what the choice of law rule might be. See Virgo, 'What is the Law of Restitution About?' in Cornish, Nolan, O'Sullivan and Virgo (eds), *Restitution: Past, Present and Future* (1998) 231 et seq.

135 [1991] 2 AC 548.

interchangeable. It followed that the defence was available to all restitutionary claims, although Lord Goff did indicate that it might not be available to a claim founded on wrongdoing because the defence should not be available to a wrongdoer or somebody who had acted in bad faith.[136]

However, the quadration of unjust enrichment and restitution no longer represents English law following *Foskett v McKeown*.[137] Lord Millett recognised that this had a knock-on effect for the application of the defence of change of position. He assumed, following the dictum of Lord Goff in *Lipkin Gorman*, that the defence was only available to unjust enrichment claims so it did not apply to claims founded on the vindication of property rights. Consequently, a defendant who has received property in which the claimant has a proprietary interest and who, in reliance on that receipt, spends money on a cruise or on some other expenditure which would not have been incurred but for the receipt of the property, must still make restitution to the claimant. This may seem harsh, since the defendant's change of position will have been innocent,[138] but it is presumably a logical consequence of characterising the claim as being founded on 'hard-nosed property rights'. This is because property rights should be treated as strong rights which should not be defeated by innocent changes in the defendant's circumstances.

The application of the defence of change of position may, however, be more complicated than Lord Millett suggested. It is possible that where the claimant seeks a personal restitutionary remedy to vindicate a property right[139] then the reliance on the property right is weaker and a defence of change of position might be applicable. This is because the claimant is not seeking to recover the property in which he or she has a proprietary interest, but simply relies on the fact that the defendant has received such property to ground the claim. Once the claim has been established the claimant only then seeks to recover the value of the benefit received by the defendant. Since this is value in which the claimant does not have a proprietary interest, a stronger case can be made that the claimant's right to it should compete with the defendant's, so that the defendant should be able to plead his or her change of position in reliance on the validity of the receipt. Where, however, the claimant seeks to recover specific property, the defendant's change of position should not be relevant. Such a claim should only be defeated if the defendant is a bona fide purchaser for value, since such a defence operates to defeat the claimant's proprietary interest so that the basis for the proprietary claim fails.

This application of the change of position defence is appropriate and follows from distinguishing between unjust enrichment and vindication of property rights claims. If proprietary claims to substitute property did depend on the defendant's unjust

136 *Lipkin Gorman v Karpnale Ltd* [1991] 2 AC 548.
137 [2001] 1 AC 102.
138 If the defendant suspected that somebody had a proprietary interest in the property which he or she had received then the defendant would have been acting in bad faith and so the defence would not be available anyway.
139 This being the preferable explanation of *Lipkin Gorman v Karpnale Ltd* [1991] 2 AC 548. See Virgo, *The Principles of the Law of Restitution* (1999) 14–15.

enrichment, it would follow logically that the defence of change of position should be available, which would unacceptably weaken claims to recover substitute property.

Summary

The prime reason for Birks's criticism of the vindication of proprietary rights theory is that it is inconsistent with his classification of events as consent, wrongs, unjust enrichment and other events. The usefulness of this method of categorisation can be tested by considering how equitable property rights arise. It is apparent from the previous discussion that there is an immediate inconsistency between his classification and the approach of equity, since there is no evidence that equitable proprietary rights are not created as a response to unjust enrichment. It is clear, however, that such rights can arise as a response to consent, as exemplified by the express trust.[140] Equally, such rights can arise as a response to wrongdoing, as exemplified by *A-G for Hong Kong v Reid*.[141] But there are two other situations where equitable property rights are created which do not fall within any of these earlier categories, and so must fall within the category of 'other events'. These categories relate to the creation of rights in substitute property, as recognised in *Foskett v McKeown*,[142]and rights which arise by virtue of the defendant's unconscionable conduct, as recognised in *Westdeutsche Landesbank Girozentrale v Islington London Borough Council*.[143] This category of 'other events' is therefore very large. So large in fact that it undermines the usefulness of this mode of categorisation, at least as regards the recognition of property rights.

Proprietary restitutionary claims operate satisfactorily within equity without any need to introduce artificial notions of unjust enrichment. *Foskett v McKeown* is undoubtedly an important case, but it is not a revolutionary decision. The House of Lords' recognition of 'hard-nosed property rights' is consistent with the equitable tradition as identified in a wide variety of cases. Equally, equitable proprietary claims are principled and it is not appropriate to introduce a discretion to determine when proprietary rights should be created and how they should be vindicated.

INTEGRATION OF EQUITY AND THE COMMON LAW

Although this analysis has shown that restitutionary principles generally operate successfully in equitable contexts, situations remain where there is a tension, not with

140 The resulting trust might be considered to fall within this category, since it is sometimes categorised as depending on the common intention of the parties: see *Westdeutsche Landesbank Girozentrale v Islington London Borough Council* [1996] AC 669, 708 (Lord Browne-Wilkinson). However, Lord Millett has described the trust as arising by operation of law: *Air Jamaica v Charlton* [1999] 1 WLR 1399, 1412. This is the preferable view, regardless of the debate as to whether this type of trust is triggered by a positive intent of the transferor or the absence of the transferor's intent to pass a beneficial interest to the recipient. See *Maudsley and Burn's Trusts and Trustees: Cases and Materials* (6th edn, 2002) 180–190.

141 [1994] 1 AC 324, [1994] 1 All ER 1. See text at n 96 above.

142 [2001] 1 AC 102.

143 [1996] AC 669. See text at n 68 above.

the application of restitution within equity, but with the different approaches and results obtained when restitutionary relief is compared at law and in equity. Analysis of *Moses v Macferlan*[144] shows that there was originally a desire to incorporate equitable principles into the common law to avoid the limitations of pleading and procedure at law.[145] A similar trend can be identified more recently with the desire to avoid the restrictions on tracing at law by resorting to the equitable tracing rules.[146] But should this trend be taken to its logical conclusion so that law and equity are completely assimilated?

Historically, law and equity were administered separately and so developed separately.[147] This separate administration was fused through the enactment of the Judicature Acts 1873–75.[148] The preferable view is that this legislation only fused the administration of common law and equity courts and did not fuse the substantive law. However, the fact of administrative fusion should act as a catalyst towards fusion of the substantive law, but only where this is beneficial.[149] Fusion for the sake of fusion is not acceptable. Law and equity may involve different fact situations and so different policies which need to be preserved. This is most noticeable with the trust and, to a lesser extent, fiduciary obligations. The recognition of a trust or a fiduciary relationship is important because it immediately signals certain policy assumptions, such as the fact that the trustee is responsible for others requires strict compliance with duties.[150]

But it does not follow that fusion is invariably a bad thing.[151] There has already been a degree of integration, such as the assimilation of equitable grounds of restitution within the common law action of unjust enrichment.[152] There are four other areas relating to the law of restitution where the integration of law and equity would be desirable.

144 (1760) 2 Burr 1005.
145 See *Roxborough v Rothmans of Pall Mall Australia Ltd* (2002) 185 ALR 335, 361 (Gummow J); Birks (1984) CLP 1.
146 See text at n 153 et seq below.
147 Beatson, *The Use and Abuse of Unjust Enrichment* (1991) 245; Getzler, 'Equitable Compensation and the Regulation of Fiduciary Relationships' in P Birks and F Rose (eds), *Resulting Trusts and Equitable Compensation* (2000) ch 13.
148 See Burrows (2002) OJLS 1, 4. See also Burrows, 'Fusing Common Law and Equity: Remedies, Restitution and Reform', *Hochelga Lectures, 2001* (2002).
149 There need not be a 'competition to the death' as Birks has suggested: (1999) 23 Melbourne University Law Review 1, 24.
150 See *Maudsley and Burn's Trusts and Trustees: Cases and Materials* (6th edn, 2002) 679; Cane, *Responsibility in Law and Morality* (2002) 200–202; Birks (2000) 34 Israel Law Review 3. However, the content of the duties themselves are becoming less strict. See especially the new statutory duty of care: Trustee Act 2000, s 1.
151 As Jackman suggests in *The Varieties of Restitution* (1998) 11: 'Those conceptual differences would exist whether or not law and equity were fused in their substantive content, and the law would be no more explicable in terms of a single unifying principle or concept than at present.' See also Justice Gummow in the foreword to Jackman (1998) at v; Getzler, 'Patterns of Fusion' in Birks (ed), *The Classification of Obligations* (1997) ch 7.
152 See text at n 84 et seq above.

Tracing

Although the matter is not free from doubt, it seems that there remains a crucial distinction between the tracing rules at law and in equity.[153] In essence, tracing at law does not require proof of a fiduciary relationship, but it is not possible to trace through a mixed fund, whereas tracing in equity does require proof of a fiduciary relationship but it is possible to trace through a mixed fund. This distinction has been subject to sustained criticism by commentators and the judiciary, most notably in *Foskett v McKeown*,[154] but it seems to have survived the onslaught, just. It is, however, only a matter of time before the House of Lords gets the opportunity to assimilate the rules, and it should do so. The function of these rules, whether at law or in equity, is exactly the same. The distinction between the rules derives from historical origins which are no longer significant. The tracing rules should exist simply as rules of evidence to identify in which assets the claimant has a proprietary interest and regardless of the origin of the proprietary right being traced.[155] It would follow that a claimant would be able to trace either at law or in equity through a mixed fund and without needing to establish a fiduciary relationship.

Fault or strict liability[156]

The unjust enrichment principle involves strict liability whereas equitable causes of action for the most part require proof of fault. This difference is most marked when the actions for money had and received and unconscientious receipt are compared. Both claims are available when the defendant has received property in which the claimant had retained a proprietary interest, either a legal interest, for the action for money had and received, or an equitable interest, for the action for unconscientious receipt. The common law claim does not require proof of fault, as appears to have been the case in *Lipkin Gorman v Karpnale Ltd*,[157] but the action for unconscientious receipt requires proof of unconscionability.[158] This fault requirement has been criticised, most notably by Lord Nicholls of Birkenhead.[159] According to Lord Nicholls it would be more appropriate to distinguish between two distinct forms of liability, one grounded on the commission of a wrong, for which fault is required and there would be no defence of change of position, and one grounded on the defendant's unjust enrichment, for which liability would be strict but the defence of change of position would apply. In fact,

153 Although some of the judges in *Foskett v McKeown* [2001] 1 AC 102 were clearly in favour of assimilating the tracing rules, this was *obiter*.

154 See especially *Foskett v McKeown* [2001] 1 AC 102 at 128 (Lord Millett) and 113 (Lord Steyn). See also *Nelson v Larholt* [1948] 1 KB 339, 342–343 (Denning J); *Bristol and West Building Society v Mothew* [1996] 4 All ER 698, 716 (Millett LJ).

155 Birks, (1996) 26 UWALR 1, 89; Smith, *The Law of Tracing* (1997) 5; Khurshid and Matthews (1979) 95 LQR 78.

156 See Birks in Swadling and Jones, (eds), *The Search for Principle: Essays in Honour of Lord Goff of Chieveley* (1999) 235 et seq.

157 [1991] 2 AC 548.

158 *Bank of Credit and Commerce International (Overseas) Ltd v Akindele* [2001] Ch 437.

159 'Knowing Receipt: The Need for a New Landmark' in Cornish, Nolan, O'Sullivan and Virgo (eds), *Restitution: Past, Present and Future* (1998) 231–245. See also Birks (2000) King's College LJ 1, 10. See now *Twinsectra v Yardley* [2002] UKHL 12, [2002] 2 WLR 802, 831 (Lord Millett) and *Dubai Aluminium Co Ltd v Salaam* [2002] 3 WLR 1913, 1933 (Lord Millett).

equity has recognised a strict liability claim, initially as regards the recovery of money by the next-of-kin which had mistakenly been paid to charities by the personal representatives of the deceased's estate.[160] This should be developed to create a new cause of strict liability action in equity, where the defendant has received property in which the claimant had a beneficial interest, and this would be the mirror-image of the common law claim.[161] The imposition of strict liability is justified both at law and in equity because, where a defendant has received property in which the claimant has a proprietary interest, the strength of that proprietary interest requires the defendant to make restitution of its value. The quid pro quo for recognising a strict liability claim should be that the defendant is able to rely on the defence of change of position. This is what happened in *Lipkin Gorman*, so why should it not apply in equity?

It does not follow that fault should be excised from equity completely, since the reliance on unconscionability is vital to equity's recognition of equitable proprietary rights in the first place.[162] But, as regards personal claims to recover the value of money which has been misappropriated, there is no longer any reason why liability at law should be strict and liability in equity should necessarily depend on fault. A strict liability personal claim should be generally available in equity, although such a claim would need to be grounded on the vindication of proprietary rights rather than unjust enrichment. Indeed, in *Dubai Aluminium Co Ltd v Salaam*[163] Lord Millett appears to have recognised this strict liability claim when he said that 'it can also be based simply on the receipt, treating it as a restitutionary claim independent of any wrongdoing.'

Compound Interest

Following the decision of the House of Lords in *Westdeutsche Landesbank Girozentrale v Islington London Borough Council*,[164] it is clear that compound interest is only available in respect of certain equitable claims because the jurisdiction to award such interest is equitable. Consequently, in that case, the plaintiff could only obtain simple interest in respect of a common law claim for money had and received. But, there is no reason why compound interest should not be available for common law restitutionary claims, where it is an appropriate measure of the defendant's enrichment. This was the view of Lords Goff and Woolf, dissenting.[165] This must be right. There may be cases where, regardless of the origins of the claim, it is appropriate to assess the interest which should be awarded as compound rather than simple interest to ensure that the policy of the law of restitution, namely to remove benefits

160 *Ministry of Health v Simpson* [1951] AC 251, [1950] 2 All ER 1137. See also *GL Baker v Medway Building and Supplies Ltd* [1958] 2 All ER 532 where this strict liability personal claim was extended to *inter vivos* trusts. Such a claim is only available, however, where the claimant has exhausted the remedies against the people who had made the mistake.

161 Cf Smith (2000) 116 LQR 412.

162 As illustrated by the law concerning the recognition of constructive trusts. See text to n 65 above.

163 [2002] 3 WLR 1913, 1933. See also *Twinsectra Ltd v Yardley* [2002] UKHL 12, [2002] 2 WLR 802, 831.

164 [1996] AC 669, [1996] 2 All ER 961. For analysis of the award of this type of interest see Elliott [2001] Conv 313, 332–340.

165 [1996] AC 669 at 696 (Lord Goff), 736 (Lord Woolf). See Rose, 'Interest', in Birks and Rose (eds), *Lessons of the Swaps Litigation* (2000) ch 11.

from the defendant, is fulfilled. Compound interest should be available where, for example, it could be shown that, if the defendant had not had the benefit of the claimant's money, the defendant would have had to borrow the equivalent amount from a bank and would have paid compound interest to that bank. In such circumstances the defendant would have saved this amount of interest which constitutes the value of the benefit obtained from the claimant.[166] This is another situation, like the rules in tracing, where developments in equity should be transplanted to the common law, since there is no longer anything peculiar about the equitable jurisdiction which means that it should be confined to equity.

Wrongdoing

The distinction between the law of tort and equitable wrongdoing is unnecessary and both forms of wrongdoing should be integrated.[167] This would mean, for example, that equitable remedies such as an account of profits would be of general application, regardless of whether the wrong was characterised as arising at law or in equity.

CONCLUSIONS

Three key lessons can be learnt from this excursion through the territory where restitution and equity intersect.

First, restitution and equity are, for the most part, integrated: it is unjust enrichment which is not.[168] But this is not a cause for any concern. In most cases restitution within equity is concerned with awarding remedies for equitable wrongdoing or to vindicate equitable proprietary rights and there is no need in such cases to resort to the unjust enrichment principle. Crucially, no trust is triggered by unjust enrichment.[169] If the judiciary and commentators now feel able to disassociate restitution and unjust enrichment, the knee-jerk reaction against the law of restitution within equity can be avoided. Unjust enrichment needs to be controlled and it should not be allowed to interfere unnecessarily with the equitable way of doing things.

Secondly, whilst equity is powerful and influential, its contribution to the development of the law of restitution must not be over-emphasised. In many cases the common law provides perfectly adequate claims without any need to resort to equity, either for a cause of action or to modify the common law approach. In *Roxborough v Rothmans of Pall Mall Australia Ltd*,[170]Gummow J issued a cautionary reminder against the 'mesmeric fixation upon the (not always well understood) potential of equitable, particularly trust, remedies where what the common law offers will meet the case.'

166 See Virgo, *The Principles of the Law of Restitution* (1999) 27–28.
167 Birks (1999) 23 Melbourne University LR 1, 19.
168 Although the unjust enrichment principle can be employed in contexts traditionally associated with equity, see text at n 84 et seq above. But this is distinct from applying the principle within equity itself in the sense of that body of rules traditionally associated with the Chancery courts.
169 Cf Birks (1999) 28 UWALR 13.
170 (2002) 185 ALR 335, 348.

Finally, there is real danger in assuming that equity stands for flexibility and vagueness. This is simply not what equity is about.[171] Equity is principled and equity needs to be clear.[172] Exactly the same is true of restitution. Both equity and restitution need to be expounded clearly and coherently. Where there is confusion it is the task of the commentator and the judge to seek clarity, predictability and coherence and to rationalise the law. This is precisely what Edward Burn has achieved in his published works. His exposition of equity has been marked by clarity of thought and analysis and our understanding is much clearer as a result of it. But the rapid development of the law of restitution requires further rationalisation, especially as regards its application within equity. Where necessary this rationalisation may require integration of common law and equity but, for the most part, equity continues to have a distinct and a vital role, particularly in its application to restitutionary claims.

171 Birks (1999) 23 Melbourne University LR 1, 19.

172 *Cowcher v Cowcher* [1972] 1 WLR 425, 430 (Bagnall J). Cf *Hussey v Palmer* [1972] 1 WLR 1286, 1289–1290 (Lord Denning MR).

CHAPTER 6

Professional Liability in the Will-Making Process

Sir Christopher Slade

INTRODUCTION

Following the common practice of Parliamentary draughtsmen, this essay will begin with a definition. It will throughout refer to solicitors rather than barristers, since much more commonly they are the professionals involved in the will-making process. All references to solicitors, however, should be treated as including barristers unless the context otherwise requires. Barristers instructed in this process nowadays enjoy no such privileged position as they would have been thought to do before the decision in *Rondel v Worsley*.[1]

When Professor Burn and I were called to the Bar in the early 1950s, the Chancery courts were much more frequently occupied in the construction of badly drafted wills than they are today. One simple reason may have been a lower quality in the general standards of drafting at that time. Another reason could perhaps have been a somewhat relaxed approach to these functions, resulting subconsciously from a widespread belief that negligence in the drafting of a will, or in advice for its preparation, or in arranging its due execution, would give rise to no legal liability to anyone beyond a contractual liability in nominal damages to the testator or his personal representatives. The main purpose of this essay is to demonstrate how later successive decisions of the courts would now render any such confidence misplaced.

THE EARLIER LAW

In those earlier days there was good foundation for the belief that the solicitor concerned in any such case could be liable to no one except his own client, with whom alone he had privity of contract. In a Scottish appeal in the House of Lords, *Robertson v Fleming*,[2] Lord Campbell LC had treated this proposition as axiomatic, saying:

1 [1969] 1 AC 191.
2 (1861) 4 Macq 167.

> I never had any doubt of the unsoundness of the doctrine, unnecessarily (and I must say unwisely) contended for by the respondent's counsel, that A employing B, a professional lawyer, to do any act for the benefit of C, A having to pay B, and there being no intercourse of any sort between B and C, – if through the gross negligence or ignorance of B in transacting the business, C loses the benefit intended for him by A, C may maintain an action against B, and recover damages for the loss sustained. If this were law, a disappointed legatee might sue the solicitor employed by a testator to make a will in favour of a stranger, whom the solicitor never saw or before heard of, if the will were void for not being properly signed and attested. I am clearly of opinion that this is not the law of Scotland, nor of England, and it can hardly be the law of any country where jurisprudence has been cultivated as a science.[3]

Lord Cranworth[4] stated the law in much the same terms, as did Lord Wensleydale.[5] If any doubts remained as to possible differences between the laws of England and Scotland, the Court of Appeal in *Groom v Crocker*[6] appeared to remove them by holding that a solicitor's duty to his client lies in contract rather than in tort.

I remember Roxburgh J, no doubt mindful of these authorities, once expressing the view, in a case in the early 1950s, that the moral responsibility of a lawyer entrusted with the preparation of a will was a particularly high one, since no one would be likely to have an effective legal remedy if he did the job badly.

Nowadays, however, lawyers who are concerned with the drafting or execution of wills, or in advice for their preparation, can no longer afford to adopt a relaxed approach to their task. Since the early 1950s, the law in this context has developed by successive stages so that their moral responsibilities may now be accompanied by legal duties owed to a wide range of persons, with what may be dire consequences in the event of breach.

NEGLIGENT SOLICITORS ARE HELD LIABLE TO PAY SUBSTANTIAL DAMAGES TO A TESTATOR'S PERSONAL REPRESENTATIVE

One of the first chinks in the defensive armour of the lawyers was revealed by the decision in *Otter v Church Adams Tatham & Co*.[7] In that case, the plaintiff, as sole administratrix of the estate of her son, Michael, sued the defendant firm, claiming that they had been negligent in failing to advise him that he ought to execute a disentailing assurance or will relating to certain settled property, if he wished to ensure that it formed part of his estate when he died. Negligence was found by the judge. It was, however, strongly contended that the damages flowing from the breach of contract could be only nominal, on the grounds that the plaintiff administratrix could have no better right than Michael himself would have possessed had he lived and, had he lived,

3 (1861) 4 Macq 167 at 177.
4 (1861) 4 Macq 167 at 184–185.
5 (1861) 4 Macq 167 at 199–200.
6 [1939] 1 KB 194.
7 [1953] Ch 280, [1953] 1 All ER 168.

he could have made the property part of his estate by executing a disentailing assurance or an appropriate will. Upjohn J, while stating that the matter was free from authority, rejected this argument.[8] He held that the damages which might fairly and reasonably be expected to flow from the defendant's breach of contract were to be ascertained at the time when the damage accrued, that is to say after Michael's death; and that, as he had been deprived of the opportunity of increasing his estate by making the settled property his own absolute property, the measure of damages was (effectively) the loss to his estate caused by the loss of this opportunity.

Following that decision, no solicitor, who failed in his duty of care to an intending testator, could safely assume that any consequent liability to the testator's personal representatives would necessarily be limited to nominal damages; a claim for substantial damages might well be open to them. As yet, however, there was no authority which established that his duty could arise in tort as well as in contract, still less that it could be owed to persons other than the testator himself.

SUBSEQUENT DEVELOPMENTS IN THE GENERAL LAW OF NEGLIGENCE

During the next few years, however, there were significant developments in the general law of negligence. The landmark decision of the House of Lords in *Hedley Byrne & Co Ltd v Heller & Partners Ltd*[9] established that, even in the absence of a contractual relationship, a negligent misrepresentation could give rise to liability for financial loss resulting from it, if the person making the representation had some special skill and knew or ought to know that the other party, in seeking information, was relying on that skill.

Very shortly after the *Hedley Byrne* decision, Plowman J, in *Clark v Kirby-Smith*,[10] had to consider the possible impact of its ratio on a solicitor-client relationship. In that case a solicitor, whose express instructions were to give a notice under the Landlord and Tenant Act 1954, failed to do so, so that his client lost his right of renewal. To determine the measure of damages it became relevant to consider the basis of the solicitor's liability. Plowman J firmly rejected an argument that the *Hedley Byrne* decision had altered this basis, saying the following:

> [Counsel in this case] argues that the result of the decision of the House of Lords in *Hedley Byrne & Co Ltd v Heller & Partners Ltd* is that negligence is a tort whether it arises out of negligent mis-statements made by a person who is not under any contractual or fiduciary obligation to give information or advice, which represents that state of affairs with which the House of Lords was concerned in the *Hedley Byrne* case, or whether, as here, it arises out of the contractual relationship of solicitor and client. I do not accept the argument that the *Hedley Byrne* case is an authority for saying that the liability of a solicitor to his client for negligence is a liability in tort.

8 [1953] Ch 280 at 287.
9 [1964] AC 465, [1963] 2 All ER 575.
10 [1964] Ch 506, [1964] 2 All ER 835.

> A line of cases going back for nearly 150 years shows, I think, that the client's cause of action is in contract and not in tort: see, for example, *Howell v Young* and *Groom v Crocker* where Sir Wilfrid Greene MR said: 'In my opinion, the cause of action is in contract and not in tort. The duty of the appellants was to conduct the case properly on behalf of the respondent as their client, subject to any proper exercise by the insurers of the right of control conferred upon them by the policy. The relationship of solicitor and client is a contractual one' – he refers to the cases – 'It was by virtue of that relationship that the duty arose, and it had no existence apart from that relationship.[11]

No less firmly, in *Bagot v Stevens Scanlan & Co Ltd*[12] Diplock LJ rejected an argument that the *Hedley Byrne* decision had altered the legal basis of the relationship between an architect and his client. He quoted the passage from Plowman J's judgment quoted above and said:

> I think that all those words apply equally to the relationship between architect and client. I can see no reason why they should not, and I can see nothing in the relationship of architect and client which can be said to give rise to the kind of status obligation which arises from the origins of the common law in the case of master and servant, common carrier, innkeeper, bailor and bailee.[13]

In *Cook v Swinfen*,[14] Lord Denning MR, with whose judgment Danckwerts LJ and Winn LJ agreed, stated categorically: 'An action against a solicitor is always one for breach of contract'.[15]

In the face of all this contrary authority, it must have taken some courage for Oliver J (as he then was) in *Midland Bank Trust Co Ltd v Hett Stubbs & Kemp*[16] to hold, as he did, that the *Hedley Byrne* decision was inconsistent with and destroyed the reasoning upon which *Groom v Crocker* was based. He declined to follow *Clark v Kirby-Smith*, *Bagot v Stevens Scanlan & Co Ltd* and *Cook v Swinfen*, and held that a duty of care owed by a solicitor to his client would arise concurrently in contract and in tort.

It is convenient at this point to digress from the chronological sequence by mentioning that the decision of Oliver J in the *Midland Bank* case was approved and applied by the House of Lords in *Henderson v Merrett Syndicates Ltd*[17] where it was held that the claimant Names at Lloyds were free to pursue their remedies against the defendant managing agents either in contract or in tort. Very recently, the possibility of concurrent liability in contract and tort on the part of professional advisers has been re-affirmed by the House of Lords in *Johnson v Gore Wood*.[18] In this case Lord Cooke of Thorndon described the *Henderson* case as having 'finally established in English

11 [1964] Ch 506 at 510.
12 [1966] 1 QB 197.
13 [1966] 1 QB 197 at 206.
14 [1967] 1 WLR 457.
15 [1967] 1 WLR 457 at 461.
16 [1979] Ch 384.
17 [1995] 2 AC 145.
18 [2002] 2 AC 1, [2001] 1 All ER 481.

law the legitimacy of recognising that professional advisers may owe to the same client a duty to exercise reasonable care and skill derived from both contract and tort law'.[19]

NEGLIGENT SOLICITORS ARE HELD LIABLE TO PAY DAMAGES TO A DISAPPOINTED BENEFICIARY

In the year following the *Midland Bank* decision, it fell to Megarry J in *Ross v Caunters*[20] to consider whether the duty of care owed to his client by a solicitor instructed in a will-making process could be owed to a third party. In that case, solicitors who prepared a will for a testator and sent it to him for execution failed to warn him that, in view of section 15 of the Wills Act 1837, the will should not be witnessed by a beneficiary. One of the witnesses to the testator's signature of the will was the husband of a residuary beneficiary, so that the gift to her was void by virtue of the section. She claimed damages against the solicitors for negligence in respect of these lost benefits. Counsel for the firm admitted negligence but, in reliance on *Groom v Crocker* and *Robertson v Fleming*, submitted that a solicitor could be liable in negligence to his client in contract only and to no one other than his own client. It was pointed out that the *Hedley Byrne* case concerned a negligent misrepresentation of fact, namely the giving of an inaccurate reference. The principle thereby established, it was submitted, did not include statements or opinions of law or acts or omissions in the giving of legal advice.

Megarry J rejected these arguments, expressing his 'most respectful concurrence in an exhaustive and convincing discussion of a complex subject' by Oliver J in the *Midland Bank* case. He summarised his conclusions as follows:

(1) Despite the dicta in *Robertson v Fleming*,[21] and what was said in *Groom v Crocker*[22] and other cases in that line, there is no longer any rule that a solicitor who is negligent in his professional work can be liable only to his client in contract; he may be liable both to his client and to others for the tort of negligence.

(2) The basis of the solicitor's liability to others is either an extension of the *Hedley Byrne* principle[23] or, more probably, a direct application of the principle of *Donoghue v Stevenson*.[24]

(3) A solicitor who is instructed by his client to carry out a transaction that will confer a benefit on an identified third party owes a duty of care towards that third party in carrying out that transaction, in that the third party is a person within his direct contemplation as someone who is likely to be so closely and directly affected by his acts or omissions that he can reasonably foresee that the third party is likely to be injured by those acts or omissions.

19 At 46 D–E.
20 [1980] Ch 297.
21 (1861) 4 Macq 167.
22 [1939] 1 KB 194.
23 [1964] AC 465, [1963] 2 All ER 575.
24 [1932] AC 562.

(4) The mere fact that the loss to such a third party caused by the negligence is purely financial, and is in no way a physical injury to person or property, is no bar to the claim against the solicitor.

(5) In such circumstances there are no considerations which suffice to negative or limit the scope of the solicitor's duty to the beneficiary.[25]

IN *WHITE v JONES*, A DISAPPOINTED BENEFICIARY IS GIVEN A REMEDY IN A CASE WHERE THE TESTATOR'S ESTATE HAS SUFFERED NO LOSS

Some fifteen years elapsed before the correctness of the landmark decision in *Ross v Caunters* fell to be tested by the House of Lords in *White v Jones*.[26] In that case, the negligence of the defendant solicitors consisted of delay in carrying out the instructions of a testator for a new will, followed by the death of the testator before the will was executed. The claim in negligence was brought by a disappointed beneficiary. Lord Goff of Chievely described the principal issue falling for their Lordships' decision as being:

> whether in the circumstances of cases such as *Ross v Caunters* and the present case the testator's solicitors are liable to the disappointed beneficiary.[27]

The majority approved the decision in *Ross v Caunters* and held that they were liable. Lord Goff, who was one of the majority, and with whose reasons Lord Browne-Wilkinson and Lord Nolan agreed,[28] explained that a primary consideration which led him to conclude that disappointed beneficiary should have a remedy against the testator's solicitor was as follows:[29]

> In the forefront stands the extraordinary fact that, if such a duty is not recognised, the only persons who might have a valid claim (i e the testator and his estate) have suffered no loss, and the only person who has suffered a loss (i e the disappointed beneficiary) has no claim: see *Ross v Caunters*[30] per Sir Robert Megarry VC. It can therefore be said that, if the solicitor owes no duty to he intended beneficiaries, there is a lacuna in the law which needs to be filled. This I regard as being a point of cardinal importance in the present case.

Lord Goff expressed his conclusions thus:

> It seems to me that it is open to your Lordships' House, as in the *Lenesta Sludge* case[31] . . . to fashion a remedy to fill a lacuna in the law and so prevent the injustice which would otherwise occur on the facts of cases such as the present. In the *Lenesta Sludge* case . . . the House made available a remedy as a matter of

25 [1932] AC 562 at 322–323.
26 [1995] 2 AC 207.
27 [1995] 2 AC 207 at 254.
28 [1995] 2 AC 207 at 276 and 295.
29 [1995] 2 AC 207 at 259–260
30 [1980] Ch 297 at 303A.
31 [1994] 1 AC 85.

> law to solve the problem of transferred loss in the case before them. The present case is, if anything, *a fortiori*, since the nature of the transaction was such that, if their solicitors were negligent and their negligence did not come to light until after the death of the testator, there would be no remedy for the ensuing loss unless the intended beneficiary could claim. In my opinion, therefore, your Lordships' House should in cases such as these extend to the intended beneficiary a remedy under the *Hedley Byrne* principle by holding that the assumption of responsibility by the solicitor towards his client should be held in law to extend to the intended beneficiary who (as the solicitor can reasonably foresee) may, as a result of the solicitor's negligence, be deprived of his intended legacy in circumstances in which neither the testator nor his estate will have a remedy against the solicitor.[32]

A DISAPPOINTED BENEFICIARY IS GIVEN A REMEDY IN A CASE WHERE THE TESTATOR'S ESTATE HAS ALSO SUFFERED LOSS

The second of the two passages from Lord Goff's speech quoted above could at first sight be read as suggesting that the remedy which the House of Lords was willing to afford to a disappointed beneficiary in *White v Jones* was confined to those cases in which the estate itself had suffered no loss. Should the remedy be available to the disappointed beneficiary in a case where the estate itself has suffered loss, but where any remedy given to the estate will be of no advantage to the beneficiary?

That was the situation which arose in *Carr-Glynn v Frearsons*.[33] In that case, a disappointed beneficiary brought a claim in negligence against the solicitor draughtsman of a will, who had failed to advise the testator to serve a notice of severance of a joint tenancy of a property. The result had been that the property did not fall into the testator's estate and a specific testamentary gift to the plaintiff of the testator's interest in the property consequently could not take effect. The estate's remedy would have been of no advantage to the beneficiary, because any damages recovered in the action would have fallen into residue, rather than passing under the specific gift to the plaintiff contained in the will. Lloyd J dismissed the claim, holding first that the defendants had not been negligent and secondly that, in any event, where a solicitor's breach of his duty of care to a testatrix in preparing her will resulted in a loss *to the estate*, the solicitor owed no duty of care to an intended beneficiary under the will, whose gift was thereby rendered ineffective.

The Court of Appeal, by what Thorpe LJ described as 'a permissible incremental extension of the holding in *White v Jones*',[34] reversed the decision of Lloyd J on the second, as well as the first point. In so far as they found negligence, their decision has been criticised by R Kerridge and A H R Brierley,[35] who submit that the Court set the standard of care expected of solicitors at an unrealistically high standard. They

32 [1994] 1 AC 85 at 268B–E.
33 [1999] Ch 326.
34 [1999] Ch 326 at 237B.
35 'Negligence and Conflicts of Interest in the Will-Making Process' (1999) 115 LQR 201 at 205–206.

suggest that the Court should have considered, but failed to consider, as the central problem, 'the extent to which a solicitor is under a duty to prod a client into taking an intended course of action which appears to be sensible and reasonable, but which may cause the client some, albeit slight, inconvenience'. This is an interesting point, of which echoes may be heard in future cases where the alleged negligence of solicitors consists of a failure to act or advise, rather than faulty advice.

The relevance of the point, however, is likely to depend on the particular facts of the case before the court. The more important feature of the decision of the Court of Appeal in *Carr-Glynn* so far as the development of the law is concerned, related to the problems of *double liability*. Chadwick LJ, who gave the leading judgment, agreed with the trial judge that it would be unacceptable if solicitors were to be at risk of two separate claims for identical loss at the suit of both the personal representative and a beneficiary, when recovery by one would not bar recovery by the other. He twice stressed the point[36] that it would not be right to fashion a remedy to avoid injustice to the disappointed legatee if that itself would lead to the injustice of imposing a double liability on the solicitors, by exposing them to claims for loss of the relevant property at the suit of both the personal representatives and the specific legatee. On the other hand, as he observed,[37] it would be equally unacceptable and unjust if, in such circumstances, the loss which the personal representatives were able to recover on behalf of the estate passed to someone who was not the beneficiary intended by the testatrix, leaving the intended beneficiary without recompense.

The court in the *Carr-Glynn* case was thus faced with a puzzling dilemma. Chadwick LJ,[38] with whose reasoning Thorpe LJ and Butler-Sloss LJ agreed, found the answer to this dilemma essentially in the following propositions (my summary, not his):

(1) On the facts, the service of a notice of severance was part of the will-making process and the plaintiff was as much an intended beneficiary of that process as she was of the specific gift in the will. Accordingly, provided no double liability was imposed on the solicitors, it would be consistent with the decision in *White v Jones* to hold that she was a person 'in relation to whom the assumption of liability by the defendants towards their client, the testatrix, ought to be extended'.

(2) In a case of this nature, however, the duties owed by the solicitors are limited by reference to the kind of loss from which they must take care to 'save harmless' (that is to say protect) the persons to whom these duties are owed: see per Lord Bridge of Harwich in *Caparo Industries plc v Dickman*[39] cited by Lord Hoffmann in *Banque Bruxelles Lambert SA v Eagle Star Insurance Ltd*.[40]

(3) The loss from which the testator and his estate are to be 'saved harmless' is the loss which those interested in his estate, whether as creditors or beneficiaries, will suffer if effect is not given to his testamentary intentions.

36 *Carr-Glynn v Frearsons* [1999] Ch 326 at 336F–G and 336H–337A.
37 *Carr-Glynn v Frearsons* [1999] Ch 326 at 334C–D.
38 *Carr-Glynn v Frearsons* [1999] Ch 326 at 336–337.
39 [1990] 2 AC 605 at 627.
40 [1997] AC 191 at 212.

(4) The duties owed by the solicitors to the testator and to a specific legatee are not inconsistent but complementary. To the extent that the duty to the specific legatee is fulfilled, the duty of the testator is cut down.

(5) 'Justice will be done to each of the three interests concerned – the specific legatee, the estate and the solicitors – if solicitors who, in the course of carrying out the testator's testamentary instructions, have failed to take care to ensure that the relevant property forms part of the estate are liable to compensate the specific legatee for the loss which he has suffered as a result of the breach of duty owed to him; and are liable to compensate the estate for the loss (if any) suffered by the other persons interested in the estate for breach of the duty owed to the testator.'[41]

It was, I think, necessarily implicit in the judgment of Chadwick LJ that the court would have regarded the personal representatives themselves as having no right of recovery in respect of the lost half share of the relevant property, at least if the estate was solvent.

THE PRINCIPLE OF *WHITE v JONES* IS NOT APPLIED IN A CASE WHERE THERE IS NO NEED TO FASHION AN INDEPENDENT REMEDY FOR A BENEFICIARY

In *Worby v Rosser*,[42] proceedings were brought by three beneficiaries under a will made in 1983 against a solicitor who prepared a later will which, after contested proceedings, was refused probate. The plaintiffs sought to recover from the solicitor the substantial costs which they incurred in resisting probate of the later will. It was said that the solicitor owed a duty to them as beneficiaries named in the 1983 will to take care that the testator did not execute a later will in which he lacked testamentary capacity and was subject to the malign influence of a third party. The Court of Appeal rejected the claim, holding that there was no lacuna which required to be filled, as there had been in *White v Jones* and the *Carr-Glynn* case. In the words of Chadwick LJ:

> If the solicitor's breach of duty under his retainer has given rise to the need for expensive probate proceedings, resulting in unrecovered costs, then, prima facie, those costs fall to be borne by the estate for the reasons which I have already sought to explain. If the estate bears the costs thereby and suffers loss then, if there is to be a remedy against the solicitor, it should be the estate's remedy for the loss to the estate. There is no need to fashion an independent remedy for a beneficiary who has been engaged in the probate proceedings. His or her costs, if properly incurred in obtaining probate of the true will, can be provided for out of the estate. If there has been a breach of duty by the solicitor, the estate can recover from the solicitor the additional costs (including the costs to which the beneficiary is entitled out of the estate). The practical difficulties, which would be likely to arise if solicitors were held to owe duties directly to

41 *Carr-Glynn v Frearsons* [1999] Ch 326 at 338 per Chadwick LJ.
42 [1999] Lloyds Rep PN 972.

> beneficiaries under an earlier will, provide powerful support for the view that it would not be appropriate to provide a remedy in circumstances in which it is not needed.[43]

The Court of Appeal accepted that in a case where a solicitor's negligence in regard to the preparation or execution of a will was the cause of expensive probate proceedings after the testator's death, this could give rise to a claim for damages against the solicitors at the suit of the testator's personal representatives for the benefit of the estate generally. On the particular facts of that case, the testator's personal representative would have had a good cause of action for the loss suffered and, if they had pursued this claim, the solicitor would have been exposed to no double liability.

THE PRINCIPLE OF *WHITE v JONES* IS NOT APPLIED IN A CASE WHERE IT WOULD EXPOSE THE DEFENDANTS TO A DUPLICATED LIABILITY

The recent case of *Corbett v Bond Pearce*[44] was another case where solicitors' negligence in regard to the will-making process had led to expensive probate proceedings. Its facts, however, were otherwise different in essentials from those of *Worby v Rosser*, since the defendants were being exposed to risks of double liability. The case well illustrates the anxiety of the courts to ensure that the application of the *White v Jones* principle does not have the result of exposing solicitors to duplicated claims for essentially the same monetary loss, brought by personal representatives and disappointed beneficiaries. It was a case in which the claimant before the court was the testatrix's personal representative, a claim by the disappointed beneficiaries having been previously made and settled. Its somewhat complicated facts were in summary as follows.

In February 1989, a testatrix had executed a valid will disposing of her estate. Subsequently she decided she wished to dispose of the property rather differently, that is to say partly by two inter vivos gifts of properties known as 'Lamellyn' and 'Tolcarne' and partly by a will in a different form. She instructed the defendant firm accordingly and they sent her a fair copy of a new will for execution. The provisions of this will, which contained no gifts of 'Lamellyn' and 'Tolcarne' were in accordance with her instructions. In September she signed, but did not date, this will. The reason why she did not date it, as the defendants knew, was that she did not wish it to take effect on her death until the lifetime gifts of Lamellyn and Tolcarne were complete. The two deeds of gift were duly executed on 25 December 1989. Shortly thereafter a member of the firm appended the date 26 December 1989 to the September will. The testatrix died in 1991.

It was common ground that the defendants' failure to procure the execution by the testatrix of a valid will on the terms of the September will or to procure such a will that could not be admitted to probate without a probate action had constituted negligence on the part of the defendants. If the September will was invalid, the whole of her

43 [1999] Lloyds Rep PN 972 at 978.
44 [2001] EWCA Civ 531, [2001] Lloyds Rep PN 501.

residuary state would pass to the claimant and a Mrs A. This would not give effect to her intentions because, as soon as the two deeds of gifts were executed, she intended that the benefits received by the claimant and Mrs A should be limited to certain properties specifically devised by the September will, and that the other residue should go to B and C.

Following her death, the claimant objected to the admission to probate of the September will. In 1996 the Court of Appeal held that that will was invalid by reason of a lack of testamentary intention on the part of the testatrix at the time of its execution. It ordered that the February will be admitted to probate. Subsequently it ordered that the costs of all parties in that court and the court below should be paid out of the estate. These costs amounted to some £150,000.

In August 1995, before the determination of the probate proceedings, B and C, the disappointed beneficiaries, issued proceedings against the defendants to recover damages in reliance on *White v Jones*. The proceedings were eventually settled in December 1997 on the basis of the payment to the disappointed beneficiaries of £275,000, representing the full amount of their claim with interest. This sum was calculated by reference to the amount of the net residuary estate undiminished by the costs of the probate proceedings.

Meantime the claimant had himself issued proceedings against the defendant. These were amended in 1997 by withdrawing his claim as a beneficiary under the February will and substituting a claim as the testatrix's personal representative. In that capacity he sought in effect reimbursement to the estate of the costs of the probate proceedings.

The Court of Appeal rejected his claim. It did so in reliance on the statement of principle by Lord Hoffmann in *Banque Bruxelles Lambert SA v Eagle Star*:[45]

> A duty of care such as the valuer owes does not, however, exist in the abstract. A plaintiff who sues for breach of duty imposed by the law (whether in contract or tort or under statute) must do more than prove that the defendant has failed to comply. He must show that the duty was owed to him and that it was a duty in respect of the kind of loss which he has suffered. Both of these requirements are illustrated by *Caparo Industries plc v Dickman*.[46]

As it happened, I gave the leading judgment in *Corbett v Bond Pearce* (with which Brooke LJ and Longmore LJ agreed). My reasoning in summary was as follows.[47] The scope of the duty of care owed by the defendants to the testatrix had to be determined by reference to the kind of damage from which they had to take care to keep her harmless. This kind of damage was (exclusively) the loss which those who would become interested in her estate, whether as beneficiaries or creditors, would suffer if effect was not given to her latest testamentary intentions. In the light of the *Carr-Glynn* decision,[48] the defendants were indisputably liable to compensate the

45 [1997] AC 191 at 211G–212B.
46 [1990] 2 AC 605, [1990] 1 All ER 568.
47 [1990] 2 AC 605 at 509–510.
48 *Carr-Glynn v Frearsons* [1999] Ch 326.

residuary beneficiaries under the September will for the full amount of the residuary estate, undiminished by the costs of the Will action, and they had been right in doing so. However, the defendants could not at the same time be under a liability to the testator's personal representatives for the same costs. Admittedly, on a strict analysis, the damages which the claimant sought to recover did not represent precisely the same sum as that which had formed part of the award to the disappointed beneficiaries. In substance, however, the two sums represented the same monetary loss. This was the relevant point. To subject the defendants to liability for the relevant costs at the suit of the claimant would in substance have involved the duplicated liability which the Court of Appeal, in giving a remedy to the disappointed beneficiary in the *Carr-Glynn* case, was so explicitly determined to avoid.

THE RELEVANCE (IF ANY) OF 'WINDFALLS'

As I stated in my judgment in *Corbett v Bond Pearce*,[49] I was fortified in my conclusion by the consideration that no injustice was caused by dismissing the claim. For if it had succeeded and there had proved to be a residue for distribution, the money recovered from the defendants would have inured for the benefit of the residuary beneficiaries named in the February will, who were not intended by the testatrix to take any part of residue and would thus have taken a windfall.

However, the mere fact that the grant of a remedy under the *White v Jones* principle would have resulted in an unintended windfall for the residuary beneficiaries named in the February will was not the basis of my decision. It had been argued in *White v Jones* that the grant of a remedy to the disappointed beneficiary against the solicitor would have the undeniable and fortuitous effect of substantially increasing the size of the testator's estate, because it would not be possible to recover any part of the estate which had lawfully devolved upon others by an unrevoked will or on an intestacy, even though that was not in fact the testator's intention. Lord Goff saw no substance in this point saying:

> I cannot however see what impact this has on the disappointed beneficiary's remedy. It simply reflects the fact that those who received the testator's estate, either under an unrevoked will or on an intestacy, were lucky enough to receive a windfall; and in consequence the estate is, so far as the testator and the disappointed beneficiary are concerned, irretrievably lost.[50]

In *Corbett v Bond Pearce* the fatal obstacle to the claimant's claim was not the prospect that its success would give him an unintended windfall. The fatal obstacle was the determination of the court not to subject the defendant firm to liability twice over for essentially the same wasted costs.

49 [2001] EWCA Civ 531, [2001] Lloyd's Rep PN 501 at 510.
50 [2001[EWCA Civ 531, [2001] Lloyd's Rep PN 501 at 510.

THE RELEVANCE OF THE STATUTORY RIGHTS TO RECTIFICATION OF WILLS

In the second paragraph of this essay, I suggested two possible reasons why proceedings for the construction of wills are nowadays much more rare than they were in the 1950s, namely improvement in standards of drafting, combined with the realisation that careless drafting may nowadays give rise to substantial claims resulting in liability for more than nominal damages. Perhaps there may be a third reason. Section 20 of the Administration of Justice Act 1982, which came into force on 1 January 1983, provided as follows:

> (1) If a court is satisfied that a will is so expressed that it fails to carry out the testator's intentions, in consequence:
> (a) of a clerical error, or
> (b) of a failure to understand his instructions,
>
> it may order that the will shall be rectified so as to carry out his intentions.

This is an important new provision, even if the prospects of successful applications being made thereunder may be limited by the considerations to which Chadwick J (as he then was) referred in *Re Segelman*:[51]

> Although the standard of proof required in a claim for rectification made under section 20 (1) of the 1982 Act is that the court should be satisfied on the balance of probabilities, the probability that a will which a testator has executed in circumstances of some formality represents his intentions is usually of such weight that convincing evidence to the contrary is necessary.

The relevance of section 20 of the Administration of Justice Act 1982 was considered by the Court of Appeal in *Walker v Geo H Medlicott & Son (a firm)*[52] (another case in which I happened to be a member of the court). In that case a testatrix had instructed a member of the defendant firm of solicitors to draft a will for her. He did so and she duly executed the will. In the action the plaintiff, her nephew, claimed that contrary to her instructions, the solicitor in drafting the will, had negligently failed to include in it a specific devise of a house in his favour.

The facts of the case thus differed from those of *Ross v Caunters*, *White v Jones* and *Glynn v Frearsons*. The alleged negligence (if any) of the defendants consisted not of the failure to see that a will was properly attested or of the failure to draw it up at all, or of the failure to advise the testatrix to take some action to ensure that the relevant asset would fall into her estate, but of the failure to draft the will in accordance with the testatrix's instruction. The court was told by counsel that neither of them was aware of any decided case in which the court had had to consider a claim in negligence brought against solicitors arising out of the allegedly bad drafting of a will which had been actually executed.

51 [1996] Ch 171 at 181.
52 [1999] 1 All ER 685, [1999] 1 WLR 727.

A claim against solicitors of that nature brought by a disappointed beneficiary could be said to give rise to questions of principle which did not arise in *Ross v Caunters*, *White v Jones* or *Carr-Glynn v Frearsons*. For in none of those cases would the disappointed beneficiary have had any remedy at all if he had none in negligence. In *Walker v Medlicott*, however, the court considered that, if the claims of negligence made by the plaintiff were well founded he would, on the evidence, also have had a good claim for rectification of the will. In view of the importance attached by the majority of the House of Lords in *White v Jones* to the absence of any alternative remedy available to the plaintiff, it could, just possibly, have been argued that a solicitor/draughtsman of a will assumes no responsibility to intended beneficiaries who, due to the failure of the solicitor to carry out his instructions in the drafting of the will, take no benefit under the will in its form as executed. Rightly, however, in my view, no such argument was submitted on behalf of the defendants, who accepted from the start that they had owed a duty of care to the plaintiff in drafting the will.

In the outcome, the Court of Appeal in *Walker v Medlicott* saw no sufficient grounds for disturbing the finding of the trial judge that negligence on the part of the defendants had not been proved. The court, however, gave a further or alternative reason for dismissing the plaintiff's appeal, namely that the plaintiff had failed to discharge his duty to mitigate the loss suffered in consequence of any such negligence, by seeking rectification of the will. Reference was made to the general principle exemplified by the decision of Harman J in *Pilkington v Wood*[53] that the duty to mitigate does not ordinarily go so far as to oblige the injured party to embark on a complicated and difficult piece of litigation against a third party. The court in no way disputed the soundness of this basic rule, but pointed out that there were crucial differences between the facts of that case and those before it. As Simon Brown LJ put it:

> In that case, it will readily be seen, the defendant was admitting negligence and yet contending that the plaintiff should embark on complicated litigation with only doubtful prospects of success. Here, by contrast, the defendant was denying negligence and contending that the plaintiff would have no greater difficulty in establishing a claim for rectification than in establishing liability against him. Indeed, . . . his difficulties in the negligence action were greater given the real possibility that this whole unfortunate case is explicable in terms of a non-negligent but rectifiable misunderstanding by Mr Medlicott of the testatrix's intentions.
>
> It seems to me an entirely different thing in these circumstances, and altogether more reasonable than in *Pilkington v Wood*, to require the plaintiff to pursue an alternative remedy, namely, to look first for rectification before suing his solicitor. Were the rectification claim to fail, then by definition the plaintiff could not have succeeded against his solicitor. Miss Wicks rightly accepts that no less convincing evidence is required for an action against the solicitor than for a claim for rectification.

53 [1953] Ch 770, [1953] 2 All ER 810.

I recognise, of course, that even were the claim for rectification to succeed, that would still leave the plaintiff with some loss, if only for the costs and delay of achieving rectification. But in my judgment that consideration cannot begin to justify suing the solicitor first. Rather there are other powerful considerations here which to my mind make it reasonable to require the plaintiff to sue his solicitor only as a last resort: if, say, through no fault of his own, it had been too late to obtain rectification, or if the solicitor would not subsequently meet the costs of obtaining it.

The first such consideration stems from an important distinction, . . . between this case and the previous run of cases – *Ross v Caunters*, *White v Jones* and *Carr-Glynn v Frearsons* – namely that whereas in each of those the disappointed beneficiary would have had no remedy at all but for his claim in negligence, here he has. There can be no doubt that this consideration (the want of an alternative remedy) played a large part in deciding the majority of the House of Lords to develop the law as they did and to overcome their misgivings about thereby adventitiously enhancing the size of the estate. Whilst, however, in common with my Lords, I conclude that the duty now held to exist in these cases must logically extend also to someone in the plaintiff's position, I see no reason why as a matter of policy the law should not require of him that he seeks initially to mitigate his loss by pursuing a claim for rectification.

The second and related consideration is that referred to by Mummery LJ as the obvious possibility of abuse in this class of case. Where, as here, there is always the risk of a family manufacturing a negligence claim in order to enhance the value of the estate from which the family will benefit at the expense of the solicitor, the court is justified in requiring the plaintiff instead to pursue his remedy of rectification. I hasten to say that there has been no suggestion whatever in the present case that this plaintiff or his witnesses have been guilty of any such deceit. I make the point merely to indicate why the situation here is, in a number of respects, so very different from the norm.

Overall I regard the circumstances of the present case as so special as to take it outside the general rule to which I referred at the outset of this judgment: this case is exceptionally one in which the plaintiff should properly be required first to have taken the risk of claiming rectification, assuming he wished to risk litigation at all.[54]

Mummery LJ summarised the position in these words:

His [the plaintiff's] essential complaint was that the will did not represent his aunt's wishes as a result of a failure on the part of [the solicitor] to carry out the instructions of the testatrix in the drafting of the will. If he wished to establish that case, rectification was obviously the appropriate remedy and should have been sought by him within the time limit set by statute. If, on the one hand, he

54 [1953] Ch 770 at 743–744.

> had succeeded on rectification, he would have inherited the house; any damages for negligence would have been confined to the costs in putting right the terms of the will. If, on the other hand, he had failed on the rectification application, he would also have failed in his negligence claim; he would not have been entitled to inherit the house and he would not have suffered any loss and damage recoverable from the solicitor.[55]

As Lord Goff recognised in the passage from his speech in *White v Jones* quoted above,[56] the application of the principle of that decision against a negligent solicitor, for the purpose of compensating a disappointed beneficiary at the solicitor's expense, may leave beneficiaries named in the relevant will, as executed, with a windfall not intended by the testator. In any such case, the solicitor might be forgiven for regarding the principle as a somewhat blunt instrument. If, on the other hand, a disappointed beneficiary who has a good claim for rectification of the will is required to pursue that claim before suing the solicitor, that will have the advantage of avoiding this apparent anomaly.

While it seems clearly right that the disappointed beneficiary should be so required, it has to be recognised that a successful claim for rectification could give rise to problems of its own. Beneficiaries named in the will as executed might find themselves deprived of their reasonable expectations. They might have acted to their detriment in reasonable reliance on such expectations. Their disappointment might at best have caused them distress and at worst nervous shock. While this would perhaps have been inconceivable 40 years ago, nowadays, as the law of negligence has more recently developed, it is at least possible that such persons might themselves have a good cause of action against the negligent solicitor in tort, thus exposing him to further perils. This possibility could perhaps provide a suitable subject for a very high-powered moot, but it will not be pursued further in this essay.

PROOF OF CAUSATION

It need hardly be added that any claimant who seeks to recover substantial damages arising out of a solicitor's negligence in the course of a will-making process has to do more than show that such negligence occurred and that in the event the claimant suffered loss. He has to prove a causal link between the negligence and the loss, sufficient to justify making the solicitor pay substantial damages. Simple logic requires that to show such causal links he must first satisfy the court as to what would have happened if there had been no negligence.

In some cases of this category, the negligence of the solicitor will consist of a positive act, for example the drafting of a will otherwise than in accordance with his instructions. In perhaps a greater number of cases, at least so far as the reports

55 [1953] Ch 770 at 742 F–G.
56 Text at n 32 above

indicate, it will consist of an omission, for example the failure to give requisite advice or to take other appropriate steps to ensure that the will is duly executed before the testator's death.

The leading case on causation in the context of solicitor's negligence, appears to be *Allied Maples Group Ltd v Simmons and Simmons*.[57] In that case Stuart Smith LJ stated the relevant principles in terms which drew a clear distinction between the case where the defendant's negligence consists of some positive act and the case where it consists of an omission or non-feasance, saying:

> (1) What has to be proved to establish a causal link between the negligence of the defendants and the loss sustained by the plaintiffs, depends in the first instance on whether the negligence consists of some positive act or misfeasance, or an omission or non-misfeasance. In the former case, the question of causation is one of historical fact. The court has to determine on the balance of probability whether the defendant's act, for example careless driving, caused the plaintiff's loss consisting of his broken leg. Once established on balance of probability, that fact is taken as true and the plaintiff recovers his damage in full . . .

Stuart Smith LJ continued as follows:

> (2) If the defendant's negligence consists of an omission, for example to provide proper equipment, give proper instructions or advice, causation depends, not upon a question of historical fact, but on the answer to the hypothetical question, what would the plaintiff have done if the equipment had been provided or the instruction or advice given? This can only be a matter of inference to be determined from all the circumstances. The plaintiff's own evidence that he would have acted to obtain the benefit or avoid the risk, while important, may not be believed by the judge, especially if there is compelling evidence that he would not. In the ordinary way, where the action required of the plaintiff is clearly for his benefit, the court has little difficulty in concluding that he would have taken it . . .
>
> Although the question is a hypothetical one, it is well established that the plaintiff must prove on balance of probability that he would have taken action to obtain the benefit or avoid the risk . . .[58]

In the passage quoted, Stuart Smith LJ was not of course concerned with the case now under consideration where the claimant is not the solicitor's client, but a person in relation to whom the assumption of liability by the solicitor towards his client, the testator, should in law be extended. Nevertheless, the claimant, whether he be the testator's personal representative or a disappointed beneficiary, will still have to show a sufficient causal connection between the negligence and the loss suffered. Perhaps in most such cases this may present little difficulty. Nevertheless, it has to be borne in

57 [1995] 1 WLR 1602.
58 [1995] 1 WLR 1602 at 1609–1611.

mind that, where the claim is based on an omission or non-feasance by the solicitor, the claimant will have to satisfy three separate conditions to establish his claim, namely by showing: first, what action or advice should in all the circumstances have been taken or given by a reasonably competent solicitor; secondly, what on the balance of probability the testator would have done or what would have happened if such action or advice had been taken or given; and thirdly, that the loss suffered was thus in fact caused by the omission or non-feasance.

EXAMPLES OF NEGLIGENCE

In what has been said above, attention has been focussed principally on the consequences of a solicitor's negligence in the will-making process, rather than on the duties which fall on him in such process and the features which constitute such negligence. The cases dealing with breach well illustrate the broad scope of such duties. The categories of such negligence are not closed and it may take a variety of forms, depending on the particular facts of any given case. Some examples, to be found in the decisions mentioned above, beyond the mere faulty drafting of a will, are the failure to advise a testator to increase his estate by executing a disentailing assurance (*Otter v Church Adams Tatham & Co*) or by severing a joint tenancy (*Carr-Glynn v Frearsons*); the failure to procure the execution by the testator of a will which complies with the provisions of the Wills Act 1837 (*Corbett v Bond Pearce*); assisting a testator to execute a will when it should be realised that he lacks testamentary capacity (*Worby v Rosser*); delay in carrying out the instructions of a testator for a new will (*White v Jones*).

CONCLUSIONS

These five cases well illustrate the risks to which a solicitor may be exposed in undertaking to assist a client in the will-making process. His duties may extend far beyond the mere reproduction of a clear and intelligible draft in accordance with his client's instructions. Furthermore, as the law has developed, his obligations or liabilities may now extend to a class of persons far wider than that of the testator and his personal representatives.

As will have appeared, however, these risks are mitigated by the anxiety of the courts to ensure that the burden of responsibility imposed by the law on solicitors involved in the will-making process is not unreasonably onerous. A recent example is to be found in *X v Woollcombe Yonge*,[59] on the facts of which Neuberger J rejected a claim that a solicitor who on 26 June had been instructed to prepare a will for a testatrix in bad health had been negligent in failing to have the will ready for execution before she died on 30 June. The courts, as has been shown, will also be anxious to ensure that any application of the principle of *White v Jones* will not expose solicitors to duplicated claims for what is essentially the same loss. They will have to be satisfied that the negligence in truth caused the loss. If the principle is to be applied, they will further

59 [2001] WTLR 301.

have to be satisfied that there is a real need to give an independent remedy to the disappointed beneficiary. They will also ordinarily expect a disappointed beneficiary to exhaust such remedies for rectification of an incompetently drafted will as he may possess under section 20 of the Administration of Justice Act 1982 before pursing his remedies (if any) against the draughtsman.

With these safeguards, the incremental development in this field of the common law over the past half-century has in my view been as healthy as it has been striking.

CHAPTER 7

Form and Substance

Lord Templeman

The historical accounts in Cheshire and Burn's *Modern Law of Real Property* of the law of leases[1] and the law of mortgages,[2] together with the striking note comparing sham transactions for the evasion of rent regulation with schemes for tax avoidance,[3] have led me to reflect on the resolution by the courts of conflicts between the form and substance of transactions as recorded by the participants.

Laws are imposed by the legislature, the judiciary and by public authorities. Laws are communicated by words and expressions. Such is the fecundity of language that the actions required to conform with a law may be obscure. Similarly the language employed by the citizen to record his actions may, by accident or design, obscure the legal nature and effect of the facts described.

The task of interpreting and enforcing the law falls to the judiciary. In construing the common or judge-made law, a judge should have regard to the object and effect of the law, the principle of logic as between laws, and the principle of fairness between citizens and between the citizen and public authorities which the law may be presumed to require. In construing statute law the judge should have regard to the intentions of the legislature as derived from the language of the statute and as derived from the principles of logic and fairness which the legislature may be presumed to intend. But in determining the nature and effect of the actions of the citizen and deciding whether those actions are in conformity with the law, a judge must struggle with the intended as well as unintended obscurities, ambiguities and contradictions of the language employed by the citizen in reporting and explaining his actions.

In *Ensign Tankers (Leasing) Ltd v Stokes* [4] the citizen taxpayer who acquired a 25 per cent interest in a film claimed to have incurred a tax deductible 'cost' of 14 million

1 Cheshire and Burn, *Modern Law of Real Property* (15th edn, 1994) 34–37, 357ff; (16th edn, 2000), 34–37, 381ff.
2 Cheshire and Burn, *Modern Law of Real Property* (15th edn, 1994) 657ff; (16th edn, 2000) 716ff.
3 Cheshire and Burn, *Modern Law of Real Property* (15th edn, 1994) 366 n 1; (16th edn, 2000) 391 n 9.
4 [1992] 1 AC 655.

dollars in the production of the film. But the sum of 11.75 million dollars, part of the total cost of 14 million, was raised by a 'loan' which the taxpayer was not personally liable to repay and which was only recoverable by the 'lender' out of the 75 per cent of the profits of the film which belonged to the 'lender'. The tax deductible cost to the taxpayer was only 3.25 million dollars and not the 14 million dollars claimed. The taxpayer was not guilty of fraud because all the relevant facts and documents were made available to the Revenue, but it was for the court to analyse and construe the facts and to disregard the language of the taxpayer which inaccurately described the legal nature and effect of those actions.

One of the earliest examples of the courts giving effect to the substance of a transaction rather than its form, is to be found in the law of mortgages. For over 500 years the traditional form of mortgage of land consisted of a covenant to repay a debt with interest on a fixed date and a conveyance or lease of the land. In the precedent in *Cheshire and Burn*, the borrower 'demises to the lender all the property specified in the schedule hereto TO HOLD the same unto the lender for the term of 3000 years . . . Provided that if the borrower shall on the first day of July next pay to the lender the principal sum with interest thereon from the date hereof . . . the term hereby created shall cease'.[5] In form therefore the mortgage was a lease subject to a condition subsequent whereby the lease was cancelled if the debt was repaid on the fixed date. But failure to pay would be fatal and the conventional picture of the borrower's innocent children being evicted, weeping, into the snow drifts was not far wrong, given the changes in climate. Thus in Littleton's *Tenures* of 1481 in s 332, after referring to the French and Latin derivation the author says 'it seemeth that the cause why it is called mortgage is, for that it is doubtful whether [the debtor] will pay[6] at the date limited such sum or not, and if he doth not pay, then the land which is put in pledge upon condition for the payment of money is taken from him for ever, and so dead to him'.[7] Equity, however, from an early stage took the view that in substance the lease was only security for repayment of the loan and that if the lender were repaid even after the fixed date, he would be bound to surrender the lease. In order to determine whether a conveyance is a redeemable mortgage 'equity has always looked to the real intention of the parties, to be gathered not only from the terms of the particular instrument but from all the circumstances of the transaction and has always admitted parol evidence . . .' per Lord Parker of Waddington in *G & C Kreglinger v New Patagonia Meat Co*.[8]

In transactions between lender and borrower, the lender and his draftsmen have the whip hand; and in the case of a mortgage the courts have come to the rescue of the borrower by giving effect to the substance of the transaction rather than its form. In transactions between landlord and tenant, the landlord and his draftsmen have the whip hand even in those few decades when the supply of land to let has exceeded the

5 Cheshire and Burn's *Modern Law of Real Property* (15th edn, 1994) 664–665; (16th edn, 2000) 724–725.
6 Original: 'si le feoffor voyt payer'.
7 Translation from Sir Edward Coke, *The First Part of the Institutes of the Laws of England, or, A Commentary on Littleton* (F Hargrave and C Butler (eds), 19th edn, 1832), vol II, sect 332, 205a.
8 [1914] AC 25 at 47.

demand. But the courts have been less ready to come to the rescue of tenants. Leases commonly contain covenants by the tenant to pay the rent, to keep the premises in repair, to insure, to carry out other works and to use the premises for specified purposes only. The severity of the obligations imposed on the tenant vary but not necessarily in relation to the length of the term granted or to any improvements by the tenant.

Leases contain an express provision entitling the landlord to forfeit the lease if the rent is not punctually paid or, as appears from the precedent in *Cheshire and Burn*: 'If there shall be any breach or non-observance of any of the covenants by the tenant hereinbefore contained, then and in any such case the lessor may, at any time thereafter, into and upon the demised premises, or any part thereof, in the name of the whole, re-enter, and the same have again, repossess and enjoy as in his former estate.'[9] In the same way as the lease in a mortgage is regarded by the courts, ignoring form in favour of substance, as security for the repayment of a loan, so one would have expected the courts, ignoring form in favour of substance, to have regarded the tenant's covenants as security for payment of the rent and the preservation of the value of the landlord's reversion. So long as any material breaches of covenant were remedied, relief from forfeiture could have been granted just as redemption could be granted notwithstanding breach of the covenants in a mortgage. So far as the payment of rent is concerned the courts indeed took that view and refused to decree forfeiture of a lease for non-payment of rent on the day fixed by the lease, provided the arrears were paid up as a condition of relief against forfeiture. No such relief was granted for breach of a covenant other than the covenant to pay rent. Thus at common law breach of a covenant to insure a building against fire entailed forfeiture at the behest of the landlord even if there was no fire before the insurance was renewed, the lease had another 100 years to run and the tenant had spent large sums in erecting the building. Equity did not intervene. At first there seems to have been some hesitation whether relief against forfeiture in the case of non payment of rent might not be extended to other cases of forfeiture for breach of covenants to repair, to insure and the like, where compensation could be made; but it was soon recognised that there would be great difficulty in estimating the proper amount of compensation: 'since the decision of Lord Eldon in *Hill v Barclay*,[10] it has always been held that equity would not relieve'.[11] The threadbare nature of the excuse proffered for failure to grant relief against forfeiture for breach of covenant is apparent by the fact that the Conveyancing Act 1881 empowered the court to grant relief against forfeiture on such terms as to costs, expenses, damages, compensation and the like as seem fit.[12] Parliament apparently did not accept that judicial 'great difficulty' was a bar to fairness.

The corrective intervention of Parliament was not, however, required when landlords sought to employ the form of a licence to disguise the substance of a tenancy and thereby to circumvent the Rent Restriction Acts. Those Acts, applying a policy dating in effect from the First World War, conferred on tenants of residential property

9 Cheshire and Burn's *Modern Law of Real Property* (15th ed, 1994) 434; (16th ed, 2000) 463.
10 (1810) 16 Ves 402.
11 *Barrow v Isaacs & Son* [1891] 1 QB 417 at 425 per Kay LJ.
12 Conveyancing Act 1881, s 14(2).

security of tenure and frozen rents. The inflexibility of the Rent Acts, while preserving the homes of most tenants indiscriminately, created hardship and unfairness for some landlords over the half century of the unamended operation of the Acts. The Acts were judicially held not to apply to a licence. Landlords therefore sought to grant licences in lieu of tenancies. The first step was to enshrine an agreement for occupation of residential property in a document which bore the name of a licence and referred to the owner as the licensor and the occupier as licensee. The second step was to omit from the document provisions usually found in a lease or tenancy agreement and to include those provisions which were consistent with a licence. The final step was to include in the document a declaration that the parties were creating a licence and did not intend to create a tenancy within the Rent Acts. Both parties acted in good faith; landlords thought they were creating licences, occupiers were prepared to accept that they were not to be entitled to the protection of the Rent Acts in order that they might achieve a place in residential accommodation. But it is not possible to contract out of the Rent Acts and it is not possible to confer on the occupier of property the rights and obligations of a tenant without creating a tenancy .The substance of a tenancy is the grant for a financial consideration of exclusive possession of property for a fixed term which may be expressed or implied. Substance must prevail over form.[13]

While the Courts have, sometimes with the urging of Parliament, protected borrowers and tenants by rejecting form in favour of substance, taxpayers have been protected against the revenue from time to time by a preference for form over substance. In *IRC v Duke of Westminster*,[14] the Duke could not deduct the wages of his gardener in calculating the liability of the Duke for income tax. The Duke therefore covenanted to pay an annuity of an amount equal to half the wages of the gardener for life and, without compelling the gardener, expressed the hope that while he was employed by the Duke he would be content with half wages. The amount of an annuity was deductible for tax purposes and the House of Lords by a majority which did not include Lord Atkin and taking a delight, not for the first or last time, in protecting the interests of the individual taxpayer against the interests of his fellow taxpayers represented by the Treasury, held that the amount of the annuity was deductible. Lord Tomlin said grandly but misleadingly that 'every man is entitled if he can to order his affairs so that the tax attaching under the appropriate Act is less than it otherwise would be'.[15] But to reduce tax the taxpayer must order his affairs in substance and not merely in form, as Lord Diplock pointed out in *IRC v Burmah*.[16] Before and after the grant of the annuity, the Duke paid the gardener exactly the same amount each week. Gardeners do not work for Dukes for half wages. The substance of the matter was that the gardener waived payment of the annuity while he worked. He would only feel morally entitled to the annuity when he retired and went on pension. Recently, in the *Westmoreland Case*,[17] a subsidiary was entitled to deduct for tax purposes the sum of

13 *Street v Mountford* [1985] AC 809, 825-827; *Radaich v Smith* (1959) 101 CLR 209, 222 per Windeyer J.

14 [1936] AC 1.

15 [1936] AC 1, 19.

16 [1982] STC 30 at 32.

17 *Macniven (HM Inspector of Taxes) v Westmoreland Investments Ltd* [2001] UKHL 6, [2003] 1 AC 311, [2001] 1 All ER 865.

40 million pounds arrears of interest owed to its sole shareholder and sole creditor provided the subsidiary paid the interest. The subsidiary being insolvent and without assets could not pay the interest debt owed to its parent. The parent company paid 40 million pounds to the subsidiary which forthwith paid 40 million pounds to the parent. The subsidiary claimed successfully in the House of Lords that it had paid the interest debt and incurred a new debt. This was form not substance. The substance of the matter was that nothing happened except that the interest debt had been relabelled; it had not been paid by the subsidiary as the Act required. It remains to be seen whether the legislature will intervene to ensure that substance prevails over form in future tax affairs.[18]

The importance of ensuring that substance prevails over form is not limited to the collection of revenue. It appears from recent revelations that some company accounts are based on the motto of my first sergeant major that 'If you stick to the book you cannot go wrong'. According to the book certain transactions may be omitted from a balance sheet, certain receipts may be counted as income, and certain expenses may be regarded as capital investment. The form of a company's accounts may comply with the rules. But a company which is solvent according to the accounts may nevertheless be insolvent if the true substance and effect of certain items in the accounts are considered. A leading member of the accountancy profession was recently reported as saying 'The regulation of accountancy and auditing practice in the United Kingdom is based on principles of truth and fairness. The American system is based on rules . . . the one major flaw in the U.S. system is its basis in rules. If instead you lay down guiding principles that ask an auditor "is this a fair and truthful representation of a company's financial position?", an Enron is much less likely to happen'.[19] Substance must prevail over form.

18 See further my article 'Tax and the Taxpayer' (2001) 117 LQR 575.

19 Per Peter Wyman, Deputy President of the Institute of Chartered Accountants as reported in *The Times* 9 May 2002.

CHAPTER 8

Tackling Avoidance

Ben McFarlane and Edwin Simpson

Edward Burn's interest and expertise span at least two areas where judges have had to confront the delicate legal art of 'avoidance': the attempt by a party or parties to arrange their affairs in such a way as to avoid the application of a particular legal characterisation. He has enlightened generations of students about fine conceptual distinctions, including that between a lease and a licence, whilst somehow finding time to sit as a General Commissioner for the purposes of the Taxes Acts. In its attempt to assess the legitimacy of the courts' response to avoidance, this paper concentrates in particular on those two fields of occupation agreements and taxes.

Our starting point is that the concept of a 'sham', the principal weapon which a court can use to thwart avoidance, is a function of, and not a restraint on, the power of parties to create legal rights according to their intentions. As a result, the sham concept is of limited effectiveness in dealing with attempts to avoid either lease or tax legislation. It is therefore no surprise that the House of Lords has been willing to employ further resources to tackle such avoidance, as will be seen from the discussion of *Antoniades v Villiers*[1] and *Furniss v Dawson*.[2] The crucial question is whether these ventures 'beyond sham' are consistent with accepted legal principle. A number of possible justifications have been offered, none of them quite satisfactory. The House of Lords' most recent and most plausible attempt, in *MacNiven v Westmoreland*,[3] emphasises the importance of statutory construction, and is to be welcomed as the first comprehensive explanation of the so-called *Ramsay* principle. The new analysis, put forward by Lord Hoffmann in particular, also has attractions in the lease context, where it may assist in understanding the controversial and difficult decision of the House of Lords in *Bruton v London and Quadrant Housing Trust*.[4] However, it will be seen that there are insuperable obstacles to using a statutory interpretation approach to explain cases such as *Antoniades v Villiers*. Further, as the Court of Appeal has already

1 [1990] 1 AC 417.
2 [1984] AC 474.
3 [2003] 1 AC 311, [2001] UKHL 6, [2001] 1 All ER 865.
4 [2000] 1 AC 406.

begun to indicate,[5] the statutory interpretation approach may be of limited use even in the very tax context in which it arose, so casting renewed doubt on the decision in *Furniss v Dawson* itself. It will therefore be concluded that the courts' current approach to avoidance suffers from a crisis of legitimacy, evident both in the field of leases and of taxes.

SETTING THE CONTEXT

Background: Leases

The decision in *Street v Mountford*[6] laid down a challenge to those wishing to let out residential property without creating a tenancy giving the occupier statutory rights under the Rent Acts. Previously, if an owner of property drafted an occupancy agreement in such a way as to show that the parties had no intention to create a lease then, even if that agreement conferred a right to exclusive possession, the occupier would merely be a licensee.[7] However, the decision of the House of Lords in *Street* re-asserted the orthodox position that a lease could be found even where the owner of the property had clearly demonstrated his intention not to create a lease. Rather, the key to whether an agreement creates a lease or a licence is whether it confers a right to exclusive possession of the property in question. As a result, unless one of a number of exceptions applies,[8] an occupier with a right to exclusive possession for a certain term will have a lease,[9] and therefore acquire whatever statutory advantages attach to being a tenant, even if the parties intended to create a licence. The facts of *Street* did not bring it within any of the exceptional circumstances described by Lord Templeman and, as it was 'conceded that Mrs Mountford is entitled to exclusive possession',[10] she therefore benefited from the statutory security of tenure and rent protection which Mr Street had so carefully sought to deny her.

The emphasis on the grant of a legal right to exclusive possession in *Street*[11] therefore closed one door previously open to owners wishing to avoid a lease. Necessarily, of course, it opened another as an owner can ensure that an occupier is a mere licensee by

5 *Barclays Mercantile Business Finance v Mawson (Inspector of Taxes)* [2002] EWCA Civ 1853, [2003] STC 66 esp per Peter Gibson LJ at para 44 and Carnwath LJ at paras 69–74.

6 [1985] AC 809.

7 See e g *Errington v Errington and Woods* [1952] 1 KB 290, esp per Denning LJ at 298: 'although a person who is let into exclusive possession is prima facie to be considered a tenant, nevertheless he will not be held to be so if the circumstances negative any intention to create a tenancy'; *Cobb v Lane* [1952] 1 All ER 1199; *Murray Bull & Co Ltd v Murray* [1953] 1 QB 211, [1952] 2 All ER 1079; *Marchant v Charters* [1977] 1 WLR 1181.

8 For discussion of these exceptions see Lord Templeman in *Street* [1985] AC 809 at 818 and 826–827. The extent to which they are merely examples of the occupier failing to show a legal right to exclusive possession is considered by Millett LJ in *Bruton v London and Quadrant Housing Trust* [1998] QB 834 at 843.

9 In *Street v Mountford* itself, Lord Templeman affirms the submission of counsel that 'the grant of exclusive possession for a term at a rent' creates a tenancy: [1985] AC 809 at 816. Whilst the reference to rent is consistent with the facts of *Street*, it should not be taken to mean that a lease cannot exist without the payment of rent: see *Ashburn Anstalt v Arnold* [1989] Ch 1 at 9–10 and Law of Property Act 1925, s 205(1)(xxvii).

10 [1985] AC 809 at 818.

11 See also Millett LJ in *Bruton v London and Quadrant Housing Trust* [1998] QB 834 at 843.

taking care not to grant a right to exclusive possession. However, Lord Templeman's judgment in *Street* indicated two obstacles. First, if an owner reserves *limited* rights to enter the property then this 'only serves to emphasise the fact that the grantee is entitled to exclusive possession'.[12] After all, why would such specific reservations be necessary if the owner retained control of the use of the property? The purpose of the exclusive possession test seems to be to identify the party who has the open-ended rights over the property which entitle him to be seen as the owner of the property for the time being.[13] To create a licence, then, it is necessary to show that the occupier 'cannot call the place his own';[14] for example by ensuring that the occupier only has the right to use the land for limited purposes, or by reserving a right of *unrestricted* access to the land.[15] Secondly, and much more importantly, Lord Templeman stressed that: 'Although the Rent Acts must not be allowed to alter or influence the construction of an agreement, the court should, in my opinion be astute to detect and frustrate sham devices and artificial transactions whose only object is to disguise the grant of a tenancy and to evade the Rent Acts'.[16] The question of what counts as a 'sham' device will be considered after the background in the tax context has been briefly described.

Background: Taxes

A party or parties wishing to organise their affairs to lessen the incidence of taxation can draw encouragement from the straightforward approach suggested by Lord Tomlin in the House of Lords in *IRC v Duke of Westminster*:

> [e]very man is entitled to arrange his affairs so that the tax attaching under the appropriate Acts is less than it otherwise would be. If he succeeds in ordering them so as to secure that result then, however unappreciative the Commissioners of Inland Revenue or his fellow taxpayers may be of his ingenuity, he cannot be compelled to pay an increased tax.[17]

Of course, such a statement leaves open precisely how it is that one determines whether a taxpayer has succeeded in so ordering his affairs,[18] but the *Westminster* case makes clear that tax is to be levied by reference to a legal analysis of the taxpayer's affairs, and not according to some underlying factual substance. Just as *Street v Mountford* emphasises that it is the legal rights of the parties to an occupation agreement that matter when it comes to the application of the Rent Acts, liability for tax is equally determined by the legal effects of a taxpayer's action. Thus, in the *Westminster* case, the Duke covenanted by deed to pay his gardener weekly sums for a

12 [1985] AC 809 at 818.
13 See [1985] AC 809 at 816 and Harris, *Property and Justice* (1996) 72–73.
14 For the description of a tenant as someone who can 'exercise the rights of an owner of land, which is in a real sense his land albeit temporarily and subject to certain restrictions' and hence call the land 'his own', see [1985] AC 809 at 816 and 818.
15 See e g *Westminster City Council v Clarke* [1992] 2 AC 288, [1992] 1 All ER 695.
16 [1985] AC 809 at 825.
17 [1936] AC 1 at 19–20.
18 This will be examined in the next section.

period of seven years or for the joint lives of the parties. The deed stated that the payments would be made without prejudice to any remuneration for services to which the 'annuitant' might also be entitled. In practice, however, the gardener received only such sums of money as, together with the sum payable under the deed, amounted to the wage he had previously earned. The Revenue contended that the payments remained remuneration for services, and so could not be deducted from the Duke's total income in determining his liability for surtax. The Duke maintained that those made pursuant to the deed were annual payments out of income,[19] and so could properly be deducted. The House of Lords decided 4–1 in favour of the Duke. The Duke was obligated to pay the annuity and to pay wages. The fact that the gardener may not have pursued his additional contractual right could not change the proper legal characterisation of the payments made pursuant to the deed. Lord Tomlin expressed the majority view as follows:

> There may, of course, be cases where documents are not bona fide nor intended to be acted upon, but are only used as a cloak to conceal a different transaction. No such case is made or even suggested here. The deeds of covenant are admittedly bona fide and have been given their proper legal operation. They cannot be ignored or treated as operating in some different way because as a result less duty is payable than would have been the case if some other arrangement (called for the purpose of the appellants' argument 'the substance') had been made.[20]

Such preference for a fully legal characterisation of the facts has in the past been accompanied by a cautious judicial approach to the construction of fiscal legislation. Article 4 of the Bill of Rights 1688[21] makes clear that taxation is a matter for Parliament,[22] rather than anybody else, and judges are consequently wary of appearing to impose a tax themselves when applying statutory words. Numerous judicial statements to this effect can be cited, most notably a passage in the judgment of Rowlatt J in *Cape Brandy Syndicate v IRC*. The role of the judge, when applying a tax statute, is 'to look merely at what is clearly said. There is no room for any intendment. There is no equity about a tax. There is no presumption as to a tax. Nothing is to be read in, nothing is to be implied. One can only look fairly at the language used'.[23]

19 Within section 27 and Schedule D, Case III, Rule 1 of the Income Tax Act 1918; such payments would no longer be effective for higher rates of tax: Income and Corporation Taxes Act 1988, s 683; nor, for new covenants, for basic rate tax: Finance Act 1988, s 36 introducing Income and Corporation Taxes Act 1988, s 347A.

20 [1936] AC 1 at 21.

21 1 Will and Mar Sess 2 c 2 Article 4 is in the following terms: 'That levying Money for or to the Use of the Crowne by pretence of Prerogative without Grant of Parlyament for longer time or in other manner than the same is or shall be granted is Illegall'. As to the manner in which the Bill of Rights was enacted, and for an explanation of the confusion as to its appropriate dating, see *Halsbury's Laws* (4th edn, reissue), vol 8(2), para 35, n 3.

22 Of course, this needs to be expressed carefully post-devolution, as the Westminster Parliament has given the Scottish Parliament power to increase or reduce the basic rate of income tax paid by Scottish taxpayers on their earned income by up to 3 pence in the pound: see Scotland Act 1998, Part IV.

23 [1921] 1 KB 64 at 71.

Therefore, prior to the development of the so-called '*Ramsay* principle' in *Furniss v Dawson*,[24] two crucial principles underpinned the application of taxing statutes to factual situations. First, Parliament needs to speak particularly clearly if it wishes to exact a tax; and secondly, the taxpayer is entitled to have the legal structure of his transactions respected rather than any underlying economic substance. That having been said, and as already suggested in the passage cited from Lord Tomlin, that would all change if the documentation were 'used as a cloak to conceal a different transaction'.

THE CONCEPT OF A SHAM

Lord Tomlin's reference in *IRC v Duke of Westminster* to the need to see through documents which 'conceal a different transaction' and Lord Templeman's emphasis in *Street v Mountford* of the need to 'frustrate sham devices' advert to the courts' well-established general jurisdiction to refuse to give effect to any act that is a sham. The most cited definition of that concept is Diplock LJ's well-worn dictum in *Snook v London and West Ridings Investments Ltd*:

> it means acts done or documents executed by the parties to the 'sham' which are intended by them to give to third parties or to the court the appearance of creating between the parties legal rights and obligations different from the actual legal rights and obligations (if any) which the parties intended to create . . . for acts or documents to be a 'sham', with whatever legal consequences follow from this, all the parties thereto must have a common intention that the acts or documents are not to create the legal rights and obligations which they give the appearance of creating. No unexpressed intentions of a 'shammer' affect the rights of a party whom he deceived.[25]

To understand the sham concept, it is vital to see that it is merely part of a court's general inquiry into the correct legal characterisation of an act. The first step in any such inquiry is to consider the factual indicators of the particular legal characterisation to be applied. If those indicators include the intention of a party or parties, then the sham concept may come into play as part of the search for that intention. That said, the so-called sham concept merely reflects the obvious point that only genuine manifestations of intention can be taken into account when considering whether the necessary factual indicators are present. The truth is that there is no independent set of criteria justifying the finding of a sham: the task of a court is simply to ascertain the genuine intentions of the party or parties in circumstances where those intentions are relevant; and a statement that an act is a sham is simply a consequence of ascertaining

24 [1984] AC 474.

25 [1967] 2 QB 786 at 802. The reference to documents cannot mean that either all of a document is sham, or none of it: see *Hitch v Stone* [2001] EWCA Civ 63, [2001] STC 214. Rather, each apparent creation of rights within a document must be seen as a relevant 'act', and will only be valid if accompanied by the necessary intention that those rights should genuinely be created.

that it does not reflect such genuine intention.[26] Certainly, it should not be suggested that there is a monolithic sham test capable of applying whenever a court is concerned with the intentions of a party or parties whose acts are being legally construed. Lord Justice Diplock's formula in *Snook* cannot therefore be taken as a universal set of criteria for a sham, as can be seen from an examination of *Midland Bank plc v Wyatt*.[27]

In that case, Mr Wyatt and his wife, joint beneficial owners of the family home, signed a trust deed which purported to share his equitable interest in the home between his wife and two daughters. Mr Wyatt then claimed this deed constituted a declaration of trust in order to resist the bank's claim to make absolute a charging order obtained in respect of his interest in the property. To show that this legal characterisation could apply, Mr Wyatt had to show that he had satisfied the relevant requirements for a declaration of trust, which includes proof that the intended settlor intends to divest himself of his beneficial interest in the property and to transfer it to the new beneficiaries, in this case his wife and daughters. As the legal characterisation which Mr Wyatt wished the court to adopt thus depended on a finding as to his intention, the court had to examine his actions for evidence of that intention. Of course, Mr Wyatt's action in signing the declaration of trust would generally suffice, but, despite this, the judge held that 'I do not believe Mr Wyatt had any intention when he executed the trust deed of endowing his children with the interest in [the family home], which at that time was his only real asset'. Instead, the behaviour of Mr Wyatt after signing the deed showed that 'the trust deed was executed by him, not to be acted upon but to be put in the safe for a rainy day'.[28] Hence, the legal result was that Mr Wyatt had retained his interest in the home as he had not proved an intention to transfer a beneficial interest; the trust deed failed to record Mr Wyatt's true intention, and, if one thinks that it is helpful to use the term, it is therefore possible to call that document a 'sham'. However, there was no suggestion that *Mrs* Wyatt had any intention to deceive the bank when signing the supposed trust deed. Rather, it was found that 'at the time of execution of the declaration of trust Mrs Wyatt was not aware of its import or effect. She said in evidence at that time she would have signed whatever was put in front of her without reading it'.[29] Hence the apparent requirement in *Snook,* that all the parties to a sham document must have a common intention that the document is not to represent their true intentions, was not satisfied.

The apparent inconsistency between the result in *Wyatt* and the test for a sham given in *Snook* demonstrates that the sham concept does not operate in the same way regardless of context. The concept is used when a question of legal characterisation depends on the intention of a party or parties. As the relevant legal characterisation varies, so does the specific intention which the court looks for. In *Wyatt*, the issue was whether a trust had been declared and this turned solely on the intention of the

26 This explains Diplock LJ's apparent reluctance to suggest that a sham is an independent legal concept: 'it is, I think, necessary to consider what, if any, legal concept is involved in the use of this popular and pejorative word' [1967] 2 QB 786 at 802. It may be thought ironic that a definition so reluctantly given has fostered the belief that there is such a concept.

27 [1995] 1 FLR 697.

28 [1995] 1 FLR 697 at 707 (D E M Young QC).

29 [1995] 1 FLR 697 at 706.

purported settlor, Mr Wyatt.[30] However, where, as in *Snook*, the legal characterisation depends upon rights created by agreement, the court cannot look simply to the intention of one party. This point was made clear in *Yorkshire Railway Wagon Co v Maclure*.[31] A railway company wished to raise money, but did not have the legal power to borrow. Instead, it sold part of its stock to a wagon company, whilst making a contract to hire the stock back from the wagon company and eventually to repurchase it. When sued for payment of the hire charges, the railway company argued that the purported sale and lease-back arrangement was in fact an *ultra vires* attempt to borrow, and therefore void. It seems that the railway company had envisaged a loan when initially approaching the wagon company, who were happy to provide money on that basis. When lawyers for the railway company discovered that such a transaction would be *ultra vires*, they insisted on drawing up documents compatible only with a sale and lease-back. This was of little concern to the wagon company; it seems it did not care what legal form the transaction took, provided it had the effect in practice of an advance of money secured on the stock. However, as Jessel MR put it:

> But even if the wagon company understood it as a loan, in order to set aside the deed, that is to treat it as a nullity, you must show that the railway company were parties to the understanding. You cannot have a bargain on one side, and if the railway company only sealed this document because it carried out their intention, you cannot say that is not the real contract between the parties.[32]

The crucial phrase here is 'You cannot have a bargain on one side', which is matched by Diplock LJ's statement that 'No unexpressed intentions of a "shammer" affect the rights of a party whom he deceived'. In both *Yorkshire Railway* and *Snook*, the arrangement between the parties was, at face value, a sale and hire-purchase transaction rather than a loan. The validity of this legal characterisation does not depend solely on the intention of one of the parties to the transaction; rather, as in any situation where the legal rights of the parties depend on agreement, the intention of both parties must be considered. Moreover, the relevant intention in these situations is judged according to normal contractual principles of objectivity, as can be seen from *Snook*. The plaintiff had taken part in what was, at face value, a hire purchase arrangement under which title in a car he possessed passed to the defendants. He later contended that the transaction was in fact an unregistered loan on the security of the car and hence void under the Bills of Sale Act. However, where rights arise through agreement, intention is judged objectively and as it was reasonable for the defendant to believe that the plaintiff intended to enter a hire purchase agreement, the transaction could not be characterised as a loan.

The apparent stipulation in *Snook* that, before it can be disregarded as a sham, all parties to an act or document must have the intention that it is not to create the legal rights it appears to should not be understood as something magical about the idea of a sham. Rather, the decision in *Snook* turns on the (clearly correct) assumption it makes

30 *Lewin on Trusts* (17th edn, 2000) 30–31, 70–71.
31 (1882) 21 Ch D 309.
32 (1882) 21 Ch D 309 at 314.

as to how rights arising by agreement are created. The underlying test in such situations is that A can acquire a right against B provided A has an actual, reasonable belief that B intended to create that right.[33] Where the parties have signed a document which purports to record the legal rights the parties intend to create, there is naturally a strong presumption that each party has an actual, reasonable belief that the other genuinely intends to create those rights.[34] Collusion between the parties prior to signing the document, contemplated by Diplock LJ's formula, is capable of rebutting such a presumption by ensuring that neither party can reasonably believe the document represents the other's true intention.[35] However, it is not correct to state, as per Arden LJ in *Bankway Properties v Pensfold-Dunsford*,[36] that 'a test of common subjective intention applies' before an apparent agreement can be seen as a sham. On this view, the document will only be ineffective if neither party intends that the document should be a true statement of their legal rights, either because they have entered a separate agreement on different terms to that of the document,[37] or because they have not entered an agreement at all.[38] However, the document can also be ineffective if only one party (A) intends it not to create legal rights, provided that this intention is sufficiently clear to the other party (B). For it will then be impossible for B to claim that he reasonably believed the terms of the document to represent the true intention of A. Of course, in the absence of collusion between A and B, it will in practice be difficult to show that it was not reasonable for B to believe that the document did represent A's true intentions. However, Lord Oliver's judgment in *Antoniades v Villiers*[39] does suggest that there may be cases in which the surrounding factual circumstances alone make it unreasonable for B to believe that A intends to be bound by a term contained in a document he has signed. This possibility has had little role to play in the tax context (where there is unlikely to be one of the parties to a

33 See Treitel, *The Law of Contract* (10th edn, 1999) 1, 8 and 158–159. However, no right will be created if B has an actual and equally reasonable belief that A intends to create an incompatible right: see *Falck v Williams* [1900] AC 176. See also the discussion in *Great Peace Shipping Ltd v Tsavliris Salvage (International) Ltd* [2002] EWCA Civ 1407, [2002] 4 All ER 689, 696 at para 28 of *Raffles v Wichelhaus* (1864) 2 H & C 906.

34 *National Westminster Bank v Jones* [2001] 1 BCLC 98.

35 See e g *Ferris v Weaven* [1952] 2 All ER 233. The owner of a house wished to remove his wife from the property, but could not do so himself due to her matrimonial occupation rights. He therefore hatched a plan with his brother-in-law to transfer the house to him for £30 so that the brother-in-law could evict the wife: 'the object of both the husband and the purchaser was to obtain possession of the house for the husband so that he could dispose of it'. So, although a conveyance was executed, title remained in the husband as the purchaser's participation in the plot meant that it was not reasonable for him to believe that the husband intended to transfer ownership of the property. See also *Bhopal v Whalia* (1999) 32 HLR 302.

36 [2001] EWCA Civ 528, [2001] 1 WLR 1369 at 1380. See too Arden LJ's similar analysis of sham transactions in *Hitch v Stone* [2001] EWCA Civ 63, [2001] STC 214.

37 As in *Bhopal v Wahlia* (1999) 32 HLR 302: a landlord wished to exaggerate his income in order to mislead a bank, and prevailed on the tenant to sign a document stating that the rent was set at £450 a month. However, the parties had previously agreed that the actual sum payable per month was to be £300 and neither party intended the new document to confer a new legal right on the landlord.

38 As in *Ferris v Weaven* [1952] 2 All ER 233, where there was no genuine intention to create any new legal rights: the husband was to remain owner of the property.

39 [1990] 1 AC 417 at 469. See discussion below.

transaction, as opposed to the Revenue, arguing for a sham)[40] but provides an important means by which an occupier can show that he has a legal right to exclusive possession notwithstanding a written term purporting to allow the owner of property the right to put others into occupation. In the very rare cases where surrounding circumstances make it impossible for B reasonably to believe that A intends to be bound by a term in a written agreement, then that term can be ineffective even if B honestly believes that A has assented to it. Hence it is possible for that term to be described as a sham without attributing any fraudulent or dishonest intention to either of the parties. This is an inevitable consequence of seeing the concept of a sham not as independent doctrine but rather as part of establishing the genuine intentions of the parties according to recognised tests about how legal rights are created. Of course, one may prefer to limit the use of the word 'sham' to situations where the parties have a common subjective intention that an act is not to create the legal rights it purports to; the link between sham and fraud would be maintained, but at the cost of failing to capture all the situations in which an act does not create the legal rights it purports to create.

APPLYING THE SHAM CONCEPT

Applying the sham concept to occupation agreements

Following *Street v Mountford*, the legal characterisation that an occupier has a lease can only be applied if the occupier has been granted a legal right to exclusive possession of land. Wherever the occupier's rights derive from an agreement, this will in turn depend on whether the occupier has an actual, reasonable belief that the owner intends to confer a right to exclusive possession. If the occupier has signed a document which does not purport to confer such a right, then he will have to bring forward evidence to prove that it was nonetheless reasonable for him to believe that the owner intended to grant exclusive possession. The most obvious means of doing so is to argue that the parties reached an understanding outside that recorded in the document. In *Sturolson & Co v Weniz*,[41] for example, the occupiers signed documents purporting to give them the 'right to share the premises . . . with such other person(s) as may be nominated by or approved by the Owner from time to time'. It was argued that the occupiers had nonetheless been given a joint right to exclusive possession, as they had been assured by the landlord's agent, in conversations preceding the signing of the agreement, that no one else would be put into the property. Relying on *Snook*, the Court of Appeal dismissed this argument that the sharing clause was a sham. First, there was no evidence that the owner did not intend the clause to be effective; indeed, as the occupiers knew that the owner only wished to enter an agreement which would not give them protection under the Rent Acts, they must have 'known that it was the

40 As in the *Westminster* case, where the court did not have the advantage of the gardener's side of the story. Equally, the possibility did not need to be considered by Arden LJ in *Hitch v Stone* [2001] EWCA Civ 63, [2001] STC 214 where, as in most of the tax cases, the interests of the participants in the transactions were united so far as the avoidance of tax was concerned.

41 (1984) 272 Estates Gazette 326; (1984) 17 HLR 140. The quotations in the text are taken from the judgment of Everleigh LJ: (1984) 17 HLR 140 at 144–145.

landlord's intention that the legal rights between the parties would be those that resulted from the agreement which was signed'. Indeed, the fact that the occupiers asked questions about the possible operation of the sharing clause was further proof that they 'knew that this document was governing their legal relationship'. Crucially, the agent's assurances in response to these questions were viewed by the court as indicating only that the landlord would take a 'benevolent' approach to enforcing its rights under the sharing clause. Such assurances could not make it reasonable for the occupiers to believe that the landlord intended to forego his rights under the document by granting them exclusive possession. An indication by the landlord that it might not enforce the sharing clause is very different to an indication that it does not intend that clause to create a right allowing it to insert others into the property should it so choose.

As *Sturolson* shows, an occupier will have difficulties in showing that a clause is a sham even if there is evidence of discussions with the landlord or his agent as to the likely effect of that clause. The occupier's problems are still more acute if no such negotiations have taken place. In such a case, the occupier will have to rely solely on the surrounding factual circumstances to show that it is reasonable for him to believe that, nothwithstanding the terms of the written document, the owner of the property intends to grant exclusive possession. In *Markou v da Silvaesa*,[42] the occupation agreement denied the occupiers a right to use the property between 10.30 a m and noon; it required the owner to provide attendance and services which would involve unrestricted access to the property; and it gave the owner the power to enter the property to remove 'such articles of furniture as he may see fit'. The Court of Appeal allowed an appeal against a possession order granted to the owner in summary proceedings, as it was at least arguable that these terms of the agreement were a sham. The only real evidence put forward by the occupiers was that the terms had not been enforced by the owner, but, as Ralph Gibson LJ emphasised, this could not suffice to render such terms ineffective. However, the Court of Appeal accepted the argument that 'apart from any evidence which the [occupiers] could give to show that the agreement was sham, the terms of the written agreement themselves provide evidence that it was 'a sham' in that the parties cannot be supposed to have intended the agreement to operate between the parties'. Hence, there may be circumstances where a clause is in itself so 'astonishingly extreme' that, even without bringing evidence of a separate agreement outside the document, it is reasonable for an occupier to believe that it cannot be 'a true statement of the nature of the possession intended to be enjoyed'.

It is interesting to compare the reasoning in *Markou* with the dissenting speech of Lord Atkin in *Westminster*.[43] In that case, there was no direct evidence that the Duke intended the payments to take the place of the wages due to his gardener. However, Lord Atkin thought it highly improbable that the Duke would bind himself to provide both the annuity and the wages without receiving any additional services; indeed, he thought there was an 'urgent necessity . . . to relieve the Duke from the obligations

42 [1986] 1 EGLR 80, (1986) 18 HLR 265. The Court of Appeal decision is reported at *Crancour Ltd v da Silvaesa*. The quotations in the text are taken from the judgment of Ralph Gibson LJ: (1986) 18 HLR 265 at 274–276.

43 [1936] AC 1.

which would exist if the deed stood alone'.[44] It would not be enough for the Duke to remain bound to pay the wages, trusting that the servant would not enforce this right, as 'the arrears would be a debt due to the servant and could be attached by any creditor of the servant, and would on death be assets of his which his personal representative would be bound to recover'.[45] The sheer improbability of the Duke's claim that he remained bound to pay both wages and annuity payments led to Lord Atkin's conclusion that a letter written to the servant before the execution of the deed of annuity must have concluded a contract preventing the servant from claiming any sum for his services apart from the annuity payments. As a result, on Lord Atkin's dissenting view of the facts, the provision in the deed that the annuity payments were without prejudice to the servant's right to receive previously agreed wages could be seen as a sham.

Nonetheless, it should be stressed that in a case such as *Markou* the occupier is asking the court to find that he has acquired a right to exclusive possession in the face of a written agreement denying such a right and in the absence of any representations by the owner which may lead the occupier reasonably to believe that the written agreement is not conclusive as to his rights. Moreover, whilst there are good reasons for which the Duke might have wished to protect himself from any claim to previously agreed wages, the owner in a case such as *Markou* has every reason to intend that the terms denying exclusive possession are effective.

As well as the possibility of the occupier arguing that it was reasonable for him to believe that the owner did not intend to be bound by written terms denying exclusive possession, it might instead be claimed that those terms are ineffective because the owner could not reasonably have believed that the occupier intended to be bound by them: after all, why would anyone agree to pay money to live in a property which they do not have a right to occupy between 10.30 am and noon? However, two points are crucial. First, if the occupier believes that the owner will be 'benevolent' and is unlikely in practice to enforce such a clause, then it may be reasonable for the owner to believe that the occupier has accepted that clause. Secondly, and most importantly, it is abundantly clear in practice that many occupiers of property have a very weak bargaining position when negotiating occupation agreements: indeed the very term 'negotiation' will be inappropriate in the large number of cases where an occupier, urgently seeking accommodation, will agree to whatever terms are offered.[46] The vulnerabilities of the occupier's position may make it more likely that the occupier can take advantage of legislation designed to relieve from unfair bargains, such as the Unfair Terms in Consumer Contract Regulations 1999.[47] Yet those same vulnerabilities make it far harder for an occupier to show that particular terms are shams, as they

44 [1936] AC 1, 13.

45 [1936] AC 1, 10; and, at 11: 'The embarrassments, however, are not all on the Duke's side . . . the servant . . . would incur [additional] liability to income tax; for salary or wages that he is entitled to, but voluntarily forgoes, must be included in his total income'.

46 See the observation of Lord Templeman in *Antoniades v Villiers* [1990] 1 AC 417 at 458: 'in a state of housing shortage a person seeking residential accommodation may agree to anything to obtain shelter'.

47 Unlike their 1994 counterpart, it is clear that the 1999 Regulations can apply to land transactions. See [2002] Conv 99.

make the owner's belief that an occupier has accepted the terms all the more reasonable. Indeed, in the *Westminster* case, this point may equally tell against Lord Atkin's dissenting view of the facts. In the midst of a period of profound economic hardship, the Duke may have genuinely intended to leave himself open to the risk that the gardener might pursue his wages as well as the annuity, confident that in practice he would not do so for fear of losing his job. In the absence of regulatory regimes governing such employment, the Duke could afford to rely on the gardener's 'benevolence' about enforcing his rights.

It is therefore clear that it will be difficult for an occupier to show that a term purporting to deny exclusive possession is a sham in the conventional sense. The decision of the Court of Appeal in *Antoniades v Villiers*[48] is a demonstration of this. In separate but identical agreements with the two occupiers, the owner reserved the right to put others into occupation of the property, a flat consisting of four rooms. The occupiers' contention that this clause was a sham and that they nonetheless enjoyed a joint right of exclusive possession was rejected by the Court of Appeal. As Bingham LJ put it, 'The issue was whether, the written agreements apart, the landlord agreed to give the occupants, jointly or severally, exclusive possession of the flat or any part of it'.[49] There was no evidence to suggest that an agreement had been reached independently of the written document. Further, it could not be said that the very terms of the sharing clause made it reasonable for the occupiers to believe that the owner did not intend that clause to create a legal right. First, there was enough room in the flat for a further occupier; indeed, the occupiers had put up a guest in the flat for over a month. Secondly, the owner was 'determined' that the occupiers should not have a right to exclusive possession, precisely because he wanted to avoid the operation of the Rent Acts. This determination was clear to the occupiers from the terms of the agreements which 'stipulate[d] with reiterated emphasis that the occupants shall not have exclusive possession'.[50] When the case went to the House of Lords, it seems that only Lord Oliver (and perhaps Lord Jauncey) were able to disagree with this analysis of the facts and therefore find that the sharing clause was a sham in the orthodox sense. Instead, the remainder of their Lordships were obliged to venture beyond the traditional understanding of the sham doctrine in order to justify their finding that exclusive possession had been granted. This development, and the conceptual difficulties it creates, will be considered further after a consideration of the application of the sham concept in the tax context.

Applying the sham concept to disapply a favourable tax consequence

The Revenue has generally been even less successful than have occupiers when seeking to argue that transactions designed to secure a tax advantage are shams. To some extent this may be because the Revenue is less deserving of the court's sympathy; and there is certainly a reluctance amongst the fact-finding Commission-

48 [1990] 1 AC 417.
49 [1990] 1 AC 417 at 446.
50 [1990] 1 AC 417 at 446.

ers[51] to reach a conclusion which, in the fiscal context, may be viewed as coming near to a finding of fraud.[52] But there is a more significant reason. Although tax avoidance schemes can involve extremely complex legal structures, and although the taxpayer may candidly admit that the sole underlying purpose is to secure a tax advantage, there is no incentive at all for a taxpayer not actually to intend the scheme to create the legal rights it purports to create. It is true that there have been doubts expressed in certain cases as to whether any 'real' money was intended to be passed around the complicated routes involved.[53] But in the vast majority of cases the taxpayer will have taken great pains to ensure that the legal structures sought are indeed created, so as to attract the desired fiscal analysis.[54] Where the test for the existence of a particular legal entity sought by a taxpayer turns upon one or more parties' intentions, then clearly only real intentions will count; but there is unlikely in most cases to have been anything so obvious as a conventional sham.[55]

Whilst the courts have not often relied upon the sham concept to tackle tax avoidance schemes, they have carefully honed their powers of statutory construction and of transaction characterisation in order to do so. Although a taxpayer may have avoided the trap of a sham, it still remains to determine whether he has succeeded, in Lord Tomlin's terms, in arranging his affairs 'so that the tax attaching under the appropriate Acts is less than it otherwise would be'. The various stages involved in determining that success are as follows.

To begin with, and just as in the case of the distinction between a lease and a licence,[56] the label attached to a transaction by the parties will not be decisive of the application

51 Appeal from the Commissioners on a question of fact lies only on *Edwards (Inspector of Taxes) v Bairstow* [1956] AC 14 principles; although, of course, if the Commissioners have applied the wrong legal test of what amounts to a sham, appeal will lie for error of law.

52 Although see the discussion above at the end of the last section.

53 E g *W T Ramsay v IRC* [1982] AC 300 at 322–323 per Lord Wilberforce: 'In some cases one may doubt whether, in any real sense, any money existed at all. It seems very doubtful whether any real money was involved in *Rawling*: but facts as to this matter are for the commissioners to find. I will assume that in some sense money did pass as expressed in respect of each transaction in each of the instant cases'. And *Ensign Tankers Ltd v Stokes* [1992] 1 AC 655, per Lord Goff at 682: 'I am prepared (with some hesitation) to accept that the composite transaction which I have just described should not be called a sham, in the narrow sense in which that word has been used in this context'.

54 Thus Lord Steyn, when recognising that the transactions in *IRC v McGuckian* [1997] 1 WLR 991 at 1001G–H were clearly not shams, stated: '[o]n the contrary, tax avoidance was the spur to executing genuine documents and entering into genuine arrangements'.

55 There are occasional examples, as in *Hitch v Stone* [2001] EWCA Civ 63, [2001] STC 214 where the Court of Appeal considered a capital gains tax scheme adopted in connection with the disposal of a farm. The Commissioners' determination that elements in the documentation recording the transactions between the Hitch family and a tax adviser were sham was upheld on *Edwards v Bairstow* principles. That some of the legal rights purportedly created by the documentation formed part of the real arrangements did not prevent the finding that other elements were shams. For criticism of Arden LJ's 'test of common subjective intention', see above.

56 See e g *Facchini v Bryson* [1952] 1 TLR 1386, esp per Denning LJ at 1389–1390; *Addiscombe Garden Estates Ltd v Crabbe* [1958] 1 QB 513, esp per Jenkins LJ at 522; *Welsh Development Agency v Export Finance Co Ltd* [1992] BCLC 148 at 160 per Dillon LJ: '[b]ut the question can also arise where, without any question of sham, there is some objective criterion in law, by which the court can test whether the agreement the parties have made does or does not fall into the legal category into which the parties have sought to place their agreement'.

of the legislation to the facts.[57] Thus a court may hold that a trade is carried on by a partnership even though a document states that there is none;[58] and a description of a series of payments as an annuity or a rent-charge does not determine its character.[59] It is the true legal nature of a transaction which falls to be taxed, and that true legal nature is determined by the courts and not the parties.

Next, the courts are entitled to look at all the circumstances of a case in determining its legal nature, and will not be blinded by the parties' own written account, even if contained in a deed. Thus, in *IRC v Mallaby-Deeley*,[60] the taxpayer covenanted under seal to pay for the completion of a book 'The Complete Peerage' in instalments. Four years later, the taxpayer enacted a further deed varying the payments to make them appear to have been paid out of annual income, and so capable of being deducted. The further deed did not recite the earlier situation, but that did not stop the court from looking behind it to discover its true legal effect. As Sir Wilfrid Greene MR explained, that was wholly consistent with *Westminster*:

> . . . the method of approach to this problem which appears to me to be the correct one does not fall within any discredited portion of the old doctrine [i.e. a substance doctrine], but falls within its permissible limits because it does not involve putting upon a transaction between parties a character in law it does not possess. It involves discovering what is the character in law of the transaction which was entered into.[61]

Equally, the courts have asserted their right, rather than any right of the parties, to identify the stages within a composite transaction which are relevant for particular tax purposes. Thus, in Lord Wilberforce's words in *WT Ramsay v IRC*:

> If it can be seen that a document or transaction was intended to have effect as part of a nexus or series of transactions, or as an ingredient of a wider transaction intended as a whole, there is nothing in the doctrine to prevent it being so regarded: to do so is not to prefer form to substance, or substance to form. It is the task of the court to ascertain the legal nature of any transaction to which it is sought to attach a tax or a tax consequence and if that emerges from a series or combination of transactions, intended to operate as such, it is that series or combination which may be regarded.[62]

A court need not therefore apply the legislation to apparently discrete 'steps' in a transaction formulated by the taxpayer, if the relevant legal concept for tax purposes

57 *Secretary of State in Council of India v Scoble* [1903] AC 299. See also, outside the context of tax or occupation agreements: *Bridge v Campbell Discount Co Ltd* [1962] AC 600, [1962] 1 All ER 385 (definition of penalty clause) and *Schuler AG v Wickman Ltd* [1974] AC 235, [1973] 2 All ER 39 (definition of contractual condition).

58 *Fenston v Johnstone* (1940) 23 TC 29.

59 *IRC v Land Securities Investment Trust* [1969] 2 All ER 430, [1969] 1 WLR 604.

60 [1938] 4 All ER 818; see also *IRC v Wesleyan and Assurance Society* [1946] 2 All ER 749.

61 [1938] 4 All ER 818 at 824.

62 [1982] AC 300 at 323–324. In fact two conjoined appeals heard and decided together: *W T Ramsay v IRC* and *Eilbeck v Rawlings*.

can only be recognised by taking account of a number of the steps together. Thus, in *Ramsay*, in the context of capital gains tax, the taxpayer argued that at one stage in a series of transactions a step gave rise to an apparent gain, and that a later step gave rise to an apparent loss. The appropriate statutory provisions, it was argued, should be applied to each separate stage to determine the fiscal consequences. The avoidance scheme would then 'work' if, as was hoped, the gain should prove to be non-chargeable, and the loss allowable. The purchaser of the scheme would then have the allowable loss available to set off against a gain made in a 'real' transaction, the existence of which was the reason for the purchase of the off-the-peg scheme in the first place. Lord Wilberforce described the hoped-for effect thus:

> In each case we have a taxpayer who has realised an ascertained and quantified gain: in *Ramsay* £187,977, in *Rawling* £355,094. He is then advised to consult specialists willing to provide, for a fee, a preconceived and ready-made plan designed to produce an equivalent allowable loss. The taxpayer merely has to state the figure involved, i.e. the amount of the gain he desires to counteract, and the necessary particulars are inserted into the scheme.[63]

The House of Lords, however, was not prepared to allow the stepped structure of the transactions to determine the application of the fiscal regime. Instead, it collapsed the scheme into a single step for tax purposes, and applied the legislation to it as one potentially taxable disposition, giving rise to no gain or loss at all. On that basis, no question arose as to whether the intermediate gains or losses should be regarded as chargeable or allowable.

It would, of course, be unacceptable if taxpayers had no way of predicting in advance the stages which should properly be taken together for tax purposes: no one would argue that the fiscal regime should operate by ambush. One might think, if it is legal analysis of factual events that counts for tax purposes, that contractually linked steps, or steps which must follow one another pursuant to some equitable obligation, might reasonably be regarded together; but the decision in *Ramsay* went further than that. Lord Wilberforce made clear that the Commissioners:

> are not, under the *Westminster* doctrine or any other authority, bound to consider individually each separate step in a composite transaction intended to be carried through as a whole. This is particularly the case where (as in *Rawling*) it is proved that there was an accepted obligation once a scheme is set in motion, to carry it through its successive steps. It may be so, where (as in *Ramsay*) there is an expectation that it will be so carried through, and no likelihood in practice that it will not.[64]

Rather than using the existence of a legal obligation as the relevant indicator, the House relied upon the factual interdependence of the separate stages in the scheme. In each case the manufactured loss was dependent upon the corresponding gain: '[t]he

63 [1982] AC 300 at 322.
64 [1982] AC 300 at 324.

one could not occur without the other';[65] '[t]he loss could not be incurred without the gain . . .'.[66] The transactions were self-cancelling in this very precise sense, and their interdependence justified applying the legislation to the scheme as a whole.[67] Applying the legislation in this way was not to trespass upon the factual substance of the matter; it merely recognised the parties' own intentions with respect to what they were doing.[68] Equally, the House's approach did not amount to a finding of sham: it did not deny that the parties intended to create the legal relationships they appeared to. Instead the case called for an unusual combination of the inevitably judicial functions of statutory interpretation and transaction construction. The only question was the treatment called for by the tax legislation, properly interpreted, of what had actually taken place, properly construed.

Despite this inherent orthodoxy of the *Ramsay* decision, it quickly gave rise to the view that the House of Lords had adopted a 'new approach' in connection with avoidance schemes of this extreme type. Although now widely known as the '*Ramsay* principle', the truth is that this 'new approach' owes a great deal more to the House's decision in *Furniss v Dawson*.[69]

GOING BEYOND SHAM: *ANTONIADES v VILLIERS* AND *FURNISS v DAWSON*

Going beyond sham in the lease cases: *Antoniades v Villiers*

Despite the limited reach of the sham concept, the House of Lords found that the occupiers in *Antoniades v Villiers* jointly enjoyed a right to exclusive possession. No clear *ratio* can be derived from the judgments of their Lordships. Lord Oliver's approach is consistent with the traditional test, which examines the reasonableness of an occupier's claimed belief that the owner intended to grant exclusive possession. He differs from the Court of Appeal's decision only in his assessment of the facts, accepting that no reasonable person 'acquainted with the circumstances in which the parties had come together and with the physical lay-out and size of the premises' could seriously have contemplated that the sharing clause was anything but 'a smoke-screen to cover the real intentions of both contracting parties'.[70] The point seems to be that, despite the occupier's signing of a document containing the sharing clause, the

65 In respect of the *Ramsay* appeal, at 328D.
66 In respect of the *Eilbeck* appeal, at 332C.
67 See [1982] AC 300 at 328F for the *Ramsay* appeal: '[t]he true view, regarding the scheme as a whole, is to find that there was neither gain nor loss, and so I conclude' and 332E for the *Eilbeck* appeal: '[t]he only conclusion, one which is alone consistent with the intentions of the parties, and with the documents regarded as interdependent, is to find that . . . there was neither gain nor loss and so I conclude'.
68 Nor is such an approach unique to tax cases. It has been regularly emphasised that, to determine the true legal effect of the parties' dealings, the court must look at the circumstances as a whole, not accepting an attempt by the parties to present factually interdependent steps as separate. Note in particular *Antoniades v Villiers* [1990] 1 AC 417, [1988] 2 All ER 309, in which the House of Lords construed two supposedly separate occupation agreements as one. In the further context of legislation relating to charges see e g *Re George Inglefield* [1933] Ch 1 and *Re Curtain Dream plc* [1990] BCLC 925.
69 [1984] 1 AC 474
70 [1982] AC 300 at 469.

surrounding factual circumstances made it impossible for the owner reasonably to believe that the occupier was genuinely assenting to that clause.[71] Lord Jauncey took a similar line, emphasising that a genuine sharing clause would produce 'bizarre results';[72] not only would it authorise the owner to put an unlimited number of people into occupation, but the actions of those new occupiers would also increase the initial occupiers' liability for such things as the power consumed in the flat.[73]

The judgments of Lord Oliver and Lord Jauncey are therefore consistent with the approach of the Court of Appeal in *Hadjiloucas v Crean*,[74] in which it was emphasised that Lord Templeman's injunction in *Street v Mountford* to thwart 'sham devices and artificial transactions' called for no more than the application of standard principles of contract law.[75] These principles mean that a sharing clause can be ineffective even if the owner did genuinely intend it to create legal rights, provided the surrounding factual circumstances make it impossible for the owner reasonably to believe that the occupier is assenting to that clause. However, it is clear that the other three judgments in *Antoniades* go beyond such orthodoxy. Lord Templeman provides two grounds for denying effect to the sharing clause. First, it was said that Mr Antoniades could never insert others into occupation as:

> Until that power is exercised Mr Villiers and Miss Bridger are jointly in exclusive occupation of the whole of the flat making periodical payments and they are therefore tenants. The Rent Acts prevent the exercise of a power which would destroy the tenancy of Mr Villiers and Miss Bridger and would deprive them of the exclusive occupation of the flat which they are now enjoying. Clause 16 [the sharing clause] is inconsistent with the provisions of the Rent Acts.[76]

This reasoning cannot be supported, as it assumes the very thing it purports to prove. The Rent Acts can only apply if the occupiers are lessees, which will only be the case if they have a right to exclusive possession. As the Rent Acts can therefore only apply if the sharing clause, which seems to deny such a right to exclusive possession, is found to be invalid, those Acts cannot also be the means by which such invalidity is proved. It is worth asking why such a seemingly fallacious argument was not only employed by Lord Templeman, but also adopted by the Court of Appeal when giving a

71 As Lord Oliver notes, counsel for the occupiers argued that 'neither party intended to be bound' by the sharing clause: [1990] 1 AC 417 at 469. However, as pointed out in the Court of Appeal, it is clear that the owner did genuinely intend to deny the occupier a right to exclusive possession. As a result, it is submitted that Lord Oliver's judgment demonstrates that, for the sharing clause to be invalid, there is no need for the parties to have a common subjective intention that it should not create legal rights.

72 [1982] AC 300 at 476.

73 Lord Jauncey was of the opinion that a number of such clauses in the occupation agreement were 'reasonable only so long as the two licensees are occupying the flat alone': [1982] AC 300 at 476.

74 [1988] 1 WLR 1006

75 See esp per Mustill LJ at 1022: 'I do not read Lord Templeman's speech [in *Street v Mountford*] as suggesting that special techniques are to be applied any differently from those of the ordinary law of contract'.

76 [1990] 1 AC 417 at 462.

combined judgment in *Aslan v Murphy (Nos 1 and 2)* and *Duke v Wynne*.[77] It can only be justified by an assumption that the Rent Acts can apply even if the sharing clause has not independently been shown to be ineffective, and therefore contains an intriguing suggestion that the term 'tenancy', as used in those Acts, may mean something other than its standard definition, and can therefore encompass a situation where exclusive occupation is enjoyed as a matter of fact. An attempt to justify the decisions in *Villiers*, *Aslan* and *Duke* by such a process of statutory interpretation will be discussed below.[78]

Secondly, Lord Templeman held that the clause was:

> not a genuine reservation to Mr Antoniades of a power to share the flat and a power to authorise other persons to share the flat. Mr Antoniades did not genuinely intend to exercise the powers save possibly to bring pressure to bear to obtain possession. Clause 16 was only intended to deprive Mr Villiers and Miss Bridger of the protection of the Rent Acts. Mr Villiers and Miss Bridger had no choice in the matter.[79]

Hence, the sharing clause was a 'pretence' which 'was only designed to disguise the grant of a tenancy and to contract out of the Rent Acts'. This reasoning is crucial as it aims to provide a means, independent of the Rent Acts, to render the sharing clause ineffective. It also seems clear that Lord Templeman contemplates going beyond the sham doctrine, as conventionally understood. First, his Lordship prefers to condemn the clause as a 'pretence', rather than as a 'sham device or artificial transaction'.[80] Whilst the concepts of pretence and sham had been used interchangeably in the past, Lord Templeman's explicit preference for the former term does suggest that it involves the adoption of a new means by which a clause may be rendered ineffective. Certainly, Lord Templeman's application of the concept of pretence in *Villiers* goes beyond Lord Oliver's examination of what legal rights the parties intended to create, and involves the overruling of *Sturolson and Co v Weniz*: a case which, as discussed above, appears correctly to apply the orthodox 'sham test'. Moreover, the judgment of the Court of Appeal in *Aslan* and *Duke* not only seems to assume that Lord Templeman's judgment forms the *ratio* of *Villiers*, but also that the pretence test constitutes a new approach, which differs conceptually from that adopted by the Court of Appeal in *Villiers*.[81] Two crucial questions must then be answered: first, what is the scope of this new approach and secondly, how can this venture beyond the orthodox sham test be justified? These questions will be addressed in the next section, after consideration of a similar development in the tax cases.

77 [1990] 1 WLR 766 at 775.
78 See p 157.
79 [1990] 1 AC 417 at 462.
80 [1990] 1 AC 417 at 462.
81 [1990] 1 WLR 766 at 772.

Going beyond sham in the tax cases: *Furniss v Dawson*

Ramsay was not a case of a conventional sham; and, with the benefit of 20 years of hindsight, it now seems a relatively uncontroversial identification of the true legal effect of a closely interrelated sequence of transactions. It is somewhat more difficult to say the same about *Furniss v Dawson*. In *Furniss*, the House of Lords did not simply combine a factually interdependent 'scheme', throughout regarded as a single package by the taxpayer, but instead taxed a transaction as if it had been carried out in a different way from the events held by the Commissioners in fact to have taken place.

The Dawsons wished to dispose of valuable shares in family companies in favour of a quite separate company, Wood Bastow Holdings Ltd. Acting on tax motivated advice, the decision was taken not to sell directly to Wood Bastow, but first to exchange the family company shares for shares in an investment company incorporated in the Isle of Man. The Dawsons acquired Greenjacket shares in return for the shares in the family companies, and Greenjacket then sold the family company shares on for the cash consideration from Wood Bastow. The scheme was designed to defer capital gains tax, relying upon certain exceptions in the context of company amalgamations[82] to the general principle[83] that tax is charged on the disposal of assets giving rise to a capital gain. One such exception applies to exchanges of shares whereby the transferee company obtains control of the company whose shares it acquires. In such a case there is deemed to be no disposal of the former shareholding by the transferor: the new and the old shareholding are treated as the same asset.[84] If these provisions applied to the facts just described, then tax would be postponed until the Dawsons might later dispose of their Greenjacket shares.[85]

The Revenue initially sought to assess the Dawsons to tax on the basis that control of the family companies had not in fact passed to Greenjacket, because Greenjacket was throughout a nominee or bare trustee for the Dawsons. The Special Commissioners, however, took the view that Greenjacket had acquired control of the family companies within the meaning of the legislation. Reliance instead upon the so-called '*Ramsay* principle' became possible following the decision of the House of Lords in *IRC v Burmah Oil*.[86]

In *Ramsay*, the series of transactions had created an arguably distinct gain and loss which the court determined to treat as one. In *Burmah*, the scheme sought instead (using Lord Diplock's word) to transmogrify an outstanding debt of £160 million, owed by a subsidiary (Holdings) within a group of companies to its parent (Burmah), into an allowable loss. The debt, which came about as the result of a sale and repurchase of BP shares, was not, as it stood, an allowable loss.[87] The steps taken before the liquidation of Holdings were designed to turn the debt into equity, upon

82 Provided by para 6, Sch 7 to the Finance Act 1965.
83 Finance Act 1965, s 19.
84 See Lord Brightman at 520E–F.
85 One reason for the hostile attitude of the House of Lords to these facts may have been the possibility that money would meanwhile be extracted from Greenjacket by way of loan: see Lord Brightman at 524B.
86 (1981) 54 TC 200.
87 By reason of para 11, Sch 7, and s 23(1), Finance Act 1965.

which an allowable loss could be claimed when the liquidation took place. Accordingly, on 12 December, Holdings was put in funds by Burmah, through a further subsidiary (Morh), to enable Holdings to repay the existing debt to Burmah. After that stage, Holdings owed £160 million to Morh, which in turn owed the sum to Burmah, whereas previously Holdings had owed that amount directly to its parent. On 18 December, Holdings made a rights issue of shares to Burmah for the sum of £160 million, the money thus raised being promptly used to repay its liability to Morh, which in turn repaid its similar liability to Burmah. At the end of the process, Burmah was still left with an insolvent subsidiary to the tune of £160 million, but argued that, on the liquidation of Holdings, it could claim to have made an allowable loss of that amount on its subscription for the issued shares.

Unlike in *Ramsay*, specific findings of interdependence between the stages of the *Burmah* scheme were not possible. The steps taken on 18 December were not factually intertwined with those that had taken place on 12 December, and they were not economically self-cancelling. The taxpayer was not therefore seeking a step-by-step analysis of a transaction that could instead be characterised as a single taxable event. Instead, the passing of money around in a loop through Morh took place to secure a quite separate analysis for fiscal purposes from the one that would otherwise have applied: to prevent para 11, Sch 7 of the Finance Act 1965 rendering the debt non-allowable and to require that para 4, Sch 7 of the Act allow a deduction of the loss made on the subscription for shares.

Nevertheless, a unanimous House of Lords concluded that an extension of the recent 'significant change in the approach'[88] to facts of this nature was called for. 'In the same way as in *Ramsay*'s case, when the scheme was carried through to completion there was here no real loss and no loss in the sense contemplated by the legislation'.[89] So far as a justification for this extension to the reasoning in *Ramsay* was concerned, this was found in the presence throughout the events in *Burmah* of a controlling will. The scheme involved: 'inter-connected transactions between artificial persons, limited companies, without minds of their own but directed by a single master mind';[90] and 'the reality was that the decision had already been taken to carry it through to completion, and that was unquestionably the intention of the directors in this case, just as it was the intention of all parties concerned in *Ramsay*'.[91]

At this point in its development, the central emphasis of the new approach thus shifted away from factual interconnectedness, towards the presence instead of a controlling will overseeing a pre-ordained scheme.[92] What allowed a number of stages to be treated together was not factual happenstance, but the parties' intentions towards

88 At 214D per Lord Diplock.
89 At 221I per Lord Fraser.
90 At 214G per Lord Diplock.
91 At 220A per Lord Fraser.
92 In *Ramsay*, at 324, per Lord Wilberforce: 'an expectation that it will be so carried through, and no likelihood in practice that it will not'; in *Craven*, at 514, per Lord Oliver: 'that there was at [the time when the intermediate transaction was entered into] no practical likelihood that the pre-planned events would not take place in the order ordained, so that the intermediate transfer was not even contemplated practically as having an independent life'.

them. But, as Lord Oliver recognised in *Craven v White*,[93] the decision in *Burmah Oil* required a further element still. As well as the court being 'entitled to look at the composite transaction as a single transaction having a single legal result', the 'further ingredient . . . establishes . . . that if you find . . . a step inserted which has no other purpose than that of avoiding or minimising a liability to tax which, without that step, would be attracted by the transactions, you are entitled for fiscal purposes to ignore that step in assessing what is the true legal result of the series taken as a whole'.[94] This move was not necessary in *Ramsay*, where the claimed loss and gain were simply treated as one transaction, giving rise neither to a gain nor a loss. In *Burmah* however, the true legal analysis could not be found by collapsing a series of transactions into one. Rather, an inserted series of steps was treated for tax purposes as if the steps had not taken place at all. The passing of money around in a loop through Morh was simply ignored as ineffective for tax purposes, leaving *Burmah* with its original non-allowable loss.

Returning to the facts of *Furniss*, the extension of the 'new approach' called in turn for a further development to the reasoning in *Burmah Oil*. Although the facts in *Burmah* were not intertwined in the way that they had been in *Ramsay*, there was at least little conceptual difficulty in identifying the inserted 'steps' within the 'real' transaction, and in taxing the 'real' transaction without those steps. In *Furniss*, however, the correct fiscal analysis was far from straightforward. Even if only for tax purposes, it is difficult to ignore the existence of Greenjacket, given that the legislation specifically demands consideration of whether or not it acquired control of the Dawson companies as a result of the initial share exchange. Lord Brightman was clear enough in re-stating the requirements for an application of the 'new approach':

> The formulation by Lord Diplock in *IRC v Burmah Oil Co Ltd.* expresses the limitations of the *Ramsay* principle. First, there must be a pre-ordained series of transactions; or, if one likes, one single composite transaction . . . Secondly, there must be steps inserted which have no commercial (business) *purpose* apart from the avoidance of a liability to tax – not 'no business *effect*'.[95]

But Lord Brightman was far less clear in stating what it is that the 'new approach' actually calls for. At first, he appeared influenced by the simple 'excision' of the scheme that had been possible in *Burmah*:

> if the two necessary ingredients exist, *the inserted steps are to be disregarded for tax purposes* [emphasis supplied]. The court must then look at the end result. Precisely how the end result will be taxed will depend on the terms of the taxing statute sought to be applied. In the instant case the inserted step was the

93 *Craven v White* [1989] AC 398.

94 At 513F–514C.

95 [1984] AC 474 at 527. This reaffirmation of Lord Diplock's formulation was designed to reveal the error in the approach of Vinelott J and the Court of Appeal by showing that, by itself, the presence of 'enduring legal consequences' did not prevent the application of the new approach. This formulation was also taken in later cases as a correct statement of the *Ramsay* principle (as can be seen most recently by *IRC v McGuckian* [1997] 1 WLR 991) but appears to have been questioned in *MacNiven v Westmoreland* [2001] UKHL 6, [2003] 1 AC 311, {2001] 1 All ER 865, as will be discussed below.

> introduction of Greenjacket as a buyer from the Dawsons and as a seller to Wood Bastow. That inserted step had no business purpose apart from the deferment of tax, although it had a business effect. If the sale had taken place in 1964 before capital gains tax were introduced, there would have been no Greenjacket.[96]

Such a straightforward 'excision' has proved possible in a number of later cases. But in other cases, including it seems *Furniss*, nothing so straightforward is possible.[97] The difficulty in *Furniss* was twofold. First, because Greenjacket received the consideration for the onward sale of the shares to Wood Bastow, rather than the Dawsons themselves, Greenjacket certainly must feature in any analysis of the property rights created by the transactions. That need not, in itself, prevent the application of the new approach, because it can be answered that the required analysis need only hold good for fiscal purposes. But then the further difficulty emerges that the terms of the tax legislation concerned in *Furniss* expressly direct attention to whether or not Greenjacket acquired control of the Dawson companies. Lord Brightman was therefore driven to add a further element to the logic, involving a recharacterisation of the facts such that the disapplication of the exemptive provisions of Schedule 7 could be precisely justified:

> *Ramsay* says that the fiscal result is to be no different if the several steps are pre-ordained rather than pre-contracted. For example, in the instant case tax will, on the Ramsay principle, fall to be assessed on the basis that there was a tripartite contract between the Dawsons, Greenjacket and Wood Bastow under which the Dawsons contracted to transfer their shares in the operating companies to Greenjacket in return for an allotment of Greenjacket shares, and under which Greenjacket simultaneously contracted to transfer the same shares to Wood Bastow for a sum in cash. Under such a tripartite contract the Dawsons would clearly have disposed of the shares in the operating companies in favour of Wood Bastow in consideration of a sum of money paid by Wood Bastow with the concurrence of the Dawsons to Greenjacket. Tax would be assessed, and the base value of the Greenjacket shares calculated, accordingly.[98]

Clearly, had there been such a contract, Greenjacket would not have acquired control of the operating companies at all, and there could have been no question of the Schedule 7 exemption applying. But it must not be forgotten that this recharacterisa-

96 Lord Brightman [1984] AC 474 at 526G to 527F. He concluded his speech with a recapitulation of the taxable transaction: 'The result of correctly applying the *Ramsay* principle to the facts of this case is that there was a disposal by the Dawsons in favour of Wood Bastow in consideration of a sum of money paid with the concurrence of the Dawsons to Greenjacket. Capital gains tax is payable accordingly'.

97 Compare, for example, cases where it has seemed possible simply to ignore the fiscally motivated steps (*McGuckian*, *Hatton*) and those where the existence of, for instance, enduring proprietary consequences (often a genuine transfer in the ownership of shares) has caused difficulty in offering any rational basis for the application of the legislation to the facts with the inserted steps simply ignored (*Craven*, *Fitzwilliam*, *Pigott*, *Whittles*). Full references to each of these cases are below in n 151.

98 [1984] AC 474 at 526–527.

tion for tax purposes took place in the face of the Commissioners' finding of fact that Greenjacket had in fact acquired control of the Dawson company shares: there was therefore no contractual or equitable obligation to make the onward sale to Wood Bastow. Lord Brightman's solution is therefore at best a curious one. In *Burmah Oil* the analysis of the transactions in property terms was not determinative for tax purposes. Although one may question the justification for this, it nevertheless is comprehensible in its own terms: pre-planned steps with no purpose other than the avoidance of tax are simply to be ignored for fiscal purpose. In *Furniss*, however, Lord Brightman's second analysis does not simply ignore Greenjacket. Rather, Greenjacket does participate in the transaction, as recharacterised for fiscal purposes; and it does so precisely so as to modify the analysis called for by the fiscal legislation. The Dawsons were, in truth, taxed not as a result of pre-planned tax avoidance steps being ignored, but rather because of the court's recharacterisation of the role of the inserted step.

Resolving the question of whether Lord Brightman intended the *Ramsay* principle to permit recharacterisation of transactions for fiscal purposes, rather than the excision of certain particular steps, may be unnecessary following the most recent account of the new approach in *MacNiven v Westmoreland Investments Ltd*.[99] One thing, however, is clear. Just as in *Ramsay*, the outcome in *Furniss* has nothing to do with an application of conventional sham reasoning. It is not that the parties actually intended a tri-partite contract and that the accompanying documentation was designed to cloak that reality. Rather, despite the clear non-existence of such a contract, the detailed statutory regime was applied to the facts as if there had been one. As in *Antoniades v Villiers*, the House of Lords responded to an attempt to avoid a particular statutory regime by going beyond existing legal doctrine and invoking a new power to counteract such avoidance. The scope and possible justifications of such a power must now be considered.

ATTEMPTS TO JUSTIFY THE EXTENSIONS OF THE LAW IN *ANTONIADES v VILLIERS* AND *FURNISS v DAWSON*

A power to disregard acts done with the purpose of avoidance?

First, in the context of leases, it has been argued that terms can be disregarded where they are inserted for the purpose of avoiding the Rent Acts by denying a right to exclusive possession.[100] It is true that, at a number of points in his judgment in *Villiers*, Lord Templeman emphasises that this was the owner's aim in including clause 16 in the written agreement.[101] Lord Bridge also suggests that this sharing clause is ineffective as it was 'introduced into the agreement for no other purpose than as an attempt to disguise the true character of the agreement which it was hoped would deceive the court and prevent the [occupiers] from enjoying the protection of the Rent

99 [2001] UKHL 6, [2003] 1 AC 311, [2001] 1 All ER 865, considered below.
100 Bright, 'Beyond Sham and Into Pretence' [1991] 11 OJLS 136.
101 [1990] 1 AC 417 at 462 and 463.

Acts'.[102] Nonetheless, the courts have repeatedly rejected any suggestion that they have a general, non-statutory power to disregard agreed terms simply because those terms have been agreed in order to avoid a particular characterisation of the parties' dealings. Any number of examples can be given.

First, the courts have frequently had to consider situations in which parties have, for various reasons, chosen to set up a hire-purchase transaction rather than a simple loan on the security of goods. As long as the parties have genuinely intended to create the legal rights characteristic of hire-purchase, then, even if the only reason for preferring that mechanism has been the desire to avoid creating a secured loan, the agreement will be taken at face-value by the court.[103] The validity of this approach has been upheld in cases dealing with attempts to avoid the very legislation considered in *Antoniades v Villiers*. In *Kaye v Massbetter*,[104] an owner insisted that a tenancy agreement be made with a company created for that purpose, rather than with the individual who was to occupy the property. The only reason for doing so was to avoid the Rent Acts, which do not protect company tenants, yet this device was upheld by the Court of Appeal. Lord Donaldson noted that: 'it is, I think, important not to confuse the objective of the parties with the route which they say, or one of them says, was adopted to achieve this objective'.[105]

It has been suggested that the *Ramsay* principle provides an example of courts disregarding terms simply because of the purpose for which they have been agreed.[106] However, whatever view one takes of the validity of the *Ramsay* principle, it has always been clear that a finding that a particular step has been taken with the purpose of avoiding tax is a necessary, but not a sufficient, condition of that principle being applied in relation to that step.[107] Indeed, even when dissenting in *Craven v White* from the majority's more restrictive interpretation of the *Ramsay* principle, Lord Templeman stressed that the mere fact that a step has been entered upon with the purpose of avoiding tax cannot possibly justify that step's being disregarded.[108] Were it otherwise, we all might be at risk when taking money from a current account to deposit it in an ISA.

102 [1990] 1 AC 417 at 454.

103 See e g *Helby v Matthews* [1895] AC 471 at 475; *Re George Inglefield Ltd* [1933] Ch 1 per Romer LJ; *Yorkshire Railway Co v Maclure* (1882) 21 Ch D 309 per Lindley LJ.

104 [1991] 2 EGLR 97.

105 Lord Donaldson referred not only to the fact that hire purchase transactions chosen in order to circumvent the Moneylenders Acts were valid if genuinely adopted, but also to the lawfulness of using alternative means of raising money for the same end, such as the factoring of invoices and the execution of promissory notes and bills of exchange later discounted on the market.

106 Bright [1991] 11 OJLS 136.

107 See e g Lord Brightman's formulation of the principle in *Furniss v Dawson* [1984] AC 474 at 527 and Lord Oliver in *Craven v White* [1989] AC 398 at 503 and 508 as well as Dillon LJ in *Gisborne v Burton* [1989] QB 390.

108 [1989] AC 398 at 489: such an 'argument would prevent a taxpayer from availing himself of the fiscal immunities, privileges, allowances and other mitigating factors provided or permitted by Parliament. If a taxpayer mindful of the immunity from taxation enjoyed by a Manx company transfers assets to a company in the Isle of Man, the immunity of that company will continue and may be enjoyed indirectly by the taxpayer subject to an express provision by Parliament to the contrary'.

The decisions of the House of Lords in both *Norglen Ltd v Reeds Rains Prudential Ltd*[109] and *MacNiven v Westmoreland Investments*[110] provide ample confirmation that the courts do not have the power to render a transaction ineffective simply because the sole motivation for embarking on it was to benefit from the statutory consequences attaching to a particular legal characterisation dependent on that transaction's being effective. Hence the fact that the owner in *Villiers* inserted the sharing clause with the sole purpose of preventing a tenancy arising should not by itself render that clause ineffective. And the mere fact that a taxpayer has inserted a step into a transaction with the sole purpose of obtaining a tax advantage does not render the step ineffective for tax purposes.

A wider sham test based on intention to enforce a term in practice?

In the context of leases, *National Westminster Bank v Jones*[111] not only provides yet further confirmation that the courts will not disregard transactions simply because of the purpose for which they were entered, but may also seem to suggest a different ground for rendering agreed terms ineffective. Owners of a farm granted an agricultural tenancy to a company of which they were the sole beneficial owners in the hope of protecting the farm from the bank mortgagee. Neuberger J clearly stated that the artificial purpose behind the transaction 'does not by any means of itself render the transaction a sham'.[112] Instead, he interpreted *Antoniades v Villiers* as providing evidence of the court's recognition of the concept of a sham, stating that '[T]he whole point of a sham provision or agreement is that the parties intend to give the impression that they are agreeing that which is stated in the provision or agreement, while in fact they have no intention of honouring their respective obligations, or enjoying their respective rights under the provision or agreement'.[113] In a recent article,[114] Bright relies on the above quotation from *National Westminster Bank v Jones* as providing support for a wider sham doctrine, which allows the courts to disregard terms if the parties do not intend to enforce them in practice, and also allows a party who is 'innocent of the sham' to avoid suffering a disadvantage by being bound by a term which the other party did not intend to enforce in practice. Or, if the innocent party has relied on the formal agreement, he may insist, if he wishes, that the agreement is binding. The decisions in *Villiers*, *Aslan v Murphy (No 1)* and *Duke v Wynne* might then be seen as exemplifying this principle. When considering the ineffective terms in *Villiers*, Lord Bridge notes that 'No one could ever have supposed that those

109 [1999] 2 AC 1, [1998] 1 All ER 218.

110 [2001] UKHL 6, [2001] 2 WLR 377, 383 at para 15 per Lord Nicholls 'A genuine discharge of a genuine debt cannot cease to qualify as a payment for the purpose of section 338 by reason only that it was made solely to secure a tax advantage. There is nothing in the language or context of section 338 to suggest that the purpose for which a payment of interest is made is material'.

111 [2001] 1 BCLC 98. Neuberger J rejected the bank's submission that the tenancy agreement was a sham, but held in the bank's favour on other grounds which were affirmed by the Court of Appeal: [2001] EWCA Civ 1541, [2002] 1 BCLC 55. There was hence no need for the Court of Appeal to consider the question of sham.

112 [2001] 1 BCLC 98 at para 37.

113 [2001] 1 BCLC 98 at para 45.

114 Bright, 'Avoiding Tenancy Legislation: Sham and Contracting Out Revisited' [2002] CLJ 146, esp at 157–159.

provisions were ever intended to be acted on';[115] Lord Donaldson may be making a similar suggestion in *Aslan v Murphy* when condemning certain provisions as 'wholly unrealistic'.[116] It may then be possible to see *Antoniades v Villiers* not as an extension of the law, but rather as uncovering the true basis of the sham concept, thereby revealing that concept to be more extensive than was previously thought.

However, it is submitted that this wider sham doctrine is just as heretical as the notion that courts can disregard terms simply because of the purpose for which they have been agreed. The crucial point is that it elides the conceptual distinction between two different tests. The first examines what legal rights the parties intended to create; although it is often described as a sham test it is in fact simply a consequence of the underlying test by which rights arise through agreement. The second imposes an additional requirement, and thereby does require there to be an independent doctrine of sham, as it looks to the very different issue of the rights the parties intended would be enforced in practice. To confuse these tests creates important problems, both conceptually and practically.

First, the suggested wider sham doctrine denies parties the opportunity to create legal rights which they do not plan to enforce in practice. For example, it removes the possibility of the benevolence intended by the owner in *Sturolson & Co v Weniz*, who wanted to retain the right to select new occupiers whilst also intending to gain the consent of any current occupiers before doing so. Moreover, A may enter a contract with B for the supply of goods at a particular price, believing that, due to likely changes in market conditions, B will be find it impossible in practice to perform the contract. In that sense, A has no intention of being bound in practice to pay B the price for the goods; yet, if B has undertaken to provide them, there is no reason why A should not be able to claim damages for breach of contract if B does not perform.[117] Further, the suggested test is very difficult to apply to the common situations, seen in cases such as *Snook* and *Yorkshire Railway*, but also in the recent tax case of *Barclays Mercantile Business Finance v Mawson (Inspector of Taxes)*, in which both parties intend that an agreement should have the practical effect of a loan or charge but that its legal form should be different (e g as involving a sale and lease-back). As Lord Denning noted in *Campbell Discount Co Ltd v Bridge* a hire purchase transaction is 'in effect, but not in law, a mortgage of goods':[118] the legal characterisation flows simply from the parties' intentions as to their legal rights, without involving an analysis of how the agreement was intended to operate in practice. Similarly, in the company let cases, it is hard to understand exactly what enforcement in practice might

115 [1990] 1 AC 417 at 454.
116 [1990] 1 WLR 766 at 773.
117 Compare *Lewis Emanuel & Sons Ltd v Sammut* [1959] 2 Lloyd's Rep 629; Treitel, *The Law of Contract* (10th edn, 1999) 808–809. Compare also *McRae v Commonwealth Disposals Commission* (1950) 84 CLR 377, as discussed in *Great Peace Shipping Ltd v Tsavliris Salvage (International) Ltd* [2002] EWCA Civ 1407, [2002] 4 All ER 689 at 709 at paras 77–80: it does not seem that the contractual liability of the Commission, based on their undertaking that the oil tanker did exist, would have been affected if the claimant had known that the tanker did not in fact exist (although of course the claimant would have been unable to recover expenses incurred in looking for the tanker in such a case, but instead would have to prove the value of his denied expectations: see *Treitel* at 877).
118 [1962] AC 600 at 626.

involve: what evidence would show that the owner intended to enforce the terms of the lease against the company rather than the individual occupier? Finally, it is inconceivable in the world of commercial agreements generally that terms should be implicated as shams and hence ineffective simply because they are not intended to be relied upon in practice. As the Court of Appeal make clear in the recent case of *Burdis v Livsey*: 'Commercial parties may, and often do, choose not to enforce their strict legal rights without intending to create or demonstrate some different state of affairs'.[119] The fact that, as in *Burdis*, a contracting party was also well aware, before entering the contract, that a term would not be enforced in practice does not render that term invalid: otherwise, many of terms included *ex abundante cautela* in standard form contracts would be shams. Equally, in the *Westminster* case, both the Duke and his gardener would have dismissed as very unlikely any attempt in practice to enforce the Duke's obligation to pay wages as well as the annuity. However, provided there was an intention that the gardener should have a legal right to claim those wages, the arrangement could not be regarded as a sham.[120]

The conceptual flaw of the wider sham doctrine is revealed by a closer examination of the Court of Appeal's decision in *Burdis v Livsey*.[121] The Helphire company operates schemes to provide vehicle repairs and car hire to innocent victims of road accidents. The victim does not pay for such services immediately; rather, he assigns his right of action against the party responsible for the accident to Helphire, who then pursue the claim against the insurers of the culpable party. It seems that the success of these schemes has eaten into the profits of insurers, who have therefore sought to challenge their validity. The House of Lords rejected an argument that the schemes were champertous,[122] but accepted that, as they did not require immediate payment from the victim for hire and repair costs, certain agreements would be unenforceable if they did not meet the requirements of the Consumer Credit Act 1974.[123] In the light of the latter decision, Helphire modified the scheme with the aim of avoiding that Act. To do so, they ensured that the hire and repair agreements called for payment by the victim after 51 weeks, thereby bringing them within an exemption covering contracts calling for payment 'within a period not exceeding 12 months'.[124] Nonetheless, in practice no payment would be made by the victim. Instead, victims were encouraged to take out an insurance policy with a Helphire subsidiary, which purported to guarantee payment of the hire and repair costs if Helphire's claim against the party responsible had not been settled within 12 months. This subsidiary, Angel, in turn had an underwriting agreement with an independent company. However, it seems that Angel never made claims against its underwriters; nor did Helphire pursue victims who failed to claim on their insurance with Angel. Whilst some payments relating to the hire and repair costs were made by Angel to Helphire, this amounted to no more than an intra-group

119 [2002] EWCA Civ 510, [2003] QB 36, 65 at para 44.

120 In the tax context, see also *R v Dimsey; R v Allen* [2000] QB 744 at 773–774. If a settlor sets up a trust in favour of two charities, with a power to select other beneficiaries from a very wide class (excluding only residents of Jersey) then the lack of an intention to exercise such powers of appointment in practice does not by itself make the trust a sham.

121 [2002] EWCA Civ 610, [2003] QB 36.

122 *Giles v Thompson* [1994] 1 AC 142.

123 *Dimond v Lovell* [2002] 1 AC 384, [2002] 2 All ER 897.

124 Consumer Credit (Exempt Agreements) Order 1989, para 3(1)(a)(i).

accounting exercise. In effect, therefore, to recover the hire and repair costs, Helphire relied solely on their assigned cause of action against the party responsible for the accident. Therefore, in such proceedings, the defendants' insurers alleged that as Helphire would in practice never pursue the victim for hire and repair costs, the credit period under the victim's agreement with Helphire did in truth extend beyond 12 months. Hence it was argued that the agreement was regulated by the 1974 Act; was as a result unenforceable by Helphire; that therefore the victim had no liability for hire and repair costs; and that consequently damages in respect of such costs could not be recovered from the defendants.

The Court of Appeal rejected the contention that, using the concept as expounded by Lord Templeman in *Antoniades v Villiers*,[125] the Helphire scheme involved a pretence. The trial judge had not considered in detail the implications of Helphire's failure to pursue victims who had not claimed on their insurance with Angel. However, the Court of Appeal stated that 'just because the scheme was, as [the trial judge] said, "sloppily enforced" does not lead to the conclusion that the credit hire and repair agreements were intended to have some meaning contrary to their express terms. Commercial parties may, and often do, choose not to enforce their strict legal rights without intending to create or demonstrate some different state of affairs'.[126] This passage highlights the crucial distinction between intention to create particular legal rights and intention as to the enforcement of those rights. There was nothing to show that the hire and repair agreements could not be taken at face-value; the fact that Helphire did not intend to enforce their rights under the agreement in practice did not affect their intention to create those rights. Equally, the crucial factor in the court's examination of Angel's arrangements with their underwriters was that 'the documents do show an intention to create genuine insurance arrangements'.[127] Even if those arrangements were 'artificial' and 'sloppily enforced' they still proved the intention to create legal rights which is the true test of the effectiveness of any agreement.

It should be noted that, when considering Angel's arrangements with their underwriters, the Court of Appeal stated that 'In effect the risk assumed by underwriters was of the solvency of the Helphire Group'.[128] It could then be argued that Angel did have some intention that the term be relied on in practice, if not by themselves then by their potential trustee in bankruptcy. However, this merely points to the fact that the wider sham test is not only conceptually dubious but is also highly problematic to apply in practice: it is not clear whether the test should be satisfied if the underwriter contemplates a risk of an enforcement by a potential trustee in bankruptcy, whilst Angel does not plan that the term be enforced by itself or a voluntary assignee. Further practical problems can be shown by a consideration of *Duke v Wynne*.[129] The plaintiff was the owner of a large house which she had previously occupied with her husband and four children. After her family had moved out of the house, and whilst she was waiting to sell it, the owner allowed a couple with

125 [1990] 1 AC 417.
126 [2002] EWCA Civ 510, [2003] QB 36, 65 at para 44.
127 [2002] EWCA Civ 510, [2003] QB 36, 65 at para 39.
128 [2002] EWCA Civ 510, [2003] QB 36, 65 at at para 39.
129 [1990] 1 WLR 766 at 773.

two sons into occupation under an agreement which stressed her intention not to grant exclusive possession and included a sharing clause. As the house had three bedrooms, it would have been perfectly feasible for another occupier to be inserted. In such a case, how should a court determine whether the owner intended to enforce the sharing clause? How remote would the possibility of enforcement have to be to render the clause ineffective?[130]

Moreover, the question arises of what precisely is meant by 'enforcing' an agreed term. In *Bankway Properties v Pensfold-Dunsford*,[131] the written agreement contained a clause giving the landlord the power to increase the annual rent fivefold to £25,000. The landlord never believed the tenant would be able to satisfy a demand for the increased rent, but did intend to rely on the term as a means to terminate the lease. Bright argues that this term does not fall within the proposed wider sham test,[132] but it is difficult to see how the owner's intention as to the sharing clause in a case such *Antoniades v Villiers* or *Duke v Wynne* is any different. In those cases, even if the owner may not envisage the insertion of another occupier as a serious possibility, he certainly does intend to rely on the sharing clause to show that exclusive possession has not been granted and hence to terminate the occupation agreement without the obstacle of the Rent Acts. The factual difficulties of applying the wider sham test emphasise its conceptual weakness: if it is reasonable for the owner to believe that the occupier has agreed to a term which prevents a right to exclusive possession arising, why should the owner be put to the additional obstacle of showing that he intended to 'enforce' this term in practice?

It is therefore important to return to the comment of Neuberger J in *National Westminster Bank v Jones* which might seem to support the proposed wider sham test. It was made in response to a suggestion from counsel that the impugned lease could not be a sham as the owners of the farm obviously intended it to be effective, if only as part of their plan to frustrate the bank. Of course, as Neuberger J recognised, such an argument would rob the sham concept of any force. The owners' intention that the apparent lease should thwart the bank proves no more than a desire for a court to accept the lease as genuine, and is clearly not conclusive proof of the necessary intention to transfer a legal right to exclusive possession of the property. Equally, in *Midland Bank v Wyatt*, the fact that the husband wished a court to view his declaration of trust as effective as part of a plan to protect himself from creditors did not prevent that declaration from being ineffective. The crucial distinction is thus between, on the one hand, simply intending a court to accept a transaction as valid, and, on the other, intending the transaction genuinely to create the legal rights it purports to create. However, to rebut counsel's submission, and hence presumably out of a desire to distance the intention required for the owner's lease to be effective from a simple intention to have a court accept the transaction as valid should the bank contest it, Neuberger J goes too far in suggesting that an agreed term can only be effective if the parties intend to rely on it in practice. More weight should be given to his later

130 The Court of Appeal noted in *Duke v Wynne* that the owner had never suggested that there was a 'serious possibility' of her enforcing the sharing clause: [1990] 1 WLR 766 at 776.

131 [2001] EWCA Civ 528, [2001] 1 WLR 1369.

132 [2002] CLJ 146 at 160.

observation that 'A sham provision or agreement is simply a provision or agreement which the parties do not really intend to be effective, but have merely entered into for the purpose of leading the court or a third party to believe that it is to be effective'.[133]

A test based on finding the 'substance and reality' of a transaction?

To the extent that they exemplify a sham test based on intention to enforce agreed terms rather than on intention that those terms should create legal rights, cases such as *Villiers* must be condemned as inconsistent with the sham concept as correctly understood. However, it seems that the approach in such cases is yet more unorthodox. In *Villiers*, *Aslan* and *Duke* the fact that the owner had not attempted to enforce clauses denying exclusive possession seems to be viewed as decisive in its own right, not in as far as it provides an indication as to the intention of the owner. In *Villiers* for example, Lord Templeman repeatedly refers to the fact that the occupiers enjoyed exclusive occupation of the property rather than asking if they had a legal right to exclusive possession.[134] In *Duke v Wynne*, Lord Donaldson suggests that the real agreement between the parties was to grant a lease as 'the true bargain was that the defendants should be entitled to exclusive occupation unless and until the plaintiff wanted to exercise her right to authorise someone else to move in as a lodger'.[135] There is a clear link between such reasoning and the misconception, discussed above, that the Rent Acts themselves could be used to prevent the owner enforcing an agreed sharing clause. The assumption made by the courts in both cases is that the occupier can be treated as a tenant provided he is enjoying in practice the same control of the property as that legally due to a tenant. The approach can be summed up in the words of Lord Ackner in *Villiers*, who found that the sharing clause was ineffective as it was not part of 'the substance and reality of the transaction entered into by the parties'.[136]

It is crucial to note that 'substance and reality' can be used in a number of different ways in this context. When applying the sham test as correctly understood, courts have often referred to the need to disregard the bare form of a written agreement in order to examine the underlying substance. This is entirely consistent with the underlying purpose of that sham test, as it amounts to a search for the intentions of the parties as to the legal rights the agreement is to create. As has been seen,[137] such intention cannot be determined by the form of the document alone, and evidence of the parties' subsequent conduct may demonstrate that the parties intended to create legal rights different to those contained in any document. In such cases, 'substance and reality' is

133 [2001] 1 BCLC 98 at para 59.

134 [1990] 1 AC 417, esp at 459–460: eg '[t]he enjoyment of exclusive occupation for a term in consideration of periodical payments creates a tenancy, save in exceptional circumstances . . .'.

135 Further, he states that '[a]pplying the test of what was the true bargain between the parties, the court would have wanted to know what steps (if any) were being taken by the owner to fill the vacancy. If the owner was not actively seeking another occupant, it is inherently more likely that the first couple were entitled to exclusive possession of the whole in the meanwhile and so were tenants': [1990] 1 WLR 766 at 776. See also Dillon LJ's explanation of *Somma v Hazelhurst* [1978] 2 All ER 1011, [1978] 1 WLR 1014, given in *Gisborne v Burton* [1989] QB 390 at 398: 'the documents were a sham because they did not reflect what was actually happening.'

136 [1990] 1 AC 417 at 466.

137 See the discussion above.

thus used to mean the true intentions of the parties as to the legal rights the agreement is to create, and cannot be confused with a simple inquiry into the practical operation of the agreement. In *IRC v Westminster*, for example, it could be said that, in practice, the payments made under deed to the Duke's servants operated as wages. However, the Duke's tax liabilities did not depend on this 'economic reality' but rather on the reality as to what legal rights had been created by the agreement with his gardener, which depended in turn on the parties' real intentions as to the legal rights the agreement was to create.[138]

The judgment of Lady Justice Arden in *Bankway Properties Ltd v Pensfold-Dunsford*[139] illustrates the pitfalls of failing to distinguish between different meanings of 'substance and reality'. In order to claim that the clause increasing rent was ineffective, counsel for the occupant argued that 'there is a variant on the usual definition of a sham where a question arises as whether an agreement is not intended to have the effect stated but is intended to evade the operation of a statute out of which the parties cannot contract . . . the question is what was the substance and reality of the transaction entered into by the parties'.[140] A number of cases, including *Antoniades v Villiers*, were relied on to support this submission, which was accepted by Arden LJ. Some of these cases were clearly not in point:[141] in *Johnson v Moreton*[142] it was accepted that the relevant statute applied and the question was whether the protection afforded by that statute could be bargained away; in *Bridge v Campbell Discount Co Ltd*[143] the House of Lords simply made clear that the legal characterisation of a contractual term as a penalty could not be determined by the parties' use of the word 'penalty' to describe that term.

The cases that were relevant included those relating to purported hire purchase transactions, discussed in passing above. In *Re Watson*,[144] specifically referred to by counsel, the meaning given to 'substance and reality' is clear. To test whether a transaction was in reality a secured loan or a hire purchase agreement, the Court of Appeal examined what legal rights the parties had intended to create. The hire purchase characterisation was rejected, as, despite the form of the agreement, there was clear evidence that the parties had not intended to transfer ownership of the property in question. Money received by the original owner of the property therefore could not be seen as the price of a purchase, but rather represented a loan secured on the property. The parties' attempt to present the transaction as one of hire purchase was rejected not because the agreement had operated in practice as a loan, but rather because the parties had intended to create the legal rights characteristic of debtor and creditor. Indeed, the hire purchase cases, like those involving company lets, demonstrate the courts' rejection of the idea that transactions can be characterised

138 See Lord Tomlin, [1936] AC 1 at 19–20.
139 [2001] EWCA Civ 528, [2001] 1 WLR 1369.
140 [2001] EWCA Civ 528, [2001] 1 WLR 1369, 1380 at para 43.
141 See also Bright [2002] CLJ 146 at 163–164. However, Bright suggests that *Re Watson* (1890) 25 QBD 27 has little to do with the definition of a sham, a view not supported by the analysis put forward here.
142 [1980] AC 37.
143 [1962] AC 600 at 634.
144 (1890) 25 QBD 27.

according to their practical operation. As Lord Denning noted in *Bridge v Campbell Discount Co Ltd* a hire purchase transaction is 'in effect, but not in law, a mortgage of goods';[145] equally *Kaye v Massbetter* involved, in practice, the enjoyment of exclusive possession by an individual occupier.[146] Counsel for the tenant in *Bankway* further relied on *Re George Inglefield Ltd*;[147] yet in this case Lord Hanworth MR approved Lord Herschell's precise and important statement in *Helby v Matthews*, relied on by Lord Tomlin in *IRC v Westminster*, that 'it is said that the substance of the transaction evidenced by the agreement must be looked at, and not its mere words. I quite agree. But the substance must, of course, be ascertained by a consideration of the rights and obligations of the parties, to be derived from a consideration of the whole of the agreement'.[148]

Hence the cases relied on by counsel in *Bankway* provide overwhelming evidence that the 'substance and reality' which the courts should uphold is made up of the legal rights the parties have intended to create, not the way in which the parties' agreement has operated in practice.[149] This conclusion is given further support by the consideration of the tax cases conducted above. Hence, given it is clear that the landlord in *Bankway* intended to create a legal right to demand the increased rent, it is difficult to agree with Arden LJ's conclusion that the rent review clause was 'not in substance or reality a provision for the fixing of rent'. This view was based on the finding that 'the landlord never expected to receive rent of £25,000 per annum and intended that it should only invoke [the rent review clause] as a means of recovering possession'.[150] It thus seems that the meaning attributed to 'substance and reality' in *Bankway* is the same as that in *Villiers*, depending as it does on the practical operation of the parties' agreement. Whilst this approach is inconsistent with the general law relating to shams, there are hints in *Bankway* that it may be justified in particular cases on grounds of statutory interpretation. It is to this possibility, more worked out in the tax than in the lease context, that this next section must finally turn.

The development in the tax cases of a test based on statutory interpretation

The operation of the *Ramsay* principle in the tax context has now been the subject of considerable judicial scrutiny,[151] and a suggested justification for it appears slowly to

145 [1962] AC 600 at 626.
146 [1991] 2 EGLR 97. See discussion above.
147 [1933] Ch 1.
148 [1895] AC 471 at 475.
149 Contrary to counsel's contention, and suggestions in *Madell v Thomas* [1891] 1 QB 230, the need to look for the 'substance and reality' of an agreement in this sense does not only arise when the application of a statute out of which the parties cannot contract is at stake: see e g *Ferris v Weaven* [1952] 2 All ER 233; *Midland Bank v Wyatt* [1995] 1 FLR 697 and *National Westminster Bank v Jones* [2001] 1 BCLC 98.
150 [2002] EWCA Civ 528, [2001] 1 WLR 1369, 1383, para 54.
151 The leading cases in the House of Lords have been *W T Ramsay v IRC* [1982] AC 300, [1981] 1 All ER 865; *IRC v Burmah Oil Co Ltd* (1981) 54 TC 200; *Furniss v Dawson* [1993] 2 All ER 49, [1984] 474; *Craven v White* [1989] AC 398; *Ensign Tankers (Leasing) Ltd v Stokes* [1992] 1 AC 655; *Fitzwilliam (Countess) v IRC* [1993] 1 WLR 1189; *Moodie v IRC* [1993] 1 WLR 266; *IRC v McGuckian* [1997] 1 WLR 991; *IRC v Willoughby* [1997] 1 WLR 1071; *Norglen Ltd v Reeds Rains*

be coalescing in the House of Lords. Lord Oliver, whose reasoning against the Revenue in the Court of Appeal in *Furniss* had been overturned by the House of Lords, first subjected the new approach to sustained analysis in *Craven v White*.[152] How was it that clear fiscal consequences flowing from the share exchange with Greenjacket were to be ignored by an analysis of the *Furniss* facts undertaken specifically for fiscal purposes? In Lord Oliver's view:

> if the result of a judicial decision is to contradict the express statutory consequences which have been declared by Parliament to attach to a particular transaction which has been found as a fact to have taken place, that can be justified only because, as a matter of construction of the statute, the court has ascertained that that which has taken place is not, within the meaning of the statute, the transaction to which those consequences attach . . . the intermediate transfer, whose statutory consequences would otherwise have resulted in payment of tax being postponed, did not, upon the true construction of the Finance Act 1965, constitute a disposal attracting the consequences set out in paragraphs 4 and 6 of Schedule 7 to the Act.[153]

This basic premise – that the new approach must be understood as a process of statutory construction and not as a judicially crafted response to schemed transactions – has recently been examined in greater detail by the House of Lords on two occasions, in *IRC v McGuckian*[154] and in *MacNiven v Westmoreland Investments Ltd*.[155]

The facts in *McGuckian* were as follows. Mr and Mrs McGuckian owned shares in a company, Ballinamore, which had built up substantial reserves available to be distributed by way of dividend. On the advice of a tax consultant, the shares were transferred to the trustee company of a Guernsey settlement known as Shurltrust. The beneficiaries of the settlement were Mr and Mrs McGuckian and the income for the time being was to be payable to Mrs McGuckian. Four days before the substantial dividends were declared, the right to receive any dividends was assigned by Shurltrust in favour of a UK company, Mallardchoice, associated with the tax consultant involved. The assignment was made for a sum representing 99 per cent of the dividend in fact paid by Ballinamore four days later; and the consideration was only paid over after the dividends had been declared. The economic incentive for this apparent loss to the McGuckians of 1 per cent of the value of the dividends, together with certain ancillary expenses, lay in section 478, Income and Corporation Taxes Act 1970. That section could only create a tax liability if the non-resident trustee company

Prudential Ltd [1999] 2 AC 1, [1998] 1 All ER 218 and *MacNiven v Westmoreland Investments Ltd* [2001] UKHL 6, [2001] 2 WLR 377. Significant decisions by lower courts include *Whittles v Uniholdings Ltd (No 3)* [1996] STC 914, CA; *Barclays Mercantile Business Finance Ltd v Mawson* [2002] EWCA Civ 1853, [2003] STC 66 CA; *Young v Phillips* [1984] STC 520, Nicholls J; *News International plc v Shepherd* [1989] STC 617, Vinelott J; *Hatton v IRC* [1992] STC 140, Chadwick J; *Pigott v Staines Investment Co Ltd* [1995] STC 114, Knox J; *Girvan v Orange Personal Communications Services Ltd* [1998] STC 567, Neuberger J.

152 [1989] AC 398.

153 At 502E–G.

154 [1997] 1 WLR 991.

155 [2001] UKHL 6, [2003] 1 AC 311, [2001] 1 All ER 865.

(Shurltrust) received income. The sum which Shurltrust received was said, however, to be capital rather than income, since it was not a dividend but the proceeds of sale of the right to receive a dividend.

A unanimous House of Lords, overruling the Northern Ireland Court of Appeal, held that the new approach was properly applicable to this statutory and factual matrix: the facts fell 'squarely within the classic requirements for the application of that principle as stated by Lord Brightman in *Furniss v Dawson*'.[156] The inserted steps were not shams: '[o]n the contrary, tax avoidance was the spur to executing genuine documents and entering into genuine arrangements'.[157] But the House rejected any suggestion that the foundations of the quite separate *Ramsay* principle might be suspect. Mr Nugee QC submitted on behalf of the taxpayers that the scope of the principle ought to be confined as an 'extreme form of statutory interpretation'.[158] Whilst the extant decisions of the House of Lords should be respected, any underlying principle should not be further extended. Lord Steyn rejected this approach as 'a false foundation for the consideration of this appeal',[159] and identified instead two general trends in judicial approach exemplified by Lord Wilberforce's decision in the *Ramsay* case:

> The new development was not based on a linguistic analysis of the meaning of particular words in a statute. It was founded on a broad purposive interpretation, giving effect to the intention of Parliament . . . And in asserting the power to examine the substance of a composite transaction the House of Lords was simply rejecting formalism in fiscal matters and choosing a more realistic legal analysis.[160]

As such, the approach was to be regarded as both an 'intellectual breakthrough',[161] and as 'based on an orthodox form of statutory interpretation'.[162] Lord Cooke expressly associated himself with this general account;[163] the rest of the Judicial Committee, at least impliedly, did so; and this summary of formative influences upon the *Ramsay* logic was quickly cited with approval in lower courts.[164]

156 Per Lord Browne-Wilkinson at 996B–C. See also per Lord Steyn at 1002F–G: 'a classic case for the application of the *Ramsay* principle'; per Lord Cooke at 1004A–B: 'the matter is clinched by the authority of *WT Ramsay Ltd v IRC* and the subsequent cases in the same line'; per Lord Clyde at 1007E: '[t]his approach in effect accords with the guidance laid down by Lord Wilberforce in *WT Ramsay Ltd v IRC*'; Lord Lloyd endorsed the reasoning of Lord Browne-Wilkinson, Lord Steyn, Lord Cooke of Thorndon and Lord Clyde.
157 Per Lord Steyn at 1001G–H.
158 At 998H–999A.
159 At 999B.
160 At 1000G–H.
161 At 999H.
162 At 1000G–H.
163 At 1005A et seq.
164 See, for early examples, *Ingram v IRC* [1997] STC 1234 at 1270g per Millett LJ, dissenting on other grounds: 'the *Ramsay* doctrine is based on a broad purposive construction of the statute and a rejection of formalism in fiscal matters'; *MacNiven v Westmoreland Investments Ltd* [1997] STC 1103 at 1128 per Carnwarth J: '[Lord Steyn] saw this, not as innovation, but rather as bringing the approach to construction of statutes in line with the "purposive methods of construction" adopted over the 30 years in other areas of the law'.

This attempt to develop an adequate analysis of the new approach is clearly to be welcomed, but the House may have complicated the task by seeking to present the reasoning as essentially orthodox. It is undoubtedly true that some element of purposive construction is now admissible in the construction of fiscal legislation,[165] and Rowlatt J's restrictive approach set out above at the end of the first section is properly not as pervasive as it once was. But it does not take the explanation of the new approach very far simply to say that it is 'founded on a broad purposive interpretation, giving effect to the intention of Parliament'. To reiterate Lord Oliver's concerns about *Furniss v Dawson*, expressed in *Craven v White*, how can even broad purposive construction 'contradict the express statutory consequences . . . declared by Parliament to attach to a particular transaction . . . found as a fact to have taken place'?[166] Equally, it is far from clear what 'rejecting formalism in fiscal matters and choosing a more realistic legal analysis' actually means. Although this second element seems designed to focus attention back on to transaction construction rather than statutory interpretation, beyond that it offers scant guidance to fact-finding Commissioners faced with assessing the significance of a set of facts brought before them. If it is correct that Lord Steyn's two insights do somehow lie at the heart of the new approach, what is really needed is a full explanation of the connection between the two wider judicial trends and the detail of Lord Brightman's test in *Furniss*. Why precisely is it that a broad purposive approach to the construction of fiscal legislation, coupled with a realistic rather than formalistic analysis of a transaction's constituent elements, justifies the disregarding of a certain type of step in a series of preordained transactions; and even, in extreme cases, that transaction's recharacterisation?

Lord Hoffmann has now suggested a possible answer, initially hinted at in his speech in *Norglen Ltd v Reeds Rains Prudential Ltd*[167] and further developed in *MacNiven v Westmoreland Investments Ltd*.[168] The facts involved in *MacNiven* were reminiscent of the *Burmah Oil* transaction.[169] Westmoreland, a property investment company, owed £70 million, including some £40 million accrued interest, to its parent company, a tax exempt pension scheme. Despite its parlous state, Westmoreland might at least have some value to its parent if its established tax losses could be set off against future profits earned by assets transferred to it. This would only be possible, however, within section 338 of the Income and Corporation Taxes Act 1988, if the accrued interest had been 'paid'. Accordingly, the tax exempt pension scheme lent Westmoreland the money to pay the accrued interest. On the same day, Westmoreland paid its parent the interest, net of tax, and accounted to the Revenue for the tax due. As a result of this simple manoeuvre, Westmoreland owed its parent a capital sum, and the accrued interest could, it was hoped, be said to have been paid. As it happened, the parent company, being a tax exempt pension scheme, was also then able to reclaim the tax paid by Westmoreland, and managed to dispose of Westmoreland (because of the value of its available losses) for £2 million.

165 See in particular *Pepper v Hart* [1992] STC 898 and now *MacNiven v Westmoreland Investments Ltd* [2001] UKHL 6, [2003] 1 AC 311, [2001] 1 All ER 865.
166 *Craven v White* [1989] AC 398 at 502E–G: above at n 153.
167 [1999] 2 AC 1 at 13–14.
168 [2001] UKHL 6, [2003] 1 AC 311, [2001] 1 All ER 865.
169 Set out above in the text following n 86.

The Crown sought to disallow Westmoreland's claim to deduct the interest payments. They had been made within a series of transactions designed purely for the avoidance of tax and were to be disregarded. In the light of the *Burmah Oil* decision, and the reinvigorated reasoning from *McGuckian*, these facts might appear an obvious instance calling for an application of the new approach, but Lord Hoffmann and a unanimous House of Lords disagreed. As between the parties, Lord Hoffmann did not doubt that the interest had been paid, 'but the dispute between the taxpayer and the Crown [was] whether the interest was "paid" within the meaning of section 338'.[170] To argue that it had not been, Counsel for the Crown sought to formulate the *Ramsay* principle in terms owing something to both Lord Steyn in *McGuckian* and Lord Brightman in *Furniss*:

> When a court is asked (i) to apply a statutory provision on which a taxpayer relies for the sake of establishing some tax advantage (ii) in circumstances where the transaction said to give rise to the tax advantage is, or forms part of, some pre-ordained, circular, self-cancelling transaction (iii) which transaction though accepted as perfectly genuine (ie not impeached as a sham) was undertaken for no commercial purpose other than the obtaining of the tax advantage in question then (unless there is something in the statutory provisions concerned to indicate that this rule should not be applied) there is a rule of construction that the condition laid down in the statute for the obtaining of the tax advantage has not been satisfied.[171]

Lord Hoffmann could not accept that this was a principle of construction. It looked instead like an overriding legal principle, superimposed upon the whole of revenue law without regard to the language or purpose of any particular statutory provision. Whilst Parliament could impose such a 'paramount provision', subject to which everything else must be read (such as section 2(2) of the European Communities Act 1972), the judges simply lack the constitutional authority to develop the common law in this way. Instead, Lord Hoffmann argued that if the new approach is to be justified, it needs to be shown in each case precisely why it is that statutory construction yields the particular result sought by the Crown.

This return to the task begun by Lord Oliver in *Craven v White* and reinvigorated by Lord Steyn in *McGuckian* has the advantage at least of identifying a proper constitutional justification for the 'new approach'; but the complexities of analysing the existing case-law convincingly should not be underestimated. Lord Hoffmann appears to have been driven to conclude that the existing decisions can only be justified if a fundamental reappraisal of the meaning of legislation in the tax sphere is undertaken. If an adequate explanation is to be provided, it needs to be accepted that Parliament may not always intend statutory language to bear a purely legal meaning. Instead, if the context so requires, Parliament may intend the words it uses to have a commercial meaning:

170 [2001] UKHL 6, [2001] 2 WLR 377, 384 at para 19.
171 [2001] UKHL 6, [2001] 2 WLR 377, 386 at para 28.

> [t]he innovation in the *Ramsay* case was to give the statutory concepts of 'disposal' and 'loss' a commercial meaning. The new principle of construction was a recognition that the statutory language was intended to refer to commercial concepts, so that in the case of a concept such as a 'disposal', the court was required to take a view of the facts which transcended the juristic individuality of the various parts of a preplanned series of transactions.[172]

Where Parliament does intend a term to have a commercial meaning, then 'to have regard to the business "substance" of the matter is not to ignore the legal position but to give effect to it'.[173] In such circumstances, although a series of transactions may not be sham, and although the steps may have legal reality for other purposes, their 'juristic categorisation' will not be determinative for the purposes of 'statutory concepts' such as 'disposal' or 'loss'.[174]

Having reorganised our thinking in this way, Lord Hoffmann attempted to explain a selection of the leading authorities. The *Burmah Oil* case followed straightforwardly enough from *Ramsay*: 'loss' in the capital gains tax legislation was again to be taken to mean a loss in commercial terms and not a series of pre-planned transactions which had no business purpose.[175] In *Furniss*, the question 'was whether the disposal had been to one person rather than another', and the answer was that 'commercially' the transaction was a transfer by the Dawsons to Wood Bastow in exchange for a payment to Greenjacket.[176] So far as Lord Brightman's detailed formulation of the new approach was concerned, that had been misunderstood, and could not be said to be a principle of construction. It was instead a statement of the consequences of giving a commercial construction to a fiscal concept, and must logically be preceded by an analysis of the statutory language. Only by doing so could it be determined whether Parliament intended a particular term to be given a commercial meaning 'capable of transcending the juristic individuality of the component parts' of the transaction concerned'.[177]

Such an approach need not always drive one to conclude that a term is meant commercially. Lord Hoffmann accepts that there are equally terms in tax legislation that cannot be construed in that way. In such circumstances, Parliament will have intended a fully legal meaning to be given to its language, and the so-called *Ramsay* principle will have no part to play.[178] So far as the facts of *MacNiven* were concerned, it was in fact such a case. The word 'payment' was not capable of bearing a commercial meaning wider than the legal one of an act, such as the transfer of money,

172 [2001] UKHL 6, [2001] 2 WLR 377, 388 at para 32.
173 [2001] UKHL 6, [2001] 2 WLR 377, 390 at para 39.
174 [2001] UKHL 6, [2001] 2 WLR 377, 390 at para 41.
175 [2001] UKHL 6, [2001] 2 WLR 377, 391 at para 44.
176 [2001] UKHL 6, [2001] 2 WLR 377, 392 at para 46.
177 [2001] UKHL 6, [2001] 2 WLR 377, 393 at para 49.
178 [2001] UKHL 6, [2001] 2 WLR 377, 393 at para 49. Lord Hoffmann also recognised at para 50 that, although a word may have a recognised legal meaning, a particular legislative context may show that it is there being used to refer to a broader commercial context. No doubt the point could equally hold true in the other direction.

which discharges a debt. The term must therefore be understood juristically, and the taxpayer was entitled to his deduction. The interest had been 'paid' within the meaning of the legislation.

The reorientation required of this area of law if Lord Hoffmann's diagnosis is correct is considerable, and will take time to be worked out in the cases to come. No doubt Lord Hoffmann can be accused of accommodating the results of earlier decisions by doing violence to their reasoning, but to some extent that is inevitable when the House seeks to elucidate the true basis of a novel line of authority. Certainly, however questionable Lord Hoffmann's accommodation of the existing authorities may be, the move he makes potentially has very considerable explanatory force.

APPLYING AN APPROACH BASED ON *MACNIVEN* AND STATUTORY INTERPRETATION

Applying the *MacNiven* approach in the lease context

Doubts have been expressed in the past about the applicability to the lease cases of approaches developed in the tax cases. In *Gisborne v Burton*,[179] a simple scheme was put in place to deny an occupier the protection of agricultural tenancy legislation by making him a sub-lessee of the owner's wife. Relying on the *Ramsay* principle, as developed in *Furniss v Dawson*, counsel argued that the court should ignore the intermediate lease between the owner and the wife, entered into with the sole purpose of circumventing the legislation. Dillon LJ accepted this submission, stating that the *Ramsay* principle was 'applicable wherever there is a pre-ordained series of transactions which is intended to avoid some mandatory statutory provision, even if not of a fiscal nature. You must look at the scheme as a whole, instead of concentrating on each pre-ordained step individually, and you do not, as it were, blow the whistle at half-time'.[180] However, both Ralph Gibson LJ, dissenting in *Gisborne*,[181] and Lord Bingham MR in the later Court of Appeal case of *Belvedere Court Management Ltd v Frogmore Developments Ltd*[182] doubted that the *Ramsay* principle could be used, in the words of Lord Bingham, to 'entitle the court simply to ignore or override apparently effective transactions which on their face confer an interest in land on the transferee'.[183]

There seem to be two independent concerns which motivate these doubts. First, a lack of confidence in the basic legitimacy of the *Ramsay* principle naturally leads to a tendency to limit its application. In his judgment in *Gisborne*, Ralph Gibson LJ very pertinently asks how the court can disregard the apparent head lease to the owner's wife, having established that it was not a sham. This nagging concern has often surfaced in tax cases considering the *Ramsay* principle,[184] and is given full expression

179 [1989] QB 390.
180 [1989] QB 390 at 399.
181 [1989] QB 390 at 408.
182 [1997] QB 858, [1996] 1 All ER 312.
183 [1997] QB 858 at 876.
184 See e g Lord Oliver in *Craven v White* [1989] AC 398 at 502E–G: see text at n 153 above.

in Lord Hoffmann's judgment in *MacNiven*, which finally rejects the idea that the courts have a general power to regard non-sham terms or transactions as ineffective. Secondly, and exemplified by Lord Bingham's comments in *Belvedere*, it is clear that the *Ramsay* principle is limited to the recharacterisation of a transaction for the purposes of attributing statutory consequences, and does not involve a finding that apparent transfers of property have simply not occurred.[185] This reasoning, which is also given conclusive support by *MacNiven*, separates the question of characterising the transaction for the purposes of statutory interpretation and the question of what legal rights have been created by the transaction. Hence in *Furniss v Dawson*,[186] for example, the fact that the taxpayer was found to have made a taxable gain did not involve a denial that ownership of the shares had passed from Dawsons to Greenjacket to Wood Bastow. As a result, it must be admitted in *Gisborne* that the head-lease to the wife does have legal effect; it can only be irrelevant if a statutory term to be applied directs the court to look at the 'commercial reality' of the transaction, not the legal rights thereby created.

Therefore the doubts expressed in *Gisborne* and *Belvedere* about the applicability of the *Ramsay* principle to lease cases are best understood as reflecting a widespread judicial concern, also seen in the tax context, about the very legitimacy of that principle. They should not be taken as precluding the application to the lease cases of any approach developed in the tax cases, provided of course that the approach itself can be justified. Indeed, given that the new statutory interpretation approach in *MacNiven* was developed precisely to address concerns about the legitimacy of the *Ramsay* principle, such as those evident in *Gisborne* and *Belvedere*, it is both legitimate and necessary to consider whether the *MacNiven* approach can also be used to explain difficult lease cases, such as *Gisborne v Burton*, *Antoniades v Villiers* and *Bankway Properties*. This inquiry is all the more urgent as, given the limits of the sham doctrine as correctly understood, and the lack of other plausible justifications for going beyond that sham doctrine, the *MacNiven* approach seems to offer the only viable means by which to defend these decisions.

However, it is clear that there are certain statutory terms which cannot possibly be interpreted in a non-legal way. For example, one might try to argue that the otherwise difficult decision in *Bankway* may usefully be understood as an exercise in statutory interpretation. The result in the case depended on a finding that the landlord could not show that any of the grounds for possession under the Housing Act 1988 could be used against the tenant. This depends not only on the nature of the parties' agreement but also on the interpretation of Ground 8 of Schedule 2 of that Act, which obliges the court to grant possession in cases of arrears of rent. Arden LJ's interpretation of this ground is that '[t]he statutory scheme does not provide a mandatory ground for a possession order for non-payment of rent unless the rent is properly due as such'.[187] As a consequence 'the effect of the 1988 Act is that where a tenant is in a position to pay the sum genuinely reserved as rent at the time provided in the tenancy agreement or at such later date as Parliament allows, he should be free to do so and not lose

185 See text following n 97 above.
186 [1984] AC 474.
187 [2001] 1 WLR 1369, 1382 at para 51.

possession'.[188] If rent is given an orthodox legal meaning and is defined as the sum which the owner has the legal right to demand from the tenant in return for conferring exclusive possession, then, given the owner genuinely intended the agreement to confer on him a right to raise the rent to £25,000, Ground 8 should apply and the court must make an order for possession. However, Arden LJ's judgment could be seen to give 'rent' a different, non-juristic meaning in the context of Ground 8. It seems that, for the purposes of this provision, 'rent' is to mean a sum which the landlord genuinely expects to be able to receive from the tenant,[189] and therefore does not include a sum which is set at a high level with the intention that the tenant will not be able to pay it. To borrow the memorable phrase of Lord Hoffmann in *Norglen Ltd v Reeds Rains Prudential Ltd,* the decision in *Bankway* need not be seen as 'spooky jurisprudence'[190] resting on a supposed general power of the courts to disregard terms agreed between the parties. However, there is an obvious problem in the way of this attempt to justify the decision in *Bankway*: Ground 8 of Schedule 2 of the Housing Act 1988 expressly defines 'rent' as meaning 'rent which is lawfully due'. As a result, it is very difficult to see how a non-legal meaning of rent could be applied by the court.

Further, there are more subtle ways in which the nature of a particular statutory scheme may provide a limit on the effectiveness of the *MacNiven* approach. In *Gisborne v Burton*, the court had to consider agricultural holdings legislation which, unlike the Rent Acts, contained no special provision for the protection of sub-tenants. Since the Agricultural Holdings Act 1948, there had been a power, first in the Minister of Agriculture and Fisheries, then in the Lord Chancellor, to make provision to safeguard the interests of subtenants such as the defendant, yet this power had never been exercised.[191] Given this background, it may be at least highly questionable to argue that the Act was intended to give protection to a sub-tenant who, in practice, was in the position of a direct tenant of the owner.[192] Hence, whilst Dillon LJ viewed the *Ramsay* principle as directly applicable in *Gisborne*, the subsequent re-analysis of that principle as a matter of statutory interpretation makes the decision in *Gisborne* very difficult, if not impossible, to justify. Further, a court may be understandably reluctant to accept a party's claim that a transaction should be disregarded when considering the application of a complicated legislative scheme, such as the leasehold enfranchisement provisions considered in *Jones v Wrotham Park Settled Estates*[193]

188 [2001] 1 WLR 1369, 1384, para 56.
189 Or, presumably, from a local authority making housing benefit payments.
190 [1999] 2 AC 1 at 14.
191 See s 26(1)(e) of the 1948 Act; s 5(1)(d) of the Agricultural Holdings (Notices to Quit) Act 1977 and s 29 of, and para 7 of Sch 4 to the 1986 Act.
192 *Norglen Ltd v Reeds Rains Prudential Ltd* [1999] 2 AC 1, [1998] 1 All ER 218 provides a powerful analogy. The case concerned the interpretation of the Legal Aid Act 1988, and whether that Act could allow legal aid to be received by an individual to whom a company had assigned a right of action in order to avoid the statutory rule preventing companies from receiving legal aid. However, it was regarded as relevant that the Lord Chancellor had a power under s 34(1) of the Act to introduce regulations to 'prevent abuse' and also that the Legal Aid Board could take into account the fact of an assignment when deciding whether to grant legal aid. Given these protections, there was no reason to interpret the Acts as laying down a general ban on legal aid being awarded to assignees of rights of actions from companies: see [1999] 2 AC 1 at 16 per Lord Hoffmann.
193 [1980] AC 74.

and *Belvedere Court Ltd v Frogmore*,[194] which already include a number of specific safeguards for the party claiming that the transaction should be so disregarded.[195] Indeed, even when considering a more straightforward scheme such as that embodied in the Rent Acts, there is a great risk of over-simplification. It cannot be assumed that the Acts aim solely to protect occupiers: rather they aim to create a balance between the needs of owners and occupiers, with the concept of a lease being used to hold that balance.[196]

Nonetheless, an attempt can be made to explain the results in *Villiers*, *Aslan v Murphy* and *Duke v Wynne*[197] on the *MacNiven* analysis. To do so, it must be argued that when the Rent Acts specify that various protection is to be given to 'tenants' this includes, not just those occupiers who have a legal right to exclusive possession, but also those who in practice enjoy full control of the property in question: hence, in order to promote the purpose of the Rent Acts, the words 'lease' and 'tenant', when used in those Acts, are to be given a non-juristic meaning.[198] Were the Rent Acts to be interpreted in this way, then the courts' focus on the practical operation of occupation agreements as the means to test their 'substance and reality' could be justified.

There is an intriguing parallel with the decision of the House of Lords in *Bruton v London and Quadrant Developments*,[199] in which Lord Hoffmann gave the leading judgment. That case concerned the application of the Landlord and Tenant Act 1985 to a claimant who had entered into occupation under an agreement with a licensee of the property. As the licensee did not have an estate in the property, the majority of the Court of Appeal held that the occupier could not have a lease and was hence outside the 1985 Act.[200] However, the House of Lords decided that, as the occupation agreement would have sufficed to confer a lease had the licensee held an estate in the land, then the Act applied. Despite some loose comments by members of the House of Lords,[201] it is impossible to describe the occupier as having a legal right to exclusive possession; he could certainly have been removed by the owner of the property. Rather, the occupier, like that in *Villiers*, had de facto control of the property until an attempt to remove him was made by the owner or a party claiming through the owner. It may therefore be significant that Lord Hoffmann posed the question: 'Did this

194 [1997] QB 858, [1996] 1 All ER 312.

195 E g the power given to a judge under s 12(4) of the Landlord and Tenant Act 1987 to order the disposal of a property without being subject to an incumbrance.

196 Compare Romer LJ in *Re George Inglefield Ltd* [1933] Ch 1, accepting that even if the impugned transaction was within the mischief of s 79 of the Companies Act 1985, that alone 'affords no reason whatever for attempting to drag the transaction within the operation of the section by calling it something which, in truth, it is not'.

197 [1990] 1 WLR 766.

198 It is interesting to note Honoré's suggestion in *The Quest for Security: Employees, Tenants, Wives* (1982) Hamlyn Lectures, at 56 that: 'To do justice to the [tenancy] legislation, one must surely ask whether the intention was to provide the occupier with a home, especially a 'family home', or merely to make a temporary or precarious arrangement . . . If, then, what was meant was a home, the legislation should apply, even if the parties do not want it to'. Note also the nature of the Law Commission's proposal to reform the statutory regulation of rented homes, discussed below.

199 [2000] 1 AC 406.

200 [1998] QB 834. See esp Millett LJ at 845.

201 E g per Lord Slynn at [2000] 1 AC 406 at 410; per Lord Jauncey at 411; and per Lord Hobhouse at 417.

agreement create a "lease" or "tenancy" within the meaning of the Landlord and Tenant Act 1985 or any other legislation which refers to a lease or tenancy?'[202] and also that counsel for the housing trust, in the words of Lord Hobhouse, accepted that 'a contractual relationship of landlord and tenant suffices to make the provisions of the Act applicable'.[203] It can be argued that *Bruton*, like *Villiers* and the cases following it, does not involve a re-working of the general test for a lease but rather involves an attempt to further the presumed purpose of a legislative scheme by looking not for a lease in the technical sense of a legal right to exclusive possession but instead for a lease in the wider, non-juristic sense of an arrangement which confers practical control of property. The decisions can thus be seen as based on an implicit assumption that the legislature's use of the concept of a tenancy to determine the bounds of particular protection for occupiers is simply a means to achieve an underlying purpose of giving such protection to those who, in practice, occupy property as one occupies a home. Provided such occupation exists, the precise legal rights enjoyed by the occupier are therefore not decisive in determining the application of the statute. Indeed, it is interesting to note, that, following *MacNiven*, an attempt has been made to argue that the word 'lease' can have a non-juristic meaning in the context of a particular statute.[204]

However, whilst such an argument is the only possible means by which to attempt to explain the *Villiers* approach, it is unsatisfactory in principle and must be rejected. First, it rests on the idea that the terms 'lease' and 'tenancy', like terms such as 'gain', can be given a non-juristic meaning when used in a statute. It might be thought that the former terms are inherently juristic, and cannot bear a meaning which is inconsistent with their orthodox, legal definition. Certainly, the terms are in themselves more obviously juristic than 'payment', which was given a legal meaning in *MacNiven*. However, this point is not decisive, as the proper meaning to attribute to any term cannot be judged in the abstract, but only in its particular statutory context.[205] Hence, it may just be possible to justify the decision in *Bruton* by arguing that 'lease' and 'tenancy', when used in the Landlord and Tenant Act 1985, includes an occupier under an agreement which only fails to confer a legal right to exclusive possession because of the grantor's lack of title. It could be said that the purpose of the legislation is to regulate the relationship between grantor and occupier, and the lack of title of the grantor, whilst it will prevent the occupier gaining rights against the true owner or those claiming through him, should not deny the occupier the protection of the Act:[206]

202 [2000] 1 AC 406 at 413.
203 [2000] 1 AC 406 at 417.
204 See *BMBF (No 24) Ltd v IRC* [2002] EWHL 2466 (Ch), [2002] STC 1450 at para 160. The respondents had attempted to argue before the Special Commissioners that the expression 'lease', when used in s 42(3)(a) to (e) of the Capital Allowances Act 1990 was intended to bear a 'commercial meaning, rather than a strictly juristic one'. The argument was rejected 'fairly summarily' by the Special Commissioners. Of course, this hardly prevents an argument that the word 'lease' has a non-juristic meaning when used in the very different contexts of the Landlord and Tenant Act 1985 or the Rent Acts.
205 See *MacNiven v Westmoreland Investments Ltd* [2001] UKHL 6, [2001] 2 WLR 377, 393 at para 50, above n 178.
206 Compare the argument of the Law Commission in their recent Consultation Paper No 162, especially at para 9.40. It proposes that the scope of statutory protection available to residential occupiers should not be determined by reference to the distinction between a lease and a licence, as

put simply, in such a situation the fact that the occupation agreement is technically unable to confer a lease in the full legal sense is not the fault of the occupier.

However, there is an insuperable problem when considering the intepretation of the Rent Acts in *Villiers*, *Aslan v Murphy* and *Duke v Wynne*.[207] The crucial point is that to interpret 'tenancy' as used in the Rent Acts in a non-technical way is flatly inconsistent with the main authority as to the definition of a lease when used in the precise context of that legislation: *Street v Mountford*.[208] Lord Templeman's judgment in that case is founded on a rejection of the previously prevailing idea that the term 'tenancy' could be given an unorthodox meaning when used in the Rent Acts. A heresy had sprung up in the Court of Appeal which allowed an owner wishing to avoid the burdens of such legislation to do so provided he demonstrated an intention not to grant a lease.[209] It seems clear that this heresy was motivated by sympathy towards such an owner, and a consequent willingness to narrow the application of the Rent Acts.[210] Lord Templeman firmly emphasises that the orthodox, traditional definition of a lease as the grant of exclusive possession is the true test to apply. This can be defended on the simple grounds that when Parliament selects a concept such as 'lease' or 'tenancy', with an established juridical meaning, to communicate with judges, there is no reason to believe it intends an unorthodox meaning of that term to be applied. Therefore whilst the result in *Street* may be favourable to occupiers rather than owners, its methodology is avowedly neutral. Lord Templeman's discussion of *Somma v Hazelhurst*[211] does however indicate the tension, fully evident in *Villiers*, between upholding the orthodox definition of a lease and assuming a novel jurisdiction to disregard non-sham terms in an occupation agreement. Whilst the latter development, like the former, may be seen to favour occupiers of property, it can only be justified by a process of making assumptions about the purpose of the legislation. And this is the very process which is impliedly condemned by Lord Templeman's rejection of the then prevailing approach to the definition of a lease.

Indeed, the marked contrast between those earlier authorities, which narrowed the definition of a lease in order to limit the application of statutes protecting tenants, and cases such as *Villiers* demonstrates one of the dangers of the statutory interpretation approach favoured in *MacNiven*. On what evidence can a court decide between different non-technical meanings of the term 'lease' which Parliament may have intended? At one extreme, the term has been taken to refer to an arrangement which demonstrates the owner's intention to create a lease; this interpretation may be seen to recognise that the onerous burdens of the Rent Acts should not be lightly imposed. At the other extreme, the term may be taken to include any arrangement which in practice

that 'distinction is essential where the proprietary consequences of the contract are concerned, and should remain so, but it should not affect the statutory regulation of the contract as between the contracting parties themselves.' Hence, the Law Commission proposes that any situation involving an agreement that confers a right to occupy premises as a home should prima facie qualify for statutory protection. It may be argued that the courts in cases such as *Bruton*, *Villiers*, *Aslan* and *Duke* interpreted the then existing statutes as though this proposed change had already been made.

207 [1990] 1 WLR 766.

208 [1985] AC 809, [1985] 2 All ER 289.

209 See n 7 above.

210 See e g *Cobb v Lane* [1952] 1 TLR 1037.

211 [1978] 2 All ER 1011, [1978] 1 WLR 1014. The discussion is at [1985] AC 809 at 825–826.

operates to provide an occupier with control over property; this reading may be seen to promote an underlying purpose of making people secure in their homes. Three points come out of this: first, an attempt to justify the *Villiers* approach on the basis of the *MacNiven* approach to statutory interpretation is impossible to reconcile with the methodology of *Street*; secondly, a departure from the technical meaning of 'lease', insisted on in *Street,* carries as many dangers for occupiers as it does for owners, as there is no reason why the non-technical meaning adopted must necessarily extend the reach of the statute concerned;[212] finally, the *MacNiven* approach, whilst purporting to limit judicial innovation, merely transfers the creative process from the development of judicial means to disregard non-sham terms to the equally, if not more, open question of the interpretation of statutory language and the elusive notion of Parliamentary intention.

A further difficulty with applying the statutory interpretation analysis to the *Villiers* approach consists of the inevitable collapse, in the context of the Rent Acts, of the very distinction which *MacNiven* seeks to preserve between characterisation of transactions on the one hand, and the legal rights which those transactions create on the other. On the statutory interpretation approach, the sharing clause in *Villiers* does create a legal right in the owner, as it is not a sham and the courts lack any other general means by which to deny its validity. However, despite the fact that they therefore do not have a right to exclusive possession, the occupiers are nonetheless tenants for the purposes of the Rent Acts as they have practical control of the property. Yet this distinction quickly proves untenable: if the occupiers are protected by the Rent Acts, then the sharing clause will be rendered unenforceable by statute. As a result, the owner will be denied the right validly created by the agreement and the occupiers will have a legal right to exclusive possession. This circularity, as has been noted above, is a feature of the judgments in *Villiers*, *Aslan* and *Duke* and can therefore support the view that these cases are based on the statutory interpretation approach. However, it also provides a compelling reason to reject an interpretation of the Rent Acts which makes any occupier with practical control of the property a tenant, as to do so would be to render ineffective rights which the owner has validly reserved and which ensure that the occupier is not, in the technical sense of the word, a tenant.[213] Such a result is not logically indefensible, as the fact that the sharing clause is valid at common law does not prevent its being rendered ineffective by statute, but it does highlight the difficulties in extending the *MacNiven* approach beyond a determination of whether a tax is payable to the application of statutory provisions which limit the parties' freedom to contract.

212 Indeed, a number of cases concerning local authority lets may be seen to depend on a process of statutory interpretation which departs from a standard legal reading of terms such as 'lease' and 'licence' in order to narrow the application of protective legislation. See the definition given to 'licence' for the purposes of s 79(3) of the Housing Act 1985 in *Westminster City Council v Clarke* [1992] 2 AC 288, [1992] 1 All ER 695 and the use of the 'tolerated trespasser' concept in *Burrows v Brent London Borough Council* [1996] 1 WLR 1448, [1992] 1 All ER 695.

213 Applying the statutory interpretation approach to *Bankway Properties* raises the same problem. If the rent review clause does not make rent due for the purposes of Ground 8 of Schedule 2 of the Housing Act 1988, then it would be nonsensical for the landlord to have the legal right to enforce the clause.

Applying the statutory interpretation approach in the tax context

In the tax context, three particular – and they are considerable – advantages flow from Lord Hoffmann's explanation of the new approach. In the first place, not until now has a complete constitutional justification been put forward by the House of Lords explaining how it is that purposive statutory construction results in stages in transactions, found as facts to have taken place, nevertheless being ignored for fiscal purposes. The suggestion that legalistic characterisation may simply be of no concern to a tribunal concerned instead to apply the commercial meaning of a statutory term, at least explains how it is that statutory interpretation and transaction construction are to be linked together in this context.[214]

Secondly, Lord Hoffmann's account has the virtue of doing away with the rigid formulation of the factual indicators calling for an application of the *Ramsay* principle formulated by Lord Brightman.[215] Transaction construction is simply not to be at the heart of the new approach. Courts need no longer dissect transactions in search of 'pre-ordainedness' and 'inserted steps without a commercial purpose' – indicators which, in any case, only served to light the way for subsequent taxpayers seeking to find their way around Lord Brightman's formulation. At the same time, the ambiguity in Lord Brightman's formulation as to the effect of an application of the new approach is neatly finessed, and the law seemingly freed from unnecessary complications of recharacterisation.[216] The effect of Lord Hoffmann's approach, considered in the terms of Lord Brightman's account, is perhaps more akin to excision than to recharacterisation; but really it operates in an entirely different way. Instead of seeking a necessary degree of pre-ordainedness, plus the presence of inserted steps without a commercial purpose, the court begins by determining whether Parliament intended a 'legal' or a 'commercial' construct. If Parliament had in mind a commercial notion, then the taxpayer's actions may come within it quite irrespective of any element of pre-ordainedness or any presence of steps with no purpose other than the avoidance of tax. Equally, there is no need to formulate a recharacterised legal analysis of the transaction justifying the treatment called for by the legislation: the legislation simply does not call for a legal analysis of what has taken place. The House

214 In doing so it cures the deficiencies of Lord Steyn's account in *McGuckian*, considered above, see text following n 159.

215 Lord Brightman's formulation is set out in full above: see text at n 95. It owes a good deal to Lord Diplock's formulation in the *Burmah Oil* case: (1981) 54 TC 200 at 214D–E.

216 See text at n 99 ff above. Perhaps the clearest instance of this complication resulting in the non-application of the new approach is *Pigott v Staines* [1995] STC 114 at 140j–141b. In the context of a scheme concerning 'irrecoverable' Advance Corporation Tax, and involving the interpolation of a company (Staines) between a parent (British-American Tobacco) and its subsidiary (BATCo), Knox J could find: 'no . . . realistic and intellectually defensible way of treating the series of transactions as a composite whole in a way which excluded Staines' claim for repayment under section 239(3) of the 1988 Act. . . . [T]he share structure at the end of the preordained steps . . . had to be recognised in the recharacterisation which the Crown claims should be made. Mr. Moses accepted that the end result in the present case included the existence of Staines as the subsidiary of BAT and holding company of BATCo. That excluded any recharacterisation which altogether ignored Staines and treated the overall transaction as a payment of a dividend by BATCo to BAT.' An analysis of what had taken place in commercial terms clearly might escape this difficulty, but Lord Hoffmann's approach would still justify Knox J's decision if the statutory concept concerned was a legal and not a commercial one. Given the outcome in *MacNiven*, it seems likely that it was.

of Lords has therefore found a neat way around Lord Brightman's over-rigid *indicia*; and around any formerly perceived need to identify a legal recharacterisation of the transactions without the inserted steps.

Thirdly, the move deserves to be welcomed because it has its own clear limits. There is to be no scope for *Ramsay* where a legal meaning must be taken from the context to have been intended by Parliament. Perhaps the clearest example of such a case will be where Parliament has provided a detailed, often scheduled, regime providing that certain facts will satisfy a central charging notion, and that others will not. In all but the most straightforward of such instances it will be impossible to maintain that the meaning of the central charging notion is other than a legal question.

Unfortunately, from this apparently clear point follows a considerable difficulty for Lord Hoffmann's argument. Many of the cases in which the new approach has been applied appear to be clear examples of fiscal legislation where Parliament has gone to great lengths to spell out the detailed meaning of its chosen terms.[217] It is therefore far from clear that the reinterpreted *Ramsay* principle ought to have been extended to such cases at all. Given this difficulty of explaining past decisions, there is corresponding concern as to how predictable the operation of the new distinction will be in the future. Both of these problems can usefully be examined by considering the Court of Appeal's first reaction to *MacNiven*.

In *Barclays Mercantile Business Finance v Mawson*[218] the Court considered certain claims for capital allowances in respect of expenditure on the acquisition of a gas pipeline. The relevant statutory concept was one of 'incurring expenditure', in the context of section 24(1) of the Capital Allowances Act 1990. The Court of Appeal, overturning the view of Park J, held that the phrase must be given a legal meaning.[219] The rights and wrongs of that view need not be gone into here, but Peter Gibson LJ was scathing in his view of Lord Hoffmann's distinction:

> I do not doubt that it is due to my own failings that I find Lord Hoffmann's dichotomy of concepts a difficult one to apply. The touchstone appears to be whether the commercial man would say of a statutory expression 'You had better ask a lawyer' (see [2001] STC 237 at [58]). It is far from obvious to me that the commercial man, knowing anything of the dozens of cases in which the distinction between capital and income has been explored, would say that those concepts are commercial; whether a transaction is of an income or capital nature is normally treated as a question of law (see *Beauchamp v FW Woolworth plc*

217 *Pigott v Staines*, considered in the previous footnote, is an obvious example from the context of Advance Corporation Tax.

218 [2002] EWCA Civ 1853, [2003] STC 66 esp per Peter Gibson LJ at para 44 and Carnwath LJ at paras 69–74.

219 Peter Gibson LJ in the end 'took refuge' in the fact that that expression archetypically would include a payment: 'Just as in *MacNiven* it was immaterial to the meaning of 'payment' that the company borrowed money from its shareholder to whom it promptly repaid the borrowed money, so . . . it is irrelevant to the meaning of "incurred . . . expenditure" that the money used . . . was borrowed from [X] in a way which eventually brought it back to [X]. On that footing, the *Ramsay* approach does not apply'.

[1990] 1 AC 478 at 491 per Lord Templeman). Yet income and capital arc described by Lord Hoffmann as business concepts (see [2001] STC 237 at [60]).

There is little doubt that Peter Gibson LJ has a point here: Lord Hoffmann's test certainly needs further elaboration. In particular, in its current form it offers only to identify legal concepts in the abstract, which is not what is required. What is needed is a test identifying, within the context of a specific piece of legislation, when it is that Parliament is to be taken to have used a particular term in a legal sense. If the meaning of a particular legislative term is contestable in this way, then it seems inevitable that Parliament may have used it in one sense or the other. Asking the man in the street about the particular word in the abstract therefore cannot assist; what is needed is an analysis of the term in its specific statutory context.

In addition, there is a difficulty in Lord Hoffmann's description of the two categories to be identified by his distinction. If his analysis is to be applied generally in the tax context – and even more widely still – then a more pervasive term will be needed than 'commercial', which has no obvious claim to preferred status in the context, say, of inheritance tax. It may be that the obvious alternative to 'legal' is simply 'non-legal', which at least would have the advantage of being fully inclusive. If a more precise antithesis to 'juristic' thinking is required, then the well-established contest between questions of law and questions of 'ordinary' fact may suggest that 'ordinary' meaning is the best candidate. But it may be that this is not the distinction Lord Hoffmann means to draw upon. Perhaps what Lord Hoffmann means to do is extend the range of circumstances in which a specialist meaning is given to statutory term, but not a specialist *legal* meaning. Instead, Parliament is to be taken to have intended that terms should bear, for example, a specialist accountancy meaning. There is of course ample existing material supporting this idea;[220] which, if correct, will involve the courts ceding some of their authority to determine the meaning of legislation. Instead, where a term is, at root, an accountancy notion, then expert evidence as to its accepted accountancy meaning at any particular time will determine its meaning rather than legal analysis. Over time, a consequence of this can be anticipated to be a reduction in the involvement of the higher courts in questions of tax avoidance. Once a statutory concept has been held to carry a non-legal meaning, its application in later cases will be a matter solely for the Commissioners, subject only to *Edwards v Bairstow* error.[221] There may still be some room for argument as to whether a taxpayer's transactions fall within the non-legal concept,[222] but the matter will be one to be resolved on expert evidence on that question, rather than as a result of legal analysis of the taxpayer's transactions.

220 See, for example, *Gallagher v Jones* [1993] STC 537 and Freedman [1993] BTR 468. Further support for this approach can be drawn from public law where judges are increasingly willing to allow specialist tribunals a range of legitimate meaning for statutory terms within their sphere of relevant expertise: see, for example, *R v Monopolies and Mergers Commission, ex p South Yorkshire Transport Ltd* [1993] 1 WLR 23.

221 See n 51 above.

222 'Business concepts have their boundaries no less than legal ones' per Lord Hoffmann in *MacNiven* at [2001] 2 WLR 377, 396 at para 59.

Returning to the *Barclays Mercantile Business Finance* case, Carnwath LJ (junior counsel for the Crown in *Furniss v Dawson*) was also troubled by the proposed distinction, and his concerns caused him to doubt Lord Hoffmann's analysis of the earlier decisions:

> Like Peter Gibson LJ, and with similar respect to its source, I find some difficulty in understanding this dichotomy. It was a difficulty shared by both leading counsel before us. Lord Hoffmann clearly regarded *McGuckian* and *Furniss* as illustrations of 'commercial' concepts in the sense he used the term, and as therefore susceptible to *Ramsay* analysis. However, in each case, there seems a strong case for regarding the statutory concept as one of law, or certainly one on which a commercial man would look to a lawyer for advice.

Again this is a point that cannot lightly be dismissed. In the lease cases just examined, it appears that the non-legal concept which might be intended when legislation speaks of a 'tenancy' or a 'lease' is an arrangement conferring practical control of property, rather than conferring a legal right to exclusive possession. But in cases such as *Jones v Wrotham Park Settled Estates*[223] and *Belvedere Court Ltd v Frogmore*,[224] where a comprehensive legislative scheme itself provides safeguards against abuse,[225] it is very difficult to conclude that statutory terms bear a non-legal meaning. There are therefore two difficulties in the way of explaining decisions such as *Furniss* and *McGuckian* in Lord Hoffmann's terms. First, what is the alternative, non-legal meaning of the statutory concept alleged better to achieve the statute's underlying purpose? And, secondly, do the details of the particular legislative regime make it impossible to conclude that Parliament's language is to be taken other than legally?

In his analysis of *Furniss*,[226] Lord Hoffmann suggested that, unlike in *Ramsay* and *Burmah*, the question was not whether there had been a statutory 'disposal giving rise to a loss', but instead whether 'the disposal had been to one person rather than another'.[227] This is a little difficult to follow. The relevant central charging notions of capital gains tax would seem to be 'disposal', 'gain' and 'loss';[228] and it is no doubt possible to give each of them, in the abstract, a commercial meaning. But section 22(9) of the 1965 Act provides that 'the amount of the gains accruing on the disposal of assets shall be . . . subject to the further provisions in Schedules 7 and 8 to this Act'; and paragraphs 4(2) and 6(1) and (2) of Schedule 7 together provide that if, on a reorganisation whereby control is acquired by a transferee company, the transferor acquires shares in place of the original shareholding, then those shares are treated as

223 [1980] AC 74.

224 [1997] QB 858, [1996] 1 All ER 312.

225 E g the power given to a judge under s 12(4) of the Landlord and Tenant Act 1987 to order the disposal of a property without being subject to an incumbrance.

226 See text following n 176 above.

227 [2001] 2 WLR 377, 392 at para 46.

228 In the context of *Furniss v Dawson*, s 19 of the Finance Act 1965 provided that 'Tax shall be charged in accordance with this Act in respect of capital gains, that is to say chargeable gains computed in accordance with this Act and accruing to a person on the disposal of assets'; and s 23 that 'Except as otherwise expressly provided, the amount of a loss accruing on a disposal of an asset shall be computed in the same way as the amount of a gain accruing on a disposal is computed.'

the same asset as the original shares.[229] It is difficult to see how, in the face of such an explicit regime, there is scope for a commercial meaning to be given to the legislation at all; or indeed how, if such an approach is possible, it leads to a statutory question concerning whether 'the disposal had been to one person rather than another'. The stark conclusion is that, if Lord Hoffmann is correct that the new approach can be understood in the way he suggests, then cases such as *Furniss v Dawson* must be accepted as having been wrongly decided. The detailed scheduled regime, applicable on its face to the very facts in issue before the court, ousts any possible justification for holding that the statutory terms were intended to bear a non-legal meaning.

The situation may not be quite so bleak for Lord Hoffmann's analysis of *McGuckian*. Section 478(1) of the Income and Corporation Taxes Act 1970 begins with a clear statement of legislative intent, in the following terms:

> For the purpose of preventing the avoiding by individuals ordinarily resident in the United Kingdom of liability to income tax by means of transfers of assets by virtue or in consequence whereof, either alone or in conjunction with associated operations, income becomes payable to persons resident or domiciled out of the United Kingdom, it is hereby enacted as follows:–

In the face of such a purpose clause it can come as no great surprise to give a purposive construction to the legislative code which follows; and, given that 'income' is nowhere defined, to give the notion a non-legal meaning in this particular context in order to advance the legislative purpose. To do so need not mean, as Peter Gibson LJ appears to suggest, that 'income' must bear a non-legal meaning throughout the tax code. On the basis that Lord Hoffmann's purposive imposition of non-legal meanings comes to be accepted generally, it seems therefore that it may well have been appropriate in asking whether 'Shurltrust had received income or capital',[230] to approach those notions in a non-legal way. The words are to be so understood, however, because of their specific legislative context – and not as a result of asking a person in the street whether legal advice might be required to understand them.

As (re-)analysis of just the two decisions of *Furniss* and *McGuckian* shows, the courts are in for an interesting time as counsel argue which of the existing applications or non-applications of the *Ramsay* principle would have been decided differently on an application of Lord Hoffmann's distinction. If *Furniss* is indeed shown to have been wrongly decided,[231] it prompts the rather more serious question of whether there is a *Ramsay* principle worth the name needing to be explained. *Ramsay* itself, as suggested above, appears quite capable of being understood as characterisation of the relevant facts before applying a statutory concept. Perhaps matters will be clearer, and more predictable for all concerned, if the terminology is abandoned. Having determined that transactions are not shams, the only question remaining will be the

229 See Oliver LJ's judgment in the Court of Appeal in *Furniss*: [1984] AC 474 at 479–480.
230 [2001] UKHL 6, [2001] 2 WLR 377, 394 at para 52.
231 *Burmah Oil* seems almost inevitably to follow with it, relying as it does upon the detailed provisions of Schedule 7 to the 1965 Act.

application of the statute to the facts, albeit an application, in the tax context, predicated upon statutory interpretation of a kind that might have surprised Lord Tomlin.

CONCLUSION

It seems there are compelling parallels between the development of the courts' approach to attempts to avoid both lease and taxation legislation. In each, the courts have initially assumed a power to disregard agreements which goes beyond the need to detect shams, as correctly understood. In this basic sense, the developments in *Villiers* resemble those in *Furniss*. However, an urgent question of judicial legitimacy is then raised: what is the source of this power to reject agreed terms which are intended to create legal rights? Perhaps because of the constitutional issues they raise, perhaps because of the deep-pocketed litigants they involve, this question of legitimacy has been addressed most directly in the tax cases. The House of Lords judgment in *MacNiven* demonstrates that the question could no longer be side-stepped and that a radical re-thinking of the basis of approaches to avoidance was required. As a result, *MacNiven* has a major effect not just on tax cases but on any situation in which the courts must deal with a party or parties who have attempted to arrange their affairs in such a way as to avoid the application of a particular legal characterisation.

It may therefore be instructive to draw conclusions on the basis that Lord Hoffmann's account of the new approach originating in the *Ramsay* case comes to be generally accepted. How will our techniques for tackling avoidance then look? There will be a crucial distinction between two situations.

Where the relevant statutory term has a legal meaning

In the first situation, where the relevant statutory terms are deemed to have a fully legal meaning, the courts will no longer be able to rely on the so-called *Ramsay* principle to tackle avoidance: the decision in *MacNiven* conclusively rejects any attempt to argue that the *Ramsay* principle reflects a general judicial power to disregard or recharacterise a particular form of transaction. Inevitably, the focus will then shift to other judicially-established techniques of tackling avoidance. First, the courts can confidently assert that the legal characterisation of acts is a matter for them and not for the parties, so that the label attached to a transaction by the parties will not be decisive.[232] Equally, the courts are entitled to look at all the circumstances of a transaction in order to determine its legal nature, and need not assent to the manner in which the parties have recorded their dealings, nor any attempt by the parties to present elements of a transaction as discrete steps when those elements are, in truth, factually interdependent.[233] However, given the evident weakness of these powers in the face of avoidance, the crucial question will be the true extent of the courts'

232 As in *IRC v Mallaby-Deeley*, considered at text at n 60 above.
233 As in *Ramsay*, as considered at text following n 62 above.

jurisdiction to disregard sham terms or transactions. In particular, it must be asked whether decisions given in the lease context, such as *Antoniades v Villiers*, can be used either to demonstrate the greater reach of the sham concept, or to prove the existence of a similar but more powerful jurisdiction to deal with 'pretences'. It has been argued here that the sham concept is a function of, and not a limit on, the power of individuals to create legal rights according to their intention as to what legal rights they wish to create. It therefore defines what counts as an agreed term or transaction, and cannot be used to render agreed terms or transactions legally ineffective. Therefore, the decision in *Antoniades v Villiers* cannot be seen as a straightforward application of the sham concept, properly understood. Nor should it be relied on as a legitimate development of the courts' powers to tackle avoidance; each of the possible justifications for such an extension has been examined and found wanting. Indeed, the reasoning of Lord Hoffmann in *MacNiven* provides powerful confirmation of the argument advanced here that the lease cases cannot be supported by any existing common law doctrine, as such a doctrine must necessarily arrogate to judges an illegitimate power to refuse to give effect to genuine agreements.

Where the relevant statutory term has a non-legal meaning

The second situation will be where a statutory term has a non-legal meaning. In these cases, the courts will be more effective in tackling avoidance, as they will be able, without concerning themselves overmuch with inserted steps or preordainedness, simply to say that the relevant acts of the parties, regarded realistically, still amount to what the statutory language really means. The intentions of the parties as to the legal rights they wished to create, even if genuine, will not be decisive as the application of the statutory term will not depend on the purely legal effect of the transaction. As for the past, this analysis provides a useful means of justifying a number of decisions, not just in the tax context, but possibly in the lease context too:[234] the validity of these cases will depend not on the legitimacy of a supposed judicial power to apply legal characterisations regardless of agreed terms or transactions, but rather on the meaning of the relevant statutory terms in each case. As for the future, decisions reached in this way may come back to bite the judges, in that non-legal terms will inevitably develop a range of meaning attributed to them by the cases. Even a commercial term will have limits to its possible meanings, and their gradual demarcation may enable some elements of avoidance again to operate even against such non-legal terms.[235]

Deciding whether a statutory term has a legal or non-legal meaning

Following *MacNiven*, the effectiveness of the courts' efforts to tackle avoidance will therefore depend on their willingness to give statutory terms non-legal meanings. There may consequently be a risk that a court in a particular case will be tempted to interpret legislation in this way simply as a means to thwart a scheme which it views as

234 See the analysis of *Bruton v London and Quadrant Housing Trust* [2000] 1 AC 406.
235 See Lord Hoffmann at n 222, above.

unmeritorious. This danger may be countered in the future by Parliament: it is possible that the courts will be given express guidance as to whether a term is used in a legal sense, either in the legislation itself, or through a Ministerial statement preceding it.[236] Even in the absence of such statements, there will be particular terms to which a court should not give a non-legal meaning. Following *Street v Mountford*, one such example is provided by the use of 'lease' and 'tenancy', at least in the context of the Rent Acts and quite possibly when appearing in similar protective legislation. As a result, the decisions in *Antoniades v Villiers*, *Aslan v Murphy* and *Duke v Wynne* cannot be justified on the *MacNiven* approach. Equally, where the legislative regime makes clear that a non-legal meaning is excluded (as in *Furniss v Dawson* and *Bankway Properties v Pensfold-Dunsford*) there can also be no scope for such an approach to tackling avoidance. Given the repeal of the Rent Acts, the much weaker protection now given to residential tenants, and the development of purposive construction even of tax legislation, it might be thought that an analysis of the lease cases is simply of historical interest. But this is not so. On the contrary, these cases offer an intriguing hint of the future, as they demonstrate precisely the problem which will arise when a court, attempting to counter avoidance, has to apply a statutory term which has previously been given, or clearly ought to be given, a fully legal meaning. Given the limited reach of the sham concept, and given the rejection of the *Ramsay* principle as a general judicial power, will the court allow a scheme to succeed, even if it regards it unfavourably? Or will the court, like the House of Lords in *Antoniades v Villiers* and *Furniss v Dawson*, be tempted to abuse existing doctrines and commit a professional foul in order to tackle avoidance? In the contest between legislation and those who seek to avoid its effects, it is clear that, even after *MacNiven*, the final whistle has not yet been blown.[237]

236 Hence, there may also be a lesson here for both the Tax Law Rewrite and the Law Commission's project to reform the statutory regulation of rented homes. The more terminology requiring a non-legal meaning is used, the more scope there will be for the operation of the *MacNiven* analysis.

237 Compare n 180 above.

CHAPTER 9

Registered Land – A Law Unto Itself?

Charles Harpum

INTRODUCTION

Lord Birkenhead's reforms of land law, that lie at the heart of the 1925 property legislation, found their first great commentator in G C Cheshire, whose *Modern Law of Real Property* was published in 1925. Now in its 16th edition, under Edward Burn's exemplary editorship, Cheshire and Burn's *Modern Law of Real Property*,[1] continues to provide an authoritative guide to the law of real property. The importance of the 1925 legislation in the scheme of that law has, however, begun to wane over the last decade. The first victim of the reformer's axe was the Settled Land Act 1925, which now applies only to settlements created before 1997, and not to trusts of land created after 1996.[2] Secondly, and much more importantly, the Cinderella of the 1925 legislation, the Land Registration Act 1925 ('LRA 1925'),[3] is to be replaced by the Land Registration Act 2002 ('LRA 2002') with effect from 13 October 2003.[4] LRA 1925 was derived from the Land Transfer Act 1875 as amended by the Land Transfer Act 1897, the Law of Property Act 1922 and the Law of Property (Amendment) Act 1924. Although the Land Transfer Act 1875 was not the first legislative attempt to create a system of title registration,[5] it marked the effective introduction of registered conveyancing in England and Wales. Since 1875, there have therefore been two systems of conveyancing in England and Wales, the registered and the unregistered, with the former replacing the latter at an ever accelerating rate. Although 'the provisions of the Land Registration Acts were designed to operate in parallel and consistently with the property legislation governing unregistered land',[6] there have always been substantive differences between the two systems. Those differences will

1 Cheshire and Burn, *Modern Law of Real Property* (2000).
2 See Trusts of Land and Appointment of Trustees Act 1996, s 2(1).
3 The Act has not had a good press: see *Clark v Chief Land Registrar* [1994] Ch 370 at 382, where Nourse LJ endorsed a description of the Act in Megarry and Wade, *The Law of Real Property* (5th edn, 1984) 196, as 'legislation of exceptionally low quality'.
4 This is the date on which it is anticipated that LRA 2002 will be brought into force.
5 See the Land Registry Act 1862, which is finally to be repealed by LRA 2002, s 122. For the history of land registration in England and Wales, see J S Anderson, *Lawyers and the Making of English Land Law 1832–1940* (1992).
6 *Abbey National Building Society v Cann* [1991] 1 AC 56 at 77, Lord Oliver of Aylmerton.

become much more pronounced under LRA 2002. This is because the Law Commission and HM Land Registry, who jointly prepared the legislation, accepted that a system of registered conveyancing should be developed according to its own logic and potential, unconstrained by whatever the position might be in relation to unregistered conveyancing.[7]

The purpose of this essay is to examine one of the most striking substantive differences between the registered and unregistered systems in order to see how far there has been a judicial acceptance and understanding of the reasons for the differences between the two systems. The specific issue is the legal effect of registering a person as the proprietor of an estate or charge in registered land, where, had the title been unregistered, no estate or interest would have vested in him because there was no valid conveyance.

It is an appropriate time to conduct such a review. For the future, the unregistered system will be relegated to a peripheral role in conveyancing. The extension of the triggers to compulsory first registration made by the Land Registration Act 1997 and LRA 2002, means that most dispositions of unregistered land will have to be registered. Furthermore, it seems likely that some means will be found of bringing all remaining unregistered freehold land on to the register of title within a very few years,[8] leaving the principles of unregistered conveyancing to operate only in relation to dealings with those legal estates that cannot be registered.[9] In practice, therefore, the substantive principles that govern dealings with land will be those applicable to registered land in their newly recast form. It also means that, in any given case, it is more than ever inappropriate to consider what the position might have been had title been unregistered. There is also fundamental change in the underlying philosophy of land registration. Under the system of electronic conveyancing that will be introduced in time under LRA 2002, it will become impossible to transfer or create many interests in registered land except by simultaneously registering them.[10] There will, in other words be a system of title by registration, rather than (as at present) a system of registration of title.[11]

THE LEGAL EFFECT OF THE REGISTRATION OF A REGISTERED ESTATE OR CHARGE

To appreciate fully the legal effect of the registration of a person as proprietor of a registered estate or charge, it is necessary to explain and contrast three situations.

7 See *Land Registration for the Twenty-First Century: A Consultative Document* (Law Com No 254) §1.6.
8 See *Land Registration for the Twenty-First Century: A Conveyancing Revolution* (Law Com No 271) §§ 2.9–2.13 (recommending that ways in which all remaining unregistered land could be brought on to the register should be re-examined five years after LRA 2002 is brought into force).
9 Examples will include dealings with unregistered short leases that do not themselves trigger the requirement of compulsory registration and dealings with unregistered manors.
10 See LRA 2002, s 93.
11 See *Land Registration for the Twenty-First Century: A Conveyancing Revolution* (Law Com No 271) §§1.4–1.10.

(a) Where there was a conveyance of a legal estate in unregistered land prior to December 1990,[12] in an area that was not then subject to compulsory registration.[13] This was the 'pure' unregistered position and can no longer arise.

(b) Where there is a conveyance of unregistered land that triggers the requirement of compulsory registration so that the grantee or transferee becomes the first registered proprietor.

(c) Where there is a transfer or grant of a registered estate or charge.

In relation to each of these three situations, the effect of a void conveyance or transfer of the owner's legal estate will be considered, to demonstrate both the difficulties that can (or could) arise under each of them and the differences that exist (or existed) between them. A conveyance or transfer can be void for a number of reasons, of which the following are some examples which could and, in practice, do arise.

(1) It may be a forgery, which is, by definition, a nullity.

(2) It may be an *ultra vires* disposition by a local authority,[14] though when LRA 2002 is brought into force, this will cease to be an issue.[15]

(3) It may be a purported disposition by a person who either no longer exists or who no longer has the power to dispose of land because it has vested by operation of law in some other person. For example, the Registrar of Companies might strike a company off the register because he believes that it is defunct. The company is, in consequence, dissolved,[16] and its property passes by operation of law to the Crown as *bona vacantia*.[17] If the company owned land, and the officers of the company did not appreciate the fact that the company had been dissolved (or chose to ignore it), there is a risk that the company may subsequently purport to sell and convey the land. While any purchaser ought to make a search of the Companies Register to ensure that the company is still in existence, he may not do so. That conveyance would be a nullity, because the 'vendor' would no longer exist and the title to the land would be vested in the Treasury Solicitor.[18]

(4) It may be a conveyance of land which the disponor no longer owns because he has already conveyed it to another person.[19]

12 The final order extending compulsory registration to the last remaining part of England and Wales took effect on 1 December 1990.

13 For the requirement of compulsory registration, see LRA 1925, ss 123 (as substituted), 123A, and LRA 2002, ss 4–8.

14 See *Re Woking UDC (Basingstoke Canal) Act 1911* [1914] 1 Ch 300.

15 LRA 2002, ss 23–26, introduce a concept of 'owner's powers'. The effect of these provisions is that a registered proprietor (or person entitled to be registered) is taken to have power to make a disposition of any kind permitted by the general law in relation to an interest of that description (subject to certain exceptions as to charges and sub-mortgages) in the absence of a limitation reflected by an entry in the register or imposed by or under LRA 2002. However, this presumption only prevents a disponee's title from being questioned: it does not validate a transaction that the disponor did not in fact have power to make.

16 See Companies Act 1985, s 652.

17 Companies Act 1985, s 654.

18 If the company were revived subsequently, the conveyance would then be effective. It would be as if the land had never vested in the Crown: see *Allied Dunbar Assurance plc v Fowkes* [1994] 1 EGLR 122.

19 This is the familiar case of the double conveyance: see e g *Epps v Esso Petroleum Co Ltd* [1973] 2 All ER 465, [1973] 1 WLR 1071.

Situation 1: Void conveyance of an unregistered estate prior to December 1990

Any void conveyance of a legal estate in unregistered land prior to December 1990 in an area that was not subject to compulsory registration, was a nullity and had no effect in law.[20] If the person who thought that he had acquired the land went into possession, he had no title to the land and was in fact a squatter.[21] His possession was vulnerable until the limitation period, normally 12 years, had elapsed.[22] If, before the true owner's title was barred, he purported to dispose of the land to a purchaser, that purchaser merely acquired the disponor's own freehold estate that arose from his adverse possession.[23] The purchaser's title could be challenged until the limitation period had ended and the true owner's right to recover the land was barred and his title extinguished.

Situation 2: Void conveyance of an unregistered estate that triggers the requirement of compulsory first registration

Most conveyances of a legal freehold estate in unregistered land,[24] together with certain other important transactions,[25] trigger the requirement of first registration.[26] If the relevant conveyance is a nullity and the disponee[27] is mistakenly registered, what is the effect?

By virtue of the statutory provisions, notwithstanding the fact that the conveyance was void, registration will vest the relevant estate in the first registered proprietor together with the benefit of any rights appurtenant to that estate.[28] It is helpful to consider the wording of the relevant legislation, taking first registration of a freehold as the exemplar.

As regards LRA 1925, s 5 provides:

> Where the registered land is a freehold estate, the registration of any person as first proprietor thereof with an absolute title shall vest in the person so registered an estate in fee simple in possession in the land, together with all rights,

20 See e g *Boursot v Savage* (1866) LR 2 Eq 134; *Re Cooper* (1882) 20 Ch D 611, especially at 623 (where Kay J stated the principle).
21 A person may have the necessary *animus possidendi* for adverse possession if he wrongly believes that he is the owner of the land.
22 See Limitation Act 1980, ss 15, 17.
23 See *Rosenberg v Cook* (1881) 8 QBD 162. As that case demonstrates, a squatter has a fee simple absolute in possession from the moment that he takes adverse possession of land. Because of the relativity of title, there is no conceptual difficulty in there being two concurrent legal freehold titles.
24 All transfers for valuable consideration, by way of gift, in pursuance of a court order or by way of an assent have to be registered.
25 Including: (i) the assignment of a lease with more than 21 years (LRA 1925) or 7 years (LRA 2002) to run; (ii) the creation of a first legal charge over a freehold estate or over a leasehold estate having more than 21 years (LRA 1925) or 7 years (LRA 2002) to run and; (iii) the grant of a lease for a term of more than 21 years (LRA 1925) or 7 years (LRA 2002).
26 See LRA 1925, s 123 (as substituted); LRA 2002, s 4.
27 In the case where the creation of a legal charge triggers the requirement of compulsory first registration, both the owner of the legal estate and the chargee will be registered.
28 LRA 1925, ss 5 (freehold), 9 (leasehold); LRA 2002, ss 11 (freehold), 12 (leasehold).

privileges and appurtenances belonging or appurtenant thereto, subject to the following rights and interests, that is to say:

(a) Subject to the incumbrances, and other entries, if any, appearing on the register; and

(b) Unless the contrary is expressed on the register, subject to such overriding interests, if any, as affect the registered land; and

(c) where the first proprietor is not entitled for his own benefit to the registered land subject, as between himself and the persons entitled to minor interests, to any minor interests of such persons of which he has notice,

but free from all other estates and interests whatsoever, including estates and interests of His Majesty

The equivalent provisions in LRA 2002, s 11(1)–(5), are as follows:

(1) This section is concerned with the registration of a person under this Chapter as the proprietor of a freehold estate.

(2) Registration with absolute title has the effect described in subsections (3) to (5).

(3) The estate is vested in the proprietor together with all interests subsisting for the benefit of the estate.

(4) The estate is vested in the proprietor subject only to the following interests affecting the estate at the time of registration—

  (a) interests which are the subject of an entry in the register in relation to the estate,

  (b) unregistered interests which fall within any of the paragraphs of Schedule 1,[29] and

  (c) interests acquired under the Limitation Act 1980 (c 58) of which the proprietor has notice.

(5) If the proprietor is not entitled to the estate for his own benefit, or not entitled solely for his own benefit, then, as between himself and the persons beneficially entitled to the estate, the estate is vested in him subject to such of their interests as he has notice of.

While the provisions of the two Acts are not identical in their effect, they do have much in common. First, each provides for the vesting of the freehold estate in the first registered proprietor on registration. In this context, it may be noted that neither of the sections refers to the *legal* estate, but to the 'freehold estate'. Secondly, each section provides for the vesting of rights appurtenant to the estate as well as the estate itself. Appurtenant rights are those that are annexed to some land for the benefit of that land, such as the benefit of an easement or of certain *profits à prendre*. Thirdly, both sections make express provision for the case where the first registered proprietor holds as trustee. The fact that it is necessary to make express provision for that case, strongly implies that both legal and beneficial ownership are otherwise vested by statute in the

29 LRA 2002 does not use the expression 'overriding interest' unlike LRA 1925. However, by whatever name, the interests listed in LRA 2002, Sch 1 are unregistered interests that nonetheless override first registration.

proprietor on first registration. This point is reinforced in LRA 2002 by the new provision contained in section 11(4)(c). The effect of that provision, when read with section 11(4)(b), is that a first registered proprietor will not be bound by the legal estate vested in a squatter who had acquired title by adverse possession prior to first registration unless either that squatter is in actual occupation (so that he has an unregistered interest that will override first registration)[30] or the first registered proprietor has notice of his interest. The case which LRA 2002, s 11(4)(c) addresses arises where X, the apparent legal owner of unregistered land, conveys it to Y, but where in fact the true owner of the land is Z. Although Z is no longer in actual occupation of the land, he had previously acquired title to it by adverse possession.[31] In that case, X is conveying land which he does not own. Nevertheless, LRA 2002 makes it clear that Y will take free of any claims that Z might otherwise have had if Y had no notice of Z's interest. The fact that it was necessary to make express provision for Y to be bound by Z's interest where he had notice of that interest shows that Y would not otherwise have been bound by it.[32]

As a matter of construction of the two sections, therefore, it is suggested that the only possible inference is that, whenever a person is registered as first registered proprietor of an estate, registration vests in him both the legal and beneficial title. This is so even if there has been no valid conveyance of the legal estate to him. This is entirely consistent with the scheme of both LRA 1925 and LRA 2002, because each Act provides a mechanism for correcting errors in the register and for the payment of indemnity to any party who suffers loss as a result of errors in the register.[33]

Notwithstanding the analysis given above, there is some authority which suggests that, in a case where the conveyance was a nullity, registration merely vests the bare legal title in the first registered proprietor. That proprietor then holds it on a bare trust for the person who would otherwise be the owner of the land. In *Epps v Esso Petroleum Co Ltd*,[34] there had been a double conveyance of a strip of unregistered freehold land and the purchaser under the second conveyance had been registered as the first registered proprietor. In proceedings brought against the first registered proprietor for rectification of the register, Templeman J was apparently prepared to accept counsel's argument that only the bare legal title had passed to that first registered proprietor. The person to whom the land had first been conveyed 'retained or acquired . . . an equitable interest in fee simple'.[35] That assumption was not necessary for the decision because the application for rectification was unsuccessful in any event, as is explained below.

30 See LRA 2002, Sch 1, para 2.
31 The danger is that a purchaser would not be able to discover the squatter's rights in those circumstances.
32 Under LRA 1925, s 70(1)(f), rights acquired by squatters under the Limitation Acts were overriding interests whether or not the squatter remained in actual occupation. Under LRA 2002, the position of squatters is substantially weakened. In those comparatively rare situations in which a squatter has a right to be registered as proprietor, that right will not bind any registered disponee for valuable consideration of the land in question, unless it is protected either by an entry in the register (which is most unlikely) or by the squatter's actual occupation: cf LRA 2002, Sch 3, para 2.
33 See LRA 1925, ss 82, 83; LRA 2002, Sch 4, Sch 8.
34 [1973] 2 All ER 465, [1973] 1 WLR 1071.
35 [1973] 1 WLR 1071 at 1077, Templeman J.

Templeman J's assumption requires closer analysis. There are significant restrictions as to when the register will be rectified against a registered proprietor who is in possession: see LRA 1925, s 82(3) and LRA 2002, Sch 4, paras 3(2), 6(2). These provisions undoubtedly enhance the security of title enjoyed by a registered proprietor.[36] Under LRA 1925, s 82(3), the protection given to the proprietor in possession is excluded in four situations.[37] One of those situations is where rectification is sought to give effect to an overriding interest. If first registration merely vested the bare legal title in the defendant, as the plaintiff's counsel contended, so that the plaintiff was beneficially entitled to the disputed land under a bare trust, and the plaintiff was in actual occupation of that land, the defendant would not be protected from rectification as a proprietor in possession.[38] As Templeman J explained:

> If the registered proprietor is not in possession then section 82(3) does not apply, and the court will normally grant rectification: see *Chowood Ltd v Lyall (No 2)* [1930] 2 Ch 156. A fortiori if the registered proprietor is not in possession but the applicant has an overriding interest constituted by an equitable interest protected by actual occupation, the court will grant rectification . . .[39]

Templeman J went on to find that the plaintiff was not in actual occupation of the disputed strip and therefore declined to exercise his discretion to rectify the register. He did not, however, probe counsel's contention that the defendant held the disputed strip on a bare trust for the plaintiff. Had he done so, he would, it is suggested, have rejected it.

Quite apart from the issue of construction of LRA 1925, s 5, that has been explored above, if counsel's contention was correct, it might have provided a simple mechanism for side-stepping the discretionary rectification provisions in the Act. If the defendant held the disputed land on a bare trust for the plaintiff, it might have been open to the latter to require the defendant to transfer the legal title to him under the rule in *Saunders v Vautier*.[40] Under this rule a beneficiary who is of full age and capacity and is absolutely entitled under a trust, may require the trustees to transfer the property to him or at his direction. Furthermore, the beneficiary's claim would never be time-barred under the Limitation Act 1980.[41] Presumably if the principle in *Saunders*

36 See *Land Registration for the Twenty-First Century: A Consultative Document* (Law Com No 254) §8.23; *Kingsalton Ltd v Thames Water Developments Ltd* [2001] EWCA Civ 20, [2002] 1 P & CR 184 at 191, 195, and 197.

37 There were in fact five exceptions at the time when *Epps v Esso Petroleum Co Ltd* was decided. One of them was subsequently removed by the Administration of Justice Act 1977.

38 It might also be added that if the plaintiff had been in actual occupation, and the register had then been rectified, no indemnity would have been payable to the registered proprietor. Because he would have been bound by the plaintiff's overriding interest he would not have suffered loss by reason of the rectification and could not therefore have recovered indemnity under LRA 1925, s 83(1): see *Re Chowood's Registered Land* [1933] Ch 574.

39 [1973] 1 WLR 1071 at 1078.

40 (1845) 4 Beav 115; affd (1845) Cr & Ph 240. Under this rule a beneficiary who is of full age and capacity and is absolutely entitled under a trust, may require the trustees to transfer the property to him or at his direction.

41 See Limitation Act 1980, s 21(1)(b) (no period of limitation applicable to an action by a beneficiary to recover trust property from a trustee).

v Vautier could be invoked in these circumstances, not only would the provisions on rectification be avoided, but the defendant would have had no claim to indemnity. The possibility of employing the rule in *Saunders v Vautier* to circumvent the law on rectification of the register was considered in a detailed and cogent critique of *Epps v Esso Petroleum Co Ltd*[42] by Simon Palk.[43] The core of Mr Palk's criticism was as follows. Referring to LRA 1925, s 5, which, as has been explained above, provides that first registration 'shall vest in the person so registered an estate in fee simple in possession in the land', he commented as follows:

> section 5 is the most powerful vesting instrument in our property law . . . [It] alone vests a title in a registered proprietor, where no entitlement exists – it can vest a title in a minor, and even vests a title where there has been no conveyance. Given then the general power of section 5, it would be strange to think that it merely vested a legal estate without the rights of beneficial enjoyment. Without the equitable estate, registration would be a mere empty act. The power and the glory of the registered system would be brought down to naught. If the equitable estate does not vest in the registered proprietor, he will be holding the legal estate on trust . . . [He] will then be liable to a call from the equitable owner to transfer the legal estate under the rule in *Saunders v Vautier*. Registration will have counted for nothing.[44]

Nothing more seems to have been heard of the contention that, where first registration of an estate came about as a result of a void conveyance, the registered proprietor held the legal estate on a bare trust for the person whose land it would otherwise have been, until it was recently touched upon, *obiter*, by the Court of Appeal. In *Malory Enterprises Ltd v Cheshire Homes (UK) Ltd*,[45] a case that is considered in detail below, Arden LJ contrasted LRA 1925, s 5 with s 69(1), which has a similar vesting function where title is already registered.[46] In that case the issue was as to effect of a void transfer by a company that personated the registered proprietor, and the Court of Appeal held that registration of the purported transferee merely vested the bare legal title in it.[47] Arden LJ drew two distinctions between the provisions. First, LRA 1925, s 69(1), unlike s 5, referred expressly to 'the *legal estate* in fee simple in possession' and not merely to 'an estate in fee simple in possession'.[48] Secondly, unlike LRA 1925, s 5, there was nothing in s 69(1) which vested the registered estate in the new proprietor 'together with all rights, privileges and appurtenances'.[49] The implication of these dicta is that where a person has been registered as first registered proprietor following a void conveyance to him, both legal and beneficial title is vested in the first

42 [1973] 2 All ER 465, [1973] 1 WLR 1071.
43 Simon N L Palk, 'First registration of title – just what does it do?' (1974) 34 Conv (NS) 236. Mr Palk, then a Fellow of Fitzwilliam College, Cambridge, is now a Senior Lecturer at the University of Adelaide.
44 Simon N L Palk, 'First registration of title – just what does it do?' (1974) 34 Conv (NS) 236 at 250.
45 [2002] EWCA Civ 151, [2002] Ch 216.
46 LRA 1925, s 69(1) is considered below.
47 Arden LJ gave the principal judgment. Both Clarke and Schiemann LJJ concurred in it save as to one issue: see below.
48 [2002] EWCA Civ 151, [2002] Ch 216 at 232.
49 [2002] EWCA Civ 151, [2002] Ch 216 at 232.

registered proprietor as a result of LRA 1925, s 5. While the conclusion that s 5 has this effect is to be welcomed, the reasoning that led Arden LJ to it must, with respect, be questioned, and has unfortunate consequences in relation to LRA 1925, s 69(1), which are considered below. Quite why the reference to 'all rights, privileges and appurtenances' should be thought to transmit the beneficial title is a mystery. Beneficial ownership is not appurtenant to a legal estate.

Situation 3: Void transfer of a registered legal estate that is nonetheless completed by registration

The final situation that must be considered arises where there is a void transfer or grant of a registered estate and the disponee is mistakenly registered as proprietor of a registered estate or charge. It is necessary to consider the relevant statutory provisions in LRA 1925 and how they have been interpreted before examining the equivalent section of LRA 2002.

LRA 1925, s 69(1) provides:

> The proprietor of land . . . shall be deemed to have vested in him without any conveyance, where the registered land is freehold, the legal estate in fee simple in possession, and where the registered land is leasehold the legal term created by the registered lease, but subject to the overriding interests, if any, including any mortgage term or charge by way of legal mortgage created by or under the Law of Property Act 1925, or this Act or otherwise which has priority to the registered estate.

It will be noted that s 69(1) is confined to the registration of freehold and leasehold estates. It says nothing about charges.[50] As is explained below, the equivalent provision in LRA 2002 is rather different.

The effect of the subsection is that registration vests the legal estate in the registered proprietor: no significance is to be attached to the use of the word 'deemed'.[51] Indeed it is registration alone that has this effect. Vesting occurs through registration 'without any conveyance', a process judicially described as 'statutory magic'.[52] Although the subsection makes no reference to appurtenances, it does not need to do so. A *conveyance* of a legal estate in *unregistered land* will carry with it any appurtenances without express mention.[53] LRA 1925 makes express provision by which a *registered disposition of registered land* vests the relevant estate in the transferee or grantee 'together with all rights, privileges, and appurtenances belonging to or appurtenant

50 Cf LRA 1925, s 26(1) (charge to be completed by registration).
51 *Morelle Ltd v Wakeling* [1955] 2 QB 379 at 413, 414.
52 *Argyle Building Society v Hammond* (1984) 49 P & CR 148 at 153, Slade LJ. The phrase was found in Ruoff and Roper's *The Law and Practice of Registered Conveyancing* (4th edn, 1979) 64. It is not found in the equivalent passage in the current loose-leaf edition of that work at §2-08.
53 This is an ancient rule: see Co Litt 121b; Williams, *Vendor and Purchaser* (4th edn, 1936) 657; *Beddington v Atlee* (1887) 35 Ch D 317 at 326; *Godwin v Schweppes Ltd* [1902] 1 Ch 926 at 932.

thereto'.[54] However, the statutory vesting of the legal estate on registration must necessarily do likewise in any case in which there was no registered disposition.[55] The legal estate in the land in question carries any appurtenances with it.

Unlike LRA 1925, s 5, s 69(1) refers explicitly to the vesting by registration of 'the *legal* estate in fee simple in possession and where the registered land is leasehold the *legal* term created by the registered lease'.[56] This necessarily prompts the question as to whether, if there is no valid disposition, registration merely vests the bare legal title in the registered proprietor or both the legal and beneficial title. This is not a new debate,[57] but it has now become a live one because of the decision of the Court of Appeal in *Malory Enterprises Ltd v Cheshire Homes (UK) Ltd*,[58] that is considered below. Before considering that case, it is worth examining the matter in principle. There are two aspects to the issue:

(1) the practical consequences of holding that the registered proprietor is merely a bare trustee; and
(2) whether, in the light of those consequences, LRA 1925, s 69(1) should, as a matter of construction, be interpreted both literally and narrowly to mean that only the bare legal title vests by registration.

A person may be registered as proprietor of a registered estate in any of the following circumstances.

The first case is where there has been a registered disposition in his favour by the registered proprietor (or by some other person having power to make the disposition, such as a chargee). There can only be a registered disposition where the transfer or grant is valid and not for some reason a nullity.[59] There is no reason to doubt that where there is such a disposition, it will vest the estate in the disponee both legally and beneficially.[60] A registered disposition will have this effect even though it is voidable, so long as it has not been avoided.[61] If, therefore, the disponee makes a further registered disposition to a person (such as a registered chargee) before any such avoidance, that disposition will be valid and there will be no ground upon which the original disponor can seek to have the register rectified against the second disponee.[62]

The second case is where a person is entitled to be registered as proprietor by operation of law, as where a squatter establishes his title to the registrar's satisfaction.[63] It has now been settled, at least at first instance, that where a squatter is

54 LRA 1925, s 20(1). In relation to a registered disposition of a registered leasehold, LRA 1925, s 23(1) provides for the disposition to pass 'all implied or expressed rights, privileges, and appurtenances attached to the estate transferred or created'.
55 An example would be where a squatter is registered as proprietor under LRA 1925, s 75(3).
56 Emphasis added.
57 See Simon N L Palk, 'First registration of title – just what does it do?' (1974) 34 Conv (NS) 236 at 249, referring to earlier discussion of the point.
58 [2002] EWCA Civ 151, [2002] Ch 216.
59 See *Malory Enterprises Ltd v Cheshire Homes (UK) Ltd* [2002] EWCA Civ 151, [2002] Ch 216 at 232.
60 Cf LRA 1925, ss 20(1), 23(1).
61 Cf *Norwich and Peterborough Building Society v Steed* [1993] Ch 116, [1993] 1 All ER 330.
62 *Norwich and Peterborough Building Society v Steed* [1993] Ch 116, [1993] 1 All ER 330.
63 LRA 1925, s 75(3).

registered he succeeds to the estate of the registered proprietor against whom he has adversely possessed. He is not registered with the independent fee simple that he has by virtue of his adverse possession.[64] Prior to such registration, the registered proprietor will have held the registered estate on a bare trust for the squatter from the time when the limitation period expired.[65] There can be no doubt therefore that, when the squatter is registered, he will have both the legal and beneficial interests in the land in question.[66]

The third case is the one with which we are concerned, namely where a person is registered as proprietor by mistake, as where there has been a forged transfer to that person. Whether or not registration vests merely the bare legal title, the following points are clear:

(1) The register could be rectified not only against the new registered proprietor,[67] but (apparently) also against any subsequent disponee to whom that new registered proprietor made a disposition.[68]
(2) In either case, subject to what is said at (5) below, the claim to rectification might be defeated if the new registered proprietor or any subsequent disponee was a proprietor in possession because of the protection conferred on such a proprietor by LRA 1925.[69]
(3) Even if rectification were ordered, a proprietor of any registered land or charge who claims in good faith under a forged disposition has a claim to indemnity.[70]
(4) If rectification were not ordered, the former registered proprietor would be

64 See *Spectrum Investment Co v Holmes* [1981] 1 All ER 6, [1981] 1 WLR 221; *Central London Commercial Estates Ltd v Kato Kagaku Ltd* [1998] 4 All ER 948. The courts have reached this conclusion as a matter of statutory interpretation. The position where title is unregistered is different. The operation of the Limitation Act 1980 does not effect a 'Parliamentary conveyance' as was once though to be the case: see *Tichborne v Weir* (1892) 67 LT 735. The freehold estate of the paper owner is extinguished and the squatter's title is his own unchallengeable fee simple. Whether title is registered or unregistered, the squatter who acquires title by adverse possession takes it subject to any prior interests in land that have not been extinguished by the squatter's adverse possession, such as restrictive covenants or easements: see *Re Nisbet and Potts' Contract* [1906] 1 Ch 386. The position in relation to pre-existing mortgages over land under the present law is complex and may not have been finally settled. To the extent that it can arise under LRA 2002, it is dealt with by express provision: see LRA 2002, Sch 6, paras 9, 10.

65 LRA 1925, s 75(1).

66 Under LRA 2002, the treatment of squatters is fundamentally different and it will become much more difficult to acquire registered land by means of adverse possession: see LRA 2002, ss 96–98; Sch 6.

67 Depending on the facts, this could be under LRA 1925, s 82(1)(d) (entry in the register obtained by fraud), (g) (registration in the name of a person who, if the land had not been registered, would not have been the estate owner), or (h) (entry made under a mistake). See *Norwich and Peterborough Building Society v Steed* [1993] Ch 116 at 133–135.

68 See *Argyle Building Society v Hammond* (1984) 49 P & CR 148, as explained in *Norwich and Peterborough Building Society v Steed* [1993] Ch 116 at 136–138. Although the registration of the new registered proprietor came about as a result of a forged transfer, he can, nonetheless, make a valid registered disposition, because he is the registered proprietor. However, under LRA 1925, s 82(1), there are grounds of rectification that would appear to be wide enough to enable rectification to be ordered in such a case against the disponee. The position may be different under LRA 2002: see Sch 4, paras 2(1), 5.

69 See LRA 1925, s 82(3) limiting the circumstances in which rectification can be obtained against a proprietor who is in possession: see above.

70 LRA 1925, s 83(4), reversing in part the decision in *A-G v Odell* [1906] 2 Ch 47.

entitled to a payment of indemnity from the registrar.[71] The measure of indemnity for the loss of the estate would be restricted to the value of the land at the time when the new registered proprietor was erroneously registered.[72] However, it is the practice of the registrar to pay interest on that sum from the date of that erroneous registration.[73]

(5) If the former registered proprietor was still in actual occupation of the land that had been erroneously registered in the name of the new proprietor, he would have an overriding interest, namely the right to seek rectification of the register coupled with actual occupation.[74] If that were so, the limitations applicable to a proprietor who was in possession would be inapplicable,[75] and rectification of the register would almost certainly be ordered. As the registered proprietor would suffer no loss by reason of the rectification, he would recover no indemnity.[76]

If registration merely vests the bare legal estate in the person who is registered as proprietor pursuant to the forged disposition and he holds it on a bare trust for the former registered proprietor, the following would appear to be the consequences:

(1) By virtue of the rule in *Saunders v Vautier*,[77] the former registered proprietor might require the new registered proprietor to transfer the registered estate to him. As explained above, the former proprietor's right would never be time-barred. It might, however, be defeated if there had been a registered disposition of the estate by the registered proprietor to a purchaser. This is because legal and beneficial title would vest in the purchaser by virtue of that registered disposition.

(2) If the rule in *Saunders v Vautier* can be applied in this manner, the scheme laid down in LRA 1925 for dealing with mistakes in the register by means of rectification and indemnity will be circumvented. The system of rectification and indemnity goes to the root of the system of registered conveyancing, and there could be grave hardship if it could be side-stepped in this way. In the leading textbook on registered conveyancing, it is stated that:

> It is possible that a registered proprietor may, perhaps quite innocently, acquire title as a result of fraud, including forgery, and the fact that he does so cannot possibly alter the fact that he is the registered proprietor and that, as such, the legal estate is vested in him, unless and until the register is rectified against him.[78]

(3) If the former registered proprietor were in actual occupation of the land vested in the new registered proprietor, he would have an overriding interest, namely

71 LRA 1925, s 83(2).
72 LRA 1925, s 83(8)(a).
73 The statutory basis for this is said to be Land Registration and Land Charges Act 1971 s 2(5). For the future, the power to pay interest is made explicit in LRA 2002, Sch 8, para 9.
74 LRA 1925, s 70(1)(g); *Malory Enterprises Ltd v Cheshire Homes (UK) Ltd* [2002] EWCA Civ 151, [2002] Ch 216 at 232–233.
75 LRA 1925, s 83(2); *Chowood Ltd v Lyall (No 2)* [1930] 2 Ch 156; above.
76 *Re Chowood's Registered Land* [1933] Ch 574.
77 (1845) 4 Beav 115; affd (1845) Cr & Ph 240; above.
78 Ruoff and Roper, *The Law and Practice of Registered Conveyancing* (2002) §2-08.

an interest under a bare trust protected by actual occupation.[79] The consequences of this in relation to rectification and indemnity are as set out above at paragraph (5).

This interpretation of LRA 1925, s 69(1) undermines, therefore, the essential structure of land registration without any compensating gains. Does the wording of LRA 1925, s 69(1) compel such an interpretation? It is suggested that, on a purposive construction of the subsection, it does not.[80]

The background to LRA 1925, s 69(1) is, in brief, as follows. Prior to 1926, there could be no certainty whatever that the person who was named as proprietor in the register had any estate vested in him, because the applicable legislation permitted dealings off the register.[81] LRA 1925, s 69(1) was intended to address this problem and to make it plain that the legal estate was always vested in the registered proprietor for the time being. This analysis is supported by LRA 1925, s 69(4) which provides that 'The estate for the time being vested in the proprietor shall only be capable of being disposed of or dealt with by him in manner authorised by the Act'. The registered proprietor would therefore have the legal estate vested in him unless and until some other person was registered as proprietor of that estate. If the registered proprietor wished to transfer his registered estate, he was obliged to do so in the manner laid down in LRA 1925 and the rules made under it. The express reference to the legal estate must surely have been intended to draw a distinction between the registered and unregistered systems of conveyancing. In unregistered conveyancing, the legal estate passes by deed of conveyance. In registered conveyancing, the execution of a valid transfer and the payment of the price will make the purchaser the absolute owner in equity, but until he is registered, the legal estate does not pass. It does not follow that, if there is no valid transfer or grant, the registration of a person as proprietor vests only the legal and not the beneficial title to the land in him. The system of rectification and indemnity that is created to deal with such mistakes is not hindered if both the legal estate and the beneficial interest which is normally carried by that legal estate are vested in the registered proprietor. On the contrary, as explained above, if the beneficial interest *does* remain outstanding in the previous owner, he will be able to subvert the provisions on rectification and indemnity.

The decision of the Court of Appeal in Malory Enterprises Ltd v Cheshire Homes (UK) Ltd

Stated shortly, the facts in *Malory Enterprises Ltd v Cheshire Homes (UK) Ltd*[82] were these. By the deception of those who had dishonestly set it up, an English company

79 See LRA 1925, s 70(1)(g); *Hodgson v Marks* [1971] Ch 892.

80 Simon N L Palk, in 'First registration of title – just what does it do?' (1974) 34 Conv (NS) 236 at 249–250, took the view that LRA 1925, s 69(1) vested both the legal and beneficial title in the registered proprietor, though his reasons are not entirely convincing.

81 See Ruoff and Roper's *The Law and Practice of Registered Conveyancing* (2002) §2-07; and *Capital and Counties Bank Ltd v Rhodes* [1903] 1 Ch 631.

82 [2002] EWCA Civ 151, [2002] Ch 216. Leave to appeal to the House of Lords has been given: [2002] 1 WLR 3016.

called Malory Enterprises Ltd managed to obtain a land certificate in its name and address in relation to a parcel of land registered in the name of a British Virgin Island company of the same name, the claimant in the action. The dishonest company then sold the parcel of land to the defendant. It was found as a fact by the trial judge that the claimant remained in actual occupation of the land at all material times.[83] He also held that the defendant was never in possession of the land (so that it could not claim the protection against rectification of the register conferred by LRA 1925, s 82(3), as proprietor in possession). After the dispute arose, the defendant entered the parcel of land and demolished a structure on it. The trial judge[84] ordered that the register of title should be rectified retrospectively to the date when the defendant was registered as proprietor. It was also held that the defendant was liable in damages for trespass, as the claimant was in possession of the land and had the better right to possess it.

An appeal to the Court of Appeal was dismissed, and it was held as follows:

(1) The transfer by the fraudulent English company was void and did not take effect as a registered disposition under LRA 1925, s 20(1).

(2) LRA 1925, s 69(1), unlike s 5, merely vested the legal title in the registered proprietor in the absence of a valid disposition of the registered estate. The claimant's rights as beneficial owner continued. The reasons why the Court reached this conclusion have already been mentioned above.

(3) The Court accepted the trial judge's finding that, as the claimant was in actual occupation, and had a continuing beneficial interest under a bare trust, it was entitled to rectification of the register. It had an overriding interest under LRA 1925, s 70(1)(g), to which the defendant necessarily took subject. It is noteworthy that the trial judge held that no purpose would be served by refusing rectification. The defendant 'would simply be holding the legal estate for the purpose of giving effect to the interest of the [claimant] and could indeed be called upon to execute a transfer'.[85] In other words, the trial judge expressly accepted that the rule in *Saunders v Vautier* could be used to circumvent the provisions on rectification and indemnity, and there is nothing in the judgments of the Court of Appeal to suggest that this conclusion was wrong.

(4) The Court of Appeal also accepted that, as the claimant was in possession and had, by virtue of its continuing beneficial ownership, a better right to possess than the defendant, it was entitled to damages for trespass even without seeking rectification.[86]

83 This finding was unsuccessfully challenged in the Court of Appeal.

84 Maddocks J, sitting as Judge of the Chancery Division of the High Court.

85 [2002] EWCA Civ 151, [2002] Ch 216 at 224, Arden LJ.

86 Cf *Chowood Ltd v Lyall (No 2)* [1930] 2 Ch 156, where a squatter, who had acquired title to land by adverse possession prior to its mistaken first registration in the name of the plaintiffs, successfully resisted an action for trespass brought against her (because she had a better right to possess the land) and obtained rectification of the register to give effect to her overriding interest.

(5) In the alternative, the claimant had an overriding interest under LRA 1925, s 70(1)(g) by reason of its actual occupation coupled with a right to seek rectification of the register.[87]

(6) Arden LJ held that the court had no jurisdiction to order rectification of the register retrospectively. Although this accords with earlier authority,[88] both Clarke and Schiemann LJJ preferred not to decide the point.

Although the issue of whether the register can be rectified retrospectively has attracted some attention,[89] that particular point is now largely of academic interest. For the future, LRA 2002, Sch 4, para 8, makes it clear that the powers of rectifying the register[90] are prospective in effect. They 'extend to changing *for the future* the priority of any interest affecting the registered estate or charge concerned'.[91] One of the aims of LRA 2002 is to create a conclusive register.[92] A power of retrospective rectification would necessarily run counter to that objective.

The point of real importance in the case is the finding that, in the absence of a valid transfer, LRA 1925, s 69(1) merely vests the legal estate in the registered proprietor, subject to the continuing beneficial interest of the former registered proprietor. The dangers that flow from that finding have been explained above. For the reasons there suggested, the Court could have reached a different view on a purposive interpretation of LRA 1925, s 69(1). In fairness to the Court such a purposive interpretation of the subsection was not put in argument, so far as the report of the case suggests.

The final question is whether, if the decision on LRA 1925, s 69(1) in *Malory Enterprises Ltd v Cheshire Homes (UK) Ltd*[93] is upheld on appeal to the House of Lords, that outcome would have any implications for the interpretation of the equivalent provisions of LRA 2002.

The vesting provisions of LRA 2002

The nearest equivalent provision to LRA 1925, s 69(1) in LRA 2002, s 58, provides:

> (1) If, on the entry of a person in the register as the proprietor of the legal estate would not otherwise be vested in him, it shall be deemed to be vested in him as a result of the registration.

87 It is a nice point whether such an overriding interest would have given the claimant a better right to possess the land than the defendant. If, as Arden LJ held (below), the right to rectification was not retrospective (with which this writer respectfully agrees), then it should not have done. The claimant should have been left to its claim to indemnity from the registrar under LRA 1925, s 83(1)(b) (for loss suffered notwithstanding rectification).

88 See *Freer v Unwins Ltd* [1976] Ch 288, [1976] 1 All ER 634; *Clark v Chief Land Registrar* [1993] Ch 294, [1993] 2 All ER 936.

89 Cf Duncan Sheehan 'Rights to Rectify the Land Register as Interests in Land' (2003) 119 LQR 31.

90 The term 'rectification' has a narrower meaning under LRA 2002 than under LRA 1925. It is confined to an alteration of the register that both involves the correction of a mistake and prejudicially affects the title of a registered proprietor: LRA 2002, Sch 4, para 1.

91 Emphasis added.

92 See *Land Registration for the Twenty-First Century: A Conveyancing Revolution* (Law Com No 271) §1.5.

93 [2002] EWCA Civ 151, [2002] Ch 216.

(2) Subsection (1) does not apply where the entry is made in pursuance of a registrable disposition in relation to which some other registration requirement remains to be met.

The wording of that section is significantly different from that of LRA 1925, s 69(1), and its purpose is clear.

First, it does not refer to registration vesting a legal estate in the registered proprietor. It refers instead to the registration of a person as 'the proprietor of a legal estate'. 'Legal estate' has the same meaning as in the Law of Property Act 1925 ('LPA 1925').[94] Under LPA 1925, s 1(4):

> The estates, interests and charges which under this section are authorised to subsist or to be conveyed or created at law are (when subsisting or conveyed or created at law) in this Act referred to as 'legal estate' . . .

In other words 'legal estates' are not confined to the two legal estates *in land* within LPA 1925, s 1(1),[95] but also include the interests and charges that can be created at law under LPA 1925, s 1(2), including easements, rights and privileges, rent-charges, a charge by way of legal mortgage and certain rights of entry. A person can be registered as a proprietor of some of these rights, including a *profit à prendre* in gross, a franchise, a rent-charge and a charge by way of legal mortgage. If that is so, the reference in LRA 2002, s 58(1) to the registration of a person as 'the proprietor of a legal estate' cannot refer to the bare legal title. It would be meaningless to say that a person who had been registered as the proprietor of a registered charge under a forged deed of charge held that charge on a bare trust for the true owner.

Secondly, this point becomes even clearer from LRA 2002, s 58(2). Under LRA 2002, s 27(4), a registered disposition has to be completed by meeting the registration requirements that are set out in detail in Sch 2. By LRA 2002, s 27(1):

> If a disposition of a registered estate or registered charge is required to be completed by registration, it does not operate at law until the relevant registration requirements are met.

LRA 2002, s 58(2) qualifies s 58(1) to ensure that this principle is effective. A registrable disposition operates in equity only until it is completed by registration. There is nothing, therefore, in s 58(1) that should lead to the conclusion that the vesting under it is merely of the bare legal title, whatever may be the true construction of LRA 1925, s 69(1). It should also be noted that, under LRA 2002, there is no equivalent provision to LRA 1925, ss 20(1) and 23(1), by which a registered disposition vests an estate in the disponee together with appurtenances. The absence of such provisions again points to the fact that registration vests the estate in the proprietor both legally and beneficially.

94 LRA 2002, s 132(1).
95 In other words, a fee simple absolute in possession and a term of years absolute.

CHAPTER 11

Roman and English Prescription for Incorporeal Property

Joshua Getzler

Edward Burn asked me an intriguing question one afternoon as we walked in the garden of the college where we taught together in the 1990s. 'Can you prescribe for a television signal?' This was shortly before the House of Lords made its decision in *Hunter v Canary Wharf*, and the signs were already there that the appeal was going to have a major impact not only on the law of nuisance and easements, but also on our understanding of a much wider puzzle: when does English law invest or clothe an interest touching land with proprietary protection? Memory can deceive, but I think that we agreed that afternoon on a strict Romanist answer: If you cannot buy the right or be granted it as a proprietary interest then you cannot prescribe for it and the interest can sound as a personal claim only, binding a limited extent of parties.[1]

It is satisfying to be able to predict correctly on occasion, but far more difficult to articulate why a complex of legal concepts should guide the courts to one side of a decision rather than another.[2] After all, why can one not buy an easement of television reception, and therefore also be allowed to prescribe for such a right? Why indeed can parties not create any number of fanciful incidents binding property, all capable of acquisition by prescription?[3] The most elaborate recent explication of this approach is found in the judgment of Lord Hope in *Canary Wharf*:

1 Cf *Dalton v Angus* (1881) 6 App Cas 740, 823–4, per Lord Blackburn, holding that use-rights outside the conventional heads of easement law can be guaranteed by private agreement sounding as personal rights, without allowing *in rem* rights to emerge by grant or prescription (cited in *Hunter v Canary Wharf Ltd* [1997] AC 655 at 685 per Lord Goff, at 699 per Lord Lloyd, at 709 per Lord Hoffmann). A jurisprudential investigation of the problem, from a non-Hohfeldian vantage, is offered in A M Honoré, 'Rights of Exclusion and Immunities Against Divesting' (1960) 34 Tu LR 453.

2 E H Burn, *Cheshire and Burn's Modern Law of Real Property* (16th edn, 2000) 567–614 gives a magisterial treatment of the doctrinal issues.

3 The problem of fanciful incidents clouding titles was pegged in *Hill v Tupper* (1863) 2 H & C 121 at 127–128; 159 ER 51, 53 per Pollock CB; and again in *Keppell v Bailey* (1834) 2 My & K 517 at 535–6; 39 ER 1042, 1049; S C Cooper T Brougham 298, 316–318, 47 ER 106, 114 per Lord Brougham LC. The theoretical issues are explored in B Rudden, 'Economic Theory versus Property Law: the Numerus Clausus Problem', in J Eekelaar and J Bell (eds), *Oxford Essays in Jurisprudence* 3rd Series (1987) 239; T W Merrill and H E Smith, 'Optimal Standardization in the Law of Property: The Numerus Clausus Principle' (2000) 110 Yale LJ 1.

> A restraint on the owners' freedom of property can only be effected by agreement, by express grant or – in the case of the easement of light – by way of an exception to the general rule by prescription. . . . The presumption also affects the kinds of easement which the law will recognise. When the easements are negative in character – where they restrain the owners' freedom in the occupation and use of his property – they belong to certain well known categories. As they represent an anomaly in the law because they restrict the owners' freedom, the law takes care not to extend them beyond the categories which are well known to the law. It is one thing if what one is concerned with is a restriction which has been constituted by express grant or by agreement. Some elasticity in the recognised categories may be permitted in such a case, as the owner has agreed to restrict his own freedom. But it is another matter if what is being suggested is the acquisition of an easement by prescription. Where the easement is of a purely negative character, requiring no action to be taken by the other proprietor and effecting no change on the owner's property which might reveal its existence, it is important to keep to the recognised categories. A very strong case would require to be made out if they were to be extended. I do not think that that has been demonstrated in the present case.[4]

But then, what amount to 'a very strong case'? One doctrinal solution formulated by the courts only begs a series of further doctrinal questions, courting a risk of endless doctrinal regress. Lord Goff's search for a 'crumb of analysis rather than a "loaf of opinion" ' must continue.[5]

This essay for my friend and colleague Edward Burn pursues the problem raised that morning in the garden nearly ten years ago. It is cast as an investigation and comparison of the Roman law of prescription for incorporeal property and the analogous pre-modern English easement law. Edward has always been adamant that lawyers must know something of the evolution of doctrine from the Romans to our own times if they are not to fight unarmed. English prescription doctrine in relation to incorporeal hereditaments borrowed heavily from Roman law from the time of Bracton onwards, but the common law doctrines turned out to work very differently within an English property system shaped by feudal concepts. When the modern law of prescription for servitudes was developed in the late nineteenth century, the judges simplified the law by ignoring much of the history even as they invoked it, and at the same time they sought to restructure the native system with borrowings from Roman law. This essay aims to search behind those acts of purposive forgetfulness and transplantation.

4 *Hunter v Canary Wharf Ltd* [1997] AC 655 at 726.

5 *Hunter v Canary Wharf Ltd* [1997] AC 655 at 694. The technique of the majority in the *Canary Wharf* decision has been strongly criticized e g by I Dawson and A Dunn, 'Negative Easements – A Crumb of Analysis' (1998) 18 LS 510, and P Cane, 'What a Nuisance!' (1997) 113 LQR 515.

OWNERSHIP FOUNDED ON POSSESSION

In *Hunter v Canary Wharf Ltd* Lord Hoffmann began his reasoning with the axiom that titles were grounded in possession.

> Exclusive possession de jure or de facto, now or in the future, is the bedrock of English land law. As it is said in *Cheshire and Burn's Modern Law of Real Property*, 15th edn (1994), p 26:
>
> > All titles to land are ultimately based upon possession in the sense that the title of the man seised prevails against all who can show no better right to seisin. Seisin is a root of title, and it may be said without undue exaggeration that so far as land is concerned there is in England no law of ownership, but only a law of possession.[6]

Where there is a claim for an incorporeal right of property such as an easement, the analysis of title based on possession presents special difficulties. Indeed the characteristic problem of prescription for incorporeities is that prescriptive ownership at its core is based on the fact of possession. *De facto* use and possession of land implies (at least evidentially) a *de jure* ownership (and conversely *de facto* non-possession and non-use of land implies *de jure* non-ownership). Yet servitudes cannot obviously be possessed in the sense of occupied with exclusive control. The seisin of incorporeities – legally significant possession of a thing that cannot exclusively be possessed – becomes a mystery even deeper than the mystery of seisin of land itself.[7] To discover how Roman and then English lawyers dealt with this conundrum, we must first look at their most basic ideas about the relationship between use, possession, and ownership of land.

Although the Romans had a slogan that 'ownership has nothing in common with possession',[8] the points of overlap belied this claim.[9] Most simply, an original title to property arose through occupation or first possession of an unowned thing, and derivative titles also depended on conveyance or transfer of possession to transfer completely an existing title; and indeed the derivative title created by *traditio* could be seen as involving the occupation of a thing surrendered by the donor to the donee. Possession *per se* was protected from interference by third parties but could not by itself establish title in the sense of an undivided and permanent right to a thing challengeable by none. However prescriptive title served to convert legally-incepted possession into a form of ownership; and its outgrowth of bonitary ownership further protected a possessor on the way to a prescriptive title from derogation by a purported grantor and ultimately against all third parties. Thus prescription lay at the heart of the

6 [1997] AC 655, 703.

7 Cf F W Maitland, 'The Mystery of Seisin' (1886) 2 LQR 481; F W Maitland, 'The Beatitude of Seisin' (1888) 4 LQR 286, reprinted in *Collected Papers* (H A L Fisher (ed), 1911) I, pp 358, 407. *Cheshire and Burn* (16th edn, 2000) at 150–1 notes: 'no proprietary interest can be other than a mere *right* of ownership, and no matter what the nature of its subject matter may be, it must always be incorporeal'.

8 *Digest of Justinian* (T Mommsen and P Krueger (eds), translation ed by A Watson, Philadelphia, Pennsylvania, 1985) [cited as D.] 41.2.12.1. (Ulpian).

9 On the development of bonitary ownership as a fusion of possession and ownership, see Jeffrey Hackney, 'Usucapio and Trusts', ch 2 in this volume.

Roman title system and Roman ownership cannot be understood apart from the complex of concepts that made up prescription law.

THE ROMAN VARIETIES OF PRESCRIPTION

Where there was no original acquisition and no overt derivative title, the Roman law allowed a shift of title to occur by virtue of long enjoyment by a new owner, or else by loss of title to another through non-user by an old owner, in one of three ways: (1) by limitation of actions barring rival claims; (2) by acquisitive prescription creating a new positive title; or (3) by negative prescription extinguishing rival titles.[10] These categories of right-creation were founded on a continuous period of user, and may be contrasted with property rights derived from the fact of possession, whereby the possessory interdicts protected the last immediate possession. In this last instance, being the simplest type of possessory right, there was an action to defend or restore possession given to the plaintiff against any dispossessor. This possessory right exists regardless of a possible superior proprietary right in the dispossessor, and no matter how tenuous the character of the plaintiff's possession. The action was distinctly possessory not proprietary: it did not confer a title binding third parties nor did it give a ranked right to possession, and a proprietary *vindicatio* could be brought by a plaintiff independently of the possessory claim and without prejudice to that claim. It is these features that give the core sense of the dictum that 'ownership has nothing in common with possession.' The doctrine of *usucapio* brought together the discrete categories of possession and ownership: if one possessed a thing for long enough, possession could be defended or recovered as owner as well as possessor against grantor and third parties; long possession thereby provided a *causa* or source or proof of ownership.

Limitation and iniuria

By contrast with positive prescription, limitation of actions and negative prescription each create rights by barring or extinguishing the claims of others; the new title is thus delineated as if in silhouette, by the negation of correlative rights. Negative prescription creates rights by extinction of adverse rights, and so differs from titles by limitation which are created through the barring of rival or inconsistent actions. Nicholas explains the distinction thus:

> Under a system of limitation, if an action is available to me and I fail to bring it within a certain time, I am debarred from bringing it thereafter. But it is only the action which is barred; the right on which the action is based still survives. It is unenforceable or 'imperfect', but not void . . . By contrast, in a system of prescription the right itself is affected.[11]

10 B Nicholas, *An Introduction to Roman Law* (3rd edn, 1962), 120–130; W W Buckland, *Main Institutions of Roman Private Law* (1931) 121–127.

11 Nicholas, *Roman Law*, 120–121, cf 218 ff.

Both limitation and extinction focus on the old owner's non-use rather than the continuous enjoyment of the new possessor.[12]

In the Institutes the concept of limitation is explained in terms of a waiver by the plaintiff of his remedy for injury, the waiver being indicated by inaction on his part.[13] In the sphere of personal actions, the idea of waiver may have emerged from the concept of *iniuria* as based on insult or contempt. According to the Institutes '*[i]niuria* . . . in its general sense denotes all wrong conduct', and also connoted 'fault', 'delict', 'unfairness and injustice', a group approximating the category of modern torts or wrongs. The wrongfulness of *iniuria* inhered in the indignation of the plaintiff caused by the contempt shown him by the wrongdoer, and damages were given with a retributory as well as a compensatory aim.[14] The subjectivity of the wrong had to be preserved, and this was why inaction barred the plaintiff's action:

> [t]his action is extinguished by dissimulation [*dissimulatione*]. If someone lets a contempt pass – having suffered it he dismisses it from his mind – he cannot later change his mind and rekindle the contempt he overlooked.[15]

Such bar or limitation of *in personam* actions for wrongs was relevant to the definition of property rights because a waiver of an owner's right of action to redress for intentional trespass to his land could constitute a privilege in another to interfere with the owner's land without negative sanction.[16] It is not clear, however, if the same limitation by waiver applied to interdicts protecting property, or to non-contumelious delictual damage to property falling into the category of *damnum iniuria datum*.[17]

Positive prescription

'Usucapion is the acquisition of ownership by continued possession for the time prescribed by law'.[18] *Usucapio* re-ordered title to land and movables by creating a new positive right in the person in possession, rather than by barring or extinguishing an existing ownership of the prior owner. 'Its principle is perfectly simple, but its application bristles with difficulties'.[19]

The doctrine is introduced in the Institutes as follows:

12 Buckland, *Main Institutions*, 121.

13 *Justinian's Institutes* (P Krueger (ed), translation by P B H Birks and G McLeod (1987) [cited as Inst.] 4.4.12.

14 Inst.4.4.pr. There was in addition to this rule a general limitation period set at thirty years for all civil actions including *in rem* actions for land, promulgated by legislation in AD 424: Nicholas, *Roman Law*, 122; J A C Thomas, *Institutes of Justinian. Text and Commentary* (1975) 99. This development came too late to influence the jurisprudence of *iniuria* or prescription.

15 Inst.4.4.12; see also E Cahn, *The Sense of Injustice* (1949), describing how justice is commonly defined in terms of injustice, the sense of breach of right conduct or convention, of invasion, upset, contempt.

16 See J A C Thomas, *Textbook* of*Roman Law* (Amsterdam, 1976) 198–199 on *iniuria* actions to defend servitudes.

17 Nicholas, *Roman Law*, 122.

18 D.41.3.3. (Modestinus).

19 W W Buckland, *Elementary Principles of the Roman Private Law* (1912) 88–92; Buckland, *Main Institutions*, 121–127.

> To prevent uncertainty over title . . . where someone dealt with a non-owner in the belief that he was dealing with an owner, and obtained something in good faith by purchase or gift or on some other legally sufficient basis, he should become owner by usucapion, i e possession over time.[20]

The doctrine derives from the idea of *usu capere*, to acquire by use. By the time of the Justinianic law, *usucapio* had become a mode for acquiring *dominium* or title in cases where a person had enjoyed a period of use of a thing, acquired either innocently from a non-owner, or else transferred from a true owner by means of a defective conveyance.[21] Neratius states the doctrine as follows:

> The usucapion of things . . . was established so that there might be an end to litigation . . . a man may usucapt a thing which he believes to be his, although his belief is unfounded . . . a reasonable and plausible error will not prevent the usucapion of a possessor.[22]

Usucapio thus provided a good root of title where proof of an unbroken chain of valid conveyances from a true owner would have been difficult or impossible to provide; it circumvented the *probatio diabolico* of title, and thereby kept ownership 'absolute' in the sense of impervious to relatively superior titles.

Gaius explained the policy of *usucapio* in terms of balancing the interests of long possessors against those of prior owners:

> Usucapion was introduced for the public weal, to wit, that the ownership of certain things should not be for a long period, possibly permanently, uncertain, granted that the period of time prescribed should suffice for owners to inquire after their property.[23]

Usucapio can be seen as a double doctrine. It is tolerably clear that in its origins it served merely to perfect imperfect transfers by moving ownership to the informal grantee after a period in possession. But it was stretched to become a general model of prescriptive acquisition outside imperfect transfers. Buckland has inverted this historical model of development: he suggests that *usucapio* was not originally designed for 'confirming a holder's title against one previously entitled'; he surmises that '[i]ts original purpose may have been to confer a title on one who had none, where there was in fact no previous owner to be barred' – for example, a rule for the creating of a title where there was an intestacy and the agnates were left in possession without title,[24] or the owner died or departed leaving his land with no-one in possession.[25] It

20 Inst.2.6.pr.; and see Inst.Gaius.2.4.: 'ownership of things should not remain uncertain for too long a time'; D.41.3.1. (Gaius); see further W W Buckland, A *Textbook* of *Roman Law from Augustus to Justinian* (3rd edn, revised P G Stein, 1963) 241.

21 D.41.3.3. (Modestinus); Buckland, *Textbook*, 250; Nicholas, *Roman Law*, 122–125; H F Jolowicz and B Nicholas, *Historical Introduction to the Study of Roman Law* (3rd edn, 1972) 152–155.

22 D.41.10.5.1.pr.-1. (Neratius).

23 D.41.3.1. (Gaius).

24 Buckland, *Main Institutions*, 121.

25 Inst.2.6.7.

was not a rule for claiming vacant land on the fringes of settlement, nor land made vacant by abandonment, in which cases original acquisition by *occupatio* of the *res nullius* was available; *usucapio* by contrast with *occupatio* was a civil mode of original acquisition created by law to meet a social need.[26]

Usucapio was also available where a thing capable of possession was believed to be abandoned which in fact was not. In such a case the owner's property in the goods was not terminated so the new possessor could not immediately take a property in the thing by occupation; but he could eventually win a title by prescriptive possession, as occupation upon perceived abandonment was a sufficient *iusta causa* for *usucapio*.[27] The relationship between abandonment and prescriptive loss was important in the sphere of incorporeal rights, as will be shown.

Usucapio and servitudes

The various modes of servitude acquisition by long user were not part of the main Roman prescription doctrine of *usucapio*. If *usucapio* was centrally a doctrine for the perfection of purported transfers of *dominium* possessed by a putative owner in good faith,[28] then it was of inherently limited application in creating incorporeal rights over land through use over time. Earlier forms of acquisitive prescription involving presumed grant once applied equally to *res incorporales* and land,[29] but the *lex Scribonia* of c 60 BCE formally ended *usucapio* for servitudes in Roman civil law,[30] unless the servitude was usucapted with land.[31] The prohibition probably embodied a policy of protecting the *dominus* from too ready a loss of use-rights over land, for as the agricultural community of the Roman state grew to an impersonal size, it became difficult to maintain face-to-face relations with one's neighbours and so maintain immediate knowledge of activities affecting one's own land use.[32] There were also formal juristic reasons for the rule against positive prescription, as described by Paul:

> Rustic praedial servitudes, even though attached to corporeal property, are nevertheless incorporeal and so are never acquired by usucapion. Or the reason may be that the nature of these servitudes is such as not to engender clear and continuous possession. For no one can make use of a right of way in so

26 D.41.7.1. (Ulpian); D.41.7.2.pr.-1. (Paul); D.41.7.5.1. (Pomponius); cf D.41.3.18. (Modestinus) (long possession required).

27 D.41.7.4. (Paul); D.41.7.5.pr. (Pomponius); D.41.7.7. (Julian); cf D.41.7.6. (Julian). See also D.41.10.1.1. (Ulpian); D.41.10.5.pr.-1. (Neratius).

28 Inst.2.6.pr.; D.41.3.1. (Gaius); D.41.3.3. (Modestinus); D.41.10.5.1.pr.-1. (Neratius).

29 D.41.3.4.28(29). (Paul); Buckland, *Main Institutions*, 157-8.

30 D.8.1.14.pr., D.41.3.4.28(29). (Paul).

31 D.8.2.32.1. (Julian); D.41.3.10.1. (Ulpian); D.41.3.23.pr. (Javolenus).

32 Inst.2.6.pr.; Buckland, *Main Institutions*, 121–122; R Yaron, in 'Reflections on *usucapio*' (1967) 35 Tijdschrift voor rechtsgeschiedenis 191, 226-9 has surmised that the *lex Scribonia* embodied a policy of restraining the transformation of *usucapio* into a general system of prescriptive acquisition rather than a method to perfect invalid transfers.

continuous and uninterrupted a manner that his possession of it will be held to be unbroken. The same rule applies to urban servitudes as well.[33]

Usucapio had a number of quite demanding requirements. There had to be a period of uninterrupted use of a thing capable of ownership (originally two years for land); good faith by the possessor, or belief that the taking of the thing was not an interference with another's right at the time of the taking (a question of fact which was prima facie presumed);[34] and finally, there had to be a real *iusta causa*, a legitimate ground of right, or acquisition by a transaction which would ordinarily have been a legitimate basis of acquisition by transfer, such as a sale, legacy or gift.[35] Conversely there could be no *usucapio* if the thing was taken by force or was stolen.[36] These requirements were demanding and extensive, and protected owners from too-ready a loss of *dominium* to later holders, under flawed transactions beyond the true owner's control.

It may be that *usucapio* began as a mode of acquisition derivatively based on some constitution, grant, conveyance, or other conventional root of title, and was not based on user directly creating an original title. A long user might have operated as a legal fact pointing to some further legal fact constituting the right, typically grant or transfer of another's right. Following the lapse of prescriptive time, the claimant of the right was relieved from having to give factual proof of the legitimate origin of his title; the long enjoyment was taken as presumptive evidence of a rightful derivation of ownership. It was then left to the opponent of the right to disprove the title by showing an absence of legitimate origin. The development of the rule that *usucapio* could be complete without possible evidence of constitution or grant was a later refinement, abstracting from the original function of *usucapio* as a simplification of proof of title. Thus over time the juristic source of prescriptive titles, in derivative transfer by presumed grant, was concealed.

A usucapted *dominium* was taken by the new owner as a real interest burdened with any servitudes previously existing on the land, unless they had separately been extinguished by adverse prescriptive user. This rule need not suggest derivative transfer of the prior *ius* with all its characteristics, however, for servitudes were regarded as inherent in the land itself, and were also burdens on a new ownership acquired originally and naturally by *occupatio*.[37]

33 D.8.1.14.pr.; D.41.2.3.pr.-1., D.41.3.4.26(27). (Paul); D.8.2.32.1. (Julian); D.41.2.45.pr. (Papinian); D.41.3.25. (Licinus Rufinus); D.41.3.9. (Gaius).

34 'Usucapion is a matter of law, while the question whether a person is a possessor in good faith or in bad faith is a matter of fact': D.41.1.48.1. (Paul); D.41.10.5.1. (Neratius); D.41.4.2.15. (Paul). The good faith requirement was a subjective refinement of the earlier objective rule against theft: Jolowicz and Nicholas, *Historical Introduction*, 154; Buckland, *Main Institutions*, 122–123.

35 Inst.2.6.7.-11.; Buckland, *Textbook*, 242–248 (on putative and real *causa*). The classical law excluded putative *causa* or subjective belief in a valid source of right in the absence of a real but flawed transaction. Generally the flaw vitiating the transfer would be seen as an error of fact, for 'an error of law never benefits the possessor in the matter of usucapion': D.41.3.31.pr. (Paul); D.41.3.17. (Marcellus).

36 Inst.2.6.2.-3.

37 Nicholas, *Roman Law*, 115–156; and see further Jolowicz and Nicholas, *Historical Introduction*, 158 ff. For a balanced criticism of the orthodoxy that servitudes originated as a form of corporeal ownership rather than as an independent class of incorporeal rights, see G Diosdi, *Ownership in Ancient and Preclassical Roman Law* (1970) 107–116.

The acquisition of *dominium* by conveyance proper – for example by *mancipatio* and *traditio* – developed conceptually in a reverse fashion to acquisition by *usucapio*. The earlier law conceived of the grantee acquiring a new right, an original *dominium*, created upon delivery and possession of the *res*; later came the idea of a transfer of the existing *ius* of the grantor to the grantee by the act of conveyance. But as in the sphere of creation of incorporeal rights,[38] acquisition by *usucapio* deployed the idea of a new right constituted by the physical fact of delivery rather than by the legal fact of grant as a translation of right.

Extinctive prescription

In the time before Justinian, the doctrine of *longi temporis praescriptio* provided for the extinction of titles to land[39] following a lengthy period of non-use.[40] *Longi temporis praescriptio* was the method of prescription operating in provincial or non-Italic lands as a substitute for *usucapio* or positive prescription, which was confined in operation to land under Roman law. In the later empire there was only limited scope for *usucapio* of land as much land was owned provincially, leaving *longi temporis praescriptio* to do the work of defining prescriptive titles.[41] The result was two distinct systems of prescription, one negative for land and one acquisitive for movables. This was not only impractical but jurisprudentially inelegant, for in the Roman system of property based on absolute titles a regime of extinctive prescription might annihilate the title of the *dominus*, and yet leave without title or proprietary remedy (*vindicatio*) a person who had been in possession of land for the prescriptive period but had lost his possession in turn.[42] Such a person might lack a possessory action yet have no positive title, and theory allowed no *tertium quid* between remedies claiming the ownership and remedies for protecting the immediate possession of property.[43] In practice the combination of *longi temporis praescriptio* and possessory and personal actions solved this difficulty, but in principle the extinctive system sat uncomfortably with an absolute or non-relative concept of ownership.

The policy of the doctrine of *longi temporis praescriptio* was 'that long and unchallenged possession of land should not be disturbed'[44] – a formulation contrasting with the more commercial idea of maintaining certainty of titles arising from transactions that informed the original doctrine of *usucapio*. Under *longi temporis praescriptio*, the person in continuous possession for the stated period would have a full defence to a proprietary action by the prior owner, whose right was thereby extinguished. Mere non-use by the prior owner without continuous adverse

38 See Buckland, *Textbook*, 264–268.

39 The distinction from limitation was not always clearly set: cf Nicholas, *Roman Law*, 120–122; Buckland, *Main Institutions*, 131–134.

40 Ten years if parties were in proximity to the land, twenty if they were not and notice to the original owner was less likely: Buckland, *Textbook*, 250; cf Inst.2.6.pr.

41 There was also a system of positive acquisition of land with very long prescribed periods, requiring mere possession without *causa* or *bona fides*, known as *longissimi temporis praescriptio*: Nicholas, *Roman Law*, 128–129; Buckland, *Textbook*, 251–252.

42 Buckland, *Elementary Principles*, 91–92.

43 Nicholas, *Roman Law*, 121.

44 Inst.2.6.7.

enjoyment was not sufficient to raise a prescription. In addition to the defence, the person prescribing enjoyed the protection of the possessory interdicts to recover his possession if it was lost, a rule which addressed the need to provide a *tertium quid* between title and possession. These doctrines created most of the substantial security and entitlements of full ownership, save that the prescription did not formally vest the long user with a positive title to the land as *dominus*.

According to Partsch and Buckland[45] the negative rule of prescription under *longi temporis praescriptio* may have concealed a more subtle procedural position, whereby *longi temporis praescriptio* was not merely a bar or cession of rival ownerships but was a positive mode for evidencing acquisition of title, though available to the possessor only in defence. This procedure followed the model of Greek prescription, whereby the fact of long possession was taken as persuasive (but not conclusive) evidence of grant of title, leaving the onus on the prior owner to show that the right had not been lost through non-use. A trace of the positive grant fiction can be discerned in certain Digest texts.[46]

A servitude exercised over prescribed-for land was not defeated by *longi temporis praescriptio* unless the *ius* itself was separately defeated by non-use.[47] *Usucapio libertatis* was the equivalent doctrine of prescription for loss of a servitude; its operation will be discussed shortly.

The fusion of *longi temporis praescriptio* and *usucapio*

Longi temporis praescriptio and *usucapio* eventually came to converge in character and practice, as *longi temporis praescriptio* assimilated the *usucapio* requirements of possession in good faith and *iusta causa* or legitimate origin. Finally Justinian fused the two forms of prescription into one unified system of positive or direct acquisition as he sought to abolish the unequal categories of ownership and status within the empire.[48] The new doctrines of prescription were known as *usucapio* for movables, and *longi praescriptio temporis* for all types of land whether imperial or Italic. The prescriptive period for *usucapio* of movables was extended to three years, whilst the ten or twenty year regime of the original *longi temporis praescriptio* was retained for land. The older, very short period of *usucapio* for Italic land was thus discarded, for according to the Institutes:

> [t]his [period] seemed right once, when people could accept that these periods gave owners long enough to discover their property. But better opinions

45 J Partsch, *Die longi temporis praescriptio im klassischen römischen Rechte* (Leipzig, 1906) 100, cited in Buckland, *Textbook*, 249; Buckland, *Main Institutions*, 126–127.

46 D.8.5.10.pr. (Ulpian); D.39.3.1.23. (Ulpian).

47 Buckland, *Textbook*, 250; Buckland, *Main Institutions*, 127. For a similar rule for *usucapio*: D.41.3.44.5. (Papinian); 7.4.19 (Gaius); cf *praescriptio*: D.44.3.5. (Ulpian) (a hypothec might be destroyed by a lapse of time, if, when possession began, the possessor did not know of its existence).

48 Inst.2.6.pr.; C.7.31.1. Buckland, *Textbook*, 251 ff.

> prevailed . . . namely that owners should not be stripped of their property so soon, and that the benefit should not be confined to any specific area.[49]

A novel form of acquisitive prescription – *longissimi temporis praescriptio* – was then invented for protecting very long users of thirty or forty years from disturbance in cases where the strict requirements of *bona fides* and *iusta causa* could not be met.[50]

The final result, as Buckland notes, was that developed Roman prescription doctrine did not employ concepts of implied or lost grant: long enjoyment itself provided the root of title'.[51] There has been a degree of debate as to whether *usucapio* originated as a form of extinctive prescription similar to the older *longi temporis praescriptio* which then evolved into a positive form; or whether there were always elements of presumed grant at the heart of the acquisitive doctrine. But the dichotomy found within acquisitive prescription between presumption of grant and positive prescription *per se* – between derivative and original modes – may be a false distinction, for all forms of prescription, positive and negative, may originally have developed from an adjectival or evidential presumption of grant. As in the case of the earlier developed extinctive *longi temporis praescriptio*, the doctrine of positive *usucapio* which formed the heart of mature Roman prescription law may originally have been premissed on acquisition through presumed grant, through a rule shifting the onus of proof of grant from the claimant to the challenger of the right who was to disprove the possibility of grant.

The Kaser thesis: early *usucapio* as a relative title by negation

Kaser has given a different interpretation of the positive grant theory, explaining the history of *usucapio* not as a development of probative procedures for asserting or denying absolute titles, but rather in terms of a descent from a negative system of prescription whereby superior titles were vindicated through extinction of rival claims.[52] His larger thesis is that the older Roman land law used a concept of relative rights to possession (similar to the hierarchy of titles of English law), and that this older system never admitted a concept of positive prescription for absolute rights. Early *usucapio*, like *auctoritas*, is seen by Kaser as a device for asserting a superior title, rather than a system for ordering patterns of land-use through creation of new positive titles based on use.[53]

49 Inst.2.6.pr.; and see Jolowicz and Nicholas, *Historical Introduction*, 155.

50 Buckland, *Textbook*, 251.

51 Buckland, *Textbook*, 241–242; Buckland, *Main Institutions*, 121.

52 The thesis is set out in M Kaser, *Eigentum und Besitz im älteren römischen Recht* (2nd edn, 1956); M Kaser, *Roman Private Law* (R Dannenbring (transl), based on the tenth revised German edition, 3rd edn., 1980) 110–119; M Kaser, 'The Concept of Roman Ownership' [1964] Tydskrif vir Hedendaagse Romeins-Hollandse Reg 5, 8–13.

53 Jolowicz and Nicholas, *Historical Introduction*, 146–147, 153–155, for references to the Kaser debate on early and classical law; and see further Yaron, 'Reflections on *usucapio*'; A Watson, 'Acquisition of Possession and *uscapion per servos et filios*' (1967) 78 LQR 205; A Watson, *Roman Private Law around 200 BC* (1971) 17–83; A Watson, *Rome of the XII Tables: Persons and Property* (1975) 150–156; A Watson, *The Law of Property in the later Roman Republic* (1968) 21–61; A M Prichard, 'Early Usucapio' (1974) 90 LQR 234; A M Prichard, '*Auctoritas* in Early Roman Law' (1974) 90 LQR 378.

Nicholas carefully examined Kaser's views, and concluded by preferring the positive theory of *usucapio* based on presumptions shifting the probative onus for grants. According to Nicholas,

> [T]he XII Tables do not recognise *usucapio* as a method of acquiring ownership, but are concerned only with what has to be proved in a *vindicatio* [assertion of a proprietary right to possession]. The transferee in a *mancipatio*, if he needed to show title in a *vindicatio* before the one or two years had elapsed, had to call upon the *auctoritas* of the transferor, whereas afterwards his position became unimpeachable. He then needed only to show his possession for the requisite period, any better right being extinguished by the holder's failure to assert it. Kaser's view here is of course in accord with his thesis that the early *vindicatio* was concerned only with a relatively better title. It is indeed the logical corollary of it. For a system which recognises only 'relative' rights cannot admit an 'acquisitive' form of prescription which confers 'absolute' ownership. And the converse is also true: a system which thinks in terms of 'absolute' ownership cannot admit a system of merely 'extinctive' prescription. Hence Kaser argues that the transition from primitive to classical *usucapio* occurs when the character of the *vindicatio* changes and 'absolute' ownership is recognised. However, if the validity of the sharp distinction between relative and absolute ownership may be doubted, so also may that of the distinction here between the early and the mature *usucapio*. For the conception of classical *usucapio* as enabling the plaintiff in a *vindicatio* positively to prove ownership must in practice have been illusory. Good faith and the absence of theft are inherently unprovable, and *usucapio* must therefore in classical law have been not so much a method of acquiring ownership as a method of shifting the burden of proof. The plaintiff who showed that he had had possession, and that it had been acquired *ex iusta causa* . . . could reasonably say that it was for the defendant to show that there had not been usucapion. The position of Kaser's primitive litigant does not seem significantly different in this respect: once he had shown possession for the requisite period it was for the other party to show that the thing . . . was . . . incapable of being usucaped.[54]

The basic idea here is that in all forms of *usucapio*, both primitive and modern, the holder of property is expected to be able to account for how his period of enjoyment of the property commenced. The earlier law applied a wide objective test that the thing had not been stolen; the mature law added a test of acquisition without bad faith, a more demanding subjective test of propriety.[55] The strict requirement of explanation of *causa* and demonstration of good faith recedes as the present holder's period of enjoyment lengthens in time and [availability of] evidence diminishes, so that a good cause of title is presumed by the law after a time, unless disproved. By this evidential rule, prescription shifts the onus of proof of title to the challenger.[56]

54 Jolowicz and Nicholas, *Historical Introduction*, 154–155; and see 145–147 for further discussion of the relativity of titles in early law; see also Nicholas, *Roman Law*, 122–125.

55 Jolowicz and Nicholas, *Historical Introduction*, 153–155.

56 See Buckland, *Main Institutions*, 121–122; Prichard, 'Early Usucapio'.

This cogent picture of *usucapio* as acquisitive prescription, involving a presumption of valid *causa* which must be disproved by the challenger, is complicated by the existence of a separate system of *usucapio libertatis* or extinctive prescription for servitudes or *res incorporales*.

The qualities of Roman servitudes

In order to understand prescription for incorporeal property we must first grasp the nature of servitudes in Roman law. The core class of servitudes were use-rights over land appurtenant to or supplementing a larger property right in dominant land and binding a servient estate. Sometimes these were classified as positive rights to do something on another's land such as rights of way, or negative rights to restrain uses of another's land, such as rights to prevent blocking of light.[57] The binding of one estate to another was betokened by the name 'praedial' servitudes, subjecting one field to the use-rights of the owner from time to time of another field. To confuse categorizations, there could also be property use-rights independent of any dominant land-holding, representing fractional interests in the subjected land, such as usufruct or the right to fruits and use or possession, typically the life interest of a widow. Later civilians described these rights as a lesser variety of ownership and afforded them real status as 'personal servitudes', defensible directly by real actions. The entire class of real and personal servitudes was then reconceptualized as *iura in re aliena*. A third category of use right again were access rights being non-exclusive public goods, which were enjoyed by the public independently of landholding. These rights merged into the various public and common rights listed in the Institutes as *res communes* and *res publicae*.[58] A possible fourth category were those positive claims to user or negative rights to freedom from interference attached to land by natural right, as inherent aspects of *dominium*, which may also be called rights to quiet enjoyment

Praedial servitudes could be created by the contractual agreement of a servient and dominant landholder. Where servitudes were contractual in origin, there had to be some public apparent user in order to establish their conveyance, and only then were they recognized by law as enforceable proprietary rights binding all comers, rather than merely personal obligations binding only the contracting parties. A more proprietary form of servitude was created by long user indicating prescriptive rights granted by or won against neighbours. Long use here can be characterized again as a basis of right *per se*, or perhaps as secondary evidence of a primary appropriative intention or contractual grant.

Despite the contractual elements of these rights, Roman law recognized only a limited range of servitudes. Within their sphere of operation, servitudes were not absolute. The law of actions for assertion of servitudes controlled the extent or scope of servitude rights and subjected the owners of land to a reasonableness standard in their use and enjoyment of attached amenity rights. Both proprietary and personal actions

57 See Buckland, 259 ff.

58 See further J Getzler, 'Roman Ideas of Landownership' in S Bright and J Dewar (eds), *Land Law: Themes and Perspectives* (1998) 81.

were available to enforce or vindicate a servitude, and there were special negative actions to deny the existence of a servitude.[59] Although the law of actions was particularly fragmented in this area, it was clear that servitudes were protected as a property right independent of damage; generally tortious damage to an existing use was not needed to form the gist of an action. Yet user was essential in the first place to constitute a servitude as a real right, and continuous user might be necessary to prevent cancellation by prescription.

Extinctive prescription and res incorporales

The most important prescription doctrine applying to incorporeal property rights was the rule that there could be no positive acquisition of servitudes by *usucapio*; there could only be *usucapio libertatis* freeing land of the burden of existing servitudes, a mode of extinctive prescription. Paul states that:

> release from servitudes can be usucapted, because the *lex Scribonia* abolished the usucapion which creates a servitude but not that which grants liberty, removing the servitude.[60]

To stress the point: prescription against servitudes, not prescription for servitudes, was the rule.

The rule excluding positive prescription of servitudes

A text by Paul gives two reasons for the rule against positive prescription:

> Rustic praedial servitudes, even though attached to corporeal property, are nevertheless incorporeal and so are never acquired by usucapion. Or the reason may be that the nature of these servitudes is such as not to engender clear and

59 The negative actions are classical (see Inst.4.6.2), but have puzzled commentators as to their function. Buckland, *Main Institutions*, 155–156; *Textbook*, 264; and Thomas, *Textbook*, 198–199, each discuss a number of rather unpersuasive theories concerning the function of the counter-servitudes. R W Lee, *Elements of Roman Law* (4th edn, 1956), at 161–162, speculates that the counter-servitudes were the rights to freedom from burdens based on *usucapio libertatis*, but if this strong connection of the two doctrines existed, it surely would have appeared more expressly in the Roman texts. Rodger derives from the law of urban lights a general reasonableness theory making sense of this duplicated procedure for litigating *res incorporales*. The formulae of the real actions dealing with light include two groups of actions: one for the enforcement of a negative servitude preventing a neighbour blocking light by building (*altius non tollendi*), another for the positive right to block light and build (*altius tollendi*). The second type of servitude only makes sense if a builder was not free to build as he pleased, but needed to acquire a right to build if he wished to block more light than was reasonable. Rodger supports this interpretation by detailing a mesne process whereby an owner could obtain a prohibition of building work without indemnity for threatened loss of rights, and thus require the builder to deny the first owner's rights and assert a counter-servitude permitting the builder to build freely. A similar legal regime of servitudes and counter-servitudes is shown to exist for the urban rights of prospect and of water run-off (*stillicidium* and *flumen*). See A Rodger, *Owners and Neighbours in Roman Law* (1972) 38 ff, 90–123; D Johnston, *Prescription and Limitation* (1999) 3–15.

60 D.41.3.4.28(29). (Paul).

> continuous possession. For no one can make use of a right of way in so continuous and uninterrupted a manner that his possession of it will be held to be unbroken. The same rule applies to urban servitudes as well.[61]

The basic rule, then, was that enjoyment of incorporeal rights including servitudes was insufficiently physical to amount to a possession founding acquisitive prescription. Two ideas are articulated within this rule: first, that servitudes are incorporeal or intangible rights that could not be possessed, and '[w]ithout possession, there can be no usucapion'.[62] Secondly, that even if servitudes were sufficiently possessed through use or quasi-possession, this was not a continuous and apparent possession capable of grounding *usucapio*. This restrictive doctrine applied whether the servitude was continuously exercised or not.[63]

Thus 'clear and continuous' possession was central to acquisitive *usucapio*, in that there must be both continuing physical appropriation and that this possession be manifest, as a legal fact supporting the existence of *iusta causa* or lawful origin of title. The existence of an earlier regime of prescription permitting *usucapio* of servitudes, before legislative abolition by the *lex Scribonia*,[64] suggests that servitudes were once regarded as tangible physical things capable of possession (the surface of a road, the watercourse of an aqueduct). A ready binding of estates with praedial burdens through user was not regarded as inimical to utilization of land in the intimate agricultural community of early Rome, where neighbours had face-to-face relations and had easy notice of their respective land uses.[65] According to Buckland, the long enjoyment of servitudes not being *vi clam aut precario* was given protection as in ordinary *usucapio*, through acquisitive prescription, a mode deriving from Greek theories of lost grant:

> Texts suggest that in classical law the *iudex* decided whether enjoyment had lasted for such a time, without contrary evidence, as to indicate that the enjoyment had been rightful, and had been created at some time in a recognised way. It does not follow that he had a free hand: the magistrate may, after enquiry into the facts, have fixed such a length of time as he thought fit in the circumstances, and the *iudex* would be bound by this time, which would appear in the *formula*.[66]

As servitudes came to be seen as properly incorporeal and incapable of possession, this acquisitive doctrine was abandoned.

Another example of the idea that only actual possession could found prescription was the rule that there could be no *usucapio* through long enjoyment of things outside

61 D.8.1.14.pr. (Paul); see also D.8.2.32.1. (Julian).

62 D.41.3.25. (Licinius Rufinus); and see D.41.2.3.pr.,1.; D.41.3.4.26(27). (Paul); D.41.3.9. (Gaius).

63 The distinction between continuous and non-continuous servitudes was much later brought into English law from French law: see A W B Simpson, 'The Rule in *Wheeldon v Burrows* and the Code Civil', in Simpson, *Legal Theory and Legal History: Essays on the Common Law* (1987) 163.

64 D.41.3.4.28(29). (Paul).

65 Inst.2.6.pr.; Buckland, *Main Institutions*, 157–158.

66 Buckland, *Main Institutions*, 158.

patrimony. Thus there was no prescription for communal, public or religious things, because by definition the user of such things could not be an exclusive possession. For similar reason there could be no prescription against the state for the acquisition of state property.[67] This meant that the doctrines of prescription could not be used to constitute private rights over public waters, although an equivalent existed in the interdictal actions to protect rights of long user.[68]

Other areas of prescription for servitudes

Notwithstanding the principle just discussed, the positive acquisition of a servitude by prescription was possible in two broad cases:

Derivative acquisition

Usucapio of a praedial estate included prescription for all appurtenant servitudes:

> [T]he nature of servitudes is such that it is impossible to possess them, but whoever possesses a house is deemed to have possession of a servitude attaching to it.[69]
>
> . . .
>
> The rule which we observe is that servitudes can never be usucapted of themselves, but they can be with buildings.[70]

This doctrine is only a peripheral exception to the rule against usucapting servitudes. Although the classical law may have seen a new or original ownership in the creation of a real right by delivery or possession rather than a transfer of the prior ownership, this conceptualization was overlaid with the idea that the new prescriptive right was a simple translation of the older ownership, with all its qualities, made over to the usucapting owner.

67 D.41.2.45.pr. (Papinian): 'Prescription by long possession is not conceded by the law of nations for the acquisition of public lands. This is the case . . . if a person, because he alone has fished in a reach of a public river for some years, refuses someone else the right.'; D.41.3.9. (Gaius): 'Corporeal things especially are the objects of usucapion, with the exception of sacred and dedicated things, the public property of the Roman people and of *civitates*, and also freemen.' See also D.41.3.18. (Modestinus): 'usucapion does not run against the imperial treasury'; Inst.2.6.9.: 'Things belonging to our exchequer cannot be usucapted.' A similar idea can be found in the common law rule that there can be no prescription against the crown, e g acquisitions of franchises of crown rights; this rule was expressed in the maxims '*nullum tempus occurrit regi* (time does not run against the king)' and '*iurisdictio delegata non potest delegari* (the delegate of a jurisdiction has no power to delegate)', see F Pollock and F W Maitland, *The History of English Law Before the Time of Edward I*, 2 vols (2nd edn, 1898, reprinted 1968), I, 571–574.

68 D.43.8.2.9. (Ulpian); D.43.8.5. (Paul); D.43.8.6. (Julian); D.43.13.1.9.,10.; D.43.15.1.3.,5. (Ulpian), suggesting availability of legal relief, both prohibitive and reparative, for individual injury caused by loss of use of *res communes* or *res publicae*.

69 D.8.2.32.1. (Julian).

70 D.41.3.10.1. (Ulpian). See also D.41.3.23.pr. (Javolenus) (a building is to be usucapted as a unity, not as separate usucapions of soil, structure, servitudes).

Discretionary protection of long possession

A text by Ulpian offers a doctrine which seems to cut squarely across the leading principle against prescription for servitudes:

> If a man has obtained a right to channel water by long use and, as it were, by long possession, he is not required to lead evidence to establish the legal title on which his right to the water is founded, for example, to show that it rests on a legacy or on some other ground. He is entitled to an *actio utilis* to establish that he has had the use of the water, say, for so many years, and that this was not obtained by force, stealth, or *precarium.*[71]

Ulpian is indicating that the Praetor might make available a personal action analogous to a possessory interdict as a protection of water-rights positively acquired by long enjoyment – in effect, a form of positive prescription for incorporeal rights.[72] Ulpian makes clear that the action is available not just against the owner of land over which the water is channelled, as if the water right was conceived as a personal right constituted between neighbours, but could be brought 'against anyone at all who prevents one from channelling the water, as is the case with servitudes in general'.[73]

There was also a more general interdict which prohibited forcible interference with the use of a private way or other rustic servitude which had been enjoyed without force, stealth or *precarium* for one year.[74] To this can be added the interdictal protection of established and customary uses of daily and summer water and of rights of drainage.[75] These various actions might be subsumed within a more general principle of acquisition by long use outlined by Ulpian:

> [W]here it is discovered that no servitude has been imposed, the person who has for a long time acted as though there were a servitude and has done so neither by force nor *precarium* nor secretly, he is regarded as having a servitude imposed quasi-legally by reason of prolonged custom. Consequently, we will not compel the neighbour to construct dams but will construct them ourselves on his land, and this will count as a sort of servitude in respect of which we will have the right to an *actio utilis in rem* or an interdict.[76]

These examples of acquisition by long use were a significant departure from the principle excluding prescription for servitudes, even if the actions do not always

71 D.8.5.10.pr. (Ulpian).

72 Thomas, *Textbook*, p 201.

73 D.8.5.10.1. (Ulpian).

74 D.43.19.1.pr.-4. (Ulpian). Rustic servitudes may have attracted special protection because of their 'positive' quality allowing ready observation and demonstration, as where one is permitted to do some action on the land of another such as use a way or draw water, rather than requiring another to forbear on his own land, such as allowing support and light to neighbouring land. See further below, text accompanying nn 79–83.

75 See e g D.8.5.10.pr. (Ulpian); D.39.3.26. (Scaevola); D.39.3.1.23. (Ulpian, Labeo); D.39.3.2.pr. (Paul); D.43.19.2., D.43.19.5.3. (Ulpian); D.43.20.3.4. (Pomponius); C.7.33.12.4., C.3.34.1., 2., 7. See also D.39.3.26. (Scaevola), stating that judges 'normally uphold aqueducts to which antiquity of use gives some authority, even where their legal right to exist is not proved.'

76 D.39.3.1.23. (Ulpian); and see Thomas, *Textbook*, 200–202.

amount to *in rem* protections of a right as property.[77] The *actio utilis* functioned as a half-way point to real positive acquisition by the means of a presumption of grant, again operating through the procedural device of shifting the burden of proof to the challenger of the right. To illustrate, if a water right or other rustic servitude was enjoyed for a long period, a *iusta causa* involving actual grant would be presumed for the purpose of supporting an *in rem* action against any interfering person, subject to that person defending by disproving the presumed grant. The *actio utilis* could thus function as a possessory interdict obliquely establishing title.

Buckland suggests that in addition to these varied actions, there was a provincial form of general prescription for servitudes:

> An analogous rule [to *longi temporis praescriptio*] applied to acquisition of servitudes . . . It is not praetorian: . . . it was not new . . . [R]escripts [of the second century] give precision, generality and sanction to what had long been the practice in some provinces. There, where title had been disputed, the Courts had habitually taken account of the fact that the defendant had been enjoying for a long time. There was no question of a specific length of time: long and peaceful enjoyment might, if the Court think fit, be taken as evidence that there was a title behind it: time was evidence of a lost grant, not, as in *usucapio*, a root of title in itself. The rule is scarcely logical. To presume a grant is to give a title, so that it looks acquisitive, but the idea was not carried through.[78]

Usucapio libertatis

Usucapio libertatis or extinctive prescription against servitudes was triggered by two factors: the non-use or interruption of a servitude for a certain period; and continued possession by the prescribing owner of the burdened servient estate. These factors were elaborated and explained by considerable amounts of doctrine.

Non-use and interruption of servitudes

In the case of rustic servitudes it was not required that the servient owner actually interrupt or block the servitude, that is use his land in a fashion inimical to the enjoyment of the servitude by the dominant owner. Failure to exercise the servitude for the stated time was itself a legal fact sufficient to release the servient land of its burden.[79] This was because rustic servitudes, such as rights of way and *aquaeductus*,

77 Lee, *Elements of Roman Law*, 164, jumps to conclude from the texts in question that *all* servitudes could in fact be prescribed for in post-classical law; but there is no strong evidence for this view and plenty against; for example D.43.19.2. (Ulpian) expressly avoids the category of servitudes to describe the right acquired by use: 'In this interdict the praetor does not inquire whether or not he had the servitude lawfully imposed, but only whether he used it this year, not by force or stealth or *precarium*.'

78 Buckland, *Main Institutions*, 127; and see Buckland, *Textbook*, 266.

79 Thomas, *Textbook*, 201, suggests that there were also separate doctrines of voluntary renunciation of servitudes in Justinian's law; see e g D.8.2.32.pr. (Julian), but this was a question of express or implied grant or release.

were generally non-continuous or occasionally-exercised servitudes: the dominant owner would not continually walk over his way or pour water through his water-course, but would do so intermittently when desired.[80] Hence a period of non-use for the period of prescription would be apparent whether or not there was active interference in the right. It was held as a result that *usurpatio* or interference by the servient owner of rustic servitudes was unnecessary to ground *usucapio libertatis*.[81] However, *usurpatio* of a servitude was necessary in the case of continuous servitudes, such as the urban servitudes of light or support or right to beams. Those rights once commenced were exercised without any further positive act: light would pour through a window and support would be given to a wall without deeds by the dominant owner. Without some patent interruption taking place, there would be no apparent period of non-use of this type of right: only if the light was blocked or the support removed would cession of the use of the right become evident.[82] Gaius outlined the doctrine as follows:

> As with rustic praedial servitudes, these [urban] rights are lost by nonuse over a specific period, except that there is the following difference. They are not lost by nonuse in every case, but are only lost if, at the same time, the servient proprietor *acquires freedom* from the servitude by lapse of time.[83]

The notion of the servient owner 'acquiring freedom' suggests that in the case of urban continuous servitudes, positive acts of interruption or adverse user for the prescription period were essential.

Non-use and abandonment

The foundation of *usucapio libertatis* in non-use suggests an analogy to abandonment. However, the jurists drew a distinction between abandonment as intentional surrender of possession and title allowing new appropriation on the one hand, and *usucapio libertatis* as loss of right through a time of non-use on the other. First, as the text by Gaius just quoted indicates, the loss of the servitude might be conceived in terms of the servient owner acquiring a new correlative right (or freedom from duty) which extinguishes the prior existing servitude. This 'acquisition' of right or liberty is not a straightforward derivative transfer of the right from dominant to servient tenement, but more in the nature of the creation of a new right (namely, a freedom from prior duty) which accompanies the extinction by prescription of the dominant right. By contrast, when an owner abandons a thing he intentionally gets rid of it, intending that it cease to be his property, so that the old title hangs by a thread and is readily extinguished upon a new possession commencing.[84]

80 Buckland, *Main Institutions*, 154. Buckland notes that *aqueductus* as a fixed channel was partly continuous in that nothing had to be done to have the watercourse in place, ready to conduct water as need or opportunity arose.

81 D.8.2.6. (Gaius); Buckland, *Textbook*, 267–268.

82 See e g D.8.6.12.2. (Paul); Buckland, *Elementary Principles*, 114–117.

83 D.8.2.6. (Gaius) (emphasis added), and see D.8.2.32.1. (Julian); D.8.6.18.2. (Paul).

84 Inst.2.1.47.

Secondly, since a servitude could not be possessed in a full and continuous manner but only quasi-possessed by use, an isolated non-user or interruption of user could not be seen as a dispossession affecting rights:

> If I have a right of way over your land and you expel me from it by force, I will lose the right of way by nonuse over a long period, because an incorporeal right cannot be regarded as possessed and no one can be evicted from a right of way, that is, a pure right.[85]

Possession of servient tenement for requisite period

During the required period of non-use of the servitude by the dominant owner, the servient tenement had to be constantly possessed in order to ground a usucapio libertatis:

> Freedom from a servitude is acquired by lapse of time, providing possession of the house is retained [throughout the prescribed period].[86]

An interruption of the prescription period was known as usurpation.[87] The required period of uninterrupted prescription was governed by elaborate rules defining what counted as usurpation; for aggregating successive unbroken possessions;[88] and also rules concerning the effective exercise of prescriptive possession through an agent, a tenant or a slave.[89] For example, if a servient house was built up so as to block a servitude for a period less than the prescription period and then possesssion of the house changed hands, the period of prescription would have to run again;[90] in other cases, however, possession by predecessors could be summed to make up a full prescription period. If possession was effected by another, the servient owner had to be aware of that third-party possession, for 'usucapion will run only for one aware of his possession'.[91]

Requisite use of servitude by dominant owner

A parallel issue was the type of enjoyment of a servitude required to maintain the right of a dominant tenement against extinctive prescription. Failure by successive owners to use servitudes belonging to the dominant tenement could be aggregated to make up a full period of prescription causing loss of rights, mirroring the rule allowing

85 D.41.3.4.26(27). (Paul).
86 D.8.2.32.1. (Julian).
87 D.41.3.2. (Paul).
88 For example D.41.2.13.1. (Ulpian) which states: 'When we invoke some support derived from our predecessor in title, we must accept it with all its incidents and defects; thus, when we count for ourselves the period of holding of our predecessor, there is the possibility that he possessed by force, stealth or *precarium*.'
89 D.41.2.2. (Ulpian); D.41.2.49.2. (Papinian); D.41.10.5.1. (Neratius).
90 See texts in note above.
91 D.41.2.49.2. (Papinian).

aggregation of possessions of the servient tenement.[92] It was not necessary for the servitude to be exercised by a true owner to keep it alive; possession of the dominant estate and active use of the attached rights by the posssessor sufficed. Thus if a man purchased an estate in good faith from a non-owner, or took possession of the land by *precarium* or forcible ejection of the true owner or *dominus*, then any prior servitude rights over the land (including 'natural' rights such as daily water that depended for their existence on continued exercise) would be kept up:

> The fact is that when an estate has particular attributes attaching to it and is possessed in that condition, such a right is not lost; and it makes little difference whether the possession of the man, who possess it as such, is lawful or not. For this reason it can be stated with even more conviction that if water flows through a watercourse of its own volition, the right to channel water along it is retained.[93]

Exercise of a servitude could be made apparent by even a partial use:

> If water flows into part of a watercourse, then, even although it does not reach its farthest end, every part of the course is still considered to be in use.[94]

A dominant owner could keep up servitude rights through use on his behalf by a co-owner,[95] a possessor in good faith;[96] a usufructary,[97] or else by his slave or tenant or even a guest or visitor.[98] The prescriptive period for non-use was extended where it was not expected that the right be used continuously for an unbroken period;[99] but a daily right to take water for a limited time, or in limited quantity, or in tandem with others, was subject to a prescription period counted for every day of non-use by the dominant owner.[100] Failure to use a servitude through ignorance of its existence was no defence to extinctive prescription;[101] and use of a servitude without belief that one was exercising a right was also an inadequate user, for example where one used a water-course or a road believing it was subject to public or permissive use (i e *precarium*).[102] If a merged ownership of both dominant and servient estates was

92 D.8.6.18.1. (Paul); D.8.6.19.1. (Pomponius).

93 D.8.6.12. (Celsus). A servitude could even survive alienation of the dominant land and surrender of its possession without reservation, provided the land was re-acquired and the servitude exercised within the prescription period: see D.8.6.13. (Marcellus).

94 D.8.6.9. (Javolenus).

95 D.8.6.5. (Paul); D.8.6.16. (Proculus); but if the users were not co-owners but separate owners of the same water-course or other servitude, then each owner had to personally use the right to sustain his servitude, and if a right was lost it would accrue to the servient landowner and not to the other servitude owners: D.8.6.16. (Proculus).

96 D.8.6.5. (Paul); cf D.8.6.24. (Scaevola).

97 D.8.6.5. (Paul); D.8.6.20. (Scaevola); D.8.6.21. (Paul).

98 D.8.6.20., 22., 24. (Scaevola); D.8.6.21., 23. (Paul). Acquisition of ownership through others generally is discussed in D.41.1.10.pr., 2.; D.41.1.32. (Gaius); D.41.1.54.4. (Pomponius); D.41.1.59. (Callistratus); D.41.2.13.1., 11.-13. (Ulpian); D.41.2.14. (Paul); D.41.2.25.1.; D.41.2.30.5. (Paul); D.41.2.31. (Pomponius); D.41.2.44.2.-3. (Papinian).

99 D.8.6.7. (Paul).

100 D.8.6.7.; D.8.6.10. (Paul); D.8.6.16. (Proculus).

101 D.8.6.19.1. (Pomponius).

102 D.8.6.25. (Paul). On *precarium*, see generally D.43.26.1.-22.

acquired, this immediately extinguished any servitudes between the estates regardless of non-use, following the definitional principle that there could be no servitude in one's own property.[103]

A contractual, that is personal, right to create a water-course over an estate was not extinguished by non-use, as the right was held not to be constituted as a property right until the physical use began. In other words liberative prescription did not run against a personal right to the potential use of a servitude.[104] The concept of servitudes as constituted by a metaphoric delivery, through actual physical use or quasi-possession, was thus operative within the *usucapio* rules.

The mental element in possession and quasi-possession

A person could possess property (or use and quasi-possess servitudes) in a variety of ways, often simultaneously; but generally it was necessary to possess consciously, as of right, in order to prevent loss of rights by *usucapio*.[105] A strong mental as well as physical element is present in defining use or quasi-possession of a servitude for the purposes of *usucapio* – a theme which ran through many other areas of Roman property doctrine.[106]

The requisite state of mind of the dominant owner who loses a servitude by prescription was variously expressed. Sometimes the Digest speaks of a mental surrender of 'possession' through non-use, regardless of intention to continue ownership;[107] or failure to assert possession as of right;[108] or through an acquiescence (knowing if non-consensual) in an adverse use by another, again indicating an intention not to possess or maintain rights;[109] or else by tacit consent to a transfer of the right to the servient owner by grant, such consent being implied from non-use or acquiescence.[110] Generally there could not be an unknowing loss of possession. For example:

> the previous possessor is said to possess even though another has entered the pasture with the object of possessing it, so long as he is in ignorance of the entry.

103 D.7.6.5.pr. (Ulpian); D.8.2.26. (Paul); D.8.6.1. (Gaius); see further WW Buckland, 'The Conception of Servitudes in Roman Law' (1928) 44 Law Quarterly Review 426.

104 D.8.6.19.pr. (Pomponius); D.8.6.18.2. (Paul); but note that 'if I had made a watercourse and not used it, I would lose my right': D.8.6.19. (Pomponius).

105 See e g D. 41.2.3.4.-7., 11., 21., 22.; D.41.2.8. (Paul); D.41.2.12.pr. (Ulpian); D.41.10.1.pr. (Ulpian). It appears that unknowing cession of personal possession of an estate ended use of attached servitudes; but interruption of possession through an agent was not a cession of user relevant to prescription, as where a slave's possession came to an end without the owner's knowledge. See D.41.2.44.2.-4. (Papinian).

106 See e g D.41.2.3.1. (Paul); D.41.2.17.1. (Ulpian); D.41.2.27. (Proculus); D.41.2.31. (Pomponius).

107 D.41.2.17.1. (Ulpian); D.41.2.27. (Proculus); D.41.2.31. (Pomponius); D.41.2.44.2. (Papinian).

108 D.8.6.25. (Paul): 'A man is not considered to be making use of a servitude unless he believes that he is exercising a right which belongs to him. Consequently, if a man makes use of a servitude as if he were using a public roadway or a servitude belonging to someone else, he is not entitled to any interdict or action.'

109 D.8.2.5. (Paul); cf the doctrine of *patientia*; Lee, *Elements of Roman Law*, 163–165.

110 D.44.7.52.4. (Modestinus): 'By virtue of our acquiescence we are of necessity regarded as being bound by consent.'

> For just as the bond of an obligation is released in the same way that it is normally created, so also possession which is held solely by intention should not be taken away from one ignorant of the facts.[111]

Yet if possession of a thing was being maintained by a slave, tenant or other agent, an adverse use unknown to the previous possessor could result in unknowing dispossession.[112]

Grant or possession as the key?

The variant qualities of mind founding prescriptions against servitudes suggested that factual circumstances could not be encompassed within a simple rule. But this indeterminacy of doctrine also expresses a deeper jurisprudential ambivalence going beyond the frailty of legal definitions and concepts in the face of intractable fact: namely, whether creation of proprietary interests primarily involved grant or possession. Was ownership created by transfer founded on contractual grant, or was ownership constituted by physical delivery and willed possession of property? A different mental state must be defined and isolated where ownership is taken to derive chiefly from the future-directed wills of transacting parties; this is evidentially and temporally distinct from the present wills of persons in possession. The classical jurists tended to stress present possession and delivery, while the Byzantines accorded a greater role to contractual will and appropriative intention. Pragmatic Roman law never gave a simple answer, but wavered between these analytical categories of conveyance and contract as foundations of ownership. These polarities assert themselves again as we turn from Roman to English law.

THE COMMON LAW OF PRESCRIPTION

Bractonian foundations

Henry de Bracton's early thirteenth-century treatment of servitudes and prescription in his treatise *De Legibus* is the foundation of common law doctrine in this field. The intricacies of the Bractonian system need not detain us here;[113] we will instead use classical modern commentators to explicate the Bractonian heritage.

We may begin with a notable difference between Roman and English notions of prescription for real rights. Roman *usucapio* after the *lex Scribonia* did not allow positive prescription for servitudes, but only for corporeal property. English property law used adverse possession to create titles to land through limitation of actions, and did not resort to true positive (nor indeed, negative) prescription in order to create

111 D.41.2.44.4. (Papinian).
112 D.41.2.44.2.-3. (Papinian).
113 See further Henry de Bracton, *De Legibus et Consuetudinibus Angliae* (4 vols, G E Woodbine (ed), S E Thorne (transl), 1977) f 51, 222–223, 229. For a detailed exposition of Bracton's servitude law see J Getzler, *A History of Water Rights at Common Law* (2003) ch 2.

rights in corporeals through long use.[114] Despite these genetic dissimilarities, Bracton was to raid the Roman doctrine for many of his leading concepts of prescription, including prescriptive acquisition and loss of servitudes. Not surprisingly, Bracton's hybrid of the Roman and common law possessory actions does not entirely cohere. In different passages he can be found saying the following:

1. Continuous use of incorporeal rights may amount to a *causa* substituting for positive grant;
2. Continuous use of incorporeal rights may be a substantive condition for maintaining legally protected possession;
3. Continuous use is an evidential condition for bringing actions to defend possession;
4. Non-use for a period of time (long or short not specified) results in substantive extinction of the right by prescription; and
5. Non-use for a period of time (long or short not specified) results in procedural barring of the right by laches or limitation.

Maitland's analysis

Bracton's contradictory doctrines of prescription deeply influenced English property law, and left a residue of problems into modern times.[115] F W Maitland in his 1895 analysis of medieval prescription law identified the prime source of tension within the Bractonian theory as lying in the relationship between legislative limitation of proprietary actions for land, and possessory rights to servitudes founded on long or immemorial use. Maitland writes:[116]

> Seisin itself is protected, seisin of the incorporeal thing. We can see this best if we consider the modes in which the ownership of such a thing can be acquired. It can be acquired by inheritance; it can be acquired by conveyance, though . . . the grantee has never got full and secure ownership until he has got possession, actual exploited possession; it can also be acquired by long-continued user. Of the effects of long-continued user Bracton speaks somewhat obscurely; his romanesque terms, *usucapio* and the like, perplex his doctrine.[117] (When Bracton is speaking of this matter, it is not always easy to say whether he is dealing with the acquisition of good right or with the acquisition of protected

114 The evolved modern common law position was laid out in *Tichborne v Weir* (1892) 67 LT 735; *Re Nisbet and Potts' Contract* [1905] 1 Ch 391, affd [1906] 1 Ch 386; cf *Cheshire and Burn* (15th edn, 1994) 620–621, 887-909; (16th edn, 2000) 676–677, 961–992; R W Megarry and H W R Wade, *The Law of Real Property* (6th edn by C Harpum, 2000) 86–94, 1303–1334. The modern law has been further complicated by registration of title, as explained in *Powell v McFarlane* (1977) 38 P & CR 452 per Slade J; and *J A Pye (Oxford) Ltd v Graham* [2002] 3 WLR 221, 229–237 per Lord Browne-Wilkinson and at 143–145 per Lord Hope. In *J A Pye* at 229–230, Lord Browne-Wilkinson noted that the provisions for limitation periods as to registered land have again been 'fundamentally altered' by the Land Registration Act 2002, ss 96–98 and Schedule 6. See further C Harpum, 'Registered Land – A Law Unto Itself?', ch 10 in this volume.

115 The morass of the law is charted – but not analysed – in T A Herbert, *The History of the Law of Prescription in England* (1891).

116 Pollock and Maitland, *History of English Law*, II, 140–141.

117 *Bracton*, f 51b, 52, II, 156–158.

> seisin. He has a, to us, misleading habit of calling the short period which protects the disseisor against the self-help of the disseisee. . .'longum tempus,' 'longum intervallum,' etc.) We must, however, draw a marked line between land and incorporeal things. Our medieval law knows no acquisitive prescription for land; all it knows is a limitation of actions. This principle seems to be implicit in the form which every demand for land by proprietary action must take. The claimant must allege that he or some ancestor of his was seised as of right; he must deduce his title from a seisin that was rightful. He must not indeed plead 'higher up' than a certain limiting period. In Bracton's day he must allege a seisin as of right on this side of Henry II's coronation. That date will leave him a hundred years or thereabouts. He will have to tender a champion prepared to swear to this rightful seisin, as one who either saw it, or was enjoined to bear witness of it by a dying father. Thus a limit is set to the action.[118]

Maitland here isolates three differing notions of user affecting property rights in the law of Bracton's time. First, there was the relatively short limitation period on the possessory actions by petty assize (notably novel disseisin and mort d'ancestor). Secondly, there is an 'evidentiary' limitation on proprietary actions, set by the formal requirement that rightful seisin should be capable of having been witnessed within the last two generations, namely that a demandant's champion could formally, if fictitiously, swear to the existence of the controverted right by personal knowledge or else by the sacrosanct hearsay of his father. Glanvill records some ambivalence as to whether a champion who was no witness could blatantly be hired to do battle, and in 1220 it is recorded that a champion was convicted for hiring himself and lost his foot. In 1275 the Statute of Westminster the first, c 41 acknowledged the practice of hire and abolished the form of oath swearing upon one's own father's knowledge; but otherwise leaving the common-law limitation period based on a past generation's witness untouched.[119]

The preservation of the notion of direct witness through a father's sacred command supplied a human measure of title or long use, based on the possibility of direct verification without resort to hearsay evidence. Time before this point was known as 'time immemorial', in the sense of occurrences literally outside living memory.[120] This contrasts with a legislative definition of time immemorial as beyond a specified

118 Citing *Bracton*, f 373; *Bracton's Note Book* pl 1217, III, p 230.

119 Henry de Glanvill, *Tractatus de Legibus et Consuetudinibus regni Anglie qui Glanvilla vocatur (The treatise on the laws and customs of the realm of England commonly called Glanvill)* (c.1187–9) (G D G Hall (ed and transl), 1965) bk II, ch 3, 22–26; 3 Edw 1 (Statute of Westminster the first, 1275) c 41: 'Since it seldom happens that the demandant's champion is not forsworn in making oath that he or his father saw the seisin of his lord or ancestor and his father commanded him to *deraign*, it is provided that the demandant's champion be not bound to swear this; but be the oath kept in all other points.' See further J B Thayer, *A Preliminary Treatise on Evidence at the Common Law* (1898) 39–46; J W Salmond, 'The History of the Law of Prescription', in Salmond, *Essays in Jurisprudence and Legal History* (1891) 73–120, at 81–87. The quo warranto controversy of the reign of Edward I echoes this point; see M T Clanchy, *From Memory to Written Record: England 1066–1307* (2nd edn, 1993) 35–43.

120 YB 20 & 21 Edw 1, (Rolls S) 414 (1293); H Rolle, *Un Abridgment des Plusiers Cases del Common Ley* (1688) (*Rolle Abdgt*), II, 268; Salmond, 'History of the Law of Prescription', at 81–83; A W B Simpson, *A History of the Land Law* (2nd edn, 1986) 109–110.

point of legal memory. This period of legal memory was set by the lengthy limitation times for the real or proprietary actions, introduced to replace the vagaries of customary or historical memory. The cut-off date for this period was originally set at the time of the Norman Conquest, as the ultimate historical fount of all titles. Later the time was set at Richard I's coronation. The Statute of Merton 1235 then fixed time of memory for the writ of right at the commencement of the reign of Henry II in 1154, some eighty-two years before, with a shorter limitation for mort d'ancestor and writs of entry, being the last return of King John from Ireland.

These various dates were conceived as more than simple statutory limitation periods; they were statutory definitions of what shall be taken to be time of memory at law, superseding the conception derived from the rule against hearsay. Bracton, writing perhaps in the reign of Henry III after the new limitations have been introduced, expressly states that the limitation statute is supposed to clarify the limits of direct evidence at common law:

> A writ of right, like other writs, is limited within a certain time, for it does not exceed the time of King Henry [II, that is, 1154]. . . The reason is because no one can prove anything beyond that time, since he cannot speak of his own sight, nor of the sight of his father, who enjoined him to be a witness if he could hear speak of it. And hence, if any one should speak of the time of King Henry the Elder, he may lose through failure of proof.[121]

In the case of a writ of entry, Bracton similarly states that the legislative limitation is to ensure that no one should exceed the time of testimony 'within their sight and hearing', again a stylized hearsay rule in the sense of not exceeding the legislative limitation.[122] Thus the second and third concepts of limitation – the period of long possession guaranteeing seisin, and the lengthy limitation period barring proprietary actions – are both described conventionally as 'time beyond which the memory of man does not run' or 'time immemorial'.[123] The much shorter novel disseisin limitation periods are distinct because of the special nature of the action, and are not part of the limitation rules regarding proof and the limits of memory.

Maitland continued his analysis: 'Mere lapse of time may serve as a shield for the tenant, but it can not serve as a sword for the demandant'.[124] Thus there was limitation of titles by the passing of time in adverse possession barring rival titles, yet no positive title by long use:

> But further, we may doubt whether for land there is any extinctive prescription. The man who can not allege a seisin on this side of Henry II.'s day has lost every

121 *Bracton*, f 373a, IV, 170; see also f 437b, IV, 359.

122 *Bracton*, f 318a, IV, 21–22.

123 For the history of the limitation periods and their impact on the law of title, see further Pollock and Maitland, *History of English Law*, II, 51–52, 81, 141; Salmond, 'History of the Law of Prescription', at 86-90; Simpson, *History of the Land Law*, 150–155, 267–269. At 150–151 Simpson notes: 'Around these statutes arose an extraordinarily complex body of law . . . a massive body of subtle doctrine'.

124 Pollock and Maitland, *History of English Law*, II, 141.

> action for the land; but it does not follow that his right is extinct. Hereafter it may prove its vitality, if this man, having obtained seisin under some new and defeasible title, is 'remitted' to the oldest title he has. . . . [A]t a later time 'it is commonly said that a right can not die'[125] and this we may well believe to be an old, as well as a common, saying.[126]

The avoidance of true extinctive prescription in medieval English law may be ascribed to its feudal context. Legal and social status, as well as economic wealth, were formally determined by one's proprietary or tenurial rights within the feudal ladder; hence such rights were not readily to be extinguished by prescription.[127] By contrast, the Roman property right in land was more properly an economic or commercial right, with status being determined by another set of legal rights and doctrines; and a variety of modes of prescription were freely made available to clear titles and facilitate trade in land, without adverse affect on individual and family status.

In the sphere of incorporeal rights, which were outside or supplementary to the standard tenurial arrangements, the communal agricultural institutions of English feudal society may suggest some reasons why land could readily be affected by prescriptive servitudes at common law, again diverging sharply from the Roman system. Maitland noted that prescription proper was unavailable for land itself; but incorporeal things could be acquired by prescription or by long-continued user. Maitland's analysis of the doctrine of prescription for incorporeities repays careful attention:

> In particular we may see this in the case of rights of common. There is an action by which the landowner calls upon the person who asserts such rights to prove his title, the action *Quo iure clamat communam*[128]. . . a thoroughly proprietary action. Now one of the usual answers to this action is a prescriptive claim – 'I and those whom I represent have commoned here – always – from before the Norman Conquest – from time immemorial.' In most cases the Norman Conquest is mentioned. Behind the great resettlement of the land one must not go; on the other hand one can, to all seeming, be required to allege a continuous seisin ever since that remote event.[129]
>
> This is a proprietary action; but it is fairly evident that a man can acquire a legally protected possession of an incorporeal thing on much easier terms. We put this case: For some time past a man openly and peaceably, and as though asserting a right, has been turning his beasts out on my land; he may have been doing it for so long a time that I can no longer bring an assize against him as against one who has been disseising me of my land; still he can not assert a user that goes back nearly as far as the Conqueror's days. The question is whether this man is protected against my self-help. May I bar out his beasts from the

125 T Littleton, *Les Tenures* (1481), s 478, E Wambaugh, *Littleton's Tenures in English* (1903) 225–226.
126 Pollock and Maitland, *History of English Law*, II, 141.
127 Cf Simpson, *History of the Land Law*, 150–155.
128 *Bracton*, f 229b, III, 184; *Note Book*, I, 185.
129 Pollock and Maitland, *History of English Law*, II, 142–143.

> pasture or seize them if they are there? To this question the answer that Bracton gives is that against self-help this man is protected. My proper course is to bring against him some more or less proprietary action. Possibly ... the *Quo iure*, and then there may be a grand assize. It is very possible that this man should one day 'recover the common' in an assize and the next day be made a defendant in a proprietary action which will deprive him of the common for good and all.[130] The idea of a purely possessory protection for those who are enjoying 'incorporeal things,' but who can not yet say that those things are their own, is one that can not be easily managed. We seem to have before us a pasture right that is only half a right, an incorporeal right that exists and yet does not exist. But the lawyers of the thirteenth century made a strenuous endeavour to pursue this idea through all speculative difficulties. (We have been dealing with a case which ... Holmes[131] rightly treated as a good test of the so-called 'possession of rights,' and we believe that, if this test is applied to Bracton's age, the result is that an user which falls far short of establishing an indefeasible right obtains a possessory protection.)[132]

Maitland here isolated a doctrinal contradiction in Bracton as to whether user established an immediate right to protected continuing possession of servitudes, or whether long user hardened extant possessory rights into fuller property rights with a wider ambit of protection, either by barring of rival claims or by positive constitution, the law is not entirely clear which.

Salmond's analysis

Maitland did not attempt further to resolve or explain these contending conceptions of prescription. This gap is noteworthy, as Maitland was certainly aware of J W Salmond's fine essay on 'The History of the Law of Prescription' which was published in 1891.[133] Salmond there provided an analytical model of Bracton's prescription doctrine and its relationship with later medieval law. The analysis rested on three premises: first, that prescription doctrine was based on an evidential presumption that the fact of possession was evidence of right; secondly, that conversely the fact of not possessing was evidence of absence of right; and thirdly that long possession (or non-possession) increased the power of these evidential presumptions so that they eventually became conclusive, or immune to rebuttal by direct contrary evidence. An irrebuttable presumption of right led to direct prescription; a rebuttable presumption made for indirect prescription, as the fact of long possession was then taken as evidence of some other disprovable fact forming the true legal root of the title or protected seisin. At English law there was no positive prescription for corporeals; instead one pleaded descent of title from the rightful seisin of an ancestor stretching back to beyond the current limitation period. The

130 *Bracton*, f 230, III, 185 ff.; f 52b, II, 158.
131 O W Holmes Jr, *The Common Law* (Boston, 1881; M De Howe (ed), Boston, 1963) 241, 384.
132 Pollock and Maitland, *History of English Law*, II, 142–143.
133 See e g citation of Salmond, 'History of the Law of Prescription', in Pollock and Maitland, *History of English Law*, II, at 141 n 4.

reason for this was in part because a line of protected seisins of land could readily be given direct proof, rendering presumptions from the fact of long possession unnecessary; but a deeper reason was that title to land was 'of common right', a title taking effect by operation of the general custom of the common law. By contrast, most (not all) incorporeal rights, including many contractual agreements, were conceived of as being 'against common right'. These were 'specialties' or rights conferred under private law created by deed, prescription or custom.[134] Prescription proper was a specialty akin to a customary right for particular individuals, proved by usage from time immemorial. Prescription proper thus was not a principle of limitation protecting seisin, but a branch of custom law.

Salmond explained how the theory of prescriptions as specialties or singular customs disappeared from the modern law, probably in the seventeenth century:

> A custom continues to be regarded as embodying a rule of special law, superseding in its particular sphere the common law. For example, when the [owner of an estate] claimed a right of way by reason of immemorial user of it by him and his ancestors, he was according to the original theory, setting up and relying upon a rule of special law, which *ipso jure* conferred upon him the right claimed; just as if he had relied on a private Act of Parliament conferring the right upon him. But, according to the modern theory, he is regarded as setting up, not a rule of law, but a title (to wit, that of long possession), which gives him

134 Charters relating to warranty of title make a separate subject; see J G H Hudson, *Land, Law, and Lordship in Anglo-Norman England* (1994) 57, 70–77; P R Hyams, 'The Charter as a Source for the Early Common Law' (1991) 12 Journal of Legal History 173. A specialty in its widest meaning was a local or private law outside and derogating from the common law; only later did specialty come to connote a formal obligation such as a debt or covenant embodied in a deed. This is touched upon by *Glanvill*'streatment of covenant and charter (bk X, (Hall (ed), 116–132, esp at 124, 132), which states that 'it is not the custom for the court of the lord king to protect or warrant private agreements of this kind concerning the giving or receiving of things . . . nor does it even concern itself with such contracts as can be considered to be like private agreements'. D J Ibbetson, *A Historical Introduction to the Law of Obligations* (1999) 17–23, in a close reading of *Glanvill*, emphasizes the procedural or probative aspect of specialty. Recent scholarship on specialty has focussed chiefly on explaining how deed requirements came to be applied to the action of covenant around 1300, whether through application of civilian formality requirements by analogy to lease covenants (e g D J Ibbetson, 'Words and Deeds: The Action of Covenant in the Reign of Edward I' (1986) 4 Law and History Review 71; Ibbetson, *Law of Obligations*, 24–30); or as a graft from county court procedure (R C Palmer, *The County Courts of Medieval England, 1150–1350* (1982) 198–215, and R C Palmer, 'Covenant, Justicies Writs, and Reasonable Showings' (1987) 31 AmJLH 97; cf J S Beckerman, 'Procedural Innovation and Institutional Change in Medieval English Manorial Courts' (1992) 10 Law and History Review 197, 219–226); or as an apt method of proof of private will or intention to be bound in conscience (J Barton, 'The Medieval Contract', in Barton (ed), *Towards a General Law of Contract* (1990) 15–37; P Philbin, 'Proving the Will of Another: The Specialty Requirement in Covenant' (1992) 105 Harv LR 2001). R C Palmer, *English Law in the Age of the Black Death* (1993) 64–65, suggests that mid-fourteenth century use of specialty covenant was generally non-litigious, and amounted to a formal method to put into effect the final concord for land transactions. This analysis returns specialty transactions to their earliest character as creators of private or special law, privilege or jurisdiction. Elements of a substantive view of specialty are discussed further in A W B Simpson, *A History of the Common Law of Contract: The Rise of the Action of Assumpsit* (1975) 15–25; Palmer, *County Courts of Medieval England*, 263–296; J Biancalana, 'Medieval County Courts: A Review Essay' (1983) 52 University of Cincinnati Law Review 994, 1015–16; J Biancalana, 'Actions of Covenant 1200–1330' (2002) 20 Law and History Review 1.

> the right at common law. According to the modern theory, there exists a rule of common law, to the effect that the immemorial possessor of an easement acquires a right thereto, and a claimant, in proving immemorial possession, is regarded as bringing himself within the supposed rule. The radical distinction that thus came to be recognised between prescription and custom has been well expressed in the following words: 'Prescription seems to us to be the making of a right; custom the making of a law . . . Prescription is creative of a right which gets its sanction from law; custom is creative of a law which gives its sanction to rights'.[135]

The change of theory of prescription was a natural result of their quality of singularity: most laws were general, conferring rights on a claimant who could show facts bringing himself within a norm-creating rule; it was anomalous to have laws directly conferring rights on a particular individual; hence 'by a natural process of assimilation to the ordinary form, immemorial user came to be regarded as a title bringing the claimant within a supposed rule of the common law.' The same change overtook the concept of contract as a specialty, as Salmond explains: 'We no longer regard a special agreement as the source of a rule of special law excluding the common law. To say that a rent charge is against common right, has now no real meaning for us. We have come to regard agreements as titles operating at common law'.[136]

This abandonment of specialties as a category of analysis in modern law helped conceal the reasons for a fundamental rule of common-law prescription: that there cannot be a title to corporeal things made by prescription, and that only incorporeal hereditaments are things claimable by prescription. We have noticed that this rule of English law contrasts with Roman and civil law where the reverse rule held, that is, that incorporeities being things incapable of apparent possession cannot be claimed by positive prescription or *usucapio*. Salmond's explanation for the contrary English rule was as follows:

> Now, it is true, as a matter of fact, that the division between things claimable by prescription and things not so claimable, is largely coincident with that between incorporeal and corporeal hereditaments. As a matter of principle, however, these divisions have nothing to do with each other. The true rule on this point is that matters against common right are claimable by prescription, while matters of common right are not so claimable. 'Every prescription is against common right'.[137] This rule follows directly from the origin of prescription as already set forth. If a right is recognised by the common law, it cannot be regarded as also conferred by an inconsistent special law, and, therefore, cannot be claimed by either of those titles that originated as sources of special law, i e by grant or by prescription. If, on the other hand, a right is not recognised by the common law,

135 Salmond, 'History of the Law of Prescription', 97, quoting J H B Browne, *The Law of Usages and Customs* (1875) 14; see also Pollock and Maitland, *History of English Law*, I, 177–178.
136 Salmond, 'History of the Law of Prescription', 98.
137 *Robert Gray's Case* (1560) 8 Co Rep 125b, 77 ER 663, 664.

> if it is *contra jus commune*, it must be claimed by special law, that is, either under a custom, or by the titles of grant or prescription.[138]

This doctrinal approach explains Coke's dictum: 'a custome cannot be alledged generally within the kingdome of England, for that is common law'.[139]

In the early forms of action for property, the law required that seisin of the claimant or his ancestor at some recent time be shown, as the basis of a claim at petty assize and as an element of a claim of right in a higher action for proprietary title. Bracton tended to confuse this lesser requirement of proof of recent possession with the greater requirement of seisin since time immemorial (more accurately *quasi*-seisin), where a title to an incorporeal thing was claimed by prescription against common right.[140] Bracton really had no discrete concept of title by positive prescription whatsoever, only concepts of long possession as bestowing a protected seisin, as Salmond writes:

> Bracton tells us, indeed, that rights of common and other servitudes may be acquired by long possession. He gives us no indication. . .as to how long this possession requires to be, or any detailed information as to this branch of the law. . . . [T]o him prescription was merely a part of that chaos of special customs into which it was no business of his to introduce order. At first sight, however, Bracton may be thought to say very much more about positive prescription then he really does. He speaks frequently about the effect of lapse of time in creating rights, but what he is really treating of is the acquisition, not of ownership, but of possession. By what means possession or seisin was lost and gained, was in the early law of property an extremely important subject. It was the rule that possession could be retained *animo solo*; until, therefore, an ejected possessor had actually or constructively acquiesced in his ejectment, he was not regarded by law as having lost possession, nor was the ejector regarded as having gained it. If, however, the person ejected delayed re-entering upon the ejector for a certain period, he was presumed by the law to have acquiesced in his ejectment. He, therefore, lost possession, and the ejector gained it, and could be removed only by action, *per breve et judicium*. These principles applied not only to the possession of corporeal things, but also to the quasi-possession or user of incorporeal things.[141]

Bracton's discussion of prescription for incorporeal property is not, then, truly about acquisition of a title by long use, but about acquisition of seisin. The proper analogy is not with *usucapio*, but with common-law seisin of corporeal things, as Bracton writes:

> And when a long and peaceable and continuous possession has intervened, they (the possessors) begin to possess against all the world, and to have a freehold, so

138 Salmond, 'History of the Law of Prescription', 98–99.

139 Sir Edward Coke, *The First Part of the Institutes of the Laws of England, or, A Commentary on Littleton* (F Hargrave and C Butler (eds), 19th edn, 1832) [*Co Litt*] 110b; cf H E Salt, 'The Local Ambit of a Custom', in G G Alexander (ed), *Cambridge Legal Essays*, 279, 282–284.

140 Salmond, 'History of the Law of Prescription', 107–108.

141 Salmond, 'History of the Law of Prescription', 107–108.

> much so that they cannot be ejected without a writ and a judgment, for just as time is a mode of creating and destroying an obligation, so it is a mode of acquiring possession . . .
>
> It has been discussed in what way a person acquires possession of a corporeal thing by time without delivery, with or without use; now we must discuss in what way possession of an incorporeal thing is acquired, as possession of a right, such as a servitude, by sufferance (which is equivalent to consent) and long and peaceful enjoyment, without grant or express consent. For sufferance is taken for consent, and the possession of a right is acquired through use, as if the lord of the property, having a free estate, has, through sufferance, when present and cognisant of the fact, allowed his neighbours to enjoy on his estate a servitude. . .for a long time peaceably and without interruption, from such an enjoyment and sufferance there is a presumption of consent and of willingness, and so possession is acquired by the lapse of time, so that any one so using it cannot be ejected without a writ and a judgment.[142]

Bracton's concept of *longa et continua possessio* was extremely variable: it could be barely four days if the disseisee was present and took no action to make re-entry; it could range up to three years if the disseisee was absent on pilgrimage to the Holy Land. Upon lapse of this period, there must be resort to a petty assize for novel disseisin or a higher action to recover lost possession: the lapse of time gives the disseisor a protected seisin in his turn.

Bracton and the early authorities have very little to say about the requisite long user for acquiring protected possession of an incorporeal thing; for Bracton it was probably a period of time indicating acquiescence in the taking, a period measured according to the discretion of the court. In the Year Book of Edward I, it is stated that ten years' enjoyment suffices to create a legally-protected possession of a profit: 'If she had been seised of that profit for ten years, think you that she were disturbed she would not have the Novel Disseisin? She certainly would'.[143] When the possessory actions become more droitural in character, so that a title can be pleaded in bar to an action, 'this whole branch of the law falls into desuetude'.[144] Later interpreters, working with an entirely different set of concepts, confuse the protection of possession upon lapse of time, as found in Bracton and the Year Books, with the vesting of title by long user on a Roman model of *usucapio*.[145] On this matter, Salmond concludes:

> The rules found in Bracton, therefore, as to the acquisition of rights by lapse of time, do not refer to prescription in the sense in which the term is understood in

142 *Bracton*, f 52a, III, 156–157.

143 YB 21 & 22 Edw 1 c 422 (1294); and see Statute of Westminster the second (1285), 13 Edw 1, c 46 (commons).

144 Salmond, 'History of the Law of Prescription', 110.

145 E g K E Digby, *An Introduction to the History of the Law of Real Property with Original Authorities* (1st edn, 1875) 149.

> English law. They constitute part of the ancient law of possession, and are quite unconnected with those rules as to immemorial user whose history we have been considering.[146]

The confusion within medieval doctrines of prescription is noted in Littleton's *Tenures* (1481, written in the 1450s), in the discussion there of custom as a source of rights:

> And note that no custom is to be allowed, but such custom as hath been used by title of prescription, that is to say, from time out of mind. But divers opinions have been of time out of mind, &c., and of title of prescription, which is all one in the law. For some have said, that time out of mind should be said from time of limitation in a writ of right; that is to say, from the time of King Richard the First after the Conquest, as is given by the statute of Westminster the First . . . And in so much that it is given by the said statute, that in a writ of right none shall be heard to demand of the seisin of his ancestors of longer time than of the time of King Richard aforesaid, therefore this is proved, that continuance of possession, or other customs and usages used from the same time [Littleton: *puis le dit temps*; Coke's translation gives 'after the same time'], is the title of prescription, &c. And this is certain. And others have said, that well and truth it is, that seisin and continuance from [Coke: 'after'] the limitation, &c., is a title of prescription, as is aforesaid, and by the cause aforesaid. But they have said, that there is also another title of prescription, that was at the common law before any statute of limitation of writs, &c., and that it was, where a custom, or usage, or other thing, hath been used, for time whereof the mind of man runneth not to the contrary. And they have said, that this is proved by the pleading, where a man will plead a title of prescription of custom. He shall say, that such custom hath been used from time whereof the mind of man runneth not to the contrary, that is as much to say, when such a matter is pleaded, that no man then alive hath heard any proof of the contrary; nor hath no knowledge of the contrary; and insomuch that such title of prescription was at the common law, and not put out by statute, *ergo*, it abideth as it was at the common law . . .[147]

The confusion in measurement of prescription periods was compounded in the next century, when the period of limitation for the writ of right was reduced to sixty years by Henry VIII's limitation statute of 1540.[148] After this limited reform, the courts saw fit to preserve 1189, being the entrenched statutory-cum-customary measure of time immemorial for the positive proof of custom and prescription, as the measure of time for prescriptive acquisition of those incorporeal rights which were specialities against common right – but not for incorporeal rights of common right, such as rents and pasture appendant to land.[149]

146 Salmond, 'History of the Law of Prescription', 110.

147 Littleton, *Tenures*, s 170, translation (following *Co Litt*) from Wambaugh, *Littleton's Tenures*, 81–82.

148 32 Hen 8, c 2. The 1623 statute of limitations, 21 Jac 1, c 16, reduced the limitation for ejectment to twenty years, setting a still shorter period for practical recovery of real property.

149 *Co Litt* 110, 113a–114b, 122a; Sir William Blackstone, *Commentaries on the Law of England* 4 vols (1st edn, 1765–9) [*Bl Comm*], II, 30–31 and n; Salmond, 'History of the Law of Prescription', 98–103.

Blackstone's analysis did little to clear the murk of the early modern law. He described the patent inability to possess or have seisin in incorporeal things as the reason why prescriptions, providing a grant or legal origin of servitudes in lieu of possession, are generally necessary, thus inverting the Roman arguments derived from the policy of the *lex Scribonia*.

> [A]s to the several species of things which may, or may not, be prescribed for: we may in the first place, observe, that nothing but incorporeal hereditaments can be claimed by prescription; as a right [of] way, a common, etc.; but that no prescription can give a title to lands, and other corporeal substances, of which more certain evidence may be had. For no man can be said to prescribe, that he and his ancestors have immemorially used to hold the castle of Arundel: for this is clearly another sort of title; a title by corporal seisin and inheritance, which is more permanent, and therefore more capable of proof, than that of prescription. But, as to a right of way, a common, or the like, a man may be allowed to prescribe; for of these there is no corporal seisin, the enjoyment will be frequently by intervals, and therefore the right to enjoy them can depend on nothing else but immemorial usage.[150]

Blackstone further distinguished between immemorial customs for a locale; prescriptions in a person and his ancestors, which could include the incorporeal franchise rights; and prescription in a que estate, for rights attached to estates. The lines between these classes of prescriptive right were hard to draw, and this generated enormous quantities of litigation in the eighteenth and early nineteenth centuries.

Reasonableness and necessity in presumptions of grant

With the waning of the concepts of specialty rights and customs outside the common law, difficulties sprang forth as lawyers tried to make sense of precedents for which the medieval rationale had vanished. Coke tried to explain necessary, appendant incorporeal rights, such as pasture and estovers, as prescribed for by a necessarily-implied grant, rather than as common rights attaching to land as a quality of seisin, independent of long user or special right.[151] A more significant problem for modern lawyers was the well-established requirement that prescriptions, like customs, should be reasonable if they were to attract legal recognition as immemorial and binding practice. Reasonableness here had a double meaning: that the right itself be reasonable, a substantive measure; or else that the right had a reasonable origin, a procedural test. For an example of the latter requirement, some putative bargain establishing the custom or prescription might be looked for, since persons would be unlikely to have agreed to special law without good consideration and reason. An example of such reasoning is given in a 1495 case where a fugitive tried to plead that a right of sanctuary had been attached to an old Templar's house. Hussey CJ in King's

150 *Bl Comm*, II, 264, following Christopher St German, *Doctor and Student* (London, 1523–30) dialogue 1, c 8; Sir Henry Finch, *Law, or, a Discourse Thereof* (London, 1613, 1729) 132; and see Salmond, 'History of the Law of Prescription', 99–102.

151 *Co Litt* 122a–b; cf A W B Simpson, *History of the Land Law*, 111–112.

Bench held that a long-held custom to accord a privilege based on custom or long use; but that: 'a sanctuary cannot lie in prescription, for the king may not grant to a man that he shall have a sanctuary; for in a sanctuary a party cannot have his remedy, and the king may not take away a party's action by his grant', that is, such grants interfering with normal procedural rights would be unreasonable, 'yet they may be granted by parliament'.[152]

The tests of reasonableness survived strongly into the eighteenth century for customs;[153] but as prescriptions lost their legal quality as specialties, the judges began to elevate the procedural presumption of grant above substantive requirements of reasonableness. The emergent idea was that if long user indicated a voluntary grant of right some time in the past, then freedom of contract dictated that the rights had a good origin and had been supported by reason – even if they appeared now to be substantively unreasonable. By thus stressing the presumed grant, rather than the precedent fact of acquiescence in long user, as the immediate cause of right, the reasonableness doctrine for prescriptions was emptied of practical effect.

The result of the changed test for good prescriptions was that by the time of Blackstone, a new orthodoxy had hardened, namely:

> A prescription cannot be for a thing which cannot be raised by a grant. For the law allows prescription only in supply of the loss of a grant, and, therefore, every prescription presupposes a grant to have existed.[154]

According to Salmond, '[t]he rule that a prescription must be reasonable was thus wholly lost sight of, being supplanted by a new rule, which originated either as a somewhat illogical inference from the earlier or as a deliberate evasion of it'; and he continued:

> By the old theory, prescription was direct; by the new, it is indirect. By the old, immemorial user was beyond question itself a title; by the new, it is merely evidence of title. The difference is fundamental, and marks a distinct breach of logical continuity in the development of this branch of the law.[155]

Judges from the mid-nineteenth century tended to instruct juries that prescriptive rights such as easements and franchises were not bad for 'rankness' or unreasonable-

152 *Rollesley v Toft* (1495) K B 27/936, m 60, in *The Notebook of Sir John Port* (J H Baker (ed), Selden Society, CII, 1986) Case 35, 31–36 at 31.

153 Littleton, *Tenures*, s 212; *Co Litt* 140a; *Bl Comm*, I, 74–79. A powerful example of legal extinguishment of 'unreasonable' customary common rights was afforded by the case of *Steel v Houghton* (1788) 1 Hy Bl 51, 126 ER 32 (CP) which ended the right of gleaning after harvest: see P King, 'Gleaners, Farmers and the Failure of Legal Sanctions in England 1750–1850' (1989) 125 Past and Present 116; P King, 'The Origins of the Gleaning Judgement of 1788, A Case Study of Legal Change, Customary Right and Social Conflict in Late Eighteenth Century England' (1992) 10 *Law and History Review* 1; A C Loux, 'The Persistence of the Ancient Regime: Custom, Utility, and the Common Law in the Nineteenth Century' (1993) 79 Cornell Law Review 183.

154 *Bl Comm*, II, 265.

155 Salmond, 'History of the Law of Prescription', 119; and see Simpson, *History of the Land Law*, 110.

ness if they had been practiced for sufficient time;[156] though customs binding locales were more vulnerable to nullification for rankness.[157] Thus in the 1835 case of *Jenkins v Harvey* in the Court of Exchequer, Parke B stated that 'the correct mode of presenting the [prescription] point to [a jury] would have been, that, from uninterrupted modern usage, they should find the immemorial existence of the payment'.[158] In that case the issue was whether a corporation could assert a prescriptive right to levy a port duty, and the fact that there had been a modern usage to so charge implied both immemoriality and reasonableness without more. Alderson B added that the trial judge had wrongly implied that the duty was against common right and so subject to a stringent test of reasonableness; this was false as all persons paying received a compensatory service.[159] The common right concept was thus eviscerated, and survives into the early nineteenth century only as an archaism at the edge of argument.

The fiction of the lost modern grant

In the last phase of common-law development of prescription, the move from direct to indirect prescription led to invention of the fiction of the lost modern grant in the mid-eighteenth century.[160] The fixing of so distant a date as 1189 as the period of time immemorial for prescription became palpably inconvenient and unworkable; but the judges were reluctant to apply the shorter statutory periods later set for the writ of right, preferring to create convoluted rules for advising juries when they could presume facts and rights from long user.[161] However, there was never any logical objection to having an archaically period of proof, when user from time immemorial itself provided a direct title:

> But, when such user came to be regarded as not in itself a title, but merely evidence of a title, it became obvious that a very much shorter period of user might be equally effective. And, accordingly, [in the later eighteenth century], the period of twenty years came to be fixed upon as sufficient to raise a presumption of title.[162] The period was selected in analogy to the statutory limitation of the action of ejectment. Possession for twenty years constituted (in practice) a good title to a house, and it was only reasonable that it should be equally effective in the case of an easement belonging to the house. In the earlier cases we may trace a tendency to make twenty years' user not merely evidence

156 Salmond, 'History of the Law of Prescription', 110–119; *Jenkins v Harvey* (1835) 2 Cr M & R 393, 407, 150 ER 169, 176 per Parke B (Ex); *Attorney-General v Mathias* (1858) 4 K & J 579, 70 ER 241; but cf *Goodman v Saltash Corpn* (1882) 48 LT 239 (HL).

157 A celebrated example was the abolition of the right to glean: see King, 'Legal Change' and 'Gleaners'.

158 *Jenkins v Harvey* (1835) 1 Cr M & R 877, 894, 149 ER 1336, 1342 per Parke B. This ratio was followed in *Shephard v Payne* (1862) 12 CBNS 414, 432-7, 142 ER 1203, 1211-13 per Willes J (CP); affd (1864) 16 CBNS 132, 143 ER 1075.

159 *Jenkins v Harvey* (1835) 1 Cr M & R 877, 895; 149 ER 1336, 1343 per Alderson B.

160 Simpson, *History of the Land Law*, 266–269.

161 Simpson, *History of the Land Law*, 266–269; and see *Co Litt* 110a, 114b, 115a-b; *Bl Comm*, II, 30–31, 36, 265; *Dalton v Angus* (1881) 6 App Cas 740, 810-5 (HL) per Lord Blackburn.

162 See *Yard v Ford* (1671) 2 Saund 172, 85 ER 922, notes by Sjt Williams and the cases there cited.

> of user, but a title itself. But this was too bold an innovation, and it soon became settled that the new form of prescription was not direct but indirect. The chance was lost of establishing by judicial decisions a satisfactory substitute for the old rule of immemorial prescription. The fiction of the modern lost grant was invented.[163]

To understand this notorious fiction, it is necessary to investigate the meaning of 'time immemorial' and the nature of the evidential presumptions made from long user. The setting of time of memory at 1189, being the old limitation for the writ of right, was reduced by limitation act in 1540 to sixty years for land by writ of right, and reduced again to twenty years for ejectment in 1623.[164] This reduced the inconvenience of distant, fixed dates of limitation which exposed titles to contrary evidence of absence of right or superior claim. The old common-law hearsay concept of time immemorial, as the approximate limitation on evidence set by the last generation's direct witness, was often applied concurrently with the fixed statutory cut-off dates of legal memory. Coke quotes Littleton's statement that he did not know which measure of limitation of 'time immemorial' was correct at law, though Littleton inclined to the latter.[165] Coke could shed no light on the matter.[166] An analysis from 1515–16 of acquisition of liberties and franchises demonstrates the persistence of hearsay concepts of time immemorial:

> Franchises . . . may be forfeited for non-user or misuse . . . One may use franchises by a general grant before time of memory, and special prescription, and allowance in eyre since time of memory . . . *Time of memory means the memory of man and not the limitation in a writ of right.*[167]

Sir John Spelman in 1519 investigated the measurement of time immemorial pertaining to real actions, and seems to thoroughly contradict himself in cases [A] and [B] as given below:

> First, prescription is something which has continued from time whereof memory runneth not. And that constitutes a good title even if the beginning was wrongful, inasmuch as the long continuance of the possession has purged the wrong. Therefore in every prescription it is said, 'whereof the memory of man is not to the contrary' (*cujus contrarii memoria hominum non existit*). And even if no man has memory to the contrary, nevertheless [A] *if it can appear that the claimant's possession began after King Richard [I] . . .the prescription fails.* For the limitation in the writ of right is from the time of King Richard . . . But prescribing since the time of Richard is good; and if the prescription is

163 Salmond, 'History of the Law of Prescription', 120.

164 *Bryant v Foot* (1867) LR 2 QB 161, 179-82 (QB) per Cockburn CJ; *R v Oxfordshire County Council, ex p Sunningwell Parish Council* [2000] 1 AC 335, 349–352 per Lord Hoffmann.

165 Littleton, *Tenures*, s 170, in Wambaugh, *Littleton's Tenures*, 81–83; see above, text accompanying n 147.

166 *Co Litt* pp 113a; 115a.

167 Anon, 'A Reading on Magna Carta, c 9', Gray's Inn, c 1515/16, in John Spelman's *Reading on Quo Warranto delivered in Gray's Inn (Lent 1519)* (JH Baker (ed), Selden Society, CXIII, 1997) 12–13.

> traversed, the inquest shall only enquire concerning the time of men's memory. Suppose someone is seised in the time of Richard and continues all the time down to King Edward III and no longer, that does not make a prescription; but [B] if the seisin began in the time of King Edward III and continues through all the time since down to the present, that is a good prescription, for the memory of man is not to the contrary.[168]

Spelman's seemingly contradictory exposition captures the tendency of the courts to hold that if there was no hearsay evidence against the claim, thus fulfilling the common-law or customary limitation period, then this raised a further presumption that there was no evidence contrary to the grant within the statutory limitation period either. Case A involves proof of time immemorial in fact; Case B involves presumption in law. Establishing the ingredients of the short common-law prescriptive period thus went some way to establishing the longer statutory presumption in turn. However, the common-law evidential presumption was a rebuttable presumption of fact, whilst the statutory presumption established the legal facts conclusively, that is, it raised an irrebuttable legal fiction that the right was 'immemorial' in the sense of beginning before the medieval limitation points for real titles.

With the modern shortening of the limitation for property actions, the presumption of grant might have become a true conclusive presumption, whereby disproof of the possibility of an actual grant, or proof of a recent origin of enjoyment, would not prevail against the legal fact of twenty years' user or more. But the courts fumbled the nature of the presumption of grant, and sometimes spoke of factual presumptions operating after twenty years' lapse, but still capable of disproof by evidence from anytime after common law memory. Sometimes, however, the twenty-year period of user was held to raise a conclusive legal presumption of lawful origin immune to rebuttal – the fiction of the lost modern grant, a means of turning rebuttable factual presumptions into conclusive legal ones. In Blackstone's doctrine, for example, current limitation periods are sometimes used to make conclusive legal presumptions of prescription, as a substantive rule defining what counts as time immemorial. Sometimes the period of prescription or limitation raises an evidential presumption of immemoriality, as a rebuttable inference of fact from partial evidence. Sometimes a factual presumption is made which further supports a conclusive legal presumption.[169] Lord Blackburn confessed in 1881 that he could not make sense of the intricate prescriptive presumptions of the preceding century.[170] Loux has identified some telling instances of judicial creativity in explaining the presumptions of immemoriality of custom.[171] For example, in *R v Joliffe* the court of King's Bench

168 'Spelman's Reading on Quo Warranto', Lecture III, ibid, 84–85; cf text B, 122.

169 The arcane set of presumptions was observed in *Angus v Dalton* (1877) 3 QBD 85, 105, QB per Cockburn CJ; *Dalton v Angus* (1881) 6 App Cas 740, 810–812, HL per Lord Blackburn. See also Simpson, *History of the Land Law*, 266–269; Loux, 'Persistence of the Ancient Regime', at 210–212.

170 See *Dalton v Angus* (1881) 6 App Cas 740, 812–813, HL.

171 Loux, 'Persistence of the Ancient Regime', at 210–212.

upheld a jury instruction that 'slight evidence [of custom enjoyed for more than twenty years], if uncontradicted, becomes cogent proof' of immemorial usage. Abbott CJ explained this as follows:

> A regular usage for 20 years, not explained or contradicted, is that upon which many private and public rights are held, there being nothing in the usage to contravene the public policy . . . or any known rule or principle of law.[172]

This meant that if a practice could be proved for the past twenty years and was not obnoxious to law or public welfare, it could be ratified as 'immemorial custom' without more. In *Bryant v Foot*[173] the court was blunt in its pragmatic approach to the doctrine:

> If we assume [that] . . . neither judges nor juries have in reality believed . . . that customs found to be immemorial had actually existed in the time of Richard I., still, if this state of the law, created by the judges to quiet titles, to protect rights derived from long user or enjoyment, and so, to supply the want of a just and enlightened legislation, be established by these decisions, we must accept it as we find it . . .[174]

The court went on to hold that the fiction of grant was 'rendered absolutely necessary by the previous 'judicial legislation,' which established the reign of Richard I as the extent of legal memory'.[175]

The coexistence of prescription systems in the nineteenth century

The Prescription Act of 1832 sought to remove the possibility of disproof by evidence after the short modern time of common-law memory had elapsed. In the 1834 case of *Bright v Walker*, Parke B stated that the purpose of the Act was to shorten the period of prescription and to allow possession as a bar or title of itself as a matter of law, without the intervention of a fact-finding jury.

> For a series of years, prior to the . . . act, Judges had been in the habit, for the furtherance of justice and the sake of peace, to leave it to juries to presume a grant from a long exercise of an incorporeal right, adopting the period of twenty years by analogy to the Statute of Limitations. Such presumptions did not always proceed on a belief that the thing presumed had actually taken place . . . 'A technical efficacy was given to the evidence of possession beyond its simple and natural force and operation'; and though in theory it was presumptive evidence, in practice and in effect it was a bar . . . [S]o heavy a tax on the consciences and good sense of juries, which they were called on to incur for the sake of administering substantial justice, ought to [have been] removed by the

172 (1823) 2 B & C 54, 59–60; 107 ER 303, 305 (KB) per Abbott CJ.
173 (1868) LR 2 QB 497, QB.
174 (1868) LR 2 QB 497, 508.
175 (1868) LR 2 QB 497, 516. See also *Hammerton v Honey* (1876) 24 WR 603, 604, Ch.

> legislature. The act in question is intended to accomplish this object, by shortening in effect the period of prescription, and making that possession a bar or title of itself, which was so before only by the intervention of a jury.[176]

The courts, however, did not allow this attempt at statutory simplification to resolve the tangles of legal history. Litigants were allowed an election between the statutory and common-law schemes of prescription, and the chance to create an integrated doctrine of prescription for incorporeal property was missed.[177] The common-law doctrine of prescription declined further into a muddle of presumptions of mixed fact and law, requiring baroque instructions to be given to juries about the level of fictitious inference of fact they were permitted to make from the evidence of long user. Finally, the process or presumption hardened, from a search for reasonable evidence of likely grant, to an assumption that so many years' user implied a grant that was presumptively reasonable in its origin, terms and consideration, and more-or-less a final bar.[178] Blackburn J restated this approach in *Bryant v Foot* in 1867, noting that the common law since Littleton at least had accepted that time beyond living memory could be stretched to imply time beyond legal memory, and that a finding of rankness should be confined to moduses rather than prescriptions in land, and that it should be in any case nearly impossible to find rankness as a factual bar as long-standing practice tended to show reasonableness as a presumption of fact. Hence the levying of a large licence fee under a claimed prescription was not necessarily bad because it was unlikely to have been charged at such level in medieval times.[179] This was an attempt to mould the law of prescription towards Parke B's vision in *Bright v Walker* of a fictitious, conclusive presumption of right arising from long user. However, impure elements were retained in a sizeable body of case-law, whereby the court undertook a search for rebuttable evidence implied by long user, which could raise a factual presumption of grant reasonable in its origin and terms.[180] Ultimately that strain of authority was upheld by the majority in *Bryant v Foot*, and affirmed on appeal to the Exchequer Chamber.[181] The leading judgment stating the majority view was that of Cockburn CJ in the earlier Queen's Bench hearing. He protested against the search for prescriptive evidence stretching back to the twelfth century and regretted that prescriptive periods did not match modern limitation periods, leaving a morass of presumptions that were, in Sir William Evans' words, 'a perversion of legal

176 (1834) 1 Cr M & R 211, 217-8, 149 ER 1057, 1060, Ex per Parke B; and see also *Manning v Wasdale* (1836) 5 Ad & El 758, 111 ER 1353 (CP); *Drewitt v Sheard* (1836) 7 C & P 465; 173 ER 206 (NP).

177 *Dewhirst v Wrigley* (1834) Coop Pr Cas 329, 47 ER 525, 529 (Ch, KB); *Eaton v Swansea Waterworks Co* (1851) 17 QB 267, 117 ER 1282, QB; *Warrick v Queen's College* (1871) LR 6 Ch 278; *Ladyman v Grave* (1871) 6 Ch App 763; *Aynsley v Glover* (1875) 10 Ch App 283.

178 Simpson, *History of the Land Law*, 266–268.

179 (1867) 2 QB 170–77.

180 See e g *Carlyon v Lovering* (1857) 1 H & N 784; 156 ER 1417, Ex; *Rochdale Canal Co v Radcliffe* (1852) 18 Q B 287, 118 ER 108, Q B, *Ivimey v Stocker* (1865) 1 Ch App 396, LC; and see generally H J W Coulson and U A Forbes, *The Law Relating to Waters, Sea, Tidal and Inland and Land Drainage* (6th edn, by S R Hobday, 1952) 269–307; C J Gale, *A Treatise on the Law of Easements* (3rd edn, by W H Willes, 1862) 132–188; *Gale on Easements* (15th edn by S G Maurice, 1986) 150–216; (16th edn by J Gaunt and P Morgan, 1997) 169–234.

181 (1867) 2 QB 161, QB; affd (1868) 3 QB 497, Exch Ch. In Exchequer Chamber only Keating J was inclined to follow Blackburn J's experiment with conclusive presumptions.

principles'. After a brilliant review of the history of prescription law, Cockburn CJ felt unable to harden the presumptions drawn from shorter periods to presume the full span of immemorial time where evidence could be led – or indeed inferred – of an inception of right after the reign of Richard I.[182]

THE POLICY OF PRESCRIPTION DOCTRINE – AND PROSPECTS FOR REFORM

The convoluted development of common-law prescription for servitudes was given a more coherent structure by Lord Blackburn in the 1881 appeal of *Dalton v Angus*.[183] He identified a number of policies for prescription: punishing laches; quieting titles long enjoyed from disturbance; allowing acquiescence as a mode of transferring titles by factual grant; and removing uncertainty of ownership. He offered a highly selective description of the history of prescription in England which largely omitted the role of custom and specialty rights. He used a Romanist *usucapio* idea to sum up the purpose and nature of the doctrine as one of quieting titles and establishing secure and certain ownerships. The elaborate rules for evidential presumptions and implied grants were dismissed as instruments and fictions directed to a utilitarian goal of stable ownership, a goal which Lord Blackburn found clearly adumbrated in the *usucapio* of Roman law. Thus he 'wiped the slate clean', superimposing a utilitarian and Romanist pattern on the unruly English materials.[184] But it cannot be claimed that Lord Blackburn carried the law with him; eighteen judges sat at various stages of that case which 'perhaps embodies a greater variety of judicial opinion than any other leading case';[185] no clear message was produced as to how time immemorial, lost modern grant and the Prescription Act of 1832 coalesced into a workable system of prescription for incorporeal property.

The common law courts accepted then, and accept now, the coexistence of a complex common law prescription for incorporeities based on time immemorial, alongside the mechanism of shorter periods laid down by the Prescription Act of 1832.[186] Judges and jurists have since the mid-nineteenth century complained at being saddled with such complexities; lawyers can hardly be satisfied with a prescription system so scattered with historical debris.[187] In *Cheshire and Burn* the learned author notes the

182 (1867) 2 QB 179–84.

183 (1881) 6 App Cas 740, 810–29. To similar effect was Fry J's advice to the Lords (at 773), stating that all prescription doctrine was an expedient supporting the policy of quieting the possession of persons against those who acquiesce in loss of their rights.

184 S Anderson, 'Easement and Prescription – Changing Perspectives in Classification' (1975) 38 Modern Law Review 641, 655–659; for later nineteenth and twentieth-century developments, see also W S Holdsworth, *A History of English Law* (13 vols, 1922–52) VII, 343–352; W S Holdsworth, *An Historical Introduction to the Land Law* (1927) 276–288.

185 *Tehidy Minerals Ltd v Peter Norman* [1971] 2 QB 528, 547-53, CA.

186 *Aynsley v Glover* (1874) 10 Ch App 283; *Gardner v Hodgson's Kingston Brewery Co* [1903] AC 229, HL; *Tehidy Minerals Ltd v Peter Norman* [1971] 2 QB 528, CA; *R v Oxfordshire County Council, ex p Sunningwell Parish Council* [2000] 1 AC 335.

187 In *Tehidy Minerals Ltd v Peter Norman* [1971] 2 QB 528, 543, CA, Buckley LJ stated for the court that 'The co-existence of three separate methods of prescribing is, in our view, anomalous and undesirable, for it results in much unnecessary complication and confusion. We hope that it may be possible for the Legislature to effect a long-overdue simplification in this branch of the law.'

dissatisfaction expressed by appellate judges and law reform committees – and also remarks that the law is so difficult and so entrenched that rapid reform is unlikely.[188] Recent attempts by counsel to argue that the doctrinal morass is in breach of the Human Rights Act as throwing possession of property into uncertainty have been put to one side.[189] The Law Commission called for reform of the tri-partite prescription system in its recent report on land titles,[190] and is currently preparing a report on easements which is intended to revive the reform debate, last broached seriously in 1966.

The House of Lords last reviewed the policy of prescription for incorporeal heriditaments in the 1999 case of *Sunningwell Parish Council*,[191] and Lord Hoffmann's speech in particular showed an acute awareness of the historical descent of this area of jurisprudence. Like Lord Blackburn in *Dalton v Angus*,[192] Lord Hoffmann portrayed the civilian concepts of *usucapio* as an elegant alternative and model to be emulated:

> Any legal system must have rules of prescription which prevent the disturbance of long-established de facto enjoyment. But the principles upon which they achieve this result may be very different. In systems based on Roman law, prescription is regarded as one of the methods by which ownership can be acquired. The ancient Twelve Tables called it usucapio, meaning literally a taking by use. A logical consequence was that, in laying down the conditions for a valid usucapio, the law concerned itself with the nature of the property and the method by which the acquirer had obtained possession. Thus . . . the acquirer had to have taken possession in good faith. The law was not concerned with the acts or state of mind of the previous owner, who was assumed to have played no part in the transaction . . .
>
> English law, on the other hand, has never had a consistent theory of prescription. It did not treat long enjoyment as being a method of acquiring title. Instead, it approached the question from the other end by treating the lapse of time as either barring the remedy of the former owner or giving rise to a presumption that he had done some act which conferred a lawful title upon the person in de facto possession or enjoyment.[193]

Lord Hoffmann noted that under each of the three prescription systems of long user at common law, lost modern grant, and short use 'as of right' under the Prescription Act 1832, the courts imposed conditions on the prescribing possessor deriving from Roman law concepts:

188 *Cheshire and Burn* (16th edn, 2000) 636–638.
189 *Mills v MI Developments (UK) Ltd* (notice of appeal, 9 October, 2002, unreported, CA). The case is now on a reference to the European Court of Human Rights, application no. 12723/03. I am grateful to Barbara Hewson for drawing my attention to this case.
190 Law Commission, *Land Registration for the 21st Century* (Law Com no 254, 1998) paras 10.79–10.94.
191 *R v Oxfordshire County Council, Ex Parte Sunningwell Parish Council* [2000] 1 AC 335.
192 (1881) 6 App Cas 740, 817–826.
193 *R v Oxfordshire County Council, ex p Sunningwell Parish Council* [2000] 1 AC 335, 349.

> It became established that such user had to be, in the Latin phrase, nec vi, nec clam, nec precario: not by force, nor stealth, nor the licence of the owner . . . The unifying element in these three vitiating circumstances was that each constituted a reason why it would not have been reasonable to expect the owner to resist the exercise of the right – in the first case, because rights should not be acquired by the use of force, in the second, because the owner would not have known of the user and in the third, because he had consented to the user, but for a limited period . . .[194]

The nineteenth-century courts interpreted the 1832 Act so as to fit the new system to these same classical requirements of intent.[195] Hence prescription law was not so much simplified as multiplied, earning the drafters of the 1832 Act a good level of opprobrium – though responsibility lies also with the courts that chose a maximally complex interpretation of the Act.

If the Law Commission does produce legislation aiming to replace the various forms of prescription for incorporeal property with a single system modelled on the short prescription periods of the 1832 Act,[196] there will be two pitfalls. Will the new system simply add a fourth method to the three extant methods, or can the historical inheritance truly be uprooted? And will it be possible to define the states of mind and requisite action of the possessor and the owner, without our jurisprudence splintering yet again into incoherent detail? The complexity of the Roman models, and the difficulties of adapting ancient precedents to modern needs, are underscored by the failures of nineteenth-century German reformers to translate successfully the Roman prescription models into their feudal land law.[197] The English reformers will have a difficult task before them, and much legal history to give lessons and warnings – perhaps too much.

194 *R v Oxfordshire County Council, Ex Parte Sunningwell Parish Council* [2000] 1 AC 335, 350–351.
195 *Bright v Walker* (1834) 1 Cr M & R 211, 219; 149 ER 1057, 1061 (Ex) per Parke B; *Gardner v Hodgson's Kingston Brewery Co* [1903] AC 229, 239, HL per Lord Lindley; *Earl De la Warr v Miles* (1881) 17 Ch D 535, 596 per Cotton LJ.
196 As adumbrated in *Land Registration for the 21st Century*, para 10.87–10.94.
197 J Q Whitman, *The Legacy of Roman Law in the German Romantic Era: Historical Vision and Legal Change* (1990) ch 5, 151–199.

CHAPTER 12

Reading Roman Law with Edward Burn

Ann Smart

Four of us came up in 1953 to St Anne's College to read Law. All had taken the college's Entrance Examination, held in those days in January and thus later in the academic calendar than that for the other four women's colleges which took place in the preceding November.

St Anne's had recently acquired full collegiate status although on the present site only the Hartland House Building then existed. All undergraduates lived out in hostels in North Oxford, and were required to be in by 10.30 each evening; two midnight leaves a term were allowed. Male visitors had to be out of the house by 7 o' clock. A major asset in the College was the Geldart Law Library. This was open to, and accommodated when needed, all women lawyers in the University. The total in the women's colleges for the 1953 entry seems to have been ten.

There were no female Law Fellows in those days, and lawyers from St Anne's and Lady Margaret Hall were directed and largely taught by Mr Peter Carter at Wadham College. With him we were to study, for Law Moderations, Criminal Law and the English Legal System; for the third subject, Roman Law, we were to have tutorials with Mr Edward Burn. At the beginning of Michaelmas Term 1953 we duly cycled up the Banbury Road for a first meeting. Led through the hall of a big house, barely visible in the dusk, we entered a large study. Here were shelf upon shelf of books, an enormous desk, a foot-muff, comfortable chairs and an open fire. Quickly put into pairs, advised about books to acquire, given reading and an essay title for the first week, and told at what time to reappear, we stumbled out into the darkness, bewildered but excited.

In the course of the following weeks we were introduced to Roman Law, a subject which none of us knew anything about and which was far removed from our hazy and inaccurate expectations of the first steps in the Oxford Law course. The purpose, had we known it, had been set down in Constantinople in 533 AD: *ut rudis animus studiosi simplicibus enutritus facilius ad altioris prudentiae redigatur scientiam* ('and so the unformed mind of the student reared on simple ideas can be brought to knowledge of rigorous learning'). Many developments must have taken place at that early stage as we tried to adjust to the demands of a new system, but two come especially to mind. One was the sense of growing intellectual excitement, the other the nature of the teaching, as Edward Burn attempted patiently to instil into our thinking some notions of accuracy and precision together with a proper awareness of the significance of ancient texts. The major figure, Gaius, appeared for the first time and we thought about the finding of the Institutes in the Cathedral Library in Verona. When and by whom had this finding taken place and in what form? The concept of a palimpsest was new to us. What other source material survives from the classical period? What *is* the classical period? Why is it known as 'classical'? And Justinian himself: not merely how had the Digest been written, but why? Had we seen the mosaics in Ravenna? Some basic knowledge of Ancient History would have served well and that gap had to be filled fast, lest some fearful blunder left one exposed. We moved on, from Sources to Property, and then to Persons, Succession and Delict. Lectures were given in the Examination Schools by Professor Barry Nicholas, to be followed in Hilary Term by Professor HF Jolowicz; also to be attended were lectures on Criminal Law given in Trinity College by Mr P Landon.

Lectures as well as tutorials were formal affairs, both the lecturer and members of his audience wearing a gown; and gowns were worn by undergraduates for tutorials. We met as 'Mr Burn' and 'Miss X' or 'Miss Y', a new experience for those who had recently left school. One occasion comes to mind when our Tutor, from his full height, observed, 'Miss X, I believe you are incorrectly dressed.' Consternation was writ large, and huge the relief when it emerged that the offender, an Exhibitioner, was clad in a Commoner's gown. The fact that Edward Burn had a distinguished war record was of course known to us all but it was never mentioned, though I know of one exception. Asked, many years later, why he did not wear a helmet when cycling in Oxford, he replied, 'I did not wear a helmet on Juno Beach so why should I wear one in the Woodstock Road?'

Tutorials in Roman Law began again in Michaelmas Term of the second year. Roman Law I was compulsory, comprising Contracts and Quasi-Contracts, studied in connection with set Institutes texts, and the Law of Sale, studied in connection with Digest 18.1; a comparison with the English Law of Sale of Goods was also required. At that time, in addition to papers in Jurisprudence, Roman Law I, Land Law, Contract and Tort, three subjects had to be taken from a list of four, namely, a second branch of Roman Law, Constitutional Law, English Legal History and Public International Law. The second Roman Law paper was a popular choice. This consisted of Delict and Quasi-Delict, along with set Institutes texts, and the Roman Law of Damage to Property, studied in connection with Digest 9.2, also comparing Roman Law with the corresponding portions of the English Law of Tort.

We were pleased to learn again from Edward Burn, now a Student of Christ Church. When we went for tutorials to his house on the Banbury Road, we were frequently welcomed at the door by Helen Burn. There would be a brief but vigorous comment, perhaps about the roses or a tree, displaying in an instant her encyclopaedic knowledge about gardening and their large and splendid garden. We had long ago realised that at least one wall in the study was occupied entirely by books on this subject.

Professor Harry Lawson' s lectures drew large numbers at this time, as did those given by Mr Cecil Fifoot who had no difficulty in filling to capacity the Hall at Hertford College on Saturday morning; our problem was that the Sale of Goods Act proved to be a source of such hilarious comment that gales of laughter from all present made note-taking impossible. At The Lodge on the Banbury Road, demands placed upon us had increased. Critical, analytical thinking was being demonstrated and taught by Edward Burn throughout every tutorial, had we but realised it. We looked at the classification in the Institutes: how may it be criticised? Did we agree with Schulz that Gaius meant what he said in Institutes 3.88? Look for support at 4.2 and 182; but if that is correct, what is to be made of 3.91? We were challenged to explain the controversy relating to the payment of *arra*: is the Institutes text a bad reproduction of the Codex, as de Zulueta (always a favourite commentator) suggests? Should *celebranda est* be substituted for *celebrata est*? We struggled to grasp the significance of the possessory interdicts and *usucapion*, and some outline views on possession and ownership. At much the same time the Schools filled as all gathered to listen to Professor Hart giving the lectures that were shortly to become, in their published form, *The Concept of Law*. We took note of his argument about the significance to the jurists of the acquisition and loss of possession and the absence of abstract definition. With Edward Burn we looked to other Digest texts, encouraged to reflect on the development in thinking to be found in the *Res Cottidianae* (for instance, in the treatment of real contracts) and, grappling with concepts of agency and assignment, to consider whether Ulpian in Digest 19.1.13.25 should be limited by 14.3.2. *Error in substantia* proved an intractable problem as we wrestled with the views of Ulpian and Julian and attempted to make comparisons with English law. Such comparisons were expected to come readily to mind or were brought sharply to our attention by Edward Burn, the exercise characterised by lucid explanation in terms that we could understand. Rules relating to the transfer of property and risk in Roman and in English law, the distinction between contract and conveyance, the significance of the *caveat emptor* maxim, of insurance in modern law as calculated risk: these and many other concepts were engraved on our minds, assisted it must be said by attendance at the Brasenose seminars given by Professor Lawson. All benefited by the richness of the Oxford system which gave pride of place to tutorial instruction, supplementing it with seminars and lectures. Tutorials with Edward Burn were exciting, and challenging in their range and scope; encouraging too: one came away vowing to do better next time.

The one-year BCL in 1956–57 involved seven papers. These were Jurisprudence, Roman Law (consisting for one paper of the Law of Ownership and Possession, studied with Digest 41.1, and for the second the Law relating to *Condictiones*, with Digest 12.1, 4–7 and 13.1–3), Common Law, Equity, Conflict of Laws and one special subject (typically Evidence or Public International Law).

For the work on *Condictiones* all were grateful for lectures given by Barry Nicholas: the difficulties of extracting a doctrine of unjust enrichment from these texts were considerable and the clarity of the exposition and meticulous examination of the texts illuminated the subject and benefited everyone. Professor David Daube's lectures on Ownership and Possession were a riot of jokes and laughter, as well as being filled with flashing insights, but his remarkable *ex tempore* thoughts on Roman law defied attempts to commit much to paper. We moved quickly between lectures from Brasenose College to All Souls and then, as the timetable required, to Magdalen to listen to Dr John Morris on Conflict of Laws or Dr Rupert Cross on Evidence. In our early days the University Law Library was housed on the ground floor of the Radcliffe Camera, and later moved to the Upper Reading Room in the Old Bodleian Library.

In all of these difficult fields of Roman and modern jurisprudence we were guided, advised, helped and encouraged by Edward Burn. We were challenged, disciplined in our ways of thinking and taught about high standards; we were constantly exposed as undergraduates to the world of legal scholarship. It was not until some years later that one began more fully to understand and value the nature of the Oxford Law course. Many elements and personalities contributed to it, and the comments made here are no more than a brief snapshot. However they attempt to convey a most sincere appreciation of the highest quality teaching in the best Oxford tradition. Many years later it was for me, now law fellow at St Hugh's College, the greatest pleasure when Edward, on retiring from Christ Church in 1990, agreed to teach at St Hugh's. Needless to say, our undergraduates were astonished and delighted to find that they were to have tutorials in college with the author of the leading textbooks on Land Law and Trusts. Unwise it is to speak for others: but here, on behalf of all who have benefited from Edward's teaching, may I say a profound thank you.

Index

[all references are to page number]

C

D

PAGE

E

F

H

